Programming Hyperledger Fabric
Creating Enterprise Blockchain Applications

Siddharth Jain

Version 1.0, 2020-12

Colophon

Programming Hyperledger Fabric: Creating Enterprise Blockchain Applications.

Created with Asciidoctor PDF 1.5.3, based on Prawn 2.2.2

Cover designed in LaTeX by Siddharth Jain

Table of Contents

Dedication

I dedicate this book to my mother.

Preface

Hello and welcome to Programming Hyperledger Fabric. The goal of this book is to make you proficient in developing enterprise blockchain applications using the open-source Hyperledger Fabric platform. Blockchain has become a poster child for *decentralization* and "trustless computing". Developing blockchain applications is a *teamsport* in which developers from multiple companies have to come together and collaborate to create a solution. New companies can join the consortium. Indeed the business value that can be extracted from the network is directly - or even exponentially - proportional to the number of companies participating in the consortium. A blockchain acts very much like an append-only, transaction log in which data once written cannot be erased. In that regard its actually not much different from a database that is shared across multiple organizations. What makes it stand out - and its secret sauce and value proposition - is that *the database is not under the control of a single organization*. That is what its all about. Its a *peer-to-peer* database. It provides a common ground of truth that all the companies agree on and thus simplifies accounts reconciliation across organizations or tracking and tracing of products in a complex supply chain to give a few examples. The technology is not without its pitfalls such as how to purge data from an append-only ledger, how to protect data privacy, and how to make it scalable and we discuss them in this book. You will also learn a taxonomy of blockchains and how not all blockchains are alike. Also, many platforms are available to a developer for developing blockchain applications. Fabric is just one of them.

Developing blockchain applications on Fabric can be quite challenging not just because of the paradigm shift that blockchain represents from traditional applications but also because of the gamut of technologies Fabric uses under the covers - X.509 certificates, public-private keys, certificate authorities, digital signatures, distributed consensus, gRPC communication, Docker containerization to name a few. The hope is that this book will help you understand all these technologies and how they come together to create a platform. We will also put emphasis on how to *debug and troubleshoot* Fabric as that is what distinguishes the good from the great developer. To that end, we will not be afraid to run Fabric under a debugger. Indeed a lot of emphasis in this book is on *understanding the internals of Fabric. And this is only possible by studying its source code*. There are liberal references to source code of Fabric in the book.

As a developer, most of Fabric development involves two areas or components. The first is the development of *smart contracts* or *chaincode* as Fabric calls it that run on the backend when a request is received. And the other is the development of the *client application* itself that is used to make requests, manage user credentials and so on. We will cover both of these. Fabric provides SDKs for development of both smart contracts as well as client applications. It currently provides SDKs in three languages - Go, Java and JavaScript. We will use JavaScript. Besides the development of smart contracts and client applications, we will also cover deployment of the application in a production environment using Docker and how to make the system secure using TLS (transport layer security).

This book is aimed at professional software developers who are comfortable with Node.js and Unix. Bonus if you know TypeScript. You should also be familiar with databases and key-value stores in particular. I also assume a basic understanding of a client-server distributed system and networking. And familiarity with Git. You will need that to download the source code that comes with this book. No prior experience with blockchain, cryptography or Docker is required. Of course, this does not mean that if you don't know Node.js you cannot read the book. All that is needed is motivation to learn. You should expect to spend about a day on each chapter including the Further Reading section.

There is a code repository that comes with this book but is not public. To gain access to the code repository please email me at phfbook@outlook.com with a proof of the book's purchase and your GitLab username if you have one. I use a dollar sign (\$) in the book as a wildcard to mean the root folder of the code repository that comes with the book.

This is a *learning by doing* book. I don't provide lots of pre-written code in the code repository that you can just run and watch. The reader is expected to write the code. The book guides the reader as to what code to write. You may even need to adapt the code samples in the repository to your specific environment. Also as you will see in the book, writing of smart contracts is only a tiny fraction of the book. Indeed, more of your time will be spent in deployment, channel and chaincode administration and other things. Writing smart contracts is the easy part of Fabric development.

One difficulty I faced while writing this book was how to organize the content - what comes first and what comes later. In this regard if I had followed a strict linear approach starting from the bottom of the dependency tree, then the book would have started off with discussion of X.509 certs and coverage of the Fabric CA Server. The writing of smart contracts would have appeared much later in the book - perhaps even towards the end. And by that time chances are reader would have lost interest in the subject. Instead what I have done is to present chapters in a way that seems more relevant. I expect many readers will come into the book wanting to write smart contracts and so they appear earlier. The book contains a bonus chapter on Bitcoin. There is also a chapter covering LDAP which can also be considered bonus material.

Abbreviations used in the Book

Here are some common abbreviations used in the book:

- e.g. = For example
- i.e. = that is
- a.k.a. = also known as
- w.r.t. = with respect to
- SDK = Software Development Kit
- CLI = Command Line Interface = Standalone Executable = Console App for those coming from Microsoft or .NET world. All these terms are synonymous and mean the same thing - a program that can be executed from the command-line.
- UI = User Interface
- TLS = Transport Layer Security. A protocol to secure communication between two machines.
- IDE = Integrated Development Experience. Tools used by software developers for software development. Examples: Visual Studio Code, JetBrains IntelliJ

Software Versions

This book is written using following versions of various software and libraries. When things don't go as expected, its a good idea to check if you are using the same version.

Software	Version
Fabric	2.0.1
Fabric CA	1.4.6
Node.js	12
fabric-contract-api	2.1.2
fabric-shim	2.1.2
fabric-network	2.1.0
fabric-ca-client	2.2.2
ldapjs	2.2.0
bitcoin-js	5.1.6
Docker CE	19.03.4
OpenLDAP	2.4.53
tiredofit/openldap	7.1.3

Writing Conventions

Hyperlinks are used in the book and are put in the footnotes so as not to distract from the main text. Sometimes the hyperlinks refer to Fabric source code. At other times they refer to logs or documentation etc. I tested all links to work when I wrote the book but its a given that hyperlinks break over time. I felt its better to provide a link than to provide no link at all. The footnotes in the book are meant to be secondary material and reader is not expected to refer to them as they are reading the book. Because of limitations of the software used in typesetting of the book, I was unable to place footnotes at bottom of the page. Instead they appear at end of the chapter.

There are also fair amount of cross-references to other chapters in the book. The reason for this is to handle the case when a reader opens a page randomly in the book such as when the book is being used as a reference. Please don't let the cross-references be a distraction just like the footnotes.

Sometimes there are references to Fabric tickets, work items or bugs in the book. These usually start with FAB, FABC, FABN and have a number e.g., FAB-17035. A simple search on jira.hyperledger.org should lead you to the page which has all the details associated with the ticket or work item. For example, jira.hyperledger.org/browse/FAB-17035.

I have seen academic-style books with a long list of bibliography that the author themselves haven't read, as well as books that have no references to outside material. I have adopted a middle ground where I provide references to one or two articles, blog posts etc. in the Further Reading section of each chapter. Its not difficult for the interested reader to branch out from there.

I like using analogies a lot as I find that they are the most powerful tool in learning. For example, I compare Fabric to Git. Sometimes I might make analogies to things that the reader might be unaware of. When that happens I would suggest ignoring the analogy altogether rather than spending time trying to figure what its about.

Acknowledgements

There are many people I would like to thank without whom this book would not be possible. First and foremost is Pallaw Sharma and the entire executive leadership team at Johnson & Johnson Supply Chain for their unwavering support of this project. Next, I'd like to thank the people who reviewed this book and gave me permission to use their names in the testimonials. Thanks to all the people who have answered my questions on Fabric mailing list. The book is written in AsciiDoc and I would like to thank the creators of the free AsciiDoctorPDF software and for answering questions on the forum. A million thanks to Google, StackOverflow and Wikipedia whose help cannot be measured. And finally thanks to my loving family.

Writing a book is not easy and I have learnt that as I wrote this book. It is my hope you will find this book useful in your learning of Hyperledger Fabric. I have tried very hard to make it accessible even if you don't have any prior experience with JavaScript or Node.js or other prerequisites, and provide a coherent learning experience so that all the information you need to be productive with Fabric is well-organized and in one place. I welcome your thoughts and feedback. If you find the book useful, I would appreciate if you give it a rating and review. As Shakespeare said: *"They do not love, who do not show their love"*.

Siddharth Jain
Fellow, Data Management
Johnson & Johnson
Twitter: @fd97207

Chapter 1. Blockchain Primer

This chapter covers

- What is a blockchain?
- What is Hyperledger Fabric?
- How it works?
- Why should you be interested in it?
- What are the challenges facing blockchain technology?

This chapter is going to expose the reader to the Blockchain landscape at large. We will learn what is a blockchain, how it works, what is the business case for it, what are the different types of blockchains, what are the various platforms available to a developer to develop blockchain applications and what are the challenges facing this technology. On one hand Blockchain is becoming increasingly pervasive and is being touted by some to become a general purpose technology like electricity or the internet, and on the other hand there is quite a bit of pessimism as well in some circles surrounding this technology. How is it going to end? No one knows but it looks like the technology is here to stay for the foreseeable future. This chapter should be useful for technical architects, software developers and anyone who wants to familiarize themselves with this technology and get a broad overview of the overall landscape.

1.1. What is a Blockchain?

We begin our blockchain journey in this chapter by asking the first question - *What is a Blockchain?* As Figure 1. 1 shows, blockchain is many things to many people.

Figure 1. 1. The Blockchain elephant. Image by MoteOo from Pixabay. Reproduced under license. (pixabay.com/illustrations/blind-men-elephant-story-feel-see-1458438/)

For a newcomer, it is admittedly a complex and difficult to understand topic not just because of the paradigm shift it represents in how software applications are built and how they work, *but also because of the many misconceptions people have about this technology*. It is possible to approach it from many directions. Many discussions of blockchain begin with explanation of blockchain primitives such as hashes, public-private keys, digital signatures, and so on building up to what is a blockchain. We will instead attempt to explain what is a blockchain by following a top-down approach in which we start with a problem to be solved and explain how blockchain can be used to solve it and learn blockchain and its associated building blocks (no pun intended) along the way.

The origins of blockchain lie in a paper published in 2008 by a person known as Satoshi Nakamoto. [1] He invented a system using which people from around the globe could engage in monetary transactions and trade in a new currency *without using any banks in between*. The new currency as well as the system came to be known as *Bitcoin*. Interestingly, there is no mention of the word blockchain in his paper. Over time technology pundits and gurus started using the word *Blockchain* to mean the technology which was the underpinnings of *Bitcoin*. They noticed the technology could be repurposed to create many new applications and use-cases.

Imagine two friends on opposite sides of the globe who like to make bets. The loser has to pay the winner certain amount. Suppose the friends don't have any bank account. Or maybe they do, but the accounts are in different banks which don't send money to each other. Or maybe the banks involved charge high fees to transfer money and do not give a good exchange rate. So to avoid using banks, these friends meet periodically, say once a year to settle their scores when they exchange cash. In the meantime they need some way of keeping a record of who owes whom how much. So what can they do? Each person could send the other an email with a memorandum I owe you this much (known as a IOU) and when they meet each person could show their IOUs and they could settle the score. But keeping track of many emails is hard. So they could instead opt to collaborate on a shared document or spreadsheet stored on a cloud service like Microsoft OneDrive or Google Drive. Whenever a bet is won or lost, an entry is added to the document which stores *From, To* and the *Amount*. But the problem with this is that anyone can go back and change amounts thus tampering the records. And what if there are more than two people involved? What if tens, hundreds, thousands or even millions of people want to trade money using this system. Nakamoto solved all of this by inventing an *append-only, peer-to-peer, transaction log* known as the *Bitcoin*.

Let us understand what each of these terms mean.

Append-only means data once written cannot be erased. It is *immutable*. Once Alice sends money to Bob, and the transaction is recorded onto the ledger, it cannot be undone. It stays there permanently. Note that the transaction cannot be undone but its effect can be undone by performing the reverse transaction i.e., Bob sending money back to Alice. That is okay. But records cannot be deleted. That is what we mean by append-only.

Peer-to-peer (p2p) in case of Bitcoin refers to the fact that people can exchange money with each other without any banks or financial institutions in between. This is reflected in the first line of Nakamoto's paper:

A purely peer-to-peer version of electronic cash would allow online payments to be sent directly from one party to another without going through a financial institution.

— Satoshi Nakamoto, Bitcoin: A Peer-to-Peer Electronic Cash System

This has to be taken with a grain of salt because although the Bitcoin network does not use any banks, it uses powerful machines known as *miners* to facilitate the transactions between *users*. The people who run these machines are also known as *miners*. So the banks have just been replaced with something else. If the *miners* are taken out, then the Bitcoin network cannot operate.

Moving on, *transaction* is nothing but an electronic record. In case of Bitcoin, conceptually this would be a record with 3 fields: From, To, and Amount. For example, From:Alice, To:Bob, Amount: 1 which translates to "transfer 1 Bitcoin from Alice's account to Bob".

And *log*, also known as *ledger*, is a electronic spreadsheet (think Microsoft Excel) that is recording these entries. A sample log with a few transactions is shown in Table 1. 1.

Table 1. 1. A very simple transaction log documenting transfer of money.

From	To	Amount	Signature
Bob	Alice	$10	Bob's signature
Alice	John	$10	Alice's signature
Mary	Susan	$20	Mary's signature
Emily	Sue	$30	Emily's signature
Daisy	Jennifer	$40	Daisy's signature

1.1.1. How does it all work?

Well the answer to that could take a full chapter or reading of Nakamoto's paper depending on how deep you want to go into it but in brief - and simplifying a bit - the system is designed such that *each participant has a full copy of the log or ledger with them*. **Peer-to-peer** *refers to the fact that there is* **no master copy** *of this log*. In systems such as Microsoft OneDrive there is usually a *master* or *central* copy of the document and that is the copy stored on the cloud in Microsoft servers. When you edit a document on one machine, it updates the master copy and the document on another machine pulls those changes from the master copy to refresh or *sync* itself to the latest. But in case of Bitcoin there is no such master copy and *that is what peer-to-peer is all about*. Sometimes we use the word ***decentralized*** instead of *peer-to-peer* to mean the same thing. Table 1. 2 shows the topological difference between a centralized and decentralized (or peer-to-peer) network or system and cuts to the heart of what a blockchain really is all about.

Table 1. 2. Centralized vs. Decentralized network. Peer-to-peer = decentralized = no master copy.

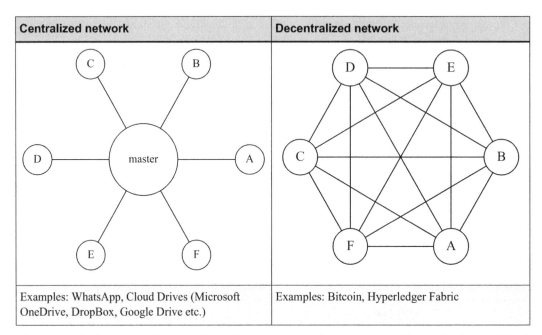

Centralized network	Decentralized network
Examples: WhatsApp, Cloud Drives (Microsoft OneDrive, DropBox, Google Drive etc.)	Examples: Bitcoin, Hyperledger Fabric

Changes to the log cannot happen arbitrarily. Any change (i.e., transaction) has to be first validated using established rules and the system ensures that when the change has to be committed, each copy of the ledger will update in exactly the same way. Meaning the copies of the ledger will never differ or *fork* from one another and will always stay in *sync*. Just like the copies of a document you store in OneDrive or Dropbox are kept in sync by the OneDrive or Dropbox software. Every transaction is further *digitally signed* and endorsed by its committer. Thus we have the additional column in Table 1. 1 that stores the digital signature of the committer. This is completely equivalent to Alice physically signing a check (or cheque depending on where you live) if she were making payment using a paper check for example. The signature serves as proof that Alice consented to and authorized the transaction to happen. The transactions don't get written to the log one-by-one. Rather transactions are batched together into *blocks* and blocks get written one-by-one. Each block holds about 1500-3000 transactions and is about 1MB in size. Each block has a pointer or reference to the previous block - hence, the concept of a *chain* or *linked list* of blocks. So this, in essence, is what a Blockchain is. It is also being commonly known as *Distributed Ledger Technology (DLT)* especially in business circles.

*We will define blockchain as a peer-to-peer, append-only, transaction log. Transactions are secured by using digital signatures, batched into blocks, and the blocks are back-linked to form a chain. In addition, blockchains usually have a feature known as a **smart contract** which is nothing but a piece of code that can respond to user input and generate a transaction in response. For example, the user input could be 2+3 and the smart contract will process that input and generate a transaction which is 5.*

The batching of transactions into blocks is done purely for performance reasons. The system would still be a blockchain if a block had only one transaction in it. Indeed, there exists a blockchain with that property - check out *Openchain*: "Openchain doesn't use the concept of blocks. Transactions are directly chained with one another, and they are no longer grouped in blocks. This means that a more appropriate term for Openchain is a transaction chain rather than a block chain." [2] The smart contract concept - while an important aspect of blockchain applications - is not something that I would say is crucial to defining what a blockchain is. The linking of blocks into a chain is just so that one can traverse the chain.

1.1.2. So what's the big deal?

We have defined blockchain as a peer-to-peer, append-only, transaction log. But isn't that what WhatsApp is? Alice, Bob and their friends could create a group in WhatsApp where they start posting these transactions. Each WhatsApp user has a complete copy of the ledger on their device. Messages can be deleted in WhatsApp but that can easily be changed to make the message log append-only. Adding a feature to make each message digitally signed by its originator is not that difficult as well. And the backend could be modified so that instead of just echoing back a message it has some smarts to do some checks such as if Alice even has the money in the account etc. So what gives? What makes blockchain so special? *The answer is that in case of WhatsApp the entire system is owned by a single entity (Facebook) whereas in case of Bitcoin there is no entity or corporation that owns it*. Have you heard of a Bitcoin corporation? And that is what the big deal is. WhatsApp is what we call a *distributed* system whereas Bitcoin is what we call a *decentralized* system. *Distributed is not the same as decentralized. Blockchain is about decentralization even though the DLT monicker uses the word distributed in it.*

The WhatsApp log is not peer-to-peer. It is a *centralized* system. There are multiple copies of the log but all of them are coordinated and managed by a *central* entity. When you send a message to your friend, you never communicate *directly* with your friend. The message first goes to the WhatsApp backend in a master log and the *client application* running on your friend's phone pulls this message from the central repository as shown in Table 1. 2. Of course we as users are never aware of the backend and to us it seems as though we are communicating directly with our friends. Also all the users in case of WhatsApp have their user accounts registered and managed by Facebook. In case of Bitcoin there is no such user registration controlled by a single organization. People can come and join or leave the Bitcoin network as they please. If a government wants to shut down WhatsApp its easy for them - they just shutdown Facebook. Shutting down Bitcoin is a different matter. For example, quoting the New Yorker: [3]

It's not clear if bitcoin is legal, but there is no company in control and no one to arrest.

It was not possible to create a completely decentralized system before the advent of blockchain technology to my knowledge. That is something it made possible which was not possible before. And that is why its a game changer.

1.2. Two Types of Blockchains: Permissioned and Permissionless

The Bitcoin project became a huge success and the underlying technology that makes it work came to known as blockchain technology. IBM saw an opportunity to create a platform or library that could be used by developers to create *enterprise* blockchain applications and that is how the **Hyperledger Fabric** - henceforth referred to as Fabric in rest of the book; Hyperledger Fabric will be quite a mouthful for me to type and you to read - project was born. Originally developed at IBM, it was then open-sourced to the Linux Foundation for further development. Although the Fabric project was born out of the success that blockchain technology achieved with the rise of Bitcoin, *there is little that Fabric shares with Bitcoin (or blockchains like Bitcoin)* when one looks under the covers. In fact I would say that Fabric and Bitcoin have *more in differences than in commonality.* Let's cover some of these differences.

First, in the Bitcoin world, the true identity of users is not even known - users are *anonymous*. What we mean is that Bob knows he is dealing with someone named Alice but he - or anyone for that matter - has no knowledge of any *personally identifiable information (PII)* associated with Alice such as her real name on a government issued ID card, her real address, phone number etc. Case in point is Satoshi Nakamoto himself whose true identity is unknown to this day. In contrast when it comes to Fabric, users have a *known identity*. Further the participants are typically businesses who come together and create a *consortium* to solve *B2B* (i.e., *enterprise*) problems such as implementing food and drug safety by secure tracking and tracing of products in the supply chain. The *users* will be employees of these companies. I like to compare this consortium to a Home Owners Association (HOA) if you are familiar with them. *Second*, in the Bitcoin world anyone can join the network whereas in case of Fabric there is a consortium that governs who can participate - thus *permission* is required to join the network. This is not as restrictive as it may sound. A consortium generally would be quite open and welcoming of other companies to join because the business value one can extract from the network is directly or even exponentially proportional to the number of participants in the network. But because of the permissioned nature, a Fabric blockchain falls somewhere *in-between* a completely centralized system like WhatsApp and a completely decentralized system like Bitcoin since membership to the club is controlled. We will see that this can be played so that it becomes a strength not a weakness. *Third*, whereas Bitcoin blockchain is viewable to the public (checkout www.blockchain.com/explorer) the data on a Fabric blockchain is visible only to members of the network. It is not public. The consortium might choose to make that data publicly accessible but that's an option not a necessity. Also keep in mind that Fabric is a platform or library you use to build blockchain applications. Bitcoin is already a blockchain application that has been built. You don't use Bitcoin as a software library or platform to build new blockchain applications the way you do with Fabric. But it does have developer API that can be used to build 3rd party apps around it. [4] A very popular platform to develop decentralized applications (or *dApps* as they are called) on top of a permissionless blockchain is *Ethereum.* The *smart contract* term was introduced and popularized by Ethereum. Ethereum dApps are basically smart contracts written in a language known as *Solidity.*

For what its worth, blockchains like Bitcoin where participants are anonymous and no permission is required to join the network have come to be known as *permissionless* blockchains whereas blockchains where identity of participants is known and permission is required to join the network have come to be known as *permissioned* blockchains although permission and identity are disjoint concepts and in theory there could be a permissionless blockchain where the identity of participants is known. A permissioned blockchain where participants are anonymous is dubious since if participants cannot be known, how would one decide whether they should be able to join or not?

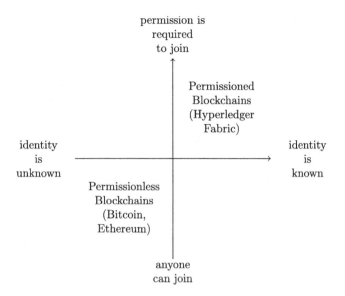

Figure 1. 2. Permissioned vs. Permissionless blockchains

The dichotomy between permissionless and permissioned blockchains will be a running theme in this chapter. Even if you pick one category out of these two, there are important differences that can arise as a result of using different platforms to build your application. This will become clear when we discuss *consensus* algorithms in the chapter. So *lesson #1 is that not all blockchains are equal and they exhibit important differences.*

As we look at various blockchains, the data being stored in the blockchain can change from one blockchain to another e.g., in case of Bitcoin the data is money exemplified in the form of Bitcoins. The block size and number of transactions in a block, who can participate, how participants are identified, what rules are used to validate a transaction, how each participant gets a copy of the ledger, how the ledger is prevented from getting forked are also things that can change from one blockchain to another. As example, how the copies of ledger are kept in sync, could not be more different between Bitcoin and Fabric. However, what does not change and is universal across blockchains is the concept of the append-only, peer-to-peer, transaction log consisting of blocks or batches of transactions linked together in a chain.

1.3. What is Hyperledger Fabric?

Hyperledger Fabric is a platform to develop blockchain applications. Its authors call it a *Distributed Operating System for Permissioned Blockchains.* [5] It is written in Go. The current version at time of this writing is 2.0. This is the version we will use throughout this book. Fabric is one of half a dozen to maybe a dozen blockchain related projects the Linux Foundation has under its Hyperledger umbrella. *Why does Hyperledger have so many projects?* I don't have in-depth knowledge of all the Hyperledger projects. But as I understand the projects form a stack of technologies. For example, Fabric and Sawtooth are platforms to develop blockchain applications.

They are different platforms just like Android and iOS are two mobile platforms. On top of platforms Hyperledger has other projects which are meant to provide additional features. The focus of this book is Fabric. That is what I know about. Some of the projects had their origins in different companies who then open sourced them to the Foundation and maybe now the Foundation is trying to make sense of it all. For example, Sawtooth project was developed at Intel. Some projects have been sunset such as the Hyperledger Composer. The projects use different consensus algorithms e.g., Hyperledger Burrow uses BFT consensus via the Tendermint algorithm. Nevermind if you don't understand the terms. Covering them will take us on a long tangent and not worth it. To cut it short, in the blockchain world there is no one-size-fits-all. You have a large menu of choices when it comes to what platform to choose.

1.3.1. What is AWS Blockchain, Azure Blockchain Workbench, IBM Blockchain (Oh My!)?

Perhaps you have heard of AWS Blockchain or Microsoft's shiny Blockchain Workbench. There's also IBM and even Oracle Blockchain. What are all these things? The big companies trying to cash in on the blockchain gold rush. That's what it is. AWS Blockchain et. al., are not platforms to build blockchain applications in the sense Fabric is. Rather they are offerings to provide Blockchain as a Service (BaaS or maybe BS!). That's the closest I can think of. An analogy will help. For example, if you have done deep learning programming you might be familiar with libraries such as Keras or TensorFlow. These are the core software components that you use to develop your application. They do the heavy lifting and are the engine of your application. Fabric fits here. On top of that, companies like Microsoft have built offerings like Azure ML Studio to provide ML as a service running in Azure cloud. That is what Azure Blockchain Workbench and AWS Blockchain etc. are. This book will not cover any of these offerings.

1.4. Why use Blockchain?

If you are reading this book, no doubt you have read some articles, whether on the web or elsewhere, on the potential of Blockchain technology to usher in a major revolution in technology and finance. Luckily people like me don't have to sell someone on the benefits and impact of this technology - that job has been done for us by Bitcoin's $200B market cap and the plethora of articles and news on the internet. This is not a business book but we will attempt to devote a few pages on why the reader should be interested in this technology. The first thing to admit is that people and enterprises have been going around doing business and living life without Blockchain before it became a thing. And they can certainly continue to do so into the future if they wish. But using Blockchain can simplify things and make life easier. Just like electronic payment systems, credit cards and e-banking have made it so much easier that its unthinkable of doing business without them whether it be an individual or a company.

The business case for Blockchain boils down to reducing two key costs of doing business - the *cost of verification* and the *cost of networking* as identified by Catalini and Gans in their article *Some Simple Economics of the Blockchain.* [6] Blockchain reduces both these costs by removing intermediaries or changing the nature of intermediation. Let's understand them.

1.4.1. Cost of Verification

Blockchain provides *a common system of record* that can be referenced and cross-checked to verify facts and information. Case in point - Bitcoin. Whereas it can take days for banks to verify a transaction and hence days to move money between accounts esp. overseas accounts, every Bitcoin transaction can be verified in seconds and there is no room for double-spend. How come this is possible? Because in case of Bitcoin there is a single logical ledger, nevermind the multiple copies of it, whereas in case of banks there are multiple ledgers and conflict resolution between ledgers can be very time consuming involving manual processes and complex methods of arbitration. Blockchain removes all of that. Enterprise supply chain is another area that is fraught with large costs of verification. Think of the global supply chain, where goods are shipped from one country to another. There are innumerable entities involved, tons of documentation and contracts (e.g., letters of credit) to manage. Using a blockchain simplifies a lot of this and reduces costs along the way. For example, BCG has done a study on pairing blockchain with internet-of-things (IoT) to cut supply chain costs. [7] Many blockchain based solutions are being developed for enterprise supply chain management. For examples, search online for TradeLens and Ambrosus.

1.4.2. Cost of Networking

This is again illustrated beautifully using Bitcoin. If you are a merchant who wants to sell goods and accept Bitcoin as a method of payment, you don't need to sign up with any credit card company. You don't need to pay them 3% commission on every transaction. Your users don't even have to register and setup an account before being able to make a purchase. You just provide users your public Bitcoin address and they can pay you in Bitcoin. The magic of all this is hard to truly appreciate until you experience it for yourself.

To operate any network requires involvement of various entities. The simplest network is the case of the two-sided marketplace - think of businesses like Amazon, Uber, Facebook etc. On one hand are buyers who want to buy products and on the other hand are sellers who want to sell products. In case you are wondering why is Facebook mentioned in the list of examples, *you* are the product and the advertisers are the buyers. Facebook is the seller in this equation. Companies like Amazon and Uber have built massive platforms with huge volumes of buyers and sellers. This is no easy task. The classic problem in building these marketplaces is how to generate the demand and supply. One does not come without the other - buyers want to use a platform where they know for sure that their demand will be met; conversely, sellers will only sell on a platform where there is a demand for their goods. Its a classic catch-22 or chicken-and-egg situation. Once the demand/supply problem has been addressed, the power of the network and the companies who control it, will grow exponentially in proportion to its size. The companies controlling the network can dictate who is allowed to participate or not, who gets paid what e.g., in case of Uber, the drivers have no control on how much a ride will cost, much less their commission; all of that is done by Uber.

Blockchains allow formation of networks where the control is not centralized in the hands of a single corporation or entity. They cannot solve the problem of bootstrapping the demand and supply, but they ensure that the governance of the network is not concentrated into the hands of a single entity. Removing this concentration of market power and allowing for operation of decentralized networks is what is meant by reduction in the cost of networking. This is also the reason we read news of people calling to break up companies like Facebook as the concentration of power is just too great and becomes a risk to users. [8]

Cost of networking = ability to form decentralized networks = anyone can join and leave as they wish = control not in hands of single entity or corporation

1.4.3. Raising Capital

Adding to above, undoubtedly the real reason blockchain is taking over the tech and financial world by a storm is because it has opened a new way to raise money for entrepreneurs through the mechanism of *Initial Coin Offering (ICO)*, *cryptocurrencies* and coin exchanges. Indeed that is how many people encounter Blockchain. Traditional methods of raising capital rely mostly on VC funding or angel investment. ICOs open up a whole new stream of securing funding for your startup. They allow entrepreneurs to raise money from the general public without doing an IPO (Initial Public Offering). Many entrepreneurs have used ICOs to escape SEC (Securities and Exchange Commission) regulation. SEC is taking increasing note of this and more information on the subject can be found on SEC website. [9] This is not a book about cryptocurrencies and how to get rich using a ICO.

1.5. How Blockchain Works?

We begin this section by noting that permissioned and permissionless blockchains work in different ways and it gives rise to important differences between them. But in both cases at a high level, there is a pool of *users* who generate *transactions* that are recorded by a pool of *bookkeepers* each of which has an *independent* copy of the ledger. All of this nicely maps to WhatsApp. The transactions in WhatsApp are messages sent by users. Further in case of WhatsApp all users are bookkeepers as well, since each user has a copy of the ledger on their device. What about the smart contract? In case of WhatsApp, the smart contract just echoes back whatever the user typed in the request.

Consider a bunch of users generating transactions and a bunch of bookkeepers recording the transactions. What can go wrong? Here are some things that can go wrong:

• How can the system ensure that a transaction cannot be changed or hacked while in transit?
• How can the system ensure that all bookkeepers' copies are identical to each other?
• How can the system ensure that every transaction makes it to the bookkeepers? In other words, how to make sure that transactions are not lost?
• How can the system ensure the ledger (or copies of it) cannot be hacked?

In both permissioned as well as permissionless blockchains, the first of the questions above is answered by using *digital signatures*. They are the digital equivalent of physical signatures. When Alice generates a transaction saying "transfer 1 BTC from my account to Bob" she also signs the transaction using a digital signature. A digital signature allows any recipient of the transaction to look at it and be sure and confident that *a) the transaction did come from Alice and b) that it has not been tampered with*. Digital signatures are explained in more detail in Section 2.1.2. Chances are you have used them previously e.g., if you have sent an email and digitally signed it or perhaps you have engaged in a real-estate transaction where you digitally signed the purchase and sale documents or maybe you have digitally signed your income tax return. Examples of their usage are numerous. Digital signatures have been around before blockchain was invented. They rely on properties of *public-private key cryptography* to achieve their magic.

For the rest of the questions, let's look at permissioned vs. permissionless blockchains individually.

1.6. How Fabric Works?

In this section we explain how Fabric works with an example. The basic idea behind Fabric is this: *a bunch of companies come together to transact business and document transactions in a ledger or database. Each company has their own ledger but will enter a record into it only when its signed-off by all the stakeholders defined in an endorsement policy. This ensures everyone always remains on the same page. That is all there is to Fabric. Really.*

Let's see how a Fabric blockchain can be used by a group of banks to record monetary transactions. The first step is for the banks to come together to form a consortium. The banks will be known as *peers* or *peer organizations* of the consortium. Each bank will spin up one or more *peer nodes* (i.e., machines or computers) which will store their respective copy of the ledger (or blockchain if you will). Each bank will also have their *users* which are the bank's customers. The peer nodes will be running application code to process requests coming in from users and generating transactions in response to those requests. Recall we use the term *transaction* to mean the record that gets written to the ledger. Fabric refers to the application code as *chaincode* although with version 1.4 it has given in and started to also refer to it as *smart contract* interchangeably. The chaincode will be developed jointly by all the banks and all peer nodes will run exact same copy of the chaincode. [10]

Now let's say Bob has an account in Bank A and he wishes to transfer $100 to Alice who has an account in Bank B. To do that Bob will draft a request that might look like following:

Listing 1. 1. Request made by a user (Bob) to transfer money to another user.

```
{
  "request_id": "JgQjxthio6kfdQ",
  "originator": {
    "name": "Bob <bob@banka.com>",
    "cert": "Bob's public X.509 certificate"
  },
  "request_args": {
    "action": "transfer",
    "from": {
      "bank": "Bank A",
      "account": "77050379840613"
    },
    "to": {
      "bank": "Bank B",
      "account": "75650548768909"
    }
    "amount": "100"
  },
  "signature": "A digital signature using which the bank can verify this request is really
coming from Bob and not someone else"
}
```

In above, Bob is trying to transfer $100 from his account #77050379840613 in Bank A to account #756505487689 in Bank B. Included with the request is an *X.509 certificate* and a *signature* (we will cover these later) which proves the request is coming from Bob and acts as his *digital identity*. Bob submits his request to all the banks in the consortium where it is evaluated *independently and in parallel*. The request triggers execution of a *smart contract* on each *peer node*. This smart contract will perform business logic specific to the application being built. In this case, the smart contract might check if Bob is authorized to perform the transaction and if he has enough balance in his account to complete the transfer. We will see how to write a smart contract using the `fabric-contract-api` provided by Fabric later on in the book. The smart contract exposes the data stored in the blockchain as a key-value store known as the *world state* with just two fundamental operations: `getState(key)` and `putState(key, value)`. For the developer writing smart contract Fabric will appear just like a key-value database. *All data in Fabric is stored as key-value pairs in a NoSQL db and Fabric provides two databases to choose from for this NoSQL db: LevelDB and CouchDB with LevelDB being the default.* So we could imagine a key-value store that stores all the users' account balances. An example is shown in Table 1. 3. Every bank will have *their own copy* of this database.

Table 1. 3. A simple key-value store storing account balances

Account (acts as key)	Balance	User
77050379840613	1000	Bob
75650548768909	200	Alice
441618027949177	400	Emily

Account (acts as key)	Balance	User
387158434152601	500	John
109514878347584	8000	Juan
…	…	…

Each peer node will execute the smart contract against the data they have and send a response back to Bob after evaluation of his request. For example, Bob might receive following responses back to his request from banks A and B:

Listing 1. 2. The request is endorsed *independently* **by each participating institution with a readwrite set and a signature**

```
{ signoff: true,
  signature: 'jsVmDvyASMjnYnYfMVXHkvzvQANQKyIg4JECwK/+HVo=',
  readset:
    [ { "account": "77050379840613", "balance": "1000" }, { "account": "75650548768909",
"balance": "200" } ],
  writeset:
    [ { "account": "77050379840613", "balance": "900" }, { "account": "75650548768909",
"balance": "300" } ],
  endorser: 'Bank A',
  request_id: 'JgQjxthio6kfdQ' }

{ signoff: true,
  signature: 'bEtmZcUw8DwZSUjEY5ArLtdyZvcNKgCsuvfK7AwwZ94=',
  readset:
    [ { "account": "77050379840613", "balance": "1000" }, { "account": "75650548768909",
"balance": "200" } ],
  writeset:
    [ { "account": "77050379840613", "balance": "900" }, { "account": "75650548768909",
"balance": "300" } ],
  endorser: 'Bank B',
  request_id: 'JgQjxthio6kfdQ' }
```

Each response comes independently and in parallel to Bob. In above both banks have signed off on the proposal as attested to by their electronic signatures. Fabric is nothing but a technology to automate what could otherwise also be done through pure manual labor. In a world without technology, Bob would take a paper to each of the companies and record their physical signatures (given by some officer or director in each company) as endorsements to his request. That officer would be doing some work to process Bob's request. In Fabric world we have codified that manual work into repeatable and predictable electronic code in the form of a smart contract.

Signing off on a proposal is not good enough. When the smart contract executes, it reads some key-value pairs from the database and would write or update some key-value pairs if the proposal were to be committed. Thus, we have:

$$(r, w) = f(x) \quad (1)$$

where: x is the input (the proposal), f is the smart contract, r are the values read from the database and *w* are the values that would be written to the database if the proposal were to be committed. The complete smart contract API is available online for reference. [11] It is possible for a smart contract to delete keys using the `deleteState(key)` method. We have said data once written to blockchain cannot be erased - that it is an append-only ledger. The presence of `deleteState` method may appear to contradict the append-only nature of the ledger. The resolution to the paradox is that the `deleteState` operation results in writing of another transaction to the ledger. When we say data cannot be erased, we mean transactions cannot be erased. However, a transaction can undo the effect of another transaction. The result of smart contract execution and the response provided back to Bob also includes *r* and *w* which are known as the *readset* and *writeset* respectively and play a very important role when the proposal has to be committed. The *readset* and *writeset* together represent a `diff` of the changes similar to the `git diff` or unix `diff` commands if you have used them before. The execution of the smart contract is a *dry-run* or a *simulation* since the changes are not committed to the ledger yet.

Once Bob has gathered the endorsements required, he will pack all the endorsements together with his original proposal into a packet, seal it with his digital signature and submit the resulting *transaction* to what is known as Fabric's *ordering service*. In practice, of course Bob will not be doing the work. He will be using some app on a device to perform these steps. This app is the *client application*. The *ordering service* is necessary to ensure that *all transactions are processed in the same order by the peer nodes*. Otherwise you can imagine a problem if two banks process transactions in different order. Transactions do not commute. Ordering service is there to take care of one and only one problem. Given two transactions T_1 and T_2:

$$T_1 \circ T_2 \neq T_2 \circ T_1 \quad (2)$$

For example, Bob might only have $100 in his account and if he tries to *double-spend* the $100 in two transactions - say T_1 is request to pay Alice $100 and T_2 is request to pay Jim $100 - we only want one of these to succeed. It doesn't matter which one but what is crucial is that it is the same transaction that succeeds and it is the same transaction that gets voided in the records of all the banks and that is what the ordering service achieves. The ordering service itself can be composed of multiple nodes managed by one or more of the banks. Prior to version 1.4 of Fabric, the ordering service was built on *Kafka* and did not provide much in terms of decentralization but with version 1.4, Fabric introduced orderer based on *Raft* which is a step towards a truly decentralized ordering service. More on the ordering service will come later.

When each bank's peer node receives a transaction, the packet is opened and each peer node will check couple of things. This phase is known as *validation* or *commit*:

- Everyone has signed off on the request. Thus we have everyone's approval or vote if you will to record the transaction.
- Everyone's read and write sets are the same. If not there is a problem. For example, if in one database Bob's account balance is $50 whereas in another its different, then this is a problem. When this happens in Fabric, user gets a *proposal response payloads do not match* error. This now needs to be addressed and debugged ad-hoc.
- The *readset* has not changed in the database since the smart contract was executed. For example, maybe Bob was trying to double spend $100 he had and when the second transaction arrives to

be committed, the peer nodes detect that Bob no longer has sufficient account balance to perform the transaction. As you can see there is a gap between when a proposal is evaluated and when its committed and a lot could be going on in that time in a busy system.

The transaction will be committed to the ledger when all checks have passed. [12] During the *commit* phase, the smart contract is not executed again. It doesn't have to. The peer nodes already know what would happen if the smart contract were to be executed. That is nothing but the *writeset*. Using induction it follows that once we start off with identical ledgers, they will continue to remain in sync. There will be no fights between the banks. Fabric allows for a configurable *endorsement policy* ranging from all participants must sign-off - this is most strict and will provide maximum security against a hacked ledger on some peer node - to at least one participant must sign (strongly discouraged). A middle ground is that a majority of the participants should sign-off. Using the strictest form of the endorsement policy will run into scalability issues as more and more participants join the network. This ***propose, collect votes, commit*** flow is illustrated in Figure 1. 3 and is very much how people make decisions in a board meeting if you have been to one.

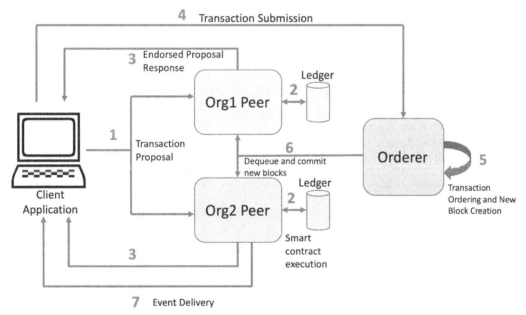

Figure 1. 3. Lifecycle of a Fabric transaction. *Step 1*, **user submits a proposal using a client app.** *Step 2*, **proposal is evaluated by each of the peer nodes independently.** *Step 3*, **peer nodes send back endorsed responses to the client together with readwrite sets.** *Step 4*, **client application packages endorsements into a transaction, digitally signs it and submits it to the orderer.** *Step 5*, **orderer is a pubsub service that performs an** *atomic broadcast* **and establishes an unambiguous order on transactions.** *Step 6*, **peer nodes can poll the orderer for new blocks or get notified via an event; they dequeue new blocks, validate transactions and commit them to their copy of the blockchain.** *Step 7*, **client application can register with a peer node to be notified when its transaction is committed to the ledger. Figure adapted from** medium.com/coinmonks/demystifying-hyperledger-fabric-1-3-fabric-architecture-a2fdb587f6cb

Steps 1-3 in Figure 1. 3 are known as *execution phase*. Steps 4-5 are known as *ordering phase* and steps 6-7 are known as *commit or validation phase*. Taken together Fabric calls it the *execute-order-validate* architecture. The entire transaction flow we have covered in this section gets executed when one runs the `peer chaincode invoke` command which we will cover later in the book in Chapter 8. The command acts as the *client application* in the transaction flow.

Sometimes I like to call blockchain as a *pseudo-centralized database* because functionally and logically it acts just like if the companies had a common shared database. But in reality each company has its own *independent* database. Since the databases remain in sync, they appear as one to an outside observer. Just like a document stored in the cloud (e.g., Dropbox, Microsoft OneDrive, Google Drive) has multiple copies of itself across many machines. However, there are two fundamental differences besides the fact that transactions in Fabric cannot be changed once they are committed (the append-only nature of the log). *First*, is that a document stored in a cloud drive is centrally managed (refer Table 1. 2) and *second* is that in case of a cloud drive anyone can start making edits and whatever changes they make get replicated to other copies of the document. Here, *there is a change management process and edits to the document cannot be made without going through that change management process.*

The above is a very simplified design as my goal was to cover how Fabric works in the simplest way possible. If one were to use the design above then the users will be able to see their account balances and changes to those balances over time, but they won't be able to see what money came from where in the transaction history. This is because the readwrite set in Listing 1. 2 is only keeping track of beginning balance and ending balance. We should also capture the `From` and `To` in our readwrite set as we saw in Table 1. 1. In fact, one can do even better. Currency notes have an identifier printed on them to track their circulation. An example is shown in Figure 1. 4 where the ID is `LG04727792`. [13]

Figure 1. 4. Image of a $100 bill showing an identifier that can be used for track and trace. By Bureau of Engraving and Printing - Public Domain, commons.wikimedia.org/w/index.php?curid=10086032

In the same way electronic currency can be ID'ed with digital identifiers to precisely track its circulation. So when Bob submits a request to transfer $1000, we would also record exactly which notes are being transferred and change their ownership from Bob to Alice. All this could happen in the background unbeknownst to Bob. See Table 1. 4 for sample illustration. In this way we have *tokenized* the underlying asset (money). *Tokenization* is a term you will hear frequently in your blockchain exploits.

Table 1. 4. Table showing tokenization of e-bills

Id	Denomination	Owner (or Account #)
ML15245960C	20	Bob
JK44900227A	20	Alice
JH85673846A	50	John
IL67881326B	100	Adam
JK91706110B	10	Nancy
…	…	…

Above exercise also exposes some considerations when using blockchain technology. Bob's account details are now shared and visible to all the banks.

Before we wrap up, let us cover the reasons why the *proposal response payloads do not match* error can happen i.e., the readwrite sets can differ across peers. Below are some:

- The reality is that the smart contract is not executed against the blockchain but against a database derived from the blockchain. This database is known as the *world state* and if you are using CouchDB without proper controls, it is easy to mistakenly tamper the world state. An admin with sufficient privileges can tamper the CouchDB even with controls in place.
- The peers executed a different smart contract. You will be surprised to learn that version 2.0 of Fabric actually supports this. [14] The idea behind the feature is that in addition to the core logic of the smart contract which should be the same across organizations, the companies might want to run some of their own idiosyncratic code in response to a request such as do some custom logging. But this portion of the smart contract should be carefully written so that there is no impact to the readwrite sets *(r,w)*.
- I have also seen it happen if one peer is running CouchDB and another is running LevelDB.
- It will also happen if the smart contract is not installed on some of the peer nodes.

Anyway, the *proposal response payloads do not match* is not an error you want to get as its kind of a red-alert and in worst case indicates a compromised ledger on one of the peer nodes. The error can be caught by the client application when it tries to package the responses into a transaction. So even though we introduced it in the validation phase as it made logical sense to introduce it there, a well-designed client application (such as the peer CLI that comes with Fabric) would raise the error before the transaction is even submitted for ordering to the orderer.

Some additional notes as we wrap up:

- Fabric allows for two kinds of peer nodes - *endorsing peers* and *committing peers*. Endorsing peers take part in steps 1-3, the execution phase. Committing peers take part in steps 6-7, the commit phase. The example that comes to mind is that of the PhD student who has to get their dissertation endorsed by three professors and then runs to the registrar's office (the committing peer) before timeout to have it recorded in the university's database. There is no reason why a node cannot be both endorsing and committing. Such a node will take part in both execution and commit phase. Indeed, in this book when we start programming Fabric, the same node will be used for both endorsement and commit. The reason is that it will just be more headache and work (need to spin up more nodes) if we separate the tasks.
- Every transaction is digitally signed by its originator. In addition it contains digital signature of every endorsing peer and the block in which it is stored is digitally signed by the orderer.
- Only way to hack the system is to steal private keys of all the peer organizations plus the orderer.
- Each peer node acts independently. It does not care what data is stored on other peer nodes. It will verify that other nodes have also endorsed the request and produced same *readwrite set* but beyond that each node is independently owned and operated and it only trusts the version of ledger it has on its system. *The peer network is decentralized.*
- *There is no consensus protocol (refer next section) that runs on the peer nodes. The peer nodes remain in sync simply because all of them receive the same transactions and in the same order from the orderer.*

1.7. Fabric's ordering service. Introduction to Consensus and CFT vs. BFT

The ordering service plays an important role in Fabric. It has only one job - batch transactions into blocks and perform what is known as an *atomic broadcast* (full definition provided shortly hereafter) of blocks/transactions. In other words, it establishes a total order on the transactions $\{T_1, T_2, T_3, ...\}$ (also known as serialization) *so there is no confusion and dispute amongst the peers on what the i-th transaction is.* Think of the ordering service as a "bouncer" in front of a busy nightclub who forces all the people (transactions in our case) to get into a line in order to enter the club (the club being the peer nodes in our case). It exposes just two endpoints: get and put. Get is an idempotent call made by a peer to get the *i*-th block of transactions. And put is a call to submit a transaction for ordering. This is the call the client application makes to submit a transaction in step 4 of Figure 1. 3. The get and put calls are known as deliver and broadcast respectively in Fabric:

```
Block deliver(int i)
void broadcast(Transaction tx)
```

Instead of a peer pulling a block from the orderer using the deliver call, it is also possible for a peer to subscribe to an event (also named deliver) to get notified when new blocks are available. The orderer keeps a copy of the ordered transactions but it does not look (i.e., peek) into the transactions to see what they contain.

The ordering service is nothing but a *pubsub* (short for *publish-subscribe*) system if you are familiar with them. There are many open source off-the-shelf pubsub systems available such as

Apache Kafka and *RabbitMQ*. Prior to version 1.4, Fabric used Kafka. Version 1.4 added *Raft* as the recommended option.

So how does one go about building a pubsub service? For starters, how about provisioning a node which does just what we described above. It collects transactions from users via the put method. How does it order them? It could attempt to order them chronologically which would be the ideal order. But here we see a problem: the server or node cannot rely on the timestamp in the user's transaction since that can be manipulated by the user to a false value. So the node could just order transactions in the order it receives them (first come first served or *FIFO* - first in first out). That would work. Remember all we are interested in is establishing an unambiguous sequence on the transactions. It need not be the chronological sequence. Indeed Fabric comes with such an orderer known as the ***Solo*** mode.

But now what if this node goes down due to a power failure? Part of a *pubsub* service's job is to ensure no transactions get lost or dropped. So we need multiple nodes to provide backup redundancy known as *Crash Fault Tolerance (CFT) which is the ability of the service to remain functional even in presence of node failures due to power crashes for example.* Another term for this is *High Availability (HA).* One of the nodes becomes a *leader* through an *election* process. The submitted transactions come to this node and it will broadcast them to all other nodes (known as *followers*). If this node fails, another node takes over through the election process. How do the other nodes know if a leader has failed? All nodes send periodic *heartbeats* to each other. If there is no heartbeat from a node within a set amount of time, that is construed to be a node failure and will trigger a *leader election* process.

The nodes run what is known as a *consensus* protocol which basically covers all of the above - how the state on nodes is replicated, how leader election happens, how failures are detected, how nodes recover etc (it makes for a gruelling backend interview). The consensus protocol also goes by various other names such as *atomic broadcast*. Wikipedia defines it as: *"In fault-tolerant distributed computing, an atomic broadcast or total order broadcast is a broadcast where all correct processes in a system of multiple processes receive the same set of messages in the same order; that is, the same sequence of messages. The broadcast is termed "atomic" because it either eventually completes correctly at all participants, or all participants abort without side effects".*
[15] Some other related terms used are *distributed database synchronization* and *state-machine replication* since the consensus protocol is synchronizing the state stored across multiple machines or equivalently replicating the state across multiple machines. Three popular popular consensus protocols are:

- ***Zab*** [16] appeared in 2011. short for *Zookeeper Atomic Broadcast*. This is what powers Apache Kafka.
- ***Raft*** [17] appeared in 2014. This is what Fabric recommends with version 1.4. Fabric uses Raft as part of the Etcd database in which ordering service stores its data in the Raft mode.
- ***Paxos*** [18] the oldest amongst the three. Appeared in 1998. Used in Cassandra database developed by Facebook for example.

All these protocols are CFT which means they can handle a certain number of node failures (of course if all nodes fail then the system cannot continue functioning; transactions or messages will start getting dropped until a node recovers) but *they do assume that when nodes are healthy they don't send wrong messages to each other about their state.* In other words, when a node receives a message from another node, that message can be *trusted*; nodes do not lie to each other. This is also equivalently stated and understood as saying that the nodes can be *trusted*. This is what **trust** means in context of consensus algorithms in blockchain or distributed-systems literature. Dealing with *untrusted* nodes falls in the realm of *Byzantine Fault Tolerance or BFT* for short. Wikipedia defines it as *"A Byzantine fault is a condition of a computer system, particularly distributed computing systems, where components may fail and there is imperfect information on whether a component has failed".* [19] Designing a BFT system is much more difficult as you can imagine. Please note that Fabric as of now (i.e., version 2.0) does not implement a BFT consensus protocol. Future versions of Fabric hope to add a BFT protocol (FAB-33).

The fact that Fabric is not BFT can lead someone to wonder is it even secure? Being BFT is not the only thing that drives security of a blockchain. *Indeed, most of the security comes from digital signatures which ensure transactions cannot be manipulated.* An attack on the ordering service (not easy by any means) can only result in some transactions being dropped or the order of transactions being manipulated and both of these though harmful cannot cause as much damage as, for example, someone being able to manipulate the dollar amount in a transaction or making himself the owner of an asset that is being transferred to someone else. Although BFT is definitely more secure, it is more difficult to implement and there is a price to be paid as well in terms of what transaction throughput you can get. In my opinion using a CFT protocol was the right trade-off for Fabric as it started with a centralized ordering service (Kafka). When all nodes of the ordering service are under control of a single organization (as when using Kafka) there is no reason why there would be Byzantine faults (i.e., malicious or *untrusted* nodes) in the system.

The thing to note here that the overall consensus in Fabric is a *2-step process*. *First*, there needs to be consensus amongst the nodes making up the ordering service and this is achieved by protocols such as Raft. *Second*, and ultimately what we are interested in the end is consensus amongst the peer nodes. And that is achieved by the fact that *if all peer nodes start out in the same state (empty ledger) and all process transactions in the same order then it logically follows that they will remain in sync. This does assume that all peer nodes are running the same code which gives the same predictable output to given input i.e., the same input should produce the same output on all the peer nodes irrespective of when and where it was run (location and time invariant).*

1.8. Blockchain vs. Shared Database

Now that we understand how Fabric works and what a Fabric blockchain is, let's take a moment to pause and appreciate the fact that a Fabric blockchain is nothing but a decentralized database. The whole discussion of blockchain vs. shared database can be equivalently framed as discussing the use of a *decentralized vs. centralized* database. And as we have noted *distributed* does not mean *decentralized*. Bitcoin, and permissionless blockchains like it are unique in that the things they have enabled (e.g., people able to exchange money anonymously and without being tracked by governments) were just not possible before. But that is not the case with permissioned blockchains you can develop using Fabric. As we have seen, it is a simple *propose, collect votes, commit* system. In principle any problem that can be solved by using Fabric, can also be solved by setting up a single shared database between the participating companies. *The problem is who is going to manage that database and can you trust that organization?* That is what blockchain aims to address. Catalini of MIT writes in *Antitrust and Costless Verification: An Optimistic and a Pessimistic View of the Implications of Blockchain Technology* [20]:

> *In cases where trusted nodes have full control over the process that updates and maintains the shared data, permissioned blockchains are very similar to the distributed databases companies have been using for decades, and provide little advantage over pre-existing solutions (except perhaps for simpler settlement and reconciliation of records across different organizations)*

So then why so much activity in this area? Are permissioned blockchains a scam perpetuated by likes of IBM? Note the use of the *trust* word in the text by Catalini above. Blockchain's whole value proposition revolves around that.

Blockchain is a way for companies to establish a common system of record without giving up control of that system in the hands of a single organization. A centralized database requires a high degree of trust in the organization managing that database. Decentralization relaxes that requirement. That is what blockchain is all about.

Permissioned blockchains provide at least three advantages over a shared database and that is the case for using them over a shared database *in addition* to the simpler settlement and reconciliation of records across different organizations acknowledged by Catalini:

- **Audit-trail**: Every transaction is digitally signed and every block is linked to its previous block and the complete history of a transaction can be traced going all the way back to the *genesis* block if needed. This kind of audit-trail functionality is needed for some regulatory compliance use-cases and is not something provided by current databases out-of-the-box even though all of them use a commit log under the hood. A commit log is nothing but the history of transactions. Virtually every database uses it to provide serialization of transactions, recovery in case of crashes and checkpointing to give a few examples. The commit log of a database does not come with digital signatures. The audit-trail functionality can be added on at the application level by a developer but at that point the developer might have invented a blockchain or something close to it.
- **Independent copy**: Your company gets to keep its own independent copy of the database. This is what decentralization is about. Note that independent copy does not mean you can do whatever you want with it. You can do reads, but you should never write anything to the ledger bypassing the normal flow of transactions where a transaction gets originated by the user, it is processed by the system, and then committed onto the ledger. We will refer to this as writing *out-of-band*. If you do that, you just shoot yourself in the foot. Your blockchain database will now be out-of-sync with the rest and most likely even corrupted. Some blockchain articles or websites portray *consensus* as some magical algorithm that replicates any change made to one copy of the ledger to all other nodes. The example that comes to mind is the shared document on OneDrive, Google Docs or Dropbox that gets magically replicated across multiple devices and users. Please note that consensus does not mean that your *out-of-band* changes will propagate to other nodes. You might fool yourself and increase your account balance, but it will remain the same on other ledgers.

- **Enhanced security**: With a shared database, there is only one password or private-key that needs to be stolen by a hacker. Whereas with a Fabric blockchain, a hacker will have to compromise private keys of all the participants in the consortium. This as we can guess makes blockchain solution much more secure. Private-key term comes from digital signatures and public-private key cryptography. Digital signatures work using two keys - a public key that you can share with anyone, its like you bank account number and a private key which you never share with anyone, its like your bank password.

1.9. Bitcoin's Proof of Work (PoW) and other consensus protocols

TL;DR: Bitcoin does not follow the *propose, collect votes, commit* architecture. You do not need anyone's permission, vote or endorsement to commit a transaction to the Bitcoin blockchain. However, you do have to demonstrate **Proof of Work**. This proof of work is very much like playing a game in the casino and winning a lottery. It takes money to play this game (in the form of compute power) and stakes are high. Because of this not everyone is interested in committing transactions to Bitcoin blockchain. Only a select group of people (*miners*) choose to do so. A winner is declared every 10 minutes and whatever transactions are selected by the winner will be committed to the blockchain in that order.

The full glory of how Bitcoin works is revealed in Chapter 16 but we need to cover some portions of it here so we can make a comparison and contrast between permissioned vs. permissionless blockchains.

Bitcoin is the first practical solution to a longstanding problem in computer science called the Byzantine Generals Problem.

— Marc Andreessen inventor of Mosaic and thought leader, NY Times 2014 - Why Bitcoin Matters

In Bitcoin, similar to Fabric, there is a pool of *users* who are generating transactions and there is a pool of *bookkeepers* who are committing the transactions to their independent copies of the ledger. In between the users and bookkeepers there is a *mining network* (similar to Fabric's ordering service) that batches transactions into blocks and announces them to the bookkeepers. This mining network is composed of nodes (known as *miners*) that are independently owned and operated i.e., its *completely decentralized*. A total order on the transactions is established as follows.

Any miner can assemble a *block* but before they can announce it to the bookkeepers they have to solve a math puzzle. We can think of this math puzzle as tossing 100 coins *all at once* and have them all come up heads. The number of coins to flip controls the *difficulty* of the math puzzle and is adjusted over time so that it takes roughly 10 minutes on average to strike lucky. You can do some math and calculate the number of trials on average it would take to get X coins all turn up heads, multiply it by time it takes to perform a trial and equate the result to 10 minutes to calculate X (the difficulty). So now even though all the miners are acting independently and they have full liberty on what transactions to include in a block and in what order, only one will be lucky enough to get all coins turn up heads. As soon as that happens, the lucky miner will announce it to the bookkeepers. The bookkeepers will commit it and system will reset. The process repeats. Transactions no longer arrive in haphazard and random order on the bookkeeping nodes. This is how it works in a nutshell. Of course the devil is in the details. How can the system ensure that the miner really flipped the coins and got 100 heads in a row? Where is their *Proof of Work (PoW)*? And how can we ensure that all *bookkeepers* will commit the block and not argue over it? We will figure out those details in Chapter 16. For now, the thing we need to note is that mining a block takes work. It requires compute power (electricity) to flip the coins and keep trying until you get the heads. This process also severely limits the transaction throughput of the system. The more difficult the challenge the longer it will take to mine a block and by extension the transaction throughput will suffer. If the challenge is made too easy then

- it increases the chances of a *collision* - two (or more) miners mining a block at the same time.
- it might not leave sufficient time for the block to disseminate amongst the bookkeepers before the next one is mined.
- it also makes it easier to attack or compromise the blockchain.

The difficulty needs to be carefully tuned to balance the opposing forces. Anyway what are the salient features as a result of this new protocol?

- One consequence is that *the more a transaction gets buried under the chain of blocks, the more difficult it becomes for it to be undone as a result of someone hacking the blockchain*. This will become clear when you read the chapter on Bitcoin, but in brief to change the *last* block, one would have to play and win the game *twice* (one for the last block and one for the next yet-to-be-mined block) before someone else gets lucky and mines the next block. Tossing 100 coins and have all of them turn out to be heads is hard as it is. Doing this *twice* becomes all the more difficult. Other miners in the race have to only win *once* as they are not trying to change or mutate the *last* block. To change a block N blocks away from the tail becomes exponentially more difficult. ***The cost of hacking the blockchain outweigh its benefits***.
- It is also possible for two blocks A and B to be mined at the same time (*collision*). Some bookkeepers will commit block A to their copy of the blockchain and others will commit block B. This introduces a ***fork*** (or *branch*) in the ledger. The solution is to just wait and let the system keep running until there is no more collision. Chances are a collision won't happen when the next block C is mined. And the miner who mines it will be using either version A or B of the blockchain. We illustrate this in Figure 1. 5 where we have chosen the miner to mine C on top of B.

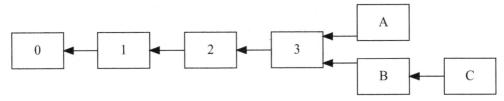

Figure 1. 5. Illustration of forks in a Proof-of-Work (PoW) blockchain

At this point there are two versions (or branches/forks) of the blockchain and one is *longer* than the other. As soon as that happens all nodes will switch to the *longer* version. In case there is a collision once again (and we get two blocks C and D at the same time; C on top of B and D on top of A), we keep waiting until a *longer* branch emerges and as soon as that happens, all nodes will switch to the *longer* branch. The *longest chain always wins*. ***The winner is not decided by how many copies of it exist (i.e., how many nodes have that version of the ledger), but by the length***.

- As a corollary, to hack a PoW blockchain, all you need to do is to manufacture a longer chain. But this is easier said than done. The PoW makes it extraordinarily difficult for a hacker to attack and manufacture a longer chain unless they seize control over more than 50% of the miners (more accurately 50% of total compute power) in the system. This is known as *51% attack* in the Bitcoin literature.

Again, note that transactions in any blockchain (be it Bitcoin or Fabric) are already protected against tampering by digital signatures. What PoW does is to prevent a hacker from changing the order of transactions or deleting them.

Table 1. 5. Fabric vs. Bitcoin Terminology

Fabric	Bitcoin
Ordering Service / Orderer	Mining / Miners
Peers	Full Nodes

The PoW protocol has several limitations associated with it such as power consumption, latency and transaction throughput (discussed in further detail in Section 1.11.1). As a result many other consensus protocols have been developed recently with the aim of addressing these limitations. We discuss two of these in Section 1.11.1. A survey can be found in the paper by Salimitari and Chatterjee. [21]. Also see the paper by Bano et. al. [22].

1.10. Permissioned vs. Permissionless Blockchains

As we have seen, there are fundamentally two kinds of blockchains. On one hand are blockchains such as Bitcoin. Anyone can join the network and start participating in it. These are also known as *permissionless* or sometimes *public* blockchains. On the other hand are blockchains where there is a consortium controlling who can join the network. Almost all enterprise blockchains fall into this category. There is good reason for a consortium to exist in these cases because only organizations with a legitimate business reason should be part of these networks. Also almost invariably the identity of users is not anonymous in these networks. The user behind every transaction is known. Such blockchains are known as *private*, *permissioned* or often just *enterprise* blockchains. There are many ways permissioned blockchains differ from permissionless blockchains but all of them stem from three fundamental differences. These three fundamental differences are: ***identity***, ***permission*** and ***consensus***. For permissionless blockchains identity is unknown, permission is not required to join and consensus is driven by proof of work. For permissioned blockchains identity is known, permission is required to join the network and consensus is driven by voting and an associated endorsement policy.

In principle there could be a permissioned blockchain driven by proof of work. Even though it will be a permissioned blockchain in the sense that someone's permission will be required to join, its characteristics would overlap with a permissionless blockchain like Bitcoin. Conversely, it is possible to create a permissionless blockchain whose consensus is driven by voting and endorsement. This blockchain will exhibit overlap with properties of Fabric. I have debated whether to title this section as permissioned vs. permissionless blockchains or Fabric vs. Bitcoin. I settled for permissioned vs. permissionless as its more natural but reader should keep in mind what when I say permissioned I mean a blockchain like Fabric or Corda and when I say permissionless I mean a blockchain like Bitcoin or Ethereum.

Let's summarize the differences between permissioned and permissionless blockchains in this section. As you read each item, try to relate it to the three essential differences of *identity*, *permission* and *consensus*.

- *Who can join*: By definition, anyone can join a permissionless blockchain whereas in case of permissioned blockchains, one needs to become a member of the club to join. The governing board of the consortium can decide whether to grant access or not only if they know who the applicant is i.e., *identity needs to be known as a prerequisite to determining whether an applicant should be allowed to join.*
- *Anonymity*: Users are pseudo-anonymous on permissionless blockchains such as Bitcoin. In case of permissioned blockchains, the identity of participants is known and not a secret.
- *Trust*: The combination of *who can join* and *anonymity* lead us to conclude permissionless blockchains as being operating under a *completely trustless* environment, whereas in case of permissioned blockchains the environment is considered *semi-trusted*.
- *Use Case*: Permissioned blockchains are designed to solve B2B or enterprise problems. A typical application would be achieving food and drug safety by secure tracing and tracking of products in the supply chain. Permissionless blockchains on the other hand are more applicable to solving B2C or even C2C problems. A typical application would be creating a marketplace that brings buyers and sellers together e.g., Uber is nothing but a marketplace that brings together riders (buyers) and drivers (sellers) to a common platform to engage in buying and selling of products (rides in this case). Permissionless blockchains seek to disrupt traditional models of building such marketplaces. Another typical application is the Bitcoin which originated and for the most part still is a completely a C2C platform.
- *Membership Service Provider*: Permissioned blockchains come with a *Membership Service Provider (MSP)* which performs authentication and authorization (*AuthN* and *AuthZ*) before someone can commit a transaction. There is no such concept in case of permissionless blockchains. That is not to say anyone can do whatever with permissionless blockchains. For example, you can only spend your own bitcoins and not of someone else.
- *Consensus*: The archetype method to implement consensus is *proof of work* in case of permissionless blockchains. There are alternative methods such as *proof of stake* that have also been developed. Permissioned blockchains like Fabric on the other hand achieve consensus simply because everyone agrees to a transaction and signs-off on it before it is committed. The nodes of the ordering service in a permissioned blockchain are kept in consensus by using traditional methods of achieving synchronization in a distributed database. Possible candidates are *Paxos, Raft, Zab*. [23]

- *Mining Network*: In case of permissionless blockchains, the mining network is completely decentralized and free for all. Anyone can become a miner. In case of permissioned blockchains, the ordering service can range from being centralized (if using Kafka) to being decentralized (if using Raft). Even if using Raft, the ordering service is under control of and operated by the consortium. Random computers cannot become part of the cluster of nodes that make up the ordering service. This is again why permissioned blockchains are considered *semi-trusted* networks. Some critics use the permissioned nature of permissioned blockchains to downplay them as not being open or fully decentralized, but the fact is that becoming a Bitcoin miner is not easy at all. It requires heavy investment of money to buy expensive machines and mining is out of reach of most individuals. There are mining *pools* that have been formed which consist of collective power of many individual miners. And the more compute power a pool has, the more influence they have over what blocks get mined. So even in case of permissionless blockchains the water runs deep when you analyze whether its really free and open for all.
- *Forking*: It is possible for two different blocks to be mined at the same time in case of permissionless blockchains. When that happens, the ledger forks. The forks, when they happen, get resolved very quickly as eventually a longer chain will emerge, and very often this will happen as soon as next block is mined since the probability of a collision - the simultaneous generation of two blocks - two times in a row is very small. Nevertheless *forking* is a possibility in case of permissionless blockchains since every miner is an independent agent behaving autonomously. The exercises in the chapter on Bitcoin ask the reader to calculate the probability of forking. *Forking* does not happen in case of permissioned blockchains since the ordering nodes work in concert to establish a total order on the transactions and always reach an agreement on the state of the system before advertising it to the peers or bookkeepers.
- *Conflict Resolution*: When we have a distributed ledger with many copies, in theory conflicts can always arise. *In a centralized system there is a master-copy that can be used to resolve conflicts. But how can they be resolved in a decentralized network when there is no master-copy to arbitrate?* A *fork* is nothing but a conflict. In case of blockchains driven by proof of work, the conflict resolution happens *automatically* and there is a simple mantra to resolve conflicts - *the longer chain always wins*. Also conflicts are expected to happen - not frequently, but sometimes when two blocks get mined at the same time. In case of permissioned blockchains like Fabric, a conflict never happens so long as the system is running smoothly and no peer nodes have been hacked. If there is conflict amongst peers, that can be settled by the orderer as the orderer establishes unambiguous order on the transactions. And its the job of Raft or Zab to ensure there is never any conflict amongst the orderer nodes - that is what consensus is about after all.
- *Attack*: The only way to attack a permissionless blockchain driven by *proof of work* is to manufacture a longer chain. The exercises at end of the chapter on Bitcoin challenge the reader to calculate the probability someone can attack a *proof of work* based blockchain. The only way someone has even a remote chance of making this happen is to seize control of more than 50% of the compute power of the network - known as the *51% attack* in literature. In contrast, to attack a permissioned blockchain like Fabric, a hacker would need to steal the private-keys of all the peers plus the orderer. Its just like a database but one that is protected by multiple passwords instead of just one.
- *Immutability*: Transactions in a permissionless blockchain cannot be considered final as there is always the possibility that someone might present a longer chain (the attack scenario) or the

ledger might *fork*. However, as the exercises in the Bitcoin chapter show, the probability of a transaction getting voided becomes vanishingly small with the number of confirmations. For many practical purposes, 1 confirmation is enough. Still from theoretical standpoint, the *transaction finality* (when a transaction is considered permanent and immutable) is what we term *probabilistic*. In case of permissioned blockchains there is no forking of the ledger and *transaction finality* is considered *immediate*.

- *Performance*: The *proof of work* involves solving a very time-consuming math problem. The difficulty of this problem is adjustable but if it is made too easy then *forks* will happen more often. Because of the time consumption in *proof of work*, permissionless blockchains can only support 2.5-20.0 tx/s depending on the block size and difficulty of the puzzle. Permissioned blockchains do not do any *proof of work* and because of this, they are able to support much higher transaction rates. For example, the authors of Fabric claim it can support 3500 tx/s. [24]. This claim needs to be qualified with a caveat which is that 3500 tx/s is *only possible when we are taking endorsement from only one or two (maybe three) peers*. As soon as you increase the # of peers required to endorse a request the transaction rate is expected to suffer. I don't know by how much and leave that as an exercise for the aspiring reader!

- *Size*: Permissionless blockchains are designed to be able to support tens of thousands of nodes whereas the distributed database synchronization technologies used in permissioned blockchains are typically used with tens of nodes. No one has run an Apache Kafka cluster with tens of thousands (or even hundreds) of nodes to my knowledge. In fact it is known that its performance takes a hit as more nodes are added. Even Fabric acknowledges that Kafka and Zookeeper are not designed to be run across large networks. [25] *Can you imagine getting a sign-off from thousands of participants - if Fabric were to be used to create something like Bitcoin - before recording onto the ledger?* As I write this there are in excess of 10,000 nodes in the Bitcoin network (bitnodes.io/). This is one area where *proof of work* shines over permissioned blockchains by enabling operation of a completely decentralized network that can scale to virtually unlimited number of nodes.

- *Cryptocurrency*: Permissionless blockchains use a cryptocurrency as a form of payment for the service they are providing to the user e.g., execution of every smart contract on Ethereum requires *gas*. *Why can't they use normal currency (e.g., USD)?* Because users on a permissionless blockchain are anonymous. Using normal currency requires identification, bank account details etc. Permissioned blockchains do not need a cryptocurrency (or tokens) to function. Indeed tokens are being introduced in Fabric only in version 2.0 (as an alpha feature) as something which a developer could use but doesn't have to. In permissioned blockchains, payment can happen using normal currency since the participants (enterprises) are known and identified. Permissioned blockchains can use a simple annual subscription to cover development of the common chaincode and cost of running any shared infrastructure. Permissionless blockchains typically use a "pay-for-use" model where a user has to pay in proportion to how much computational resource the smart contract uses; otherwise someone can abuse the system by executing a long-running smart contract. One question that naturally arises is *why does every permissionless blockchain use its own cryptocurrency? Why can't all of them use the same cryptocurrency such as Bitcoin?* I am not really sure why. Maybe because using a native token keeps the blockchain isolated and self-contained and it does not need to interact with other blockchains. For example, if a blockchain uses Bitcoin as cryptocurrency then when user submits a transaction and wants to make payment in Bitcoin, the Bitcoin blockchain has to be consulted to verify that the user indeed owns the bitcoins.

- *Error Correction*: Errors and mistakes are a fact of life in software development. In permissioned blockchains, the consortium can intervene to correct mistakes and undo "faulty" transactions resulting from software bugs. In case of permissionless blockchains there is no such recourse. The classic case study in this area is the infamous DAO attack in which a hacker stole ~$150M by exploiting a software vulnerability in a smart contract. [26] The hacker argued that what they did was legit since by definition DAO agreed to be bound by terms of its the smart contract and that the blockchain after all is supposed to be an immutable append-only ledger; transactions once committed cannot be undone.

Our findings are summarized in the table below:

Table 1. 6. Permissionless vs. Permissioned Blockchains

Property	Permissionless	Permissioned
Who can join	anyone	restricted
Anonymity	pseudo-anonymous	identity is known
Trust	trustless	semi-trusted
Use Case	B2C, C2C	B2B (enterprise)
Membership Service Provider	not applicable	applies
Consensus	mainly Proof of Work (PoW)	peer nodes remain in consensus simply because everyone agrees to a change before its committed to the ledger
Mining network	decentralized (each miner is independent)	semi-centralized (miners work together, they co-operate)
Forks	possible	do not occur
Conflict Resolution	automatic (longest chain wins)	conflicts are not expected to occur
Attack	51% attack	an attacker will need to steal private keys of all the peers plus the orderer
Transaction Finality	probabilistic	immediate
Performance	2.5-20 tx/s	3500 tx/s
Size	10^3 - 10^4	tens
Cryptocurrency	needed	is not needed
Error correction	difficult (blockchain is after all supposed to be append-only ledger)	consortium can intervene to correct errors and mistakes

Property	Permissionless	Permissioned
Examples	Bitcoin, Ethereum	Fabric, Corda

From business point of view permissioned blockchains are appealing since:

- No cryptocurrency is needed. More traditional forms of funding/operation such as an annual or monthly subscription are possible.
- Transaction throughput is much higher.
- Most importantly, there is a consortium who can intervene and correct mistakes that should not have happened.

Table 1. 7. Blockchains vs. Database

Property	Shared (or centralized) Database	Permissioned Blockchain (Fabric)	Permissionless Blockchain (Bitcoin)
Transaction Throughput	High	Closer to what you can get from a database than a permissionless blockchain (e.g., authors of Fabric claim 3500 tx/s in their whitepaper)	Very low (2.5-10 tx/s). [27]
Security	OK	More secure as it acts like a database that is protected by multiple passwords	Best
Topology	centralized	semi-centralized as you need permission to join	fully decentralized

1.11. Challenges facing Blockchain Technology

In this section we cover the challenges facing blockchain technology.

1.11.1. Challenges facing permissionless blockchains

- ***Transaction throughput***: Bitcoin can support only 2.5-5 tx/s and comes nowhere close to the rate of transactions processed by credit card companies such as Visa and MasterCard. The low transaction rate directly follows from the difficulty in mining a block. This difficulty can be dialed down but then it would increase chances of fork as well as make the blockchain more susceptible to attacks by making it easier for an attacker to amass required compute power to execute a successful attack. One way to increase transaction rate is to increase the block size (# of transactions in a block). Another solution much discussed and in news is the *Lightning Network* which increases tx throughput by overlaying a separate network on top of Bitcoin, creating a direct 1:1 *channel* between two users over which they can engage in multiple transactions and storing only the aggregated amount on the Bitcoin blockchain. For example, say you go on vacation with a friend for a week. Every day the two of you have expenses - sometimes your friend pays, sometimes its you. You keep a track of who paid what and at the end of the vacation the total expense is divided and shared between the two. There is a single transaction that happens at the end which equalizes the share of expenses. You don't pay each other every day. Similarly on the Lightning Network the users conduct multiple transactions; the debit and credit is aggregated and only the final amount needs to be stored on the Bitcoin blockchain when the channel is closed.

- *Energy consumption*: Proof of work has been severely criticized for how wasteful it is in terms of energy consumption. The amount of energy consumed by the global Bitcoin mining network is estimated to be 66.7 terawatt-hours per year and rivals energy consumption of countries like the Czech Republic. On one hand it is wasteful. On the other hand it is a necessary price to pay to secure the blockchain by making the possibility of 51% attack impossible and economically infeasible.

- *Latency*: The Bitcoin blockchain adds blocks at the rate of one block every 10 minutes on average. So at minimum a merchant has to wait for 10 minutes for their transaction to even be recorded onto the chain. And 60 minutes or 6 confirmations is considered a safe rule of thumb when one wants to be certain that the transaction won't be voided. This means Bitcoin cannot be used for real-time transactions. The *Lightning Network* mentioned earlier claims to solve the latency problem in addition to the transaction throughput. It does not provide any numbers but since there is a dedicated 1:1 channel between two users, it should be possible to transact on this at internet speed.

All above challenges follow from the *Proof of Work (PoW)* protocol used in permissionless blockchains. Hence, many researchers have recently worked on developing other forms of consensus. Covering each and every one of them is outside the scope of this book, but we will cover two promising alternatives in brief which are *Proof of Stake (PoS)* and *Proof of Elapsed Time (PoET)* and provide references for further reading for the interested reader. It helps to go back to the drawing board and recall the goal of consensus is to handle concurrency in a distributed system by establishing a total order on the transactions and eliminating the simultaneous generation of two blocks. In case of *proof of work* all the miners are competing with each other and are in a race to mine the next block. PoW effectively acts as a lottery system which randomly selects who is going to assemble the next block. The secret sauce is that the lottery winner is not decided by any central entity (think of a casino owner). The selection process is completely decentralized, autonomous and fair above all. What about a round-robin counter that cycles among the miners? We could do that. In fact, we can just dial down the difficulty of mining a block and that would automatically increase the tx throughput we can get from PoW. But the difficulty is set high for a reason - to make it very difficult for someone to hack the blockchain. That is the problem alternate consensus algorithms have to struggle with - *the tx throughput needs to be increased but at the same time the blockchain needs to be hack proof*. Both PoS and PoET implement an alternate lottery system that dictates who will be the next miner to mine a block, also known as the *leader*. The details differ between the two.

- *Proof of Stake (PoS)*: In this method, miners will stake a deposit in return for the opportunity to mine the next block. In the most naive version of the protocol, the higher the stake the higher the chances of getting chosen to mine the next block. The stake acts like a collateral which will be forfeited if the miner is found to have cheated. In this way it is in the miner's own interest not to attack or compromise the blockchain as they stand to lose money otherwise. Silvio Micali of

MIT has done influential work in this area and has developed an alternate cryptocurrency Algorand based on PoS. Readers interested in details of how *proof of stake* works are referred to the white papers on Algorand's website. Also see Ethereum's FAQ. [28] One criticism for PoS is that if chances of winning the lottery are proportional to the amount of cryptocurrency staked by the miner, then this centralizes control in hands of rich people and the "rich get richer". To address this, in improved versions of the protocol, other criteria are also involved besides just the amount of cryptocurrency staked by the miner such as users voting who they want to mine the next block (known as *Delegated Proof of Stake*). But here also the user's vote is weighted by his or her stake.

- *Proof of Elapsed Time (PoET)*: This is a conceptually simple and elegant way of achieving consensus. It operates simply like this: in every iteration, all the miners will go into sleep for a random amount of time. The miner who wakes up first, will get the right to mine the block. For this to work, we need to be certain that each miner did select the time to be random and did not wake up before that time elapsed - this is the miner's *proof of elapsed time*. There are two ways in which PoET can be implemented - software mode and hardware mode. In the software mode, also known as simulation mode, no special hardware is required. The hardware mode requires use of Intel SGX capable processor which provides a trusted execution environment (TEE). The advantage of hardware mode is that it provides Byzantine Fault Tolerance (BFT) which is securing the blockchain against malicious miners - a must for permissionless blockchains. The software mode is only Crash Fault Tolerant (CFT). PoET was developed as a consensus mechanism for *Hyperledger Sawtooth*, another platform to develop permissioned blockchains under the Hyperledger umbrella of blockchain projects operated by the Linux Foundation. Some people argue that it can be used for permissionless blockchains as well. Others argue that to be unlikely since to make it BFT requires using special processors made by Intel (at least currently) and is anti-thetical to the completely trustless mantra and requirement of permissionless blockchains. More details on PoET can be found online including a security analysis. [29] [30] [31]

1.11.2. Challenges facing permissioned blockchains

- *Data Privacy*: Use of a blockchain allows for companies to collaborate by creation of a common data-sharing platform that reduces the cost of verification to near zero. Companies like this and are drawn to blockchain because of this but at the same time they want to protect their data since data is the new gold in the digital age. A simple example of the dilemma is as follows: consider a bunch of companies in healthcare that come together to form a blockchain to track and trace movement of drugs in the pharma supply chain. A company could mine the ledger and gain competitive business intelligence about a competitor such as their manufacturing volumes - how much drugs are they producing. Translating this example to Bitcoin, if the identity of users of Bitcoin were not anonymous, then effectively everyone's bank account would be in public domain and anyone could see or calculate your account balance. This is a difficult nut to crack. One solution that is often proposed is *Zero Knowledge Proofs (ZKP)*, also known as *Zero Knowledge Asset Transfer (ZKAT)* - in simple terms a ZKP serves as evidence of the fact that something happened without revealing the details of that something. From Wikipedia: *"a zero-knowledge proof or zero-knowledge protocol is a method by which one party (the prover) can prove to another party (the verifier) that they know a value x, without conveying any information apart from the fact that they know the value x*". [32] The typical example given is that of proving your age using your driver's license at a bar. A driver's license gives a whole bunch of confidential information to the bar without even answering the question whether you are over the drinking age limit in a true or false manner. A ZKP would provide a true or false answer and not reveal any confidential information such as your birthdate, where you live etc. ZKP is not a panacea and magical solution to data privacy concerns. *And ZKP does reveal some information - namely the answer to the boolean question itself.* In Chapter 12 we will show how to protect data privacy by storing *digital fingerprints* on the blockchain which will serve as unambiguous proof of some fact such as ownership of an asset. The fingerprints by themselves are unintelligible. A key is always needed to unlock a fingerprint and that key is always stored off-chain and shared out-of-band on a need-to-know basis. Using clever designs we can even circumvent disclosing the key. Another solution to data privacy is *channels* and *private data collections* in Fabric. *Channels are nothing but separate ledgers or blockchains connected to the same ordering service.* They allow two parties to communicate in private without the entire consortium listening to the conversation. But in some ways they create fragmentation and take us back to the problem blockchain was supposed to solve - to create a single common ground of truth.

- *Interoperability*: Another key challenge facing enterprise blockchains is that of interoperability. The idea here is that, continuing the supply chain example from before, it would be foolish to assume that there will be one consortium and blockchain for the entire industry. Instead what is more likely to happen is that there will be multiple consortiums and blockchains. So in some sense we are back to the drawing board from where we started. Multiple blockchains effectively means multiple systems of record. How do we make these blockchains interoperate with each other and create a single system of record which is the holy grail we set out to achieve? Do we create a blockchain of blockchains? There is no easy answer to this question. An interesting read can be found on IBM blog [33] and the announcement of collaboration between Hyperledger Fabric and Enterprise Ethereum Alliance (EEA) to pave way for interoperability. [34]

- *Immutability*: The *append-only* or *immutable* aspect of blockchain - the fact that data cannot be erased - is hailed as a positive feature until you realize your specific business use-case might be subject to some regulation requiring the purging of data that is beyond a certain age.

- *Developer Experience*: In the opinion of this author, the tools, frameworks, platforms, libraries that are currently available to develop blockchain applications especially permissioned ones lack maturity. The feature set is not rich or complete, bug count is high, documentation is missing or in some cases even incorrect, and learning curve is extremely steep. These are certainly the reasons for writing this book.

1.11.3. Challenges common to both

- *Last-mile problem*: This problem refers to the interface and boundary that connects the physical asset to its digital representation. An example serves to highlight the problem: let's say a blockchain is developed to prove authenticity of art and trace its provenance. This is not a fictitious example, see Verisart on the internet. You, an art collector, go to an exhibition and purchase an artwork after having satisfied yourself that it is genuine based on the certificates and other data stored in the blockchain. What blockchain brings to the table is that cost of verification is greatly reduced. Verifying authenticity of art is an expensive process otherwise. The art lands on your doorstep. Your friend, an expert curator, visits you and upon examining the art claims it is fake. What happened? While the shipment was in transit, the original was stolen and replaced by a fake. How to fix this? We have to resort to old-fashioned techniques such as putting the art in a box protected by a lock whose key only you have. This problem is non-existent when the assets in the problem are purely digital such as Bitcoins but whenever a physical asset is present, the last-mile problem is also present in some form or the other. Another example is someone taking apart or cloning the label on a drug and affixing it to a counterfeit. To protect against this the label needs to be such that its not possible to take it apart without destroying it and its not possible to clone it just like its not possible to clone currency notes (one way to achieve this is to use holograms). High tech solutions to the last-mile problem try to make use of IoT (internet of things) sensors to detect tampering of physical assets. Using IoT is not a guaranteed way to foolproof the system; there is always a cat and mouse chase between those who want to protect and those who want to hack.

Here again we see a dichotomy between permissionless and permissioned blockchains as the challenges they face are quite different. In both cases we see *the strengths of blockchain also become its weaknesses*. For example, *proof of work* is a really novel mechanism that enables a group of decentralized independent nodes to reach consensus and arguably the most important innovation that came from Bitcoin. But that is also its weakness - it wastes energy and limits throughput of the system.

1.12. Which Blockchain Platform should I use?

When I started my blockchain journey, I was shocked to find the huge number of platforms, frameworks, libraries (call them whatever you want) available to develop blockchain applications. I remember reading somewhere about as many 21 platforms - I am sure there are more. That immediately sent my head spinning. Even under Hyperledger there are at least half a dozen (or maybe even more as this book goes to print) blockchain platforms - Fabric is just one of them. What are all these platforms doing? Which one should I choose for my application? I haven't researched each and everyone of the platforms available. The impression I gathered is that Ethereum and Fabric are two of the most popular platforms for developing blockchain applications. Ethereum is a blockbuster blockchain, the world's decentralized computer, and its huge popularity and footprint is evident by the fact that it has its own StackExchange. Smart contracts or business logic (the application code) in Ethereum is written in a programming language known as *Solidity*. However, it is a public blockchain which disqualifies it for most enterprise applications. A private instance of Ethereum can be deployed to create a permissioned blockchain but it doesn't come with things like the *Membership Service Provider (MSP)*. For this reason, many forks of Ethereum tailored for developing permissioned blockchains have been developed - all of them are collectively known as *Enterprise Ethereum*. [35] *Quorum* developed by JP Morgan and *Hyperledger Besu* are two of them. A detailed discussion of pros and cons of each platform is well beyond the scope of this book and gradually I have come to the opinion that just as there are many programming languages, there are and will be many blockchain platforms available to a developer to choose. Buying a car is easier than choosing what platform to use for developing a permissioned blockchain. I was drawn to Fabric because it was built for the enterprise from the ground-up, supported writing chaincode in JavaScript, boasted high throughput in comparison to Ethereum verified by independent tests (see *Performance Analysis of Private Blockchain Platforms in*

Varying Workloads, [36] and *Untangling Blockchain: A Data Processing View of Blockchain Systems* [37]), had good enterprise footprint thanks to work of IBM with Merck, Walmart etc., did not require a cryptocurrency to function, and was backed by Linux Foundation which is a trusted name in computing and open-source. However, please don't take that as an endorsement of any kind and make your own decisions.

In the age of clever marketing where every blockchain platform claims to offer the best in class, performance, features etc. I think perhaps the most important criteria should be the footprint of the platform i.e., how many businesses and users are using it. Unfortunately I don't know of a website that tracks the market share of permissioned blockchain platforms similar to sites that track market share of web browsers for example. That is understandable. It is very difficult to know how many businesses are using a certain platform. But not all is lost. The question count on StackOverflow (SO for short) can be used as a proxy for market share. After all, the more a platform is used, the more there will be buzz about it, the more questions will get asked on StackOverflow. The hypothesis is validated by looking at the question count of programming languages. JavaScript, Java and Python are some of the most popular languages and also have the highest question count on SO. So let's see where the platforms land in terms of the question count on SO. Very luckily SO provides a web based query engine that can be used for data mining and the question count of some popular blockchain platforms for developing permissioned blockchains is shown in Figure 1. 6 at the time of this writing. [38] We can see that Fabric comes out on the top - however once again I would advise the reader to do their own due diligence before choosing a blockchain platform.

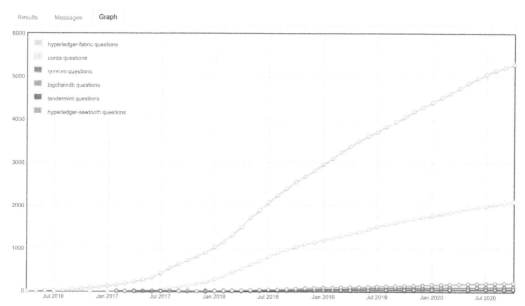

Figure 1. 6. Cumulative question count of some popular permissioned blockchain platforms on StackOverflow

1.13. Summary

Blockchain = Decentralization

- Blockchain can be understood as an append-only, peer-to-peer (or decentralized), transaction log.
- Transactions are secured by digital signatures, batched into blocks and back-linked into a chain where each block has a pointer to the previous block.
- Blockchain technology has its origins in Bitcoin - a peer-to-peer cryptocurrency that allows people to engage in financial transactions without any banks in between.
- Blockchain is a *teamsport* - the value you can extract from the network is exponentially proportional to the number of players in it.
- There are two kinds of blockchains: permissioned (where a consortium governs who can participate) and permissionless (where anyone can participate and participants are usually pseudo-anonymous). [39]
- Many blockchain platforms exist today. Two of the most popular ones are Ethereum for permissionless blockchains and Hyperledger Fabric for permissioned blockchains.
- Fabric blockchain is a simple peer-to-peer, append-only ledger where each addition has to be first endorsed (i.e., consented to or signed off) by the participants before it can be committed to the ledger.
- It is a way for enterprises to establish a common system of record without giving up control of that system in the hands of a single organization. If all you care about is a common system of record, that can be had by setting up a shared database between companies. Problem is who is going to manage it and can you trust that organization?
- To hack Fabric blockchain one would need to steal the private keys of all the participants plus the orderer.
- Permissionless blockchains powered by Proof of Work are handicapped by low throughput and high latency whereas permissioned blockchains struggle with protecting data privacy and achieving interoperability. The last-mile problem is common to both blockchains and is present whenever a physical asset is involved in the problem.

Fun Facts for this chapter: Did you know that there are 33 occurrences of the word decentralized and 40 occurrences of the word consensus in this chapter? The word smart contract is used 36 times and there are 0 occurrences of Docker.

1.14. Further Reading

- A very good alternate and comprehensive introduction to blockchain technology can be found in *NIST.IR.8202 Blockchain Technology Overview* available free of charge at nvlpubs.nist.gov/nistpubs/ir/2018/NIST.IR.8202.pdf. I highly recommend this article.

[1] bitcoin.org/bitcoin.pdf
[2] docs.openchain.org/en/latest/general/overview.html
[3] www.newyorker.com/magazine/2011/10/10/the-crypto-currency
[4] bitcoin.org/en/bitcoin-for-developers
[5] arxiv.org/pdf/1801.10228.pdf
[6] www.nber.org/papers/w22952.pdf
[7] www.bcg.com/publications/2018/pairing-blockchain-with-iot-to-cut-supply-chain-costs.aspx

[8] www.bloomberg.com/news/articles/2019-05-09/facebook-co-founder-chris-hughes-calls-to-break-up-the-company

[9] www.sec.gov/ICO

[10] With version 2.0 it is possible to run different versions of the chaincode on different peers but ignore that for now. I anyway do not recommend it.

[11] hyperledger.github.io/fabric-chaincode-node/release-2.0/api/

[12] To be accurate, Fabric persists the transaction even if its invalid; this is in contrast to many other blockchains like Bitcoin and Ethereum. But it marks the transaction as invalid using a bit mask and of course ignores the invalid transactions when constructing the *world state*.

[13] I initially tried to scan a $20 bill I had to create the image in Figure 1. 4 but the scanner did not work. Then I tried another scanner and it did not work as well. It turns out that scanners (at least here in the US) have special software to prevent scanning of US currency notes to protect against counterfeiting. Try scanning a note and let me know if you succeed!

[14] hyperledger-fabric.readthedocs.io/en/release-2.0/whatsnew.html

[15] en.wikipedia.org/wiki/Atomic_broadcast

[16]   marcoserafini.github.io/papers/zab.pdf;   also   see   www.tcs.hut.fi/Studies/T-79.5001/reports/2012-deSouzaMedeiros.pdf

[17] raft.github.io/

[18] www.cs.utexas.edu/users/lorenzo/corsi/cs380d/past/03F/notes/paxos-simple.pdf

[19] en.wikipedia.org/wiki/Byzantine_fault

[20] ide.mit.edu/sites/default/files/publications/SSRN-id3199453.pdf

[21] arxiv.org/pdf/1809.05613.pdf

[22] arxiv.org/pdf/1711.03936.pdf

[23] we call these methods traditional although a chronological look shows that Zab and Raft were actually developed after Bitcoin's Proof of Work.

[24] dl.acm.org/ft_gateway.cfm?id=3190538&type=pdf

[25] hyperledger-fabric.readthedocs.io/en/release-1.4/orderer/ordering_service.html#raft

[26] www.coindesk.com/understanding-dao-hack-journalists

[27] can be verified against www.blockchain.com/explorer?view=btc_txperday

[28] github.com/ethereum/wiki/wiki/Proof-of-Stake-FAQ

[29] sawtooth.hyperledger.org/docs/core/releases/latest/architecture/poet.html

[30] www.researchgate.net/publication/320246838_On_Security_Analysis_of_Proof-of-Elapsed-Time_PoET

[31] www.hyperledger.org/blog/2018/11/09/hyperledger-sawtooth-blockchain-security-part-one

[32] en.wikipedia.org/wiki/Zero-knowledge_proof

[33]   www.ibm.com/blogs/blockchain/2018/10/blockchain-interoperability-i-do-not-think-it-means-what-you-think-it-means/

[34]   www.hyperledger.org/announcements/2018/10/01/enterprise-ethereum-alliance-and-hyperledger-to-advance-the-global-blockchain-business-ecosystem

[35] For the longest time in my study of blockchain, I couldn't figure out what is Enterprise Ethereum. I have now given it away but try figuring it out yourself on the internet. I thought Enterprise Ethereum would be some platform or library like Fabric but I couldn't find its repo or samples or any tutorial on it. Turns out Enterprise Ethereum is none of that. Its just a name given to all the many forks of Ethereum to develop enterprise blockchains. And the Enterprise Ethereum Alliance or EEA is just a standards body like the Internet Engineering Task Force or IETF.

[36] ieeexplore.ieee.org/document/8038517

[37] arxiv.org/pdf/1708.05665.pdf

[38] To see latest results, goto data.stackexchange.com/stackoverflow/query/1165722/question-count-or-score-growth-over-time-by-tag-comparison?ShowScore=0&Tag1=hyperledger-fabric&Tag2=quorum&Tag3=bigchaindb&Tag4=corda&Tag5=tendermint&Tag6=hyperledger-sawtooth#graph

[39] There exist other taxonomies as well. E.g., see medium.com/@kctheservant/in-what-we-trust-1457f9bc11b.

Chapter 2. A Closer look at Fabric

This chapter covers

- How identities are managed in Fabric
- Steps to provision a Fabric network
- Decision points when developing Fabric applications

In the previous chapter, we did a pretty good deep dive into Fabric's transaction flow in Section 1.6. We also learned a whole host of new terms like *peers, orderer, smart contract, transactions, digital signatures, client application, endorsement policy, consensus, Kafka, Raft* etc. However two questions were left unanswered:

- *How does the network of peers and orderer come into existence in the first place?*
- *How are identities managed in Fabric?*

In this chapter let's try to answer these two questions and go down the rabbit hole a little further. Let's start with the second question first since it also plays a big role in how a network is provisioned. In fact, let's take a step back and understand how exactly does Fabric identify users.

2.1. How does Fabric identify users?

Fabric identifies users using a combination of X.509 certificates and digital signatures. An X.509 identity consists of a public and private key-pair. The public key is meant to be shared and stored inside an X.509 certificate. The private key is meant to be a secret and should never be shared with anyone. A digital signature proves ownership of the private key without giving away the key itself.

Fabric being a permissioned blockchain, everything ranging from Bob (our brave user in Section 1.6) to even the peers and orderer nodes have an identity in Fabric. In our day-to-day use of computers we generally prove our identity with a username and password combination. This process starts from when you log into your computer and is used again and again to check your email, connect with friends on Facebook and LinkedIn and so on. This username/password type of authentication is however a poor choice when you have to interact *across* organizations as is the case in Fabric. For example, you cannot use your Facebook password to log into LinkedIn. [40] *Your Facebook identity is separate from your LinkedIn identity.* In case of a blockchain users come from different organizations and thus their identity is registered, issued and managed by different organizations. But their requests still need to be processed by all the peer orgs and they need a *single unified identity when interacting with different organizations*. This is accomplished by using a *combination* of *X.509 certificates* and *digital signatures*. For example, in Section 1.6, Bob included a X.509 certificate and a digital signature with his request.

So let's spend some time learning what this *X.509 certificate* is. It is like a driver's license. An example certificate could look like below:

Listing 2. 1. Example X.509 certificate

```
Certificate:
    Data:
        Version: 3 (0x2)
        Serial Number: 15569805412580877457449304940592314946479982712
    Signature Algorithm: ECDSA-SHA256
        Issuer: C=US,ST=North Carolina,O=Hyperledger,OU=Fabric,CN=fabric-ca-server
        Validity
            Not Before: Mar 27 17:39:00 2020 UTC
            Not After : Mar 27 17:44:00 2021 UTC
        Subject: C=US,ST=North Carolina,O=Hyperledger,OU=client,CN=bob
        Subject Public Key Info:
            Public Key Algorithm: ECDSA
                Public-Key: (256 bit)
                X:
                    18:87:34:37:f9:8c:09:64:86:07:f4:33:74:e6:7a:
                    b0:14:08:3f:a7:89:b0:9e:9f:32:78:d3:4c:7e:ed:
                    5e:11
                Y:
                    54:bc:34:dd:82:b9:f0:48:a1:8c:9f:7c:a2:a4:ad:
                    c8:12:b8:a6:ce:44:bf:9c:b7:c1:30:33:77:46:52:
                    28:08
                Curve: P-256
        X509v3 extensions:
            X509v3 Key Usage: critical
                Digital Signature
            X509v3 Basic Constraints: critical
                CA:FALSE
            X509v3 Subject Key Identifier:
                FB:71:EC:2D:EF:B5:F1:57:FE:0C:E9:46:B3:62:DC:FC:A0:A5:75:77
            X509v3 Authority Key Identifier:
                keyid:2B:3F:D3:1D:A6:E7:92:CA:BB:D1:B9:9E:29:7E:3B:CF:9D:EB:7E:63
            X509v3 Subject Alternative Name:
                DNS:WITSC02X6385JGH
            Unknown extension 1.2.3.4.5.6.7.8.1

    Signature Algorithm: ECDSA-SHA256
         30:44:02:20:4c:c9:a0:f8:54:0d:f4:4b:2c:9e:7f:ea:f1:af:
         ...
```

That's a lot of stuff and you don't have to understand all of it yet. But note there is a Subject field which specifies who this certificate is for. The next thing to consider is that just like a driver's license is issued by the local Department of Licensing, who issues this X.509 certificate to Bob? The answer is Bob's bank. In a world without technology, the certificate would be a piece of paper that is signed by an officer in the bank. In the world of computers, X.509 certificates are issued by entities known as *Certificate Authorities*. Notice the Issuer field in Listing 2. 1. That tells who issued this certificate to Bob. Certificate Authorities form a *chain of trust*. When Bob presents his certificate to someone, they will check who issued the certificate. If the issuer is not a known and trusted person, Bob will be asked to present the certificate of the issuer and a *recursive* check happens which is illustrated in Figure 2. 1. The Issuer field acts as a *link or pointer to another X.509 certificate. We keep on navigating the chain of issuers until we find an issuer that we trust or the recursion stops.* The recursion stops when we reach a certificate where `Subject` = `Issuer` i.e., the `Issuer` *pointer* loops back to self. This is known as a *self-signed certificate.* All valid X.509 chains terminate in this way. A more detailed flowchart of X.509 certificate validation will appear in Figure 4. 2. Every X.509 certificate is digitally signed by the `Issuer` making it legit. Otherwise, anyone can cook up whatever certificate they want and claim to be whoever they want.

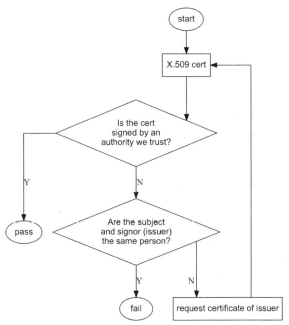

Figure 2. 1. How an X.509 certificate is verified by recursively navigating the chain of issuers until you find someone you trust.

Note that an X.509 certificate by itself does not prove identity. X.509 certificates are meant to be public and shared. ***If identity was being verified by using the certificate alone, then anyone could pretend to be Bob by using his certificate.*** A *digital signature* is also needed to prove identity. Inside every X.509 certificate is something known as a *public key.* Associated with every *public key* is its corresponding *private key. The private key is meant to be a secret and never shared with anyone* so its never part of the X.509 certificate. It is like a password. When Bob sends his request, he also signs it with his private key and that signature can be digitally verified to establish the *message is coming from Bob and only Bob.* If someone had Bob's X.509 certificate and public key they could use it in a message but they won't be able to sign it since they don't have Bob's private key. *If they sign it using another key, the message will fail verification and the bank will reject it as a spoof request.* We explain this in the next sections.

We began this section by observing that your Facebook username and password cannot be used to login to LinkedIn for example. The only reason an X.509 certificate works as an identification mechanism across organizations is that both organizations trust the issuer of the certificate. For this reason when it comes to the public internet, X.509 certificates are issued by well-known third parties such as Verisign, Geotrust, Sectigo etc. whom everyone trusts and who naturally charge for issuing X.509 certificates. This is an example of *identity federation* - making identity information portable across otherwise autonomous security domains.

2.1.1. Hash Functions: The heart of Digital Cryptography

Throughout this book we will simply use the term hash when we actually mean a *cryptographic hash*. Chances are you are familiar with hash functions. You may even have written a hash function if you have implemented the GetHashCode method in C# or hashCode in Java. A cryptographic hash function (denoted by $\phi(x)$) has following properties from Wikipedia: [41]

- it is *deterministic*, meaning that the same message always results in the same hash (this is true for any hash function)
- it is *quick to compute* the hash value for any given message (this also applies for any hash function)
- it is infeasible to generate a message that yields a given hash value. This is known as *one-way* property of hash functions. They are *irreversible*. Given the output, it is impossible to know the input (known as *pre-image attack*).
- it is also resistant to a *second pre-image attack* namely given an input, find another input which will give same hash.
- it is infeasible to find two different messages that will yield the same hash value (*collision resistance*). It is because of this property that the MD5 hash function is no longer considered a secure cryptographic hash function as its vulnerable to collisions.   [42] *Note that all hash functions suffer from collisions since they map an infinite range to inputs to a finite output range. However, a cryptographic hash guarantees that you cannot find inputs that will yield collisions.*
- a small change to a message should change the hash value so extensively that the new hash value appears uncorrelated with the old hash value. This is known as *avalanche effect*.

Collision Attack: Find x and y s.t. $\phi(x) = \phi(y)$. This is easiest for a hacker since both x and y are free to choose. Obviously $x \neq y$.

Pre-image Attack: Given y, find x s.t. $\phi(x) = y$ i.e., reverse engineer the hash function.

Second pre-image Attack: Given y, find x s.t. $\phi(x) = \phi(y)$. If we let z = \phi(y) then this reduces to a pre-image attack where z is given and we have to find x s.t. $\phi(x) = z$.

You might be wondering aren't pre-image and second pre-image attacks the same thing. Why have two names? The answer is that in case of a pre-image attack, the attacker tries to reverse-engineer the hash function whereas a second pre-image attack can be carried out if one can discover what set of modifications we can make to an input so that it yields the same output. An example where one would have to perform a pre-image attack is to crack a password (e.g., refer Exercise 15.2). An example where a second pre-image attack would be involved would be faking or spoofing a document - the assumption being that the recipient uses a hash (commonly referred to as a *checksum* in these scenarios) to verify authenticity of the document.

So in summary what we want from a hash function is to *return a random number but one that is fully determined by the input* (two opposing requirements if you will; random numbers are about tossing coins whereas determinism is about avoiding randomness).

2.1.2. Digital Signatures: The most important blockchain primitive

Digital signatures are the most important blockchain primitive used to secure data in any blockchain (be it Fabric, Bitcoin or any other). 99.9% of Fabric blockchain is built upon and relies on the security provided by digital signatures. Functionally, they play exactly the same role as physical signatures which provide proof of authenticity of a physical document. But since we are dealing with bits and bytes in this book, there is a different process to sign and prove ownership of electronic data. Make sure you understand this section as it is foundational to this whole book.

Problem Statement: A sender (Alice) sends an electronic message M to a receiver (Bob). When Bob receives the message, how can he be sure that:

- Alice, and only Alice, could have crafted M - this is equivalent to proving Alice as the *originator* and *owner* of the message or as lawyers like to call it *nonrepudiation* which means that Alice cannot deny signing the message or contract.
- that the message M has not been tampered with - this proves the *authenticity* of the message.

This is done as follows. *In addition to sending the message M, Alice also signs it and sends the signature sig to Bob*. The signature is computed as follows. First, the message is hashed giving $\phi(M)$ where ϕ is the hash function. This is also known as a *message digest*. Then, the digest is encrypted using Alice's private key to give the *digital signature*. Encryption can be viewed as a black box process whose details do not concern us - it is only the output that matters. We thus have

$$sig = enc(\phi(M), s) \quad (1)$$

where, *sig* is the signature and *s* is the secret - the private key in our case. *The encrypted digest (i.e., sig) can only be decrypted using Alice's public key to give back $\phi(M)$*. This is illustrated in Figure 2. 2 in the general context of a sender and a receiver. Public-private keys work in vice-versa as well - data can be encrypted using public key and decrypted using the private key. The first option (encrypt with private key of *sender*) is used when the message is intended to be public i.e., the recipient could be anyone whereas the second option (encrypt with public key of *recipient*) is used when the message is intended for a specific recipient ("for your eyes only"). An example is sending encrypted email where the message is encrypted with public key of the *recipient*.

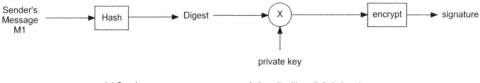

(a) Sender composes a message and signs it with a digital signature

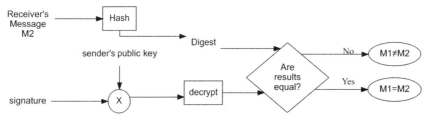

(b) Receiver uses the signature to verify the authenticity and owner of the message

Figure 2. 2. How digital signatures work. Note that the signature is a function of the message itself and so *cannot* be bundled with the message. It has to come separately.

Listing 2. 2 shows sample code that maps to each of the steps in Figure 2. 2. The code can also be found under $/illustrating-digital-signatures. To run the code you will need to install the bitcoinjs-lib and secp256k1 packages first. The code below has been tested with version 5.1.6 of bitcoinjs-lib and version 4.0.1 of secp256k1. The folder $/illustrating-digital-signatures contains a package.json that you can npm install to get the required dependencies.

Listing 2. 2. Illustration of how digital signatures work. Below code shows both send and receive operations happening in the same program. In practice, the receive operation and check will happen on receiver's machine or computer.

```
const bitcoin = require('bitcoinjs-lib');
const secp256k1 = require('secp256k1');
const keyPair = bitcoin.ECPair.makeRandom();                    ❶
const messageSent = 'From: Bob, To: George, Amount: 1BTC';      ❷
const messageReceived = messageSent;                            ❸
const digest = bitcoin.crypto.hash256(messageSent);             ❹
const sigObj = secp256k1.ecdsaSign(digest, keyPair.privateKey); ❺
const observed = bitcoin.crypto.hash256(messageReceived);       ❻
secp256k1.ecdsaVerify(sigObj.signature,
    observed, keyPair.publicKey)                                ❼
```

❶ Generate a new public-private key pair.

❷ This will be the actual message sent by the sender.

❸ We set messageReceived equal to messageSent to be able to test the code. In practice, received message will be whatever the receiver receives.

❹ Compute hash of the message. This is also known as *message digest*. The sender performs this step.

❺ Sign the digest using the private key. Note it is the digest that is signed not the message. The sender performs this step.

❻ The receiver computes the digest of message s/he receives.

❼ The receiver decrypts the signature using the sender's public key and verifies it matches the digest of the message it received. If verification succeeds, message is authentic and was sent by the sender.

Don't let presence of `bitcoinjs-lib` throw you off. We use `bitcoinjs-lib` to generate a ECC (Elliptical Curve Cryptography) key pair and compute a double SHA256 hash. Its not used for anything else. `secp256k1` library is named after the parameters of the elliptic curve used in Bitcoin's digital signature algorithm. `secp256k1` is slightly different from the curve that Fabric uses (`secp256r1`). [43] The signature it computes with the `ecdsaSign` method is what is called a *ECDSA (Elliptic Curve Digital Signature Algorithm)* signature. *Note from Equation 2.1 and Listing 2. 2 that the signature is a function of the message itself and thus cannot be bundled with the message. It has to be sent separately from the message.* [44]

Exercise 2.1

You might be wondering why do we compute a message digest in Figure 2. 2? Since both the sender and receiver have to compute the digest on the message sent and received, it should be possible to cancel this operation out like the way we cancel common variables on both sides of a math equation and work directly with the message i.e., sender feeds the raw message to the encrypter and receiver compares decrypted message with the received message. This is shown in following code:

```
const bitcoin = require('bitcoinjs-lib');
const secp256k1 = require('secp256k1');
const keyPair = bitcoin.ECPair.makeRandom();
const messageSent = 'From: Bob, To: George, Amount: 1BTC';
const messageReceived = messageSent;
const bSent = Buffer.from(messageSent);
const sigObj = secp256k1.ecdsaSign(bSent, keyPair.privateKey);
const bReceived = Buffer.from(messageReceived);
secp256k1.ecdsaVerify(sigObj.signature, bReceived, keyPair.publicKey);
```

Try running the above code and see what you get. Explain your findings. *Hint*: refer the Wikipedia article for details on the entire ECDSA encryption and decryption process. [45]

2.2. How are identities issued and managed in Fabric?

X.509 identities are issued by Certificate Authorities (CAs). A CA can be provisioned using the `fabric-ca-server` (Chapter 13). `cryptogen` (Chapter 4) provides us with a shortcut to generate X.509 identities without provisioning a full-blown CA server. Identities are stored in a Wallet by the client application.

Certificate Authorities play a very important role in Fabric as they are the ones who issue X.509 credentials to users and even the peer and orderer nodes. Provisioning *certificate authorities* is the very first step in Fabric and has to happen even before you provision the peer or orderer nodes since in order to provision them, you need their identities. *How does one create or provision a*

Certificate Authority (CA)? Fabric provides a way to do this using the *Fabric CA* component that comes with Fabric. However, note that *Fabric CA* is an *optional* component of Fabric - you don't have to use it if you don't want to and its not developed or prioritized as actively as rest of Fabric. You can develop your own CA. The `java.security` and `javax.security` packages in Java and the `crypto` package in Node.js have all the necessary functions you will need to develop a CA of your own. Different organizations are likely to have their own CAs although its also possible to have a common central CA who issues credentials to everyone. [46] The organizations will also need to establish a *mutual chain of trust* which is done by *exchanging the certificates of the CAs themselves* and adding them to a trusted repository or folder on each peer node so that when a request comes in, the certificates in that folder can be referenced to establish if the issuer is trusted and thus if the request is genuine.

X.509 certificates can also be generated using the `openssl` or `certtool` command line tools that come with Linux or Mac. These tools are useful while prototyping and to generate the self-signed certificate that can be used to bootstrap a CA server. In production one usually needs some database to manage issued credentials and an endpoint that can be accessed from remote machine, hence the need to run a CA server. The Fabric CA is further made up of a server component known as `fabric-ca-server` which issues certificates and a client component `fabric-ca-client` that can be used to make requests to the server from a remote machine through a command line. There is also a Node.js client that is also named `fabric-ca-client` which can be used by a Node.js application to communicate with the server. [47] The server exposes just a handful of APIs:

- `register`: used to create an account for a user much like the way you sign up for a Facebook account for example.
- `enroll`: used to obtain a X.509 certificate for a registered user. A user needs to be registered in the system before he or she can be enrolled.
- `certificate`: used to retrieve certificate of a previously enrolled user.
- `identity`: can be used to check if a user exists (i.e., is registered) in the CA db. user need not be enrolled.

2.2.1. How client application interacts with Fabric CA?

With the above background in place, let's see how Bob gets his X.509 certificate when he makes his request. We assume the use of *Fabric CA* in the discussion. Refer Figure 2. 3 to understand the process.

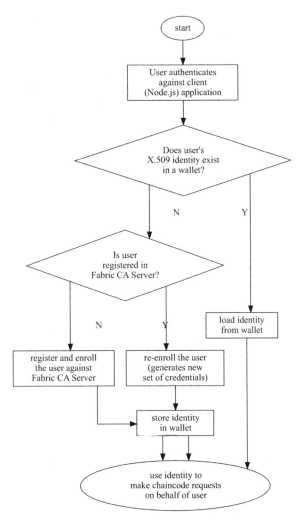

Figure 2. 3. How a client application retrieves X.509 identity of a user

First, Bob submits a username and password to the bank's *client application* (the website essentially) to log into it. The client application verifies that username and password against an identity provider such as Azure AD or an LDAP server. Client application then checks if Bob's X.509 identity is already cached in a *wallet* - think of it as something that is used to store X.509 credentials. If a cached identity is found in the wallet, the client application uses it. Otherwise, client application has to first register Bob against Fabric CA (assuming he was never registered previously) - this just creates a user record in CA db - and then client application has to enroll Bob in a separate call. When the client application submits an *enrollment request*, it basically drafts up a X.509 certificate with the attributes it would like in that certificate. The Fabric CA reviews that *certificate signing request* and signs the certificate making it legit and returns it back to the client application. [48] *The private key associated with the X.509 certificate is generated on the client and it is never sent to the CA server.* Once the client application gets the signed certificate, it can securely store it in a *wallet* so that it doesn't have to retrieve it from Fabric CA every time Bob logs in. There are a total of three calls that happen between client application and Fabric CA in the worst case - is user registered, `register` user, `enroll` user. And per call there will be a round-trip between Fabric CA and CA db. A client application written in Node.js would use the `fabric-ca-client` package to communicate with a Fabric CA. Once the client application has Bob's X.509 certificate it can use it to make a chaincode invocation request on peer nodes. *The thing to note in all of this is that the X.509 certificate does not reside on the user's machine. It resides in the wallet of the Node.js application that runs on a web server. Thus Bob never sees his X.509 certificate. Everything in* Figure 2. 3 *happens behind-the-scenes to him.* The chaincode request is drafted by the Node.js app running on a web server. This is what would be known as a *thin client* architecture. The word client in this case is referring to the end user's device. A *thick client* architecture would store a user's X.509 credentials on the user's device itself and the request would also be constructed on the user's device. But the downside of this is that the user is now tied to that device.

2.2.2. Idemix Certificates

For completeness, we mention that there is one other way by which users can provide identity besides an X.509 certificate. They are known as *Idemix certificates*. They provide a way to keep identities anonymous and unlinkable through the use of zero-knowledge proofs. Their value-proposition seems to be centered around developing Bitcoin like applications where the participants remain unknown and their identity is untraceable. Be aware that contrary to whatever you might read in Fabric docs, the truth is that *Fabric does not support Idemix*. For example, see FABN-689 which is about adding support for Idemix in Node SDK. And look at following code for the peer: [49]

```
func serve(args []string) error {
    // currently the peer only works with the standard MSP
    // because in certain scenarios the MSP has to make sure
    // that from a single credential you only have a single 'identity'.
    // Idemix does not support this *YET* but it can be easily
    // fixed to support it. For now, we just make sure that
    // the peer only comes up with the standard MSP
    mspType := mgmt.GetLocalMSP(factory.GetDefault()).GetType()
    if mspType != msp.FABRIC {
        panic("Unsupported msp type " + msp.ProviderTypeToString(mspType))
    }
}
```

Now that we have seen how the client application gets a user's X.509 certificate and built some knowledge around how identities are issued and verified in Fabric, lets move on to the next topic which is a discussion of the two databases Fabric provides for its key-value store and their pros and cons.

2.3. Choosing the right database for your key-value store

All Fabric transactions are recorded onto an append-only ledger - the blockchain. This list of transactions can be read and processed to create a key-value store or database. Fabric provides us with two options for the key-value store: *LevelDB* (default) and *CouchDB*. In fact, *for the chaincode developer, interaction to the blockchain will happen through read/write calls to the key-*

value store. The smart contract does not interact with the underlying blockchain when it is invoked. This is for performance reasons. Reads of the key-value store do not result in any transactions as there is nothing that is changed as a result of reads. Fabric calls this key-value store as the *world state. Both LevelDB and CouchDB are NoSQL databases.* For comparison, Corda, another popular platform for developing enterprise blockchains, uses a relational database for its data store. *All peers on the network (thus all organizations making up the consortium) should use the same database type and its not possible to change the type later,* so choosing the database type is an important decision to be made prior to deploying the Fabric network. For information, there is a database called Couchbase - *please note that Couchbase is not the same as CouchDB* just as Java is not the same as JavaScript.

The most important thing to note between LevelDB and CouchDB is that LevelDB is a database *embedded* within the peer process whereas CouchDB runs in a separate process. CouchDB has more bells-and-whistles but of course they come at the price of increased operational and maintenance cost. For example, if you want to query the blockchain data from a standalone CLI, you should use CouchDB. It exposes a REST API for querying the database that can be accessed using the familiar `curl` command. LevelDB does not provide a server or CLI for querying the data outside of peer process. This may tempt you to use CouchDB for the data store but ask yourself do you want the ledger data to be queried and accessible outside of the smart contract? This could lead to mining of competitive business intelligence if you are not careful. In addition, according to Fabric docs, *"the blockchain data structure is optimized to validate and confirm transactions and is not suited for data analytics or reporting. If you want to build a dashboard as part of your application or analyze the data from your network, the best practice is to query an off chain database that replicates the data from your peers. This will allow you to understand the data on the blockchain without degrading the performance of your network or disrupting transactions".* [50]

Table 2. 1 below lists the pros and cons of LevelDB vs. CouchDB.

Table 2. 1. LevelDB vs CouchDB

LevelDB	CouchDB
Embedded database	Standalone database like MySQL with a client/server architecture
No CLI or UI to query the db from outside Fabric. DB exists only inside the peer process	Both CLI as well as a Web UI are available to query the database independently of Fabric
More performant (faster transactions)	Less performant
Key-value store	Feels like a key value store, with the querying ability of MongoDB for objects stored as JSON
Can be considered more secure as the only access is through Fabric	Need to implement proper security measures (such as who can access) since DB runs independent of Fabric process
-	`getQueryResult` API [51] works only with CouchDB

2.4. Introducing Docker

We now move to the other question with which we began this chapter: how did the network come into existence in the first place? Docker is a technology that allows software to be packaged and run inside isolated *containers*. Maybe you have heard of it. It is quite popular these days among DevOps and is a complete book unto itself. Fabric components can be run as binaries (command line executables) or as Docker containers. Fabric provides Docker *images* for all its components - peer, orderer and CA. CouchDB comes with its own Docker image. *A Docker image is a template that is used to instantiate a container just like a Java class is a template used to instantiate an object.* A container goes through three stages in its lifecycle. First, it is *created* from an image. At this point the container exists but is not running. The second stage is when container starts *running*. Finally when the command used to run the container (think of it as the main function) *exits*, so does the container. In most cases the container never exits since it typically runs some server process which listens indefinitely for incoming connections. In this book we will see how to run Fabric with and without Docker. The Fabric peers can be run in two modes - dev (development) and net (production). Prior to version 2.0 of Fabric, the smart contract or chaincode would always run inside a Docker container in net mode so you could not avoid taking a dependency on Docker i.e., *installing and running Docker daemon was a prerequisite for Fabric prod deployment*. With 2.0 Fabric supports *external builders* which allow a developer to run chaincode without taking a hard dependency on Docker in production. [52] This feature is very new and only supported for chaincode written in Go at time of this writing.

Within Docker there are several ways one can go about containerization. From simplest to most advanced these are *containers, services, and stacks*. Container is the most basic unit. A Docker *service* is used to run multiple identical copies of an application in multiple containers (aka horizontal scaling) and Docker *stack* is a powerful way to manage an application composed of multiple services. We will create containers in this book without using any abstraction layer provided by a service or a stack. The problem using Docker services is that there is no way to copy some files (such as private-public keys and X.509 certificates) to the container before it starts. With standalone containers one can create the container, perform some intermediate steps such as copying files to the container, and then start the container. If you are using services you will either need to use what are known as *bind mounts* or some other means to inject any credentials or config into the container at runtime.

Regardless of the option chosen (services, stack or containers), you will need to create an ***overlay*** network. An overlay network is what allows containers on multiple computers (known as *hosts* in Docker) to communicate with each other. There are two ways to go about creating an *overlay* network. The simplest way is to run Docker in what is known as ***swarm*** mode, although its possible to create an overlay without a swarm. [53] We will be creating a swarm in this book to make use of *overlay* networking.

Below are the latest Docker images for Fabric peer, orderer, CA and CouchDB at time of this writing that we will be working with in this book:

• hyperledger/fabric-peer:2.0

- hyperledger/fabric-orderer:2.0
- hyperledger/fabric-ca:1.4
- couchdb:2.3.1

The images can be found on DockerHub. [54]

2.5. Securing communication between machines using Transport Layer Security (TLS)

Fabric is a distributed system and many nodes have to work together to process transactions. *Transport Layer Security (TLS) is a protocol that is used to secure machine to machine communication.* [55] It is the same protocol that is used to secure communication when you access your bank account from a web browser so your Internet Service Provider (ISP) cannot see what messages are being sent between the two. TLS provides *two* things:

- Verifying identity of the server so you can be confident you are really communicating with your bank and not some server that is owned by a hacker.
- TLS encrypts messages being sent over a channel so that an eavesdropper who is listening to the channel (think of someone tapping your phone) cannot decode the messages.

Fabric allows us to secure communication between peers, orderer and Fabric CAs using TLS if one wants. TLS also uses X.509 certificates for identity verification. An example TLS certificate is shown in Figure 2. 4.

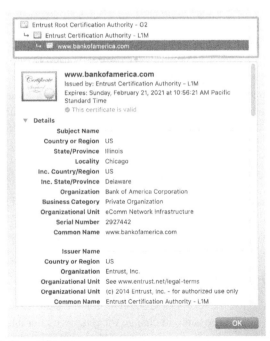

Figure 2. 4. Example TLS certificate

A peer node can have two X.509 certificates associated with it. Both certificates are ID cards it uses to establish identity but in different contexts. One context is when its signing off on transactions and another context is when its communicating with another peer or orderer and TLS is enabled. It is even possible to use different TLS certificates when communicating with different machines although it will just cause more certificate management headaches without much benefit.

The default mode of TLS provides *one-way* authentication in which *it is the server which proves its identity to a client* before a secure connection is established. For example, when you connect to your bank's website using your web browser, the bank's website sends a X.509 certificate to the browser. The browser validates this certificate against a list of trusted CAs it has. This proves to your web browser that the website it is connecting to is indeed owned and operated by the bank. *The client is not verified by the server in one-way auth i.e., the server allows any machine to connect to it. Client or mutual authentication* enables *two-way authentication* in which the client (your web browser in this case) also has to send down a X.509 certificate to the server that the server will validate to establish identity of the client. In case of the bank-scenario such client auth is unnecessary as the user will authenticate to the bank using a password and they could be accessing the bank's website from any location and machine such a cafe, airport or the library. *The bank wants to authenticate the user but does not want to restrict what machine the user is using to connect to the bank.*

In case of Fabric you may want to secure the network by allowing only *known machines* to connect to your node. Fabric supports this *two-way* authentication and it is tempting to use it but it does increase more certificates to manage. Since the peers in Fabric are engaged in a p2p communication protocol where the same peer A might act as client to one peer B and server to another peer C, it is possible for the peer to use two different TLS certificates: one to be used in client mode and another to be used in server mode. And remember a third certificate for the non-TLS purposes. A piece of advice is not to go overboard with TLS and clientauth. TLS must definitely be used whenever passwords are being sent such as when communicating with an authentication server. But depending upon how much headache you are willing to endure you might want to dial it down in other circumstances. A large proportion of questions and issues on Fabric are related to TLS, client auth and other errors having to do with CAs and X.509 certificates.

2.6. Steps to provision a Fabric network

We are now ready to perform a walkthrough of how to provision a Fabric network. This is a lengthy process and there are a number of decisions that need to be made. Some of these decisions have to be made collectively and others can be made on a per organization basis. Let's review some of them:

2.6.1. Collective Decisions

• Decide whether you will use LevelDB or CouchDB for the state store. Refer to Table 2. 1 for pros and cons of each. It is not possible to change the database later and all peers must use same db type to be safe and free of unexpected side-effects as a result of mixing LevelDB and CouchDB.

- Decide if you will use Kafka or Raft for the orderer. Raft is recommended by Fabric due to easier setup. This should be an easy decision. Use Raft unless you are on version 1.3 or earlier.
- Decide if you will use X.509 or Idemix certificates. We only cover X.509 certificates in this book.
- What language will be used for development of smart contracts? Fabric supports three languages - Go, Java and JavaScript. We will only cover JavaScript in this book. Fabric 2.0 does claim to support different organizations writing smart contracts in different languages although if you ask me, I am of the firm opinion that the smart contracts or chaincode is *communal property* that needs to be *jointly developed and co-owned in a shared repo*.

2.6.2. Individual (i.e., per organization) Decisions

- You will need a CA to issue X.509 certificates. Decide if you will use Fabric CA or some other CA. If you use Fabric CA, will the Fabric CA and your client application authenticate users against the same LDAP database?
- Decide what will you use for user registration and authentication. Will you create a new database of users for your application or is there an existing users database that you would like to use? If there is an existing database, are you able to authenticate against it by connecting directly to it, or is the authentication brokered by a Single Sign-On service like Ping Identity or OneLogin?
- Decide if you will use any containerization technology like Docker to deploy your peers, orderer nodes and CA. You don't have to containerize if you don't want to. It is possible to run the peers, orderer and CA servers using binaries (command line executables) but the chaincode will run inside a Docker container unless you are using *external builders* (a new feature in Fabric 2.0).

2.6.3. Provisioning Steps

At a super high-level, the provisioning of a Fabric network can be divided into following stages:

1. Provision CA servers (Chapter 13; Chapter 4 shows a shortcut and also covers the next step in the list)
2. Register and enroll the peer and orderer nodes and the admin users who will manage the nodes, create channel and install/commit chaincode (Chapter 14)
3. Provision peer, orderer and any CouchDB nodes (Chapter 5)
4. Create a channel and join peer nodes to it (Chapter 7)
5. Install, approve and commit chaincode (Chapter 7)
6. Provision client application (Chapter 8)

All the steps above have to be executed per organization with exception of a few such as creating a channel and committing the chaincode. Figure 2. 5 shows some applications that each peer organization might be running once the network is deployed.

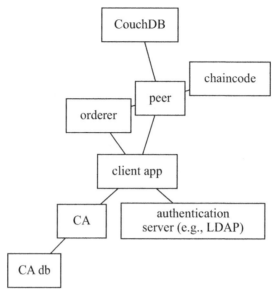

Figure 2. 5. Each peer organization might be running above applications in Docker containers or as binaries on multiple hosts (computers or virtual machines).

PROVISIONING CA SERVER

To provision CA server one can use the `hyperledger/fabric-ca:1.4` Docker image or the `fabric-ca-server` binary that ships with Fabric. You can also develop your own CA and not use the one provided by Fabric. Irrespective of whether you are using Fabric CA or not, before you can provision a CA server, you need to provision the database that server will use - unless you are using a local file based db like sqlite3 for the CA db. In addition, before the CA server can be provisioned, you need to generate a self-signed certificate to bootstrap the CA. This certificate provides the identity of the server itself. How do we get this certificate? This is a "chicken-and-egg" problem since we need a CA server to get a certificate in the first place. When using Fabric CA, there are two ways to solve this problem: one is by using the `fabric-ca-server init` command and another is by using `openssl` or `certtool` CLI to generate a self-signed certificate. Once we have the CA's cert in hand, the server can be started with `fabric-ca-server start` command. Central to provisioning of Fabric CA is the `fabric-ca-server-config.yaml` file which contains important configuration information such as connection string to the CA db and path to the CA server's own X.509 certificate and private key. [56]

Next we can provision any intermediate CA server(s). As mentioned earlier, CAs form a hierarchy or chain. A X.509 certificate has a reference to its issuer. One can keep navigating the chain of issuers until it terminates at a CA whose issuer is the CA itself (known as a self-signed certificate). Intermediate CAs help in spreading out the risk. If a root CA is compromised, it compromises all the certificates that can be traced to it vs. compromise of an intermediate CA will only impact the certificates under its tree. See Figure 2. 6 for illustration.

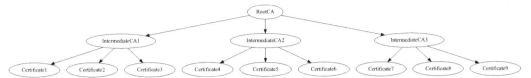

Figure 2. 6. Use of intermediate CAs spreads out the risk. For example, if the Intermediate CA2 is compromised, it only affects the certificates that can be traced to it; namely Certificates 4, 5, 6. The rest of the certificates are not compromised.

REGISTER AND ENROLL PEER, ORDERER AND ADMIN USERS

In order to provision peer and orderer nodes we need their identity. We get those identities in this step by registering and enrolling the peer and orderer nodes against the CAs. This includes getting TLS certificates as well. Fabric CA exposes a flag known as `enrollment.profile` which can be used to configure what type of certificate you want to be issued when enrolling a user [57] - TLS or non-TLS. Getting the identities of peer and orderer nodes is not enough. We also need to get identities of the people having admin privileges over those nodes. To register and enroll the peer, orderer and admin users one can use the `fabric-ca-client` CLI that ships with Fabric or one could also do this through a Node.js app utilizing the `fabric-ca-client` Node.js package. This Node.js app could be bundled together with the main client application or could be developed as a separate app.

PROVISION PEER, ORDERER AND ANY COUCHDB NODES

If you are using CouchDB for your key-value store then the first step is to provision that db before a peer node can be started. At this stage you have everything you need to provision a peer node using either the `hyperledger/fabric-peer:2.0` Docker image or the `peer` binary that ships with Fabric.

But to provision an orderer node you need what is known as a *genesis block*. This block is generated by running the `configtxgen` tool and takes as input a file known as `configtx.yaml` - this is a very important file in Fabric that should be *jointly developed in a shared repo* just like the smart contracts since it contains channel configuration and policies which impact everyone. These configuration and policies are copied by `configtxgen` from the yaml file into the *genesis block*. Among other things, the *genesis block* contains what is known as the *Membership Service Provider (MSP)* information of all the companies participating in the consortium. For the most part, this is nothing but the X.509 certificates of the CAs (and the admin users if using older versions of Fabric) of each peer organization packaged nicely in a particular directory structure that Fabric expects. The peer organizations will have to manually exchange these certificates with each other out-of-band through email or whatever means. The MSP enables the orderer to do things like verify that the peer who signed a transaction is who they claim they are and have the authority to endorse the transaction. Recall that X.509 certificate verification involves checking if the X.509 chain of issuers can be traced to an issuer who is from a list of trusted CAs. Once you have the *genesis block* you will be able to provision an orderer node either directly through the `orderer` binary that ships with Fabric or using the `hyperledger/fabric-orderer:2.0` Docker image.

At this stage we have provisioned the network of peers, orderers and CAs - however we cannot perform any transactions on it as we haven't provisioned the chaincode. In fact before we can do it we need to provision a *channel*. All the steps of provisioning a channel and chaincode below have to be done by an *admin* user.

CREATE CHANNEL AND JOIN PEER NODES TO IT

A *channel* is analogous to a chat room in WhatsApp. Peers will join a channel just like we join a chat room in WhatsApp with our friends. A channel has a blockchain or ledger associated with it. All peers that have joined the channel will get the transactions broadcasted to the channel. *Remember there is 1:1 correspondence between a channel and a blockchain.* And just as a user can join multiple chat rooms in WhatsApp, similarly a peer can join multiple channels in Fabric. The blockchain is the channel's log in exactly the same way as we have the message log of a chat room in WhatsApp. Different channels have distinct and separate blockchains in exactly the same way as we can have multiple chat rooms in WhatsApp. The channel/chatroom analogy has really helped me whenever I got stuck or confused trying to understand relationship between channels and blockchain, what happens when a peer joins multiple channels etc.

To create a channel, we first need to generate a *channel configuration transaction*. This is done using the `configtxgen` tool and the same `configtx.yaml` file that we used to generate the genesis block. This *channel configuration transaction* is processed by special system chaincode to create a channel. Only an admin from one peer org needs to perform the channel creation step. This is much like we need only one user to create a chat room in WhatsApp. Once a channel is created the admins from other peer organizations join their peer nodes to it. Now at this stage we have an interconnected network of peers and orderers and a channel to transact on but there is no chaincode deployed on this channel.

INSTALL, APPROVE AND COMMIT CHAINCODE

The process of provisioning the chaincode differs from Fabric 1.x to 2.0. Fabric 2.0 still supports the old protocol of version 1.x for deploying the chaincode but also adds a new chaincode lifecycle and deployment process. The main problem with the chaincode deployment process of 1.x is that one organization gets to set the *endorsement policy* governing the chaincode. *Other organizations have to simply trust that this policy has been set correctly.* The new chaincode lifecycle of 2.0 overcomes this limitation and is the most important improvement in 2.0 over the previous version in my opinion.

The 1.x protocol of chaincode deployment consists of two steps - installing the chaincode on the peer nodes and instantiating the chaincode over a channel. The new lifecycle works as follows and consists of four steps: *package, install, approve, commit*. First, the chaincode has to be packaged by an admin into a tar file and installed on the target peer nodes. Then the admin will approve the chaincode for his or her organization - this is where the admin sets the endorsement policy which will apply when the chaincode runs on his or her node. When all admins have installed the chaincode on their peer nodes and set approval policy, *only one admin needs to commit the chaincode*. At this stage if there is a mismatch between the endorsement policies, the commit will fail. Fabric provides a `checkcommitreadiness` command that can be used to check if a chaincode is ready to be committed.

The channel creation, join peer nodes to channel, install, approve and commit chaincode are all done using the peer CLI that ships with Fabric. As of this writing, it is not possible to do any of this from a Node.js app. A Node.js app would provide a friendly UI to perform these actions and could potentially be used by people who are not Fabric developers such as people in Ops. Fabric plans to develop a fabric-admin package which will provide ability to install, approve and commit chaincode from a Node.js app but the channel provisioning would still need to be done from the CLI. [58] Note that version 1.4 of the fabric-client Node package has support for channel creation and chaincode provisioning APIs but this package is deprecated and not suggested to be used with Fabric 2.0. In v2.0, fabric-network is the only recommended API for developing client applications. [59]

Now you have a network that is ready to process requests. The next thing to do would be to provision your client application.

PROVISIONING THE CLIENT APPLICATION

For this, you would follow the normal steps of provisioning a Node.js app. One thing you will need to do is to authenticate requests coming in to your application as you don't want anonymous users accessing it. To do that, depending on your individual setup you might either use SAML, OAuth or LDAP based authentication server. You might even have to provision a new server - for example if you are a startup. As bonus, this book will show how to setup an OpenLDAP server for user authentication in Chapter 15. LDAP is a specification and many implementations (free and paid) are available. It is crucial to enable TLS on the LDAP server and have it refuse non-TLS connections since user passwords will be sent to the LDAP server. *Nowhere else is TLS more important than here.* Another crucial thing is to store passwords as salted hashes not as plain text. That way even if someone steals the LDAP database, the attacker will not be able to determine the original passwords. As a bonus it is recommended to also enable clientauth on the LDAP server to tightly control what machines can access it.

2.7. Fabric Consensus and Forks

Let's take a closer look at Fabric consensus and understand what it is and what it is not. At this stage you should re-read Section 1.7 to refresh your memory of Fabric consensus and concepts such as CFT and BFT. We noted in that section that Fabric consensus (Raft or Zab) relies on a *trust* assumption amongst the orderer nodes. We also defined what *trust* means in this context. Messages amongst ordering nodes can take arbitrarily long to be delivered, can be duplicated, and can be lost, *but they can be trusted when received.* But we did not answer one question which is *why would a node act maliciously? i.e., why would it send the wrong message about its state to other nodes?* Nodes after all are running deterministic and predictable code. And all of them would run the same orderer code downloaded from the Fabric repository or Docker image. They are not human beings who can act in unpredictable and arbitrary ways. The answer is that the code on the node gets compromised and that causes it to go rogue. This can happen due to an attack or the organization managing the node itself may decide to do bad things and modify the code deliberately. Thus the assumption that all the nodes are running the same code gets violated and causes the *trust* to breakdown. When all ordering nodes are managed by a single organization, it is perfectly reasonable to assume there will be no Byzantine faults. In other words, the nodes (or messages coming from them) can be fully trusted. *Why would the same organization run one version of code on some of the ordering nodes and another version on others? It does not make sense.*

The only advantage or feature enhancement provided by Kafka over the Solo orderer is protection against a single point of failure, known in other words as Crash Fault Tolerance (CFT). Raft adds the ability to form a decentralized ordering service.

In the context of Fabric's ordering service, Zab and Raft are CFT protocols in which the constituent nodes vote to elect one node as leader. The leader node then processes all transactions submitted by client applications. If the leader node goes down (i.e., *crashes*), a new node is elected leader and continues processing of transactions. The followers blindly trust the order of transactions that is output by the leader node. That's all there is to it. There is no message passing and voting to come to any consensus amongst the nodes about the transactions. *The only time there is a consensus is when the leader has to be elected.* So much so for calling themselves a consensus protocol!

The Raft based ordering service stores its data in a database known as Etcd. From its online documentation: *"Etcd is a strongly consistent, distributed key-value store that provides a reliable way to store data that needs to be accessed by a distributed system or cluster of machines".* [60] The Raft protocol is simply the engine that powers this database and *synchronizes the state of the key-value store across the machines.* Etcd is not unique to Fabric. It is a general purpose key-value store also used by other projects - most notably Docker itself in the *swarm* mode to synchronize the global cluster state across nodes. What does the key-value store store? In case of Fabric, this key-value store is storing (block_id, block). The Raft based ordering service also orders transactions on *first-come-first-served basis. A Raft cluster of* n *nodes can handle maximum* Math.floor{(n-1)/2} *failures*. This translates to 1 failure for 3 nodes, or 2 failures for 5 nodes, or 3 failures for 7 nodes. Most common configuration for Raft is 3, 5, or 7 nodes. Raft is named after *Reliable, Replicated, Redundant, And Fault-Tolerant.*

Table 2. 2 is a summary of the most noticeable feature enhancements or improvements in Fabric ranging from 1.x to current stable release of 2.0 in my opinion. *If you ask me, version 1.4 is the MVP (minimally viable product) for Fabric because with version 1.3 or less the ordering service is under control of a single organization and thus the network is not fully decentralized.* This is because the Kafka cluster of Zookeeper nodes can only be managed by a single org. And not to mention the fact that it takes significant operational expertise to setup, configure, and manage a Kafka cluster. [61] With v1.3, sometimes the peer orgs hire a 3rd party company to manage the ordering service and lose out on the whole value proposition of blockchain in the first place which is about reducing costs and decentralization! Another business model is to form an independent company with the peer orgs as shareholders. With 1.4 and Raft, the ordering service can be finally decentralized and peer orgs can contribute nodes to it. Version 1.4 still has one major bug in it which is that the endorsement policy is specified by the administrator of some organization and other organizations just have to trust that it was correctly set. So even calling 1.4 as a MVP is somewhat of a stretch.

Table 2. 2. Feature enhancements of various versions of Fabric

1.3	1.4	2.0
Centralized ordering service (Kafka)	Decentralized ordering service (Raft)	Endorsement policy not under control of a single organization
Debian based Docker images		Alpine based Docker images
Buyer Beware	MVP	

One advantage of Fabric consensus is that the transaction finality is *immediate* vs. being *probabilistic* if one were using Proof of Work (PoW). What this means is that forks cannot occur in the ledger - validated transactions will never be reverted or dropped. [62] A fork occurs when the copy of the ledger differs between two or more peers (definition). This however opens up the question that *if forks cannot occur in the ledger (i.e., if all copies are identical) then why does one ever need to get endorsement from more than one peer?* The answer is that the claim that forks cannot occur in Fabric is true as long as peer nodes act as good citizens, are running the same chaincode, refrain from making out-of-band changes to the ledger and are not hacked. In that case arguably one does not need endorsement from more than one peer. But what if the conditions above do not hold? Getting endorsements from one than one peer causes a timely alert in the form of `proposal response payloads do not match` error when forks do happen in the ledger and is a protective measure. Thus the claim that forks cannot occur is not something that can be taken blindly for granted. It is not some intrinsic property of the Fabric blockchain and relies on some assumptions for it to hold true.

Let's cover some ways how the ledger could be forked and bad things could happen and how getting endorsement from more than one peer protects us from mayhem:

- *Unauthorized changes*: These are changes that are committed without approval of other parties. They in effect constitute a hack (attack) on the ledger. It is practically not possible to make these changes because it requires the hacker to steal the private keys of other organizations that are involved in endorsement process plus the orderer in order to fake their signatures. A strict endorsement policy will protect against someone being able to attack the ledger and make such unauthorized changes.
- *Corrupting the ledger*: The Fabric ledger is stored in plain sight on `/var/hyperledger/production/ledgersData` on the peer nodes. The data is however stored in a binary format and so not something that can be modified by using a text editor to any meaningful purpose. Any change you make in a text editor will likely corrupt the ledger. However, *the world state derived from this ledger can be viewed and modified independently and outside of Fabric if one is using CouchDB for the world state.* [63] Nothing prevents the Curious George from modifying the ledger in this way. However if he does this, his changes will not propagate to rest of the nodes. But unfortunately it will cause havoc on rest of the system since if George's endorsement is required for a transaction to be committed and his ledger is corrupted or out-of-sync with other nodes, then the entire system suffers. *This is in sharp contrast to Bitcoin where a tampered ledger on George's node will not stop the addition of new blocks to the ledgers on other nodes. Other nodes will continue to make progress.*

In summary, a corrupted or compromised ledger on one peer node does not corrupt the copies of ledger on the other nodes and no further transactions will happen on the ledger until the conflict is resolved.

2.8. Thought Exercise: Comparing Fabric to Git

A powerful metaphor for Fabric is provided by Git itself. Fabric's transaction lifecycle of *propose, collect votes, commit* is very similar to how a developer submits a PR, waits for others to sign off on it and then commits it to the repo. Consider following similarities between Git and a Fabric blockchain:

- Both are distributed logs. Both are just a chain of transactions or commits.
- In Git each changeset has a pointer to previous changeset and in a blockchain a block has pointer to previous block.
- Fabric's process of endorsement prior to commit works very similar to code-review process at time of code check-in by a developer where a developer sends out changeset for code-review and has to obtain sign-offs from other developers before he or she is allowed to check in code.
- In both cases a commit can fail even though it was endorsed due to conflicting changes to the same content.
- Git commits can be signed just like Fabric transactions are. [64]
- Both Git and a blockchain use a data structure known as *Merkle trees* for secure verification of content. Merkle trees are covered in Section 16.3.
- Git also acts as an append-only log. Its `revert` command undoes the effect of an earlier commit by appending a new commit not by changing the history of commits. [65]

Do you think you could use Git to develop a permissioned blockchain like Fabric?

2.9. Summary

- Everything in Fabric ranging from users to the peer and orderer nodes has an identity in the form of an X.509 or Idemix certificate.
- A X.509 certificate by itself does not prove identity. Identity is proven using a combination of X.509 certificate and an associated *digital signature*.
- X.509 certificates are issued by *Certificate Authorities*. *Fabric CA* is an optional component of Fabric that can be used to provision a CA.
- X.509 certificates and their corresponding private keys are securely stored in a *wallet* by the *client application*.
- *Certificate Authorities* form a chain of trust and to validate a X.509 certificate, the chain of issuers (CAs) is examined until one finds an issuer that is trusted.
- *LevelDB* is a database that exists only embedded within the peer process whereas *CouchDB* runs and exists independently of Fabric as a standalone server.
- It is possible to run the peers, orderer and CA servers using binaries (command line executables) but the chaincode will run inside a Docker container in production unless you are using external builders (a new feature in Fabric 2.0).
- *Client authentication* is used to control what machines can connect to a server. It is also known as *mutual authentication* since by default TLS only provides one-way authentication in which only the server proves its identity to the client.

- The chaincode (smart contracts) and `configtx.yaml` should be jointly developed and co-owned by the organizations making up the consortium in a shared repository.
- If the world state db on a peer node gets corrupted - or if the node goes down for any reason - and a sign off from that peer is required for transactions to be committed, it will block the entire system and other nodes will have to suffer.
- There is nothing special in how consensus is achieved in Fabric. It is a direct consequence of all stakeholders agreeing to a change before its committed onto the ledger and this is where Fabric differs sharply from Bitcoin. Don't be fooled into thinking that Raft or Kafka drive consensus in Fabric.
- A Raft cluster of `n` nodes can handle `Math.floor{(n-1)/2}` failures.

Recall some of the new terms you learned in this chapter: public and private keys, X.509 certificate, Fabric CA, LDAP, Channel, MSP, TLS, genesis block, Docker, configtxgen, channel configuration transaction.

2.10. Further Reading

- What's new in version 2.0: hyperledger-fabric.readthedocs.io/en/release-2.0/whatsnew.html.
- Fabric FAQs: hyperledger-fabric.readthedocs.io/en/release-2.0/Fabric-FAQ.html.
- Fabric Glossary: hyperledger-fabric.readthedocs.io/en/release-2.0/glossary.html.
- KC Tam has some good articles on Fabric. I recommend watching his blog at medium.com/ @kctheservant.

[40] maybe you use the same password but the point here is that Facebook uses a completely separate database to authenticate you than LinkedIn.

[41] en.wikipedia.org/wiki/Cryptographic_hash_function

[42] en.wikipedia.org/wiki/MD5#Collision_vulnerabilities

[43] Legend has it that Satoshi deliberately choose `secp256k1` over `secp256r1` because NIST is closely influenced by NSA and leaked documents by the NSA contractor and whistle-blower Edward Snowden suggested that the NSA had used its influence over NIST to insert a backdoor into a random number generator used in elliptic curve cryptography standards. see koclab.cs.ucsb.edu/teaching/ecc/project/2015Projects/Bjoernsen.pdf

[44] Both signature and message could be in one JSON object sent to the receiver but the signature cannot be inside the message. If you try to put the signature in the message, you change the message itself. This is similar to how a file's checksum cannot be inside the file itself (for readers familiar with it).

[45] en.wikipedia.org/wiki/Elliptic_Curve_Digital_Signature_Algorithm

[46] The advantage with a central CA is that setting up the chain of trust becomes much easier. However it is antithetical to the decentralized concept underlying a blockchain.

[47] There are clients for Java and Go as well.

[48] Perhaps you have asked a professor for a recommendation letter at some point. Some professors will ask you to send them a draft letter with what you would like them to write in it. The professor just signs the letter and seals it, making it legit and as coming from him or her. It is the same thing here. No different. Fabric CA is the professor and client application is the student.

[49] github.com/hyperledger/fabric/blob/v2.0.1/internal/peer/node/start.go#L180

[50] hyperledger-fabric.readthedocs.io/en/release-1.4/couchdb_tutorial.html#use-best-practices-for-queries-and-indexes

[51] fabric-shim.github.io/master/fabric-shim.ChaincodeStub.html#getQueryResult

[52] hyperledger-fabric.readthedocs.io/en/release-2.0/cc_launcher.html

[53] codeblog.dotsandbrackets.com/multi-host-docker-network-without-swarm/

[54] hub.docker.com/

[55] previous versions of it were called Secure Sockets Layer or SSL.

[56] A sample of this file can be found at hyperledger-fabric-ca.readthedocs.io/en/latest/serverconfig.html

[57] as far as the CA server is concerned the peer and orderer nodes are also users for it

[58] www.npmjs.com/package/fabric-client/v/2.0.0-beta.2

[59] hyperledger.github.io/fabric-sdk-node/master/tutorial-migration.html

[60] etcd.io/

[61] hyperledger-fabric.readthedocs.io/en/release-1.1/kafka.html#kafka-caveat

[62] hyperledger-fabric.readthedocs.io/en/release-1.4/orderer/ordering_service.html

[63] The situation is no different than if you were using MySQL as the database for some application (e.g., a Wordpress site). DB administrators can always modify the database by accessing it directly outside of the main application.

[64] see www.linuxjournal.com/content/signing-git-commits

[65] www.atlassian.com/git/tutorials/undoing-changes/git-revert

Chapter 3. Writing Your First Smart Contract

This chapter covers:

- How to write a smart contract
- Getting basic familiarity with Node.js and TypeScript

Code for this chapter is under `$/boilerplate-contract` directory

By now you have gained a solid understanding of how Fabric works and learnt most of its jargon. In this chapter we kick the tires and get started with some real programming. We will learn how to write a simple smart contract using the `fabric-contract-api` that comes with Fabric's Node.js SDK. Smart contracts encapsulate the business or application logic. We will be writing all our smart contracts in TypeScript which is a syntactical superset of JavaScript, and adds optional static typing to the language so that we can do things like find all references where a variable is being used, jump to definition of a class and catch errors at compile time instead of run-time. In short we get all the advantages which a statically typed language such as Java provides. The only prerequisite for the coding in this chapter is to have Git, Node.js and preferably an IDE like Visual Studio Code (VS Code for short) installed on your local development machine. These are covered in Section A.1 to Section A.4, however I would recommend to go through the full list in Appendix A and install all the prerequisite software for developing Fabric applications. [66]

3.1. The Fabric Codebase

Before jumping in, let's take a moment to understand how the Fabric codebase is organized on GitHub. When things don't work as expected, you will want to refer to Fabric code and possibly run it under a debugger to understand how the internals work. You can even modify the source code and create a custom build of Fabric e.g., if you run against a bug or missing feature and don't want to wait for the fix or feature to appear in the official release. Take a look at Table 3. 1 to see the repositories which form the Fabric stack.

Table 3. 1. Fabric code repositories

fabric-sdk-node (SDK to develop client applications)		
fabric-chaincode-node (SDK to develop smart contracts)		
fabric	fabric-ca	fabric-baseimage

The full URL of a repo can be constructed by appending the repo name in Table 3. 1 to `github.com/hyperledger`. In order, we have:

- `fabric`: This repo contains code for the `peer`, `orderer` and tools such as `cryptogen` and `configtxgen`. `cryptogen` is a command line tool that ships with Fabric and can be used to generate private keys and X.509 certificates during development and testing. This repo also contains the code to build Docker images for the peer and orderer. This code is defined in a `Dockerfile`. The Dockerfiles for the peer and orderer can be found under the `images` directory in this repo. For example, the `Dockerfile` for the orderer is at `/images/orderer/Dockerfile`. The code in this repo is written in Go.

- `fabric-ca`: This repo contains code for the Fabric CA. The Dockerfiles can be found under the `images` directory of the repo. This repo also uses Go.

- `fabric-baseimage`: This repo seems largely deprecated with version 2.0 of Fabric. It contains code to build the `fabric-baseimage` and `fabric-baseos` Docker images used in 1.x. The Dockerfiles for these can be found under the `config` directory. Both 1.x peer and orderer derive from the `fabric-baseos` image. In addition the repo contains Dockerfiles for `fabric-kafka`, `fabric-couchdb` and `fabric-zookeeper` under the `images` directory.

- `fabric-chaincode-node`: This repo contains two important packages that together form the SDK which enables developers to write and run smart contracts in JavaScript. One is **fabric-contract-api** which was introduced in v1.4 of Fabric. This is the only package you will require if all you want to do is *write* a smart contract and compile the TypeScript files into JavaScript. This package is found under `/apis/fabric-contract-api`. [67] The other package is **fabric-shim** found under `/libraries/fabric-shim`. [68] This package builds the `fabric-chaincode-node` executable that is used to *run* a smart contract. Just as we have a SDK for Node.js, there are also SDKs for Java and Go but we don't list them here as we don't use Java or Go in this book. In addition, this repository contains the `Dockerfile` for the `fabric-nodeenv` image which is the base image used to build the chaincode container. [69]

- `fabric-sdk-node`: This is the SDK that enables developers to write client applications in Node.js using the **fabric-network** API introduced in v1.4 and `fabric-client` API available in earlier versions of Fabric. It also contains the **fabric-ca-client** Node.js package to communicate with a Fabric CA server. Just as we have a SDK for Node.js, there are also SDKs for Java and Go but we don't list them here as we don't use Java or Go in this book.

As a developer you will mostly be working with two libraries: **fabric-contract-api** to write smart contracts and **fabric-network** to develop client applications. Both are published as `npm` packages. The full list of Fabric repos can be found at `github.com/hyperledger?utf8=%E2%9C%93&q=fabric`.

3.2. Defining the problem: Tracking assets through a supply chain

At the heart of most blockchain applications is an asset and blockchain is nothing but a way to track and trace ownership of that asset. For example, if you examine the Fabric samples [70] all the examples follow this pattern. `Balance-transfer` is an application to track & trace money. `Fabcar` is an application to track & trace cars. `Commercial-paper` is an application to track & trace bonds. Here we consider developing an application for the pharmaceutical supply chain that aims to eliminate counterfeit drugs from entering the supply chain. The pharma supply chain consists of a drug manufacturer who manufactures a drug and sells it to a wholeseller. The wholeseller will sell it to other suppliers and middle-men until finally the drug is sold to a retail pharmacy or a hospital which sells it to the end consumer. Any time a drug changes ownership we would like the buyer to verify if the seller is the legitimate owner of the drug. This is the key business requirement and the reason why we use a blockchain is because it establishes a global registry that can be consulted for this information. This way we can prevent counterfeit drugs from entering the supply chain. So the drug is the asset in this application. At the abstract level, any asset can be modelled with a unique identifier plus metadata specific to that asset. For example, in case of a drug the metadata could have information such as the drug name, who is the manufacturer, date of manufacture, date of expiry, SKU, its possible uses, warnings, side-effects, a possible web URL etc.

What methods/endpoints should our smart contract have? We just need 3 methods to get started:

- **Create**: will allow a manufacturer to be able to create an asset in the system. Recall an asset is just a ID + some metadata.
- **Update**: will record transfer of ownership of the asset from one party to another. The owner of asset calls this endpoint and releases ownership to someone else.
- **Verify**: can be used to verify ownership of the asset before purchasing. A buyer calls this endpoint and provides the asset ID + name or ID of seller and the endpoint responds `true` or `false` depending on whether the seller is indeed the legitimate owner of the asset or not.

The `create` and `update` operations will cause writes on the blockchain ledger whereas the `verify` operation will just perform reads on the ledger. Note that we do not have a method to trace the provenance or history of an asset. We'll leave that as an exercise for the reader and provide hints on how to do it. Let's define a small network consisting of three fictitious companies:

- **Biotor** is a drug manufacturer
- **Express Medicinals** is a wholeseller
- **Key Pharmacy** is a retail pharmacy

These three companies come together to form a consortium and create a blockchain based track & trace solution. As their proof of concept becomes a success, more companies will join the consortium and the business value of the network will grow over time.

3.3. The Smart Contract Boilerplate: Getting to know Node.js and TypeScript

To help you get started writing smart contracts I have created a template that can be used as a starting point in your adventure. This template is derived from the template IBM Blockchain VS Code extension uses to create a new smart contract. The only difference is that the unit tests are stored in a `test` directory instead of the `src` directory as done by the IBM extension. To use this template, clone the code repository that comes with this book and change to the `boilerplate-contract` directory:

```
$ cd boilerplate-contract
```

You should see following files:

Listing 3. 1. Source files of `boilerplate-contract`

```
$ tree -a .
.
├────── .editorconfig
├────── .gitignore
├────── .npmignore
├────── .vscode
│         └────── launch.json
├────── package-lock.json
├────── package.json
├────── src
│         ├────── asset-contract.ts
│         ├────── asset.ts
│         └────── index.ts
├────── test
│         └────── asset-contract.spec.ts
├────── tsconfig.json
└────── tslint.json

3 directories, 13 files
```

Here is quick explanation of various files that you see above:

* `src/asset-contract.ts`: the main file containing the contract. It contains following 5 methods which provide CRUD (create/read/update/delete) operations on an asset:

  ```
  assetExists
  createAsset
  readAsset
  updateAsset
  deleteAsset
  ```

  An `asset` just contains a `value` which can be an arbitrary string. And an `asset` is identified by its ID. Take some time to go through this file and understand the code in these methods.

* `.editorconfig`: this file contains editor settings for VS Code such as whether to use tabs or space for indent, how much spaces to indent etc.
* `.gitignore`: defines files and directories that should be ignored by git.
* `.npmignore`: defines files and directories that should be ignored by npm when it packs your project.
* `.vscode`: this directory contains files specific to VS Code.
* `.vscode/launch.json`: this is an important file and it contains the configuration that enables debugging the smart contract and unit tests from VS Code.
* `package.json`: a very important file defining all the dependencies and various commands. We will dig into this in a minute. It is the equivalent of `pom.xml` if you are a Java developer.
* `src`: contains the source code of the smart contract.
* `test`: contains the unit tests.
* `tsconfig.json`: config file that tells the TypeScript compiler how to compile the source code.

- `tslint.json`: defines the rules that govern code style.

Let's dig into some of these files now.

3.3.1. `package.json`

If you are a Node.js developer you are already familiar with `package.json`. We won't cover the file line by line but mention some of the more important aspects defined in the file. Let's start with dependencies. One can see dependencies defined in two places. The core dependencies are defined in:

```
"dependencies": {
    "fabric-contract-api": "~2.1.2",
    "fabric-shim": "~2.1.2"
}
```

These contain the dependencies required at runtime. We covered them earlier. There is another section which lists dependencies required to compile and test the project. These are defined in `devDependencies`. Let's cover some of them:

- `typescript`: the TypeScript compiler which compiles TypeScript code into JavaScript. The code is not compiled into a binary but its standard practice to still say its compiled (some authors use the word transpiled). The TypeScript compiler uses the `tsconfig.json` file which tells it what files to compile, what version of JavaScript to target (we use `es2017` aka ECMAScript 2017 or ES8) and where to output the results.
- `ts-node`: `ts-node` allows us to run TypeScript code directly without first compiling it to JavaScript. We use it in this project to run our unit tests without converting them into JavaScript first. If you think about it, it must be doing some compilation (perhaps in memory) but those are details that don't concern us.
- `tslint`: this is the TypeScript linter which checks for code style violations.
- `mocha`: a popular framework used for testing JavaScript code.
- `nyc`: a popular library to generate code coverage statistics from unit tests.
- `chai`: provides assertions used in unit tests to check if something equals its expected value.
- `sinon`: allows a developer to mock, fake and spy objects in unit tests.

3.3.2. `tsconfig.json`

`tsconfig.json` is an important file configuring TypeScript settings. The settings we use are shown below in Listing 3. 2: [71]

Listing 3. 2. TypeScript settings as defined in `tsconfig.json`

```
{
    "compilerOptions": {
        "outDir": "dist",                        ❶
        "target": "es2017",                      ❷
        "moduleResolution": "node",              ❸
        "module": "commonjs",                    ❹
        "declaration": true,                     ❺
        "experimentalDecorators": true,          ❻
        "emitDecoratorMetadata": true,
        "sourceMap": true                        ❼
    },
    "include": [                                 ❽
        "./src/**/*"
    ],
    "exclude": [                                 ❾
        "./src/**/*.spec.ts"
    ]
}
```

❶ The output directory where the compiled code will be placed.

❷ The target controls what features of JavaScript are used. `es2017` is a safe target for use with Node.js 8 or higher.

❸ This affects the algorithm used to search for modules or imports. `node` mimics the Node.js module resolution mechanism (recommended). The only other option for this setting is `classic`.

❹ Changes the output produced by TypeScript compiler. `commonjs` is the most common setting.

❺ Generates `.d.ts` files for every TypeScript or JavaScript file inside your project.

❻ This allows us to use decorators such as `@Transaction` in our code.

❼ An important setting that allows us to debug JavaScript while sticking breakpoints in TypeScript source code.

❽ What files will be compiled

❾ What files will not be compiled

3.3.3. Installing dependencies

Go ahead and run `npm install` (or `npm i` for short) from the directory that contains `package.json`. You should see an output that looks like following. Don't worry about getting an output that exactly matches what you see below - just ensure you don't get any errors: [72]

```
$ npm i

> protobufjs@6.9.0 postinstall /Users/siddjain/go/src/github.com/siddjain/phf/boilerplate-
contract/node_modules/protobufjs
> node scripts/postinstall

npm WARN boilerplate-contract@0.0.1 No repository field.

added 390 packages from 1078 contributors and audited 391 packages in 7.123s

1 package is looking for funding
  run `npm fund` for details

found 12 vulnerabilities (9 low, 3 high)
  run `npm audit fix` to fix them, or `npm audit` for details
```

I wouldn't worry about running npm audit fix just yet. What's going on as we run above command? The node package manager (npm; equivalent to mvn if you come from the Java world) will install all the dependencies defined in package.json under a directory node_modules. [73]

3.3.4. Main Entry Point

It can take a minute or two for npm install to finish as it may also compile some binaries. Links to the binaries will be stored under node_modules/.bin. The bin directory can always be accessed by running npm bin:

```
$ npm bin
/Users/siddjain/phf/code/boilerplate-contract/node_modules/.bin
```

Take a look at the contents of this directory. You will find the TypeScript compiler (tsc) and other goodies stored in there. One goodie you will find is fabric-chaincode-node. The fabric-shim dependency generates this binary and Fabric uses this binary to run the smart contract written by us. This is defined under the scripts section of package.json:

```
"start": "fabric-chaincode-node start"
```

The fabric-chaincode-node is given an entry point that is defined by main in package.json:

```
"main": "dist/index.js"
```

Think of it as the main class in a Java or C program. When our TypeScript code is compiled, it results in generation of this file under the dist directory which is defined in tsconfig.json under the outDir field. You can change the output directory by changing the value of this field.

The other important section in package.json is scripts:

```
"scripts": {
    "lint": "tslint -c tslint.json 'src/**/*.ts'",
    "pretest": "npm run lint",
    "test": "nyc mocha -r ts-node/register test/**/*.spec.ts",
    "start": "fabric-chaincode-node start",
    "build": "tsc",
    "build:watch": "tsc -w",
    "prepublishOnly": "npm run build"
}
```

It defines commands that can be run like so (to give an example):

```
$ npm start
```

This will cause npm to execute the start command defined in the scripts section. npm supports a number of well-known commands. [74] In addition it allows developer to create new commands that can be executed by running (to give an example):

```
$ npm run foo
```

where foo is a command defined by the developer in the scripts section. For example, you could define "foo":"ls" under the scripts section and then run it like npm run foo. Try it.

3.3.5. Compiling TypeScript

Go ahead and compile the TypeScript code by running:

```
$ npm run build

> boilerplate-contract@0.0.1 build /Users/siddjain/phf/code/boilerplate-contract
> tsc
```

You should now see a dist directory which contains following files:

```
$ ls dist
asset-contract.d.ts asset-contract.js   asset-contract.js.map   asset.d.ts      asset.js
asset.js.map        index.d.ts          index.js                index.js.map
```

3.3.6. Checking the code for style violations

You can check the code for style violations by running:

```
$ npm run lint

> boilerplate-contract@0.0.1 lint /Users/siddjain/phf/code/boilerplate-contract
> tslint -c tslint.json 'src/**/*.ts'
```

This process is also known as linting. The style guidelines are defined in tslint.json.

3.3.7. Running unit tests

The boilerplate comes with some unit tests defined under the `test` folder. You can run the unit tests from the command line like so:

```
$ npm test
```

There will be a long output (git.io/JI35j) but it should start with something like

```
> boilerplate-contract@0.0.1 pretest /Users/siddjain/phf/code/boilerplate-contract
> npm run lint


> boilerplate-contract@0.0.1 lint /Users/siddjain/phf/code/boilerplate-contract
> tslint -c tslint.json 'src/**/*.ts'


> boilerplate-contract@0.0.1 test /Users/siddjain/phf/code/boilerplate-contract
> nyc mocha -r ts-node/register test/**/*.spec.ts
```

and end with something like

```
    10 passing (156ms)

============================== Coverage summary ================================
Statements   : 100% ( 93/93 )
Branches     : 100% ( 10/10 )
Functions    : 100% ( 23/23 )
Lines        : 100% ( 88/88 )
===============================================================================
```

The code coverage will be stored in a directory named `.nyc_output`. The unit tests can also be run inside the VS Code debugger. To do that, open the boilerplate in a new workspace and debug using the `Mocha All` configuration defined in `launch.json` and copied below. Refer to VS Code documentation if you need help.

```
{
    "type": "node",
    "request": "launch",
    "name": "Mocha All",
    "program": "${workspaceFolder}/node_modules/mocha/bin/_mocha",
    "args": [
        "-r",
        "ts-node/register",
        "--timeout",
        "999999",
        "--colors",
        "${workspaceFolder}/test/**/*spec.ts",
    ],
    "console": "integratedTerminal",
    "internalConsoleOptions": "neverOpen",
    "protocol": "inspector"
}
```

3.3.8. Running the smart contract

Ready to run the smart contract? Go ahead and give it a try:

```
$ npm start -- --peer.address localhost:7051 --chaincode-id-name mycc
```

The extra `--` is not a typo. This is how `npm` knows that the arguments after `--` should be passed to `fabric-chaincode-node` and are not meant for `npm` itself. These arguments are the address of a peer node and a name (identifier) of the chaincode and are required by `fabric-chaincode-node`. When you run above command, it will give you some output starting with

```
> boilerplate-contract@0.0.1 start /Users/siddjain/phf/code/boilerplate-contract
> fabric-chaincode-node start "--peer.address" "localhost:7051" "--chaincode-id-name"
"mycc"
```

but end in an error:

```
2020-04-02T17:55:58.872Z error [c-api:lib/handler.js]  Chat stream with peer - on error: %j
"Error: 14 UNAVAILABLE: failed to connect to all addresses...
```

This is not surprising because we don't have any peer node running. Provisioning the peer node will take us down a long path and so we'll table this for later.

3.4. Writing the smart contract

Create a new directory and copy the source files of `boilerplate-contract` into it. These are the files that were checked into source control and listed in Listing 3. 1. Edit `src/asset.ts` and define a very simple bare-bones `Asset` as follows:

Listing 3. 3. Definition of an Asset

```
import { Object, Property } from 'fabric-contract-api';

@Object()
export class Asset {
    @Property()
    public id: string;
    @Property()
    public owner: string;
    @Property()
    public createdBy: string;
    @Property()
    public lastModifiedBy: string;
    @Property()
    public metadata: string;
}
```

The fields are self-explanatory:

* id: is a string used to uniquely identify this asset
* owner: is a string used to record who is the owner of this asset
* createdBy: is a string that will store who created this asset
* lastModifiedBy: is a string that will store who last modified this asset
* metadata: is a string that will store metadata relating to this asset. This could be stored as a JSON blob. We use a string but you could replace string with a strongly typed class tailored to your use-case if you wish.

Next we will work on the three methods we identified in previous section: create, update and verify. These methods will be defined in src/asset-contract.ts.

3.4.1. create

The create method will look like following:

Listing 3. 4. The create **method to create an asset in the system**

```
@Transaction()                                            ❶
public async create(ctx: Context, assetId: string,
    metadata: string):                                    ❷
    Promise<void> {                                       ❸
        const mspId = ctx.clientIdentity.getMSPID();      ❹
        if (mspId !== "BiotorMSP") {
            throw new Error("you do not have permission to create an
                asset");
        }

        const exists =
            await this.assetExists(ctx, assetId);         ❺
        if (exists) {
            throw new Error(`The asset ${assetId} already exists`);
        }

        const asset = new Asset();
        asset.id = assetId;
        asset.owner = mspId;
        asset.metadata = metadata;
        asset.createdBy = asset.lastModifiedBy =
                ctx.clientIdentity.getID();                ❻
        const buffer =
            Buffer.from(JSON.stringify(asset));           ❼
        await ctx.stub.putState(assetId, buffer);         ❽
}
```

❶ All callable methods of a smart contract (sometimes referred to as endpoints in the book) should have the @Transaction decorator applied to them.

❷ The first argument to every method will be the Context. This is followed by the arguments needed by your method. The arguments can be strongly typed.

❸ Transactions always return a Promise which is JavaScript's way of writing an asynchronous method or function.

❹ Here we get the ID of the organization the caller belongs to. An alternative way to get this is using ctx.stub.getCreator().mspid.

❺ Helper method to check if asset exists. Part of boilerplate contract.

❻ This will return the Subject and Issuer attributes of the caller's X.509 certificate. This tells us who the caller is and who issued them their ID card.

❼ This is a standard pattern where we first serialize the object as JSON and then encode it in binary before storing in the key-value database (world state).

❽ Standard API call to store a key-value pair in the database. The key (assetID) should be valid UTF8, and should not start with underscore.

A common newbie mistake is to get the organization name from the caller's X.509 certificate and use that to check if caller is part of an organization (such as Biotor). Don't do this. This is because an attacker can impersonate themselves as belonging to another organization. To check if caller really belongs to an organization (e.g., Biotor), we need to trace the chain of issuer of the caller's X.509 certificate until we find an issuer that is known to be from Biotor (or you could use the getMSPID method which is more convenient). Don't trust the metadata (i.e., the organization attribute) in the X.509 certificate for identifying caller's organization as that can be faked.

Resist the temptation to store a lastModifiedAt timestamp which would store the time when last change was made to an Asset. This is because the smart contract will be executed on multiple peer nodes at different times. So if in the smart contract there is a system call to retrieve current timestamp, it will evaluate to different values when the contract is executed on different nodes. As a result, the writesets will be different across the nodes and the transaction will fail to be committed to the ledger in the commit stage.

The Transaction decorator is applied to all methods whose invocation can result in a transaction being appended to the ledger. The first argument to any Transaction is the Context object. It contains two fields:

- clientIdentity: contains the identity of the caller. Recall that in Fabric, callers are identified by their X.509 certificates. The complete API can be found online. [75]
- stub: the stub object provides method to read and update values in the Level or Couch DB. The complete API can be found online. [76]

The Context is followed by arguments passed by caller to the method. The create method takes two arguments from the caller - the assetId which is unique identifier of the asset and an arbitrary metadata payload which can be used to store any metadata about this asset. For a drug, this could store things like name of the drug, expiry, possible side-effects, uses, recommended and maximum allowed dosage, whether its a narcotic etc. The method performs following checks:

- It checks to see if the caller has permission to create an asset. In our problem, we place a restriction that only a drug manufacturer can create an asset. Since we have only one manufacturer (Biotor) as part of our consortium, the smart contract checks if the caller is a member of Biotor.
- It checks if the asset has not been previously created.

If the checks pass, the method creates an asset in the system. Note that we have a lastModifiedBy field to store who was the last person to make updates to an asset.

I would recommend serializing objects as JSON when storing them in the state db which is done by the call to JSON.stringify. If you don't serialize the object as JSON, you won't be able to take advantage of CouchDB's query APIs which can be used to make queries against the objects stored in the db. Non-JSON objects are stored as opaque attachments in CouchDB and are not queryable. [77] Storing objects as JSON in the key-value store keeps the code portable between LevelDB and

CouchDB and you get the benefits of CouchDB's query API if using CouchDB.

3.4.2. Buffers

For readers unfamiliar with Buffer, Buffer is a built-in class in Node.js that provides methods to handle binary data. Note that you did not have to require anything in order to use Buffer. That is why its known as a built-in class or object just like Number or String. A Buffer is nothing but a byte array. The Buffer.from method will make a copy of the string passed to it, encode it in UTF-8 by default and return pointer to the byte array. This is shown below as example:

```
> b1 = Buffer.from("Hello World")
<Buffer 48 65 6c 6c 6f 20 57 6f 72 6c 64>
```

We could try another encoding as follows:

```
> b2 = Buffer.from("Hello World", "ascii")
<Buffer 48 65 6c 6c 6f 20 57 6f 72 6c 64>
```

We can compare the contents of two buffers using Buffer.compare:

```
> Buffer.compare(b1,b2)
0
```

The two buffers are identical since the result of encoding a string composed of English alphabet is the same whether you do it in ASCII or UTF-8. The two buffers themselves are distinct objects in memory:

```
> b1===b2
false
```

We can get the length of a buffer by calling byteLength:

```
> b1.byteLength
11
```

To get a buffer with different contents try encoding the string in UTF-16 by running Buffer.from("Hello World", "UTF16le") and repeat the exercise above.

3.4.3. update

The update method is used to transfer ownership of the asset and will look like following:

Listing 3. 5. The update method to transfer ownership of an asset

```
@Transaction()
public async update(ctx: Context, assetId: string,
    newOwner: string):
    Promise<void> {
        const buffer = await ctx.stub.getState(assetId);
        if (buffer && buffer.length > 0) {
            const asset = JSON.parse(buffer.toString()) as Asset;
            const mspId = ctx.clientIdentity.getMSPID();
            if (asset.owner === mspId) {
                if (mspId !== newOwner) {
                    asset.owner = newOwner;
                    asset.lastModifiedBy = ctx.clientIdentity.getID();
                    await ctx.stub.putState(assetId,
                        Buffer.from(JSON.stringify(asset)));
                }
            } else {
                throw new Error("You do not have permission to modify
                    this asset");
            }
        } else {
            throw new Error(`The asset ${assetId} does not exist`);
        }
}
```

It uses same API calls as the create method. It checks to see if the caller is current owner of the asset in question before transferring ownership. As blockchain is an append-only ledger, when we update any key using putState, the history of the key is preserved and never lost. It can be retrieved using the **getHistoryForKey** method. There was a long standing bug in this method (FAB-16303) where it would return results in random order but with v2.0 this method returns results from newest to oldest in terms of ordered transaction height.

3.4.4. verify

The last method in our smart contract is the verify endpoint which can be called by a buyer to verify that the person or organization selling the asset is indeed the legal owner of the asset. That method is coded as follows:

Listing 3. 6. The verify endpoint

```
@Transaction(false)                                    ❶
@Returns('boolean')                                    ❷
public async verify(ctx: Context, assetId: string, owner: string):
    Promise<boolean> {
        const buffer = await ctx.stub.getState(assetId);
        if (buffer && buffer.length > 0) {
            const asset = JSON.parse(buffer.toString()) as Asset;
            return asset.owner === owner;                 ❸
        }
        return false;                                     ❹
}
```

❶ The `Transaction` is marked `false` to indicate that this method only performs reads on the ledger. It does not write anything to the ledger.

❷ This method returns a `boolean` unlike the `create` and `update` methods which don't return anything.

❸ Return `true` if the true owner (`asset.owner`) is same as asserted owner.

❹ Return `false` if asset does not exist.

The finished smart contract can be found in `$/your-first-contract` directory in the code repository that comes with the book.

3.5. Restrictions on smart contracts

There are a few things that have to be kept in mind as we write smart contracts:

• The result of invoking a smart contract (the `writeset`) should be repeatable across peer nodes. This means we should not create random variables, or use any function whose return value(s) are functions of the current time or location of execution. Time or location related calls may return different values on different peers. If these calls directly or indirectly affect what the smart contract is going to write to the ledger (the `writeset`), then chances are the writesets of different invocations will not match. When that happens, the transaction will be voided and fail to be committed to the ledger in the commit phase.

• Functions should be aware that they may read state, and write state. But they are producing a set of changes that will be applied to the state only when the transaction gets committed. *The implication is that updates to the state may not be read back in the same function call.* For example, consider following code:

```
let v1 = getState("key")
v1=="hello" // is true
putState("key","world")

let v2 = getState("key")
v2=="world" // is false,  v2 is "hello"
```

The value will update only when the transaction gets committed. For newcomers, it is easy to fall prey to this gotcha as illustrated by following code used to return an asset such as a book or mp3 and claim a token in the process. [78]

```
@Transaction()
public async query(ctx: Context, assetId: string): Promise<string> {
    let buffer = await ctx.stub.getState('token');
    const flag = buffer.toString();
    if (flag === '0') {                                        ❶
        await ctx.stub.putState('token', Buffer.from('1'));    ❷
        buffer = await ctx.stub.getState(assetId);             ❸
        return buffer.toString();
    } else {
        throw new Error('you have already claimed your token');
    }
}
```

❶ token has not been spent

❷ claim the token so it cannot be used again

❸ The developer has tacitly assumed here that token is 1 which is incorrect and a *bug* in this code.

The token will not be spent until it is committed onto the ledger. Until that happens, multiple chaincode invocations will continue to return assets and someone could use the loophole to purchase more than one book thus double-spending the token. **Exercise**: Can you think how you would fix this problem? *Hint*: the asset should be returned only *after* the transaction gets committed - the purchase is confirmed - not during when its being simulated in the endorsement phase. Add an event hook in your client application (not the smart contract) to listen to the commit event by using the addCommitListener function on the Network class (FABN-1100). The Network class will be introduced in Section 8.10.6 and has following methods on it (this is a non-exhaustive list):

```
async addCommitListener(listener, peers, transactionId) {
removeCommitListener(listener) {
```

The smart contract should be co-developed in a shared repository by all the companies participating in the consortium. The smart contract affects what data gets written to your copy of the ledger. So you would want to review (and test) it carefully before installing it onto your peer node. One of the advantages of a permissioned blockchain is that there is a consortium who can intervene to correct and undo mistakes if necessary as a result of bugs in the smart contract. In a completely decentralized system such as Ethereum or Bitcoin, there is no consortium who can intervene. The DAO attack is the definitive case study in this area that every blockchain developer should know. Because a blockchain is only as secure as the smart contract that underpins it, there is a whole industry that has emerged whose sole purpose is to audit and guarantee (insure) smart contracts.

One operating model found in permissioned blockchains is to spin off the consortium as a separate entity (organization) with the participating companies as shareholders of this entity. The smart contract development may be done by the consortium but that does not change the fact that it is essentially still being co-developed by all the companies and that you should review it very carefully before installing onto your peer node.

At this stage we have written our smart contract and are ready to put it to the test. To do that we need to provision a network which will be the topic of the next chapter.

3.6. Summary

* Smart contracts (chaincode) are written using the `fabric-contract-api`.
* `fabric-shim` package contains the code for `fabric-chaincode-node` which is the executable that runs a smart contract.
* Smart contracts only interact with the world state. They do not interact with the blockchain.
* The world state is built from the blockchain and stored in a Level or Couch DB.
* Storing the world state in a database allows for faster execution of the smart contract vs. if it had to interact with the blockchain.
* For the chaincode developer, the blockchain will appear very much like a key-value database with the familiar CRUD (create/read/update/delete) operations. They may not even realize that they are working with a blockchain.
* Each peer node will execute the smart contract independently on the data in its own independent copy of the ledger (decentralization).
* A smart contract must give repeatable result when it is executed on different nodes at different times (location and time invariant).
* Smart contracts must be carefully reviewed and tested for bugs in a test environment before running in production.

3.7. Further Reading

* Understand dependency resolution in Node.js: lexi-lambda.github.io/blog/2016/08/24/understanding-the-npm-dependency-model/
* Understand module resolution in Node.js and TypeScript: www.staging-typescript.org/docs/handbook/module-resolution.html#node

[66] That might keep you busy for a day and you should return to this chapter the next day :)

[67] github.com/hyperledger/fabric-chaincode-node/tree/v2.1.2/apis/fabric-contract-api

[68] github.com/hyperledger/fabric-chaincode-node/tree/v2.1.2/libraries/fabric-shim

[69] github.com/hyperledger/fabric-chaincode-node/tree/v2.1.2/docker/fabric-nodeenv

[70] github.com/hyperledger/fabric-samples

[71] Full documentation on `tsconfig.json` can be found at aka.ms/tsconfig.json

[72] If you get errors at this step, please ensure you are using version 12.16.1 or higher of Node.js and version 6.4.1 or higher of npm.

[73] `yarn` is another package manager for Node.js. We will use `npm` in this book.

[74] Complete list can be found at docs.npmjs.com/misc/scripts

[75] fabric-shim.github.io/release-1.4/fabric-shim.ClientIdentity.html

[76] fabric-shim.github.io/release-1.4/fabric-shim.ChaincodeStub.html

[77] hyperledger-fabric.readthedocs.io/en/release-2.0/couchdb_as_state_database.html

[78] This code is adapted from medium.com/@rahulmahadev/side-effects-due-to-speculative-execution-in-hyperledger-fabric-a0b7cd6ab1ca

Chapter 4. Generating identities required to bootstrap a network

This chapter covers:

* Using `cryptogen` utility to generate identities required to bootstrap a network
* Various types of X.509 certificates and their distinguishing characteristics

Code for this chapter is in `$/three-org-network` directory

At this stage we have written our smart contract and are ready to put it to the test. Provisioning a Fabric network is a long winded process. The first step in this process is to generate the identities used to bootstrap the peer and orderer nodes. We do that in this chapter using the `cryptogen` utility that ships with Fabric. This chapter will also provide a deeper understanding of the various forms of X.509 certificates encountered with Fabric and what distinguishes them from one another.

4.1. X.509 certificates, Certificate Authorities and the Chain of Trust

An X.509 certificate is the most widely encountered implementation of a public key certificate. Wikipedia explains it pretty well: *"In cryptography, a public key certificate, also known as a digital certificate or identity certificate, is an electronic document used to prove the ownership of a public key. The certificate includes information about the key, information about the identity of its owner (called the subject), and the digital signature of an entity that has verified the certificate's contents (called the issuer). If the signature is valid, and the software examining the certificate trusts the issuer, then it can use that key to communicate securely with the certificate's subject."* [79]

So we see an X.509 certificate in its most basic form is 4 things:

* a public key. Asymmetric key cryptography uses two keys. A private key which is never shared with anyone and its corresponding public key. The public key is what gets stored in the X.509 certificate.
* who owns that key
* how this key can be used i.e., its permitted usages.
* above 3 facts are attested to and endorsed with a digital signature by a certificate authority (CA). The CA is known as the *issuer* of the certificate.

We can represent it conceptually with the `struct` in Listing 4. 1.

Listing 4. 1. A conceptual representation of an X.509 certificate. It contains a public key, who owns that key, permitted usages of the key and an attestation by a certificate authority.

```
struct X509 {
    byte[] publicKey;    ❶
    long   keyUsages;    ❷
    string metadata;     ❸
    byte[] signature;    ❹
    *X509  issuer;       ❺
}
```

❶ public portion of a public private key pair. private key is never stored in the certificate.

❷ a bit mask defining permitted usages of this key. Different bit masks generate different kinds of X.509 certificates that are meant to be used for different purposes.

❸ metadata about the owner of the key. In case of humans it could be name, what company they belong to, department they work in etc. In case of a machine the metadata might contain the DNS name (address) of this server.

❹ attestation (endorsement) by a certificate authority who attests to the accuracy of the information in this certificate.

❺ pointer to the X.509 certificate of the issuer CA.

The certificate is useless if it isn't signed by a CA - in fact it isn't a certificate at all. It is possible for someone to sign their own certificate. The pointer field in Listing 4. 1 would loop back to itself in that case. This is known as a *self-signed certificate* and they are used to terminate a chain of certificates where we start with A → B → C and so on until we reach a certificate X that loops back to itself and legitimizes itself. X is known as a *root certificate* or a *trust anchor*. The certificates in-between are known as *intermediate CAs* and the leaf cert A is known as *end entity certificate*. We show this diagrammatically in Figure 4. 1. The latest version of X.509 certificates is version 3. The version number is something that appears in the certificate. Note that it is possible to generate multiple certificates using same public key but with different other attributes. Thus there can be a one-to-many mapping between a public key and X.509 certificates although its not something that usually happens in practice and is a purely theoretical construct.

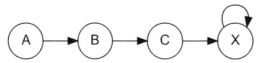

Figure 4. 1. An X.509 certificate chain with A as the end entity certificate and X as the root CA or trust anchor. B and C are intermediate CAs.

What has all of this to do with Fabric? In Fabric, users, administrators, peers and orderers communicate and exchange messages. And *X.509 certificates (plus digital signatures) are used as the user authentication mechanism* similar to how you commonly use a username and password combination on websites for user authentication. Figure 2. 1 showed a simplified gist of what it entails. Basically, we simply check the signature on the certificate. If the signature is by an issuer we trust, then we accept the claims in that certificate. Otherwise we do a recursive check where we test if we trust the issuer of the issuer and so on until we find an issuer we trust or we reach the end of recursion. This scheme effectively establishes a *chain of trust* where *a trust anchor implicitly confers trust on intermediate CAs.* The CA is usually a company that charges customers to issue certificates for them. The centralized chain of trust is is to be contrasted with a decentralized *web of trust* where individuals sign each other's keys directly. [80] What do we mean when we say do we trust an issuer? Simply that there is a database of trusted X.509 certs (or public keys) and we test to see if the issuer's cert or public key exists in that database.

4.2. Using cryptogen *to generate X.509 identities and certificates*

Fabric comes with a convenient tool known as cryptogen that can be used to generate crypto material for bootstrapping a network. You would not use this tool in production - not because it is not secure, but because for lack of a better word its like a "single-serving friend" which requires you to a-priori specify the number of users, provides limited customization of certs it generates and does not come with any database to maintain certificate revocation lists or a server that can be used to dynamically generate certs at runtime as you add more users to your application. A production setup would use Fabric CA or alternative. Provisioning the Fabric CA server and using that to generate identities has a steep learning curve and therefore to provide a more beginner friendly introduction we will take a shortcut and use cryptogen to generate Fabric identities. You will learn Fabric CA later on in the book when we start developing real-world applications.

We have three organizations: Biotor, XMed and KeyPharmacy. Further, conceptually we deal with two kinds of identities in Fabric - human beings (users and admins) and machines (peers, orderers and CAs). We can also think of two kinds of X.509 certificates: one is the normal kind which acts as an ID card similar to a driver's license. All identities whether they are human or machine need this for identification. Machines in addition need a TLS certificate to communicate when TLS is enabled. TLS secures the communication between machines by encrypting the messages that only the receiver can decrypt. TLS can be turned on or off in Fabric as we will see in the book. It is possible to generate a certificate that doubles as an ID card as well as provides TLS. We will use cryptogen to generate following identities for us per organization:

- The root CA which is referred to as just CA. The root CA issues ID cards to everyone in the organization including itself. Think of it as the HR director in a company.
- TLSCA. The TLSCA is a CA that issues TLS credentials. Think of it as the IT director in a company whose approval is needed by the peer and orderer to use a secure communication device.
- One admin
- One user
- One peer
- One orderer

Let us now begin with above preface. You should have downloaded cryptogen binary as part of the Fabric installation in Section A.8. cd into $/three-org-network folder. Make sure you are using correct version of cryptogen. The version can be checked by running:

```
$ cryptogen version
cryptogen:
 Version: 2.0.1
 Commit SHA: 1cfa5da98
 Go version: go1.13.4
 OS/Arch: darwin/amd64
```

The OS/Arch will be different on Windows or Linux. Verify you have a file crypto-config.yaml in the directory. Run cryptogen using the command below:

Listing 4. 2. Command to generate MSP directories and User, Admin, Peer and Orderer credentials (the crypto material)

```
$ cryptogen generate --config=./crypto-config.yaml
```

You should see following output:

```
biotor.com
xmed.com
keypharmacy.com
```

And a directory named crypto-config should be generated. If you run the tree command on this directory you will see it contains hundreds of files and directories! (git.io/JI3dq) What just happened? cryptogen has generated necessary X.509 certificates and private keys which act as identities of users, administrators and the peer and orderer nodes in Fabric. We will be using these identities throughout the next chapters in the book.

Let's look at some of the identities cryptogen has generated for Biotor - the drug manufacturer organization. The identities are stored under a folder named msp. If you do a search for folders named msp under Biotor's tree, you should see following folders:

Listing 4. 3. The various identities generated by cryptogen for Biotor organization

```
$ find crypto-config/peerOrganizations/biotor.com -name msp
crypto-config/peerOrganizations/biotor.com/msp
crypto-config/peerOrganizations/biotor.com/users/User1@biotor.com/msp
crypto-config/peerOrganizations/biotor.com/users/Admin@biotor.com/msp
crypto-config/peerOrganizations/biotor.com/peers/peer0.biotor.com/msp
crypto-config/peerOrganizations/biotor.com/peers/orderer0.biotor.com/msp
```

In above:

- /msp is the MSP directory for the Biotor organization. *This directory does not contain any private keys.* It simply contains the public certificates of Biotor's CA(s). In previous versions of Fabric, this folder also used to contain the certificates of all the administrators but that is no longer necessary. This directory becomes part of the genesis block when a channel is created and plays a fundamental role in user authentication which will be covered in detail in Section 7.3.
- /users/User1@biotor.com/msp contains the identity (public cert and private key) of User1 - a user belonging to Biotor organization.

- /users/Admin@biotor.com/msp contains the identity of Biotor's admin.
- /peers/peer0.biotor.com/msp contains the identity of Biotor's peer node.
- /peers/orderer0.biotor.com/msp contains the identity of Biotor's orderer node.

In above, we only create identities for 1 user, 1 peer and 1 orderer node. It is possible to create identities for more users and nodes by modifying the crypto-config.yaml file but note that the settings have to be specified in advance. Thus cryptogen assumes you know a-priori how many users you have. In practice, your client application - the website or mobile app your users will use - will have a user registration section and it will generate crypto material for new users as they register on-demand in real-time using the Fabric (or another) CA server. Also as convenience in above you generated identities for all organizations. In the real-world you will only be generating identities for your organization.

 Make a secure backup of the crypto-config directory. There are several exercises in the chapter that ask you to try variations of cryptogen. Run these exercises from a fresh empty directory to avoid modifications to the crypto-config directory you just generated.

Exercise 4.1

chmod the crypto-config directory so that it cannot be written to, to prevent any modifications to the directory caused by accidental running of cryptogen again. This is a classic unix programming problem that has cost the grade of many a student. As it happens the solution is not trivial. You might think you can change the directory permissions to 444 but if you do that, you won't be able to read any file from the directory. If you change directory permissions to 555 you will not be able to create a new file under the directory but will be able to modify existing files. Try it for yourself. So what you need to do is to walk the directory recursively and if you find a file change its permissions to 444 and if you find a directory change its permissions to 555. (*Hint*: use the find command). You might be thinking that its only the top level directory that needs its permissions changed to 555 but you will be wrong again. I wish unix had a single line command to freeze a directory but it doesn't.

Exercise 4.2

Take a look at the crypto-config.yaml file and map what you see in it to what cryptogen generates. Modify the file so that cryptogen generates credentials for 2 users and 2 administrators. For extra bonus, write a script that asks you for many organizations you want to generate crypto material and how many peers, orderers, users and admins will be per org. The script should generate appropriate crypto-config.yaml file based on user input. *Hint*: this is a trick question. cryptogen cannot be used to generate identity for more than one admin to my knowledge.

4.3. *Understanding output of* cryptogen *and its directory structure*

Perhaps the most difficult part of cryptogen is making sense of all the data it generates. For example, in present case when you run it, it should have generated 124 directories and 117 files! Listing 4. 4 shows top 3 levels of the crypto-config directory generated by cryptogen.

Listing 4. 4. Tree showing 3 levels of the crypto-config directory output by cryptogen.

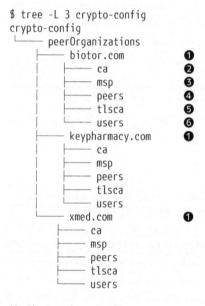

```
$ tree -L 3 crypto-config
crypto-config
└── peerOrganizations
    ├── biotor.com              ❶
    │   ├── ca                  ❷
    │   ├── msp                 ❸
    │   ├── peers               ❹
    │   ├── tlsca               ❺
    │   └── users               ❻
    ├── keypharmacy.com         ❶
    │   ├── ca
    │   ├── msp
    │   ├── peers
    │   ├── tlsca
    │   └── users
    └── xmed.com                ❶
        ├── ca
        ├── msp
        ├── peers
        ├── tlsca
        └── users

19 directories, 0 files
```

❶ The name of the folder comes from the Domain defined in crypto-config.yaml. If you change the Domain in crypto-config.yaml, the folder name will change as well.

❷ The ca folder will contain the certificate and private key of the root CA or trust anchor for this organization. Think of this as the HR director in an org.

❸ This is the OrgMSP folder for Biotor which gets copied into the genesis block. It does not contain any private keys. It will contain the CA cert(s) of Biotor.

❹ This folder will contain public certs and private keys of the peers of Biotor.

❺ The tlsca folder is similar to ca except that it contains the certificate and private key of the root CA which issues TLS certificates. Think of this as the IT director in an org.

❻ This folder will contain public certs and private keys of the users and admin of Biotor.

Let's dig into the subfolders taking Biotor as example. The ca folder has the private key and public cert of the organization's CA.

Listing 4. 5. The `ca` **folder simply contains the private key and public cert of the root CA.**

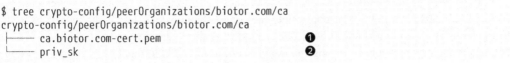

❶ Public cert of CA who will issue certs to Biotor's members.
❷ Private key

The `tlsca` folder has the private key and public cert of the organization's CA that is used to issue TLS certificates. One can use the same CA in the `ca` folder to issue TLS credentials as well - in fact it is possible to use a single certificate that can act as TLS cert as well as provide identification, but `cryptogen` generates two distinct CAs for us and separate certificates. The CA in the `ca` folder is used to issue non-TLS certs whereas the CA in the `tlsca` folder is used to issue TLS certs.

Listing 4. 6. The `tlsca` **folder simply contains the private key and public cert of the CA used for issuing TLS certs.**

```
$ tree crypto-config/peerOrganizations/biotor.com/tlsca
crypto-config/peerOrganizations/biotor.com/tlsca
├── priv_sk                                        ❶
└── tlsca.biotor.com-cert.pem                      ❷
```

❶ Private key
❷ Public cert of CA who will issue TLS certs to Biotor's members.

Next we come to the `msp` folder. This is an important one and has to have the structure defined below independent of whether you are using `cryptogen` or Fabric CA to generate it.

Listing 4. 7. Directory structure of the organization's `msp` **folder. The Org MSP folder has to obey the same structure irrespective of whether you are using** `cryptogen` **or another tool.**

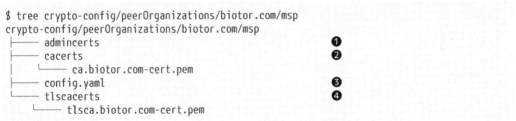

❶ In previous versions of Fabric, all administrators would need their certificates to be listed under this folder. With *NodeOUs* (Section 7.3.2) that is not necessary and so this folder is empty.
❷ This folder will contain the certificate (chain) of the CA(s) trusted to issue certificates to members of Biotor. Think of it as storing the certificate of the HR director of an organization.
❸ This is a config file to enable NodeOUs. By enabling Node OUs, we turn on attribute based access control. For example, the presence of OU=admin grants admin privilege to a caller.
❹ This folder will contain the certificate (chain) of the CA(s) trusted to issue TLS certificates to members of Biotor. Think of it as storing the certificate of the IT director of an organization.

The msp folder basically contains the full certificate chain(s) of all the CAs of an organization. In addition it contains an *optional* config.yaml file that is used to turn on Node OUs covered later in the book. The data in msp folder is copied into the genesis block which acts as the first block on the blockchain. This way when someone makes a request, Fabric can identify if the requestor really belongs to the organization by tracing the issuer chain to the certs in this directory. We will cover this in more in detail in Section 7.3.

Let us now come to the peers subfolder. It will contain identities of the peers defined in crypto-config.yaml. In our case we have defined two peers in our yaml - orderer0.biotor.com and peer0.biotor.com. So we will see subfolders corresponding to those. The presence of orderer0.biotor.com under peers subfolder may cause some confusion but the explanation to that is that its how we use an identity that determines what it is rather than its name. For example, we will use the identity in orderer0.biotor.com to bootstrap Biotor's orderer. That is perfectly okay and done by design in order to avoid a more complicated cryptogen setup otherwise in which we will have to use an OrdererOrgs section in our crypto-config.yaml and create fictitious organizations. The two peers (orderer0 and peer0) will have identical structure so we only show the subfolders of peer0 below to save space.

> The online Fabric samples define a crypto-config.yaml in which the orderers are declared under a OrdererOrgs section. If you use that approach, then configtx.yaml (in next chapter) will also change. Fabric samples create a separate orderer organization. That design defeats the whole purpose of a blockchain which is decentralization and is a relic from the days of Kafka where the peer organizations would hire a company like IBM to run the ordering service for them. Please refer to the online post *Why should organization not be both orderer and peer?* on Fabric mailing list for related discussion once you have built some muscle with Fabric. [81] We do not run orderers as separate organizations in the book as I feel there is no need to do so. Use the crypto-config.yaml and configtx.yaml under $/three-org-aliter if you want to take that approach.

Listing 4. 8. Directory structure of the `peers` **folder generated by** `cryptogen`.

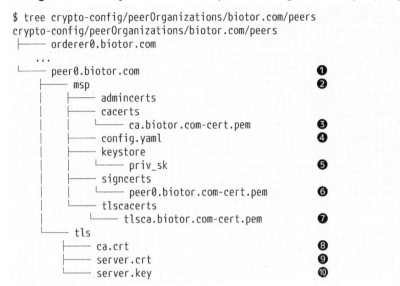

```
$ tree crypto-config/peerOrganizations/biotor.com/peers
crypto-config/peerOrganizations/biotor.com/peers
├────── orderer0.biotor.com
    ...
└────── peer0.biotor.com                        ❶
    ├─── msp                                     ❷
    │    ├────── admincerts
    │    ├────── cacerts
    │    │       └────── ca.biotor.com-cert.pem  ❸
    │    ├────── config.yaml                      ❹
    │    ├────── keystore
    │    │       └────── priv_sk                  ❺
    │    ├────── signcerts
    │    │       └────── peer0.biotor.com-cert.pem ❻
    │    └────── tlscacerts
    │            └────── tlsca.biotor.com-cert.pem ❼
    └─── tls
         ├────── ca.crt                           ❽
         ├────── server.crt                       ❾
         └────── server.key                       ❿
```

❶ The folder name is derived from what's declared in `crypto-config.yaml` under `Specs.Hostname`

❷ This `msp` folder will be given as input when starting Biotor's peer node in Section 5.5.4

❸ Certificate of the CA who issues peer0.biotor.com's certificate

❹ Config file to turn on Node OUs

❺ The private key of peer0.biotor.com. Not to be shared with anyone. It is stored under keystore folder. This private key will be used to sign all messages coming from this peer such as endorsements on transactions.

❻ The public certificate corresponding to the private key.

❼ Certificate of the CA who issues peer0.biotor.com's TLS certificate

❽ Duplicate of tlsca.biotor.com-cert.pem

❾ TLS certificate

❿ Private key corresponding to TLS certificate

Finally we come to the `users` subfolder. This stores exact same data as `peers` the only difference being that it stores identity information of Biotor's users and administrator instead of peers as we can see below.

Listing 4. 9. Directory structure of the Users **folder generated by** cryptogen.

```
$ tree crypto-config/peerOrganizations/biotor.com/users
crypto-config/peerOrganizations/biotor.com/users
├────── Admin@biotor.com
│    ├────── msp
│    │    ├────── admincerts
│    │    ├────── cacerts
│    │    │    └────── ca.biotor.com-cert.pem
│    │    ├────── config.yaml
│    │    ├────── keystore
│    │    │    └────── priv_sk
│    │    ├────── signcerts
│    │    │    └────── Admin@biotor.com-cert.pem
│    │    └────── tlscacerts
│    │         └────── tlsca.biotor.com-cert.pem
│    └────── tls
│         ├────── ca.crt
│         ├────── client.crt
│         └────── client.key
└────── User1@biotor.com
    ...
```

The TLS certs under users subfolder might seem out of place since TLS certs apply to a machine and users are not machines. However, they can be used for providing client authentication. For example, if a peer has clientAuth turned on, a user would use the TLS certs above to whitelist his or her machine so that the peer will accept connections from it.

There are many files under crypto-config/peerOrganizations/biotor.com that are duplicates. For example, all the files below are duplicates. Below commands are run from crypto-config/peerOrganizations/biotor.com.

Listing 4. 10. The organization's CA certificate appears multiple times in various places.

```
$ find . -name ca.biotor.com-cert.pem
./ca/ca.biotor.com-cert.pem
./msp/cacerts/ca.biotor.com-cert.pem
./users/User1@biotor.com/msp/cacerts/ca.biotor.com-cert.pem
./users/Admin@biotor.com/msp/cacerts/ca.biotor.com-cert.pem
./peers/peer0.biotor.com/msp/cacerts/ca.biotor.com-cert.pem
./peers/orderer0.biotor.com/msp/cacerts/ca.biotor.com-cert.pem
```

Here is another set of files which are duplicates of the same CA certificate that is used for TLS.

Listing 4. 11. The TLSCA certificate is also seen multiple times in various places.

```
$ find . -name ca.crt
./users/User1@biotor.com/tls/ca.crt
./users/Admin@biotor.com/tls/ca.crt
./peers/peer0.biotor.com/tls/ca.crt
./peers/orderer0.biotor.com/tls/ca.crt
$ find . -name tlsca.biotor.com-cert.pem
./tlsca/tlsca.biotor.com-cert.pem
./msp/tlscacerts/tlsca.biotor.com-cert.pem
./users/User1@biotor.com/msp/tlscacerts/tlsca.biotor.com-cert.pem
./users/Admin@biotor.com/msp/tlscacerts/tlsca.biotor.com-cert.pem
./peers/peer0.biotor.com/msp/tlscacerts/tlsca.biotor.com-cert.pem
./peers/orderer0.biotor.com/msp/tlscacerts/tlsca.biotor.com-cert.pem
```

Use the unix `diff` command to verify any pair of files above are duplicates.

 Please make a secure backup of all the private keys and certs of CAs and users, admins, peers and orderers. The TLS certs don't need backup as fresh ones can be generated but the other certs are like ID cards. If you lose them, you lose the associated identity.

4.4. *Using* `cryptogen` *in production*

Let's see what happens if we try to use `cryptogen` to generate identities for new users "on-the-fly" as they are onboarded onto our application. Assume we use the `crypto-config` directory generated in this chapter to bootstrap a network. Let's further call Biotor's CA as Bob (the HR director) and TLSCA as Alice (the IT director) to give them friendly names. Bob and Alice's cert are stored in the genesis block on the blockchain so that when someone makes a request, Fabric can check the issuer, verify its Bob and if so declare the request as coming from a member of Biotor. Now let's say Biotor wants to onboard another user to the platform. So we run `cryptogen` again to generate a new identity. The problem is that `cryptogen` generates a fresh set of CAs with every invocation. So the new user's cert will be signed and issued by Tom, not Bob. When this new user makes a request, Fabric will detect the cert is not issued by Bob and reject the request. There is no way to tell `cryptogen` to use Bob's credentials to issue certs of new users. This is the biggest reason preventing it from being used in production. There are other limitations as well. For example, the only way to run it is through command line. There is no way to run it from Node.js using an API or method call. Also you cannot customize the metadata associated with the certificate. The certificate will always say `C=US`, `ST=California`, `L=San Francisco` under the `Subject` and `Issuer` sections and you cannot change that. Adding to the list is that `cryptogen` cannot be run in server mode and that it does not maintain any certificate revocation lists.

There is however a way to work around the core limitation and use `cryptogen` in production if one was so determined. It is this: what if all of Biotor's users used the canonical identity generated in this chapter to make requests. That is, Biotor can onboard new users to the platform but all of them will use the canonical identity `User1@biotor.com` to make requests and perform transactions. After all maybe your application is such that you only care which organization has made the request. You don't really care about the specific person making the request. And if you did, there is a way to handle that as well. The username of the person could be made an argument to the smart contract. Thus `User1@biotor.com` would make the request on behalf of actual user. There is nothing wrong with this and its an example of the *proxy design pattern* at work.

The take away from this section is that rest assured there is no security concern w.r.t. the certificates it generates that prevents `cryptogen` from being used in production. Fabric docs just state `cryptogen` should not be used in production without explaining why and at first glance it gives the impression that there is some security issue with the certs it generates because of which it should not be used in production. But that is not the case.

4.5. Different types of X.509 Certificates

We encounter following types of X.509 certificates when working with Fabric: user, admin, peer, orderer, CAs and TLS certs. These certs are distinguished by different values in their `keyUsages` bitmask. Recall that the `keyUsages` bitmask in an X.509 certificate defines how the public key in the certificate can be used. Different values of the bitmask yield certificates specialized for different use cases. Table 4. 1 shows upfront summary of the distinguishing characteristics of various types of X.509 certificates and deep dives will come in subsequent sections.

Table 4. 1. Defining characteristics of different types of X.509 certificates.

CA	User, Admin, Peer, Orderer	TLS Server	TLS Client
X509v3 Basic Constraints: critical CA: TRUE X509v3 Key Usage: critical Certificate Sign	Public Key Algorithm: id-ecPublicKey X509v3 Key Usage: critical Digital Signature	X509v3 Key Usage: critical Key Encipherment X509v3 Extended Key Usage: TLS Web Server Authentication	X509v3 Extended Key Usage: TLS Web Client Authentication

We will be using the `openssl` utility to inspect X.509 certificates so before you begin, make sure you have `openssl` utility installed.

4.5.1. User, Admin, Peer and Orderer Certificates

X.509 certificates can be stored in various formats. The `cryptogen` tool generates the certificates in *PEM (Privacy Enhanced Mail)* format. If you try to print out the certificate using the `cat` command you will see a Base64 encoded text that looks something like below to give an example:

Listing 4. 12. Base64 encoded X.509 certificate in PEM format.

```
$ cat crypto-
config/peerOrganizations/biotor.com/users/User1@biotor.com/msp/signcerts/User1\@biotor.com-
cert.pem
-----BEGIN CERTIFICATE-----
MIICGDCCAb6gAwIBAgIQQYqjbTFRIOfk4sCFgj8j7zAKBggqhkjOPQQDAjBnMQsw
CQYDVQQGEwJVUzETMBEGA1UECBMKQ2FsaWZvcm5pYTEWMBQGA1UEBxMNU2FuIEZy
YW5jaXNjbzETMBEGA1UEChMKYmlvdG9yLmNvbTEWMBQGA1UEAxMNY2EuYmlvdG9y
LmNvbTAeFw0yMDA0MTYxOTA1MDBaFw0zMDA0MTQxOTA1MDBaMGYxCzAJBgNVBAYT
AlVTMRMwEQYDVQQIEwpDYWxpZm9ybmlhMRYwFAYDVQQHEw1TYW4gRnJhbmNpc2Nv
MQ8wDQYDVQQLEwZjbGllbnQxGTAXBgNVBAMMEFVzZXIxQGJpb3Rvci5jb20wWTAT
BgcqhkjOPQIBBggqhkjOPQMBBwNCAARgCCAuW75AZnEu+lZ9GpUwQI2P/lIZpSca
8ROxEkXcHRqQ4E+Vkj1YjDlmIl8Go67WAJpbdVBpjcRzy4q63ljmo00wSzAOBgNV
HQ8BAf8EBAMCB4AwDAYDVR0TAQH/BAIwADArBgNVHSMEJDAigCDYg7VZUwEndu4J
MIByvWjKXRalFfvzne8mPs4zCjcM7zAKBggqhkjOPQQDAgNIADBFAiEAs+vYPxr7
LwpV/iUeASYtrGgAEd+3ov8cjmHbcs/u9fYCIAaOembhV5p5F5ahgjcmF1ypyBsx
dUa91n/xmze6Yt9P
-----END CERTIFICATE-----
```

We can decode the certificate using the `openssl` utility:

Listing 4. 13. Command to print out X.509 certificate of Biotor's user in human readable form

```
$ openssl x509 -in crypto-
config/peerOrganizations/biotor.com/users/User1@biotor.com/msp/signcerts/User1\@biotor.com-
cert.pem -text -noout
```

It should give an output that resembles below:

Listing 4. 14. A User's certificate

```
Certificate:
    Data:
        Version: 3 (0x2)                                              ❶
        Serial Number:
            41:8a:a3:6d:31:51:20:e7:e4:e2:c0:85:82:3f:23:ef           ❷
    Signature Algorithm: ecdsa-with-SHA256                            ❸
        Issuer: C=US, ST=California, L=San Francisco, O=biotor.com, CN=ca.biotor.com ❹
        Validity                                                      ❺
            Not Before: Apr 16 19:05:00 2020 GMT
            Not After : Apr 14 19:05:00 2030 GMT
        Subject: C=US, ST=California, L=San Francisco, OU=client, CN=User1@biotor.com ❻
        Subject Public Key Info:
            Public Key Algorithm: id-ecPublicKey                      ❼
                Public-Key: (256 bit)                                 ❽
                pub:
                    04:60:08:20:2e:5b:be:40:66:71:2e:fa:56:7d:1a:
                    95:30:40:8d:8f:fe:52:19:a5:27:1a:f1:13:b1:12:
                    45:dc:1d:1a:90:e0:4f:95:92:3d:58:8c:39:66:22:
                    5f:06:a3:ae:d6:00:9a:5b:75:50:69:8d:c4:73:cb:
                    8a:ba:de:58:e6
                ASN1 OID: prime256v1                                  ❾
                NIST CURVE: P-256
        X509v3 extensions:                                            ❿
            X509v3 Key Usage: critical
                Digital Signature                                     ⓫
            X509v3 Basic Constraints: critical
                CA:FALSE                                              ⓬
            X509v3 Authority Key Identifier:

keyid:D8:83:B5:59:53:01:27:76:EE:09:30:80:72:BD:68:CA:5D:16:A5:15:FB:F3:9D:EF:26:3E:CE:33:0
A:37:0C:EF

    Signature Algorithm: ecdsa-with-SHA256
        30:45:02:21:00:b3:eb:d8:3f:1a:fb:2f:0a:55:fe:25:1e:01:        ⓭
        26:2d:ac:68:00:11:df:b7:a2:ff:1c:8e:61:db:72:cf:ee:f5:
        f6:02:20:06:8e:7a:66:e1:57:9a:79:17:96:a1:82:37:26:17:
        5c:a9:c8:1b:31:75:46:bd:d6:7f:f1:9b:37:ba:62:df:4f
```

❶ This denotes the version of X.509 certificate. Version 3 is latest.

❷ Certificates are assigned a unique serial number by the issuer

❸ This field contains the identifier for the cryptographic algorithm used by the CA to sign this certificate.

❹ Metadata about the issuer of this certificate

❺ Duration for which this certificate is valid.

❻ Metadata about the owner of this certificate. We see that OU=client. cryptogen adds this attribute to the certificates it generates for the users when Node OUs are enabled in the crypto-config.yaml file.

❼ id-ecPublicKey indicates that the public key in the cert is an ECC key and that it can be used with any signature algorithm - ECDSA, ECDH or even ECMQV.

❽ The public key associated with this certificate.

❾ The curve associated with the ECC key. Fabric supports only 3 curves: `prime256v1` (aka `secp256r1`), `secp384r1` and `secp521r1`.

❿ The extensions section defines the usages associated with this key.

⓫ `Digital Signature` means the key can be used for signing messages. We need this attribute as a user needs to sign every transaction request they make to Fabric.

⓬ The public key in this cert is not that of a CA. (`CA:FALSE`)

⓭ Signature of the CA. Signature by a trusted issuer legitimizes the certificate and acts as an endorsement (attestation).

The defining characteristic of a user, administrator, peer or orderer certificate is that the **Digital Signature** permission, key usage or privilege must be enabled under X509v3 `Key Usage` section. The X509v3 `Key Usage` is always marked as `critical` in any X.509 certificate. The `critical` keyword is used to mean that the public key in the cert is to be used only for that purpose. The `Digital Signature` permission allows users, administrators, peers and orderers to digitally sign messages they exchange with each other. The more accurate statement is that when a user, administrator, peer or orderer sends a digitally signed message to a recipient together with their X.509 cert, the presence of `Digital Signature` permission in the X.509 certificate tells the recipient that the public key in the cert can be used to verify the digital signature accompanying the message.

Furthermore, Fabric only supports *ECDSA* (Elliptic Curve Digital Signature Algorithm) signatures with the `Digital Signature` permission due the crypto libraries it uses under the covers. The Elliptic Curve Digital Signature Algorithm is based on the use of ECC (Elliptic Curve Cryptography) keys. The thing to note here is the ECC is a key type whereas ECDSA is a signature algorithm. ECC keys appear as `id-ecPublicKey` in the certificate. Associated with an ECC key is a curve. Fabric only supports 3 curves: `prime256v1` (aka `secp256r1`), `secp384r1` and `secp521r1`. I suggest sticking with `secp256r1` which is most common and NIST recommended. `cryptogen` only uses this curve and does not support any config parameter to change the curve type. The curve is used to lookup values of some parameters required by the ECDSA algorithm. It is also possible to *explicitly* specify the values of these parameters in the certificate instead of specifying the curve name in the certificate which would then be used to perform an *implicit* lookup.

The presence of the `OU=client` attribute is not a strict requirement for a user certificate. *It depends whether Node OUs are enabled or not.* Admin certificates are characterized by `OU=admin` in them and peer and orderer certificates have `OU=peer` and `OU=orderer` in them respectively when NodeOUs are enabled in `crypto-config.yaml` by setting `EnableNodeOUs: true`.

Exercise 4.3

Print out Biotor's admin, peer and orderer certificates. If you cd to `$/three-org-network/crypto-config/peerOrganizations/biotor.com`, from there the admin cert will be found under `./users/Admin\@biotor.com/msp/signcerts`, peer cert will be under `./peers/peer0.biotor.com/msp/signcerts/` and orderer cert will be under `./peers/orderer0.biotor.com/msp/signcerts/`. Verify that in all these certs the `Digital Signature` bit (permission) is set and all certs use an ECC key with `prime256v1` named curve.

Further verify that OU=admin in admin's cert and OU=peer in peer's certificate. *You will notice that* OU=peer *in orderer's certificate!* This is not a bug in cryptogen. As far as cryptogen is concerned, orderer0.biotor.com is a "peer". This can be confirmed if we inspect the $/three-org-network/crypto-config.yaml file where we can see that orderer0.biotor.com is declared under PeerOrgs section.

4.5.2. Printing a chain of certificates

The openssl x509 -in command cannot be used to print out a chain of certificates. If you provide it a PEM file containing a chain of certificates, it will only print the first certificate in that file. To print out the full chain, we have to convert the chain file to PKCS7 format. This is done by running:

```
$ openssl crl2pkcs7 -nocrl -certfile chain.pem > pkcs7.txt
```

And next, we have to use the pkcs7 command to decode this file like so:

```
$ openssl pkcs7 -in pkcs7.txt -print_certs -text -noout
```

The crl2pkcs7 and pkcs7 commands can be chained together using a Unix pipe to do everything in a single command. We won't encounter certificate chains in this chapter but we will encounter them later on in the book. Or you might run into them sooner as part of your work.

4.5.3. CA Certificates

Let us now look at a CA certificate and contrast its key usages to a user certificate. The minimum requirement for a CA cert is following section in the certificate:

Listing 4. 15. Minimum requirement for a CA certificate.

```
X509v3 extensions:
    X509v3 Key Usage: critical
        Certificate Sign
    X509v3 Basic Constraints: critical
        CA:TRUE
```

The X509v3 Basic Constraints section in an X.509 certificate is used to define if this certificate belongs to a CA or not. The section is always marked as critical and if the **CA** bit is set then this means the public key in the certificate can be used to verify the digital signature on a X.509 certificate. Also, if the CA bit is set then one must set the **Certificate Sign** permission as well under X509v3 Key Usage. A commonly encountered usage in addition to Certificate Sign is **CRL Sign** - the ability to sign off on certificate revocation lists. These are lists that contain certs that have been revoked. For example, imagine that your drivers license gets revoked and your name is put on an offenders list. CRL lists serve similar purpose. Another attribute that is sometimes found in CA certificates is **pathlen**. It is a non-negative integer that if set defines the maximum number of non-self-issued intermediate certificates that may follow this certificate in a valid certification path. Listing 4. 16 below shows example of these attributes.

Listing 4. 16. CA certificate with pathlen **and** CRL Sign **attributes.**

```
X509v3 extensions:
    X509v3 Key Usage: critical
        Certificate Sign, CRL Sign
    X509v3 Basic Constraints: critical
        CA:TRUE, pathlen:1
```

Since the pathlen is set to 1, we can have a chain A→X or A→B→X but A→B→C→X is not possible where X is the root cert and B, C are intermediate CAs. Figure 4. 2 shows X.509 certificate validation in more detail. [82] It is the long version of Figure 2. 1.

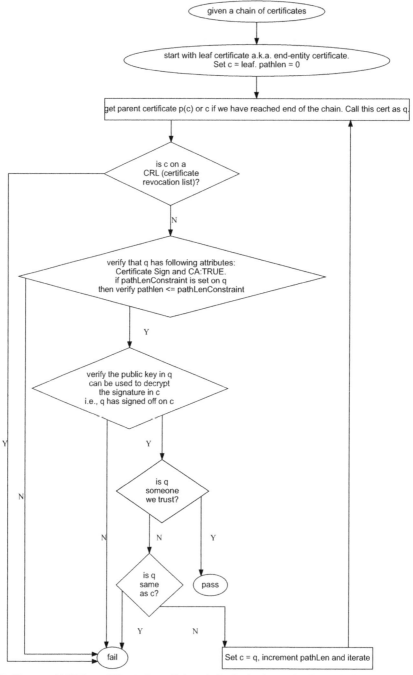

Figure 4. 2. How an X.509 certificate is validated. A chain (array) of certificates is provided to the validation algorithm where the leaf cert is the certificate which is to be validated. This flowchart does not include *hostname validation*. **The root certificate in the chain is also known**

as a *trust anchor.*

Exercise 4.4

Print out Biotor's CA certificate and confirm it has the attributes needed by a CA. The certificate can be found under `$/three-org-network/crypto-config/peerOrganizations/biotor.com/msp/cacerts/`.

4.6. TLS Certificates and TLS Protocol

TLS certificates are used to secure communication between a server and a client. Before we delve into TLS certificates, let's take a moment to understand the TLS protocol. The communication between a client and server is secured by encrypting messages that can only be decrypted by the intended receiver. If a spy intercepts the message, he or she should not be able to decode it. There are *two* ways to encrypt and decrypt electronic messages. Both require the use of keys. The only difference is that in one method the *same* key is used to encrypt and decrypt the messages (*symmetric encryption*) whereas in another method the key used to encrypt message is different from the key used to decrypt the message (*asymmetric encryption*). Symmetric encryption is much faster than asymmetric encryption. Let's say we have decided on using symmetric encryption. Look up AES (Advanced Encryption Standard) if you are interested in learning symmetric encryption. We now need a way to exchange the key between the client and the server. *The purpose of TLS certificate is to securely exchange this key.* The way it works is that the client connects to a server. The server sends back a TLS certificate. The client uses the public key in that TLS certificate to send an encrypted *pre-master secret* to the server that only the server can decrypt using the private key associated with the TLS certificate of the server. After that there is some more back and forth and eventually a *shared* secret key is computed between the client and server using which they then communicate. So the thing to note here is that the public key in TLS cert is only used to exchange (encrypt) the pre-master secret. *It is not used after that.* The relevant key usage is Key Encipherment in an X.509 certificate and appears under the X509v3 Key Usage section like so:

Listing 4. 17. The Key Encipherment **usage is critical for an X.509 certificate to be used as a TLS certificate.**

```
X509v3 Key Usage: critical
    Key Encipherment
```

Key Encipherment literally means that the key in this certificate can be used to encrypt another key and this is exactly what TLS does. Note that in most of our Fabric discussion, we use a private key to encrypt and a public key to decrypt. This is also what we showed when we discussed digital signatures in Figure 2. 2. But the process works in reverse as well. A public key can be used to encrypt and the private key can be used to decrypt as we see with Key Encipherment.

In addition TLS certificate is also used by the client to identify the server and optionally by the server to identify the client when *mutual* or client authentication is turned on on the server. *Client authentication* is not something that we encounter in our day to day lives. If your bank had client authentication on, you would have to install a certificate on your computer making it trusted by the bank. The bank would give you the cert. And imagine the amount of customers a bank may have. But client auth is a possibility in tightly controlled environments and especially intranets where there are relatively fewer computers. Anyway in order to be used for authentication purposes of TLS protocol, an X.509 certificate must have X509v3 Extended Key Usage: TLS Web Client Authentication for client auth and X509v3 Extended Key Usage: TLS Web Server Authentication for the normal *one-way* auth in which its only the client that authenticates the server; server does not do any authentication on the client and allows any machine to connect to it. It is possible for an X.509 certificate to have both TLS Web Client Authentication and TLS Web Server Authentication enabled which means the same certificate can be used for both client as well as server authentication.

It is instructive to note that the client and server auth privileges appear under the Extended Key Usage section of an X.509 certificate whereas the Key Encipherment appears under the Key Usage: critical section since the primary (critical) purpose of the TLS cert is to provide a public key to the client that can be used by the client to send a pre-master secret to the server.

What does TLS Web Server Authentication exactly mean? In addition to the X.509 validation in Figure 4. 2, the *hostname* of the server is verified by the client. Recall that a client connects to a server using an address e.g., peer0.biotor.com. In the Subject section of an X.509 certificate is a field known as the Common Name or CN for short. For example, CN=User1@biotor.com in Listing 4. 14. This common name needs to exactly match the address client used to connect to the server or the hostname validation fails. Client refuses to connect to the server. Now a days it is common for a server to be accessible from multiple addresses. For example, nsa.gov and www.nsa.gov may internally point to the same IP address. The Common Name only allows for a single address or host name. So the X.509 standard was extended to introduce a **X509v3 Subject Alternative Name** extension (subjectAltName) where alternate names of the server can be provided like so to give an example:

Listing 4. 18. Subject Alternative Name **extension is used to provide all the names by which a server is known.**

```
X509v3 Subject Alternative Name:
    DNS:nsa.gov, DNS:www.nsa.gov
```

Using this extension, a client will honor the alternate server names that appear in this section. In fact, *according to latest RFCs the* subjectAltName *is supposed to override and supersede the* Common Name. *What it means is that if* subjectAltName *is present, the client should use only that and not even look at the* Common Name *in the certificate.* The process of identifying a remote server this way is known as ***hostname validation***. The X.509 standard allows for using * wildcard in the subjectAltName. Thus a DNS address of *.nsa.gov will match foo.nsa.gov as well as bar.nsa.gov in addition to www.nsa.gov of course.

It is much more common to encounter RSA keys with TLS certificates than ECC keys and ECDSA signature algorithm. RSA keys are much longer than ECC keys and RSA encryption is also less performant than ECDSA but its use is more widespread.

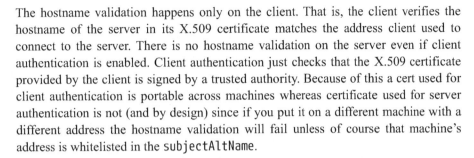

The hostname validation happens only on the client. That is, the client verifies the hostname of the server in its X.509 certificate matches the address client used to connect to the server. There is no hostname validation on the server even if client authentication is enabled. Client authentication just checks that the X.509 certificate provided by the client is signed by a trusted authority. Because of this a cert used for client authentication is portable across machines whereas certificate used for server authentication is not (and by design) since if you put it on a different machine with a different address the hostname validation will fail unless of course that machine's address is whitelisted in the `subjectAltName`.

Figure 4. 3 shows a summary of the discussion in this section.

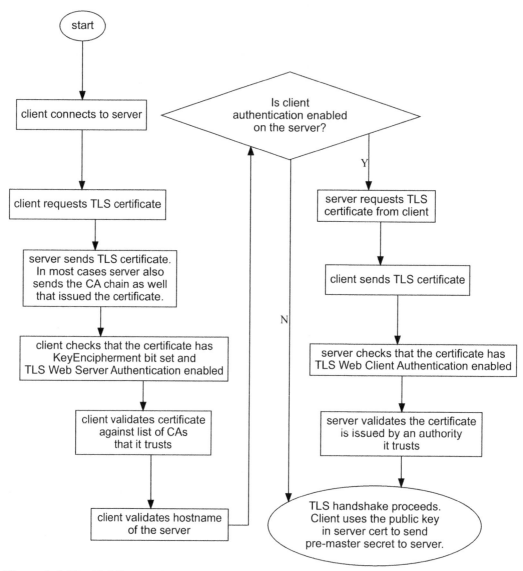

Figure 4. 3. The TLS Protocol.

Exercise 4.5

The TLS cert for Biotor peer node can be found in `$/three-org-network/crypto-config/peerOrganizations/biotor.com/peers/peer0.biotor.com/tls` folder. Look for a file named `server.crt`. Print it and verify it has the required attributes for a TLS certificate. In fact you will see it also has the `Digital Signature` attribute set on it. So we could use `server.crt` as the peer's ID card as well. The ID card is under `peer0.biotor.com/msp/signcerts`.

Exercise 4.6

Sometimes you might run into situations where a TLS certificate fails to validate. openssl can be used to debug such errors. As example, let's try to validate the TLS certificate of nsa.gov or your favorite website. Cd to $/x509-lesson and from there run following command:

Listing 4. 19. openssl **command to validate TLS certificate from a remote server.**

```
$ openssl s_client -connect nsa.gov:443 -state -nbio -CAfile Certificates.bundle -showcerts
```

When we run above command openssl will perform the TLS handshake with nsa.gov on port 443 and display useful information. The remote server will send back its TLS certificate which will be validated against the list of trusted CAs in Certificates.bundle directory. On Mac this directory can be found under /System/Library/Security. I made a copy of it under the $/x509-lesson folder. Run the command and observe its output carefully. You will see the full PEM encoded certificate chain starting from the end entity certificate going all the way to the trust anchor printed out on the console. Decode the certs using openssl. The command will also show you the cipher suite negotiated between the client and server (in my case I got ECDHE-RSA-AES256-GCM-SHA384) and the master key. This is a very useful command to keep in your arsenal of debugging tools.

 If the server you are connecting to has client authentication enabled then use the -key and -cert options to add the client key and client cert when running openssl s_client.

4.7. Summary

- An X.509 certificate contains a public key and its permitted usages. The certificate is useless unless it is signed by someone we trust.
- We come across following identities in Fabric: users, admins, peers, orderers and certificate authorities.
- cryptogen is a tool that can be used to statically generate X.509 certificates and private keys for above identities.
- Users, admins, peers and orderers all need to have the Digital Signature bit set in their X.509 certificate. That bit allows the public key in the cert to be used to verify digital signatures. That in turn enables Fabric backend to identify and authenticate the originator of a request. Thus an X.509 certificate with Digital Signature bit acts like an ID card.
- Fabric only supports ECDSA signatures from users, admins, peers and orderers. Further Fabric only supports ECC keys based on secp256r1 (aka prime256v1), secp384r1 or secp521r1 elliptic curves.
- Certificate Authorities have the Certificate Sign bit set and CA:TRUE in their X.509 certificate. In addition there is an optional pathlen attribute the controls the maximum number of allowed intermediate CAs that can appear in a chain leading up to the CA. A pathlen of 0 would mean no intermediate CAs are allowed.
- TLS certificates are used to secure communication between machines and are characterized by

presence of `Key Encipherment` attribute in the certificate. In addition they have the `TLS Web Server Authentication` and `TLS Web Client Authentication` extended key usages enabled for hostname validation and client authentication respectively.

- TLS certificates found on the web usually use RSA keys. Fabric supports RSA based TLS certs [83] but for other use cases - most importantly the endorsement of transactions and requests - it only supports ECDSA keys and signatures. ECDSA keys are smaller and faster than RSA.

- It is possible to have a certificate with both `Digital Signature` and `Key Encipherment` set. This cert can act as an ID card as well as a TLS certificate.

- The `subjectAltName` (SAN) section in a TLS certificate is very important and should list all the names by which a server is known. It is what the client will use when it does hostname validation.

4.8. Further Reading

- KC Tam's article on cryptogen and Fabric CA: medium.com/@kctheservant/identity-in-hyperledger-fabric-part-2-fc2f50214d9
- Elliptic Curve Cryptography: www.secg.org/SEC1-Ver-1.0.pdf

[79] en.wikipedia.org/wiki/Public_key_certificate

[80] en.wikipedia.org/wiki/Web_of_trust

[81] lists.hyperledger.org/g/fabric/topic/76214410#8864

[82] also see The most dangerous code in the world: validating SSL certificates in non-browser software in ACM Conference on Computer and Communications Security, 2012 p. 38-49. www.cs.utexas.edu/~shmat/shmat_ccs12.pdf

[83] I have never used an RSA based CA cert but according to lists.hyperledger.org/g/fabric/message/8841 they are permitted. The `fabric-ca-server` - which is different from Fabric - for sure does not support CA certs with RSA keys.

Chapter 5. Provisioning a Local Three Org Test or Development Network

This chapter covers:

- Deploying a multi-org network on your local computer without using Docker
- Running peer nodes in dev mode
- Understanding orderer.yaml and core.yaml config files
- Debugging network connectivity issues

Code for this chapter is in $/three-org-network directory

In previous chapter we generated the necessary identities needed to bootstrap peer and orderer nodes. In what follows you will build a three organization network and run it locally on your machine. We will be covering following steps in this chapter and using the identities we generated in previous chapter:

1. Generate genesis block
2. Provision orderer node
3. Provision CouchDB
4. Provision peer nodes

We will provision 1 peer, 1 orderer and 1 CouchDB for each organization. We have three organizations (Biotor, XMed and KeyPharmacy) so total 9 nodes will be provisioned. [84] We will show how to provision nodes for Biotor and leave it as exercise for the reader to do the same for XMed and KeyPharmacy. The web of connections is shown in Figure 5. 1.

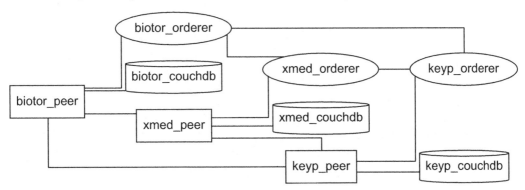

Figure 5. 1. The 3-org network of Biotor, XMed and KeyPharmacy

In what follows we will be working from the $/three-org-network directory. *All commands are to be run from that directory unless otherwise noted. A large part of this chapter is understanding three configuration files -* **configtx.yaml** *used to generate genesis block,* **orderer.yaml** *used to bootstrap orderer and* **core.yaml** *used to bootstrap a peer. Keep in mind as you are working* through this chapter that you will have access to everything and will be able to assume identity of anyone, [85] but in real-world developing a blockchain application is a team effort in which *you won't have access to another company's private keys and won't be generating their Membership Service Provider (MSP) data or provisioning their peer or orderer nodes.* They will generate their credentials and the companies will need to exchange MSP information by some means before a network can even be provisioned. This is illustrated in Figure 5. 2 which gives an overview of how the ordering service would be provisioned in practice.

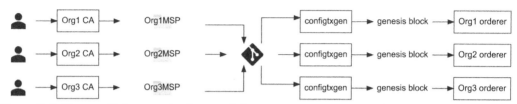

Figure 5. 2. How multiple organizations collaborate to create the ordering network. Each organization's administrator will generate the organization's MSP and upload it to a repository. The repository will also store `configtx.yaml`**. Then each organization will pull the MSP directories and** `configtx.yaml` **from the repo, use the** `configtxgen` **tool to generate the genesis block and use that to bootstrap an orderer node.**

If you have read official Fabric samples, you would have noticed they use Docker extensively. In this chapter we will see how to deploy a network *without using Docker.* Later chapters will show how to deploy the network using Docker. Docker certainly has its advantages and is recommended in production but you should also know how to deploy a network without using Docker. In particular, when you want to debug Fabric errors, you will most certainly need to deploy the network without using Docker as its not possible to attach VS Code debugger to a process running in Docker container in my experience. VS Code provides a `Remote Development` extension that in principle is supposed to enable debugging a process running inside a container but I haven't been able to use it successfully.

- IBM provides an extension for VS Code that can be used to provision a Fabric network with click of a button. You can also use it to create a Smart Contract project and install/instantiate your smart contract. Its not a bad idea to try it out, but it comes with two limitations. As of this writing, it can only deploy a single-org network and has not been updated for Fabric 2.0. For this reason we do not cover it in this book.
- We have provided a separate chapter on Debugging Fabric in the book (Chapter 6) to help the reader with troubleshooting and debugging Fabric errors. You may want to refer to that chapter for help when things don't go as expected (e.g., if you are using a different version of Fabric than in the book).

Before you begin this chapter, go ahead and install all the software and prerequisites in Appendix A. After that please create following directory structure under `$/three-org-network`:

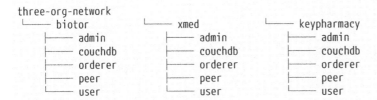

We will provision CouchDB, orderer and peer from the respectively named directories for each organization. The `admin` directory will be used in Chapter 7 and the `user` directory will be used when we perform transactions on the network (Chapter 8). Let us now do a quick review of computer networking as this chapter is all about setting up a network.

5.1. A Short Primer on Networking

The Fabric network is a distributed system consisting of many programs that have to communicate with each other. Hence a basic knowledge of computer networking is essential to provision and troubleshoot a Fabric network. When all the programs are running on the same machine (also known as *host*) as in this chapter, the knowledge you learn in this section may not play as big a role but it will be instrumental when you start to provision a truly distributed network. We learn a couple of useful commands in this section - `lsof` (list open files), `ss` (socket statistics) and `nc` (netcat) that help in troubleshooting connectivity issues. Networking gurus can safely skip this section.

We begin by noting that network communication takes place between a *server* and a *client*. A server *listens* for incoming connections by *binding* a *socket* to a *port* and an *address*. A client *connects* to the *socket* the server is listening on.

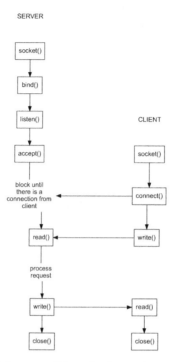

Figure 5. 3. Client-server model. A server *listens* **for incoming connections by** *binding* **a** *socket* **to a** *port* **and an** *address.* **A client** *connects* **to the** *socket* **the server is listening on. Figure adapted from stackoverflow.com/a/27017691/147530**

The address is a 4 byte IPv4 address which is commonly expressed as a.b.c.d where a, b, c and d are the 4 bytes expressed in base-10 (decimal) notation.   [86] The port is a 2 byte unsigned int. Ports less than 1024 are privileged and you need to be a privileged user (root) to use them. *Exercise:* Find the IP address corresponding to 172225221. *Answer:* 10.67.242.197.

There are two special addresses that we have to be mindful of. They are 127.0.0.1 and 0.0.0.0. We will encounter the use of both these in this chapter. 127.0.0.1 is used to mean the address of the host machine itself - hence also known as *localhost* or the *loopback interface* - the interface that loops back network traffic to the machine itself. 0.0.0.0 is a special wildcard that resolves to an empty string internally and is used to mean "no-particular-address". If you bind a server to 127.0.0.1 it will only be able to accept connections from clients on the *same* host or machine. A remote client - i.e., a client on *another* host or machine - uses the IP address of the server's host to connect to it. Say this IP address is 10.67.242.197. By binding the server to 127.0.0.1, the server is not listening on 10.67.242.197 and will refuse connections from remote clients. If you bind the server to 10.67.242.197, it will refuse connections to local clients who use 127.0.0.1 to connect to it. By resolving to an empty string, 0.0.0.0 causes the server to listen on all the *network interfaces* it can find on the host. *The practical consequence of this is that it allows both local as well as remote clients to connect to the server. So the TL;DR is to always use 0.0.0.0 for any listen address and you will see this principle being applied when we set the addresses of peers and orderers in this chapter*. On the client-side, strictly speaking its not a valid thing to ever use `0.0.0.0` as that does not resolve to any destination address. But in practice, you might be still able to connect to a local server using `0.0.0.0`.

> Local vs. Public IP Addresses: A public IP address is one that is routed on the internet. A local or private IP address is routed on the Local Area Network or LAN. It is not recognized on the internet. Local IP addresses normally range from `10.0.0.0` to `10.255.255.255` or `172.16.0.0` to `172.31.255.255` or `192.168.0.0` to `192.168.255.255`. Direct access to the internet using a private IP address is not possible. In this case, the connection to the internet is via *NAT (Network Address Translation)* which replaces the private IP address with a public one.

You can test this for yourself using the following Node program: [87]

Listing 5. 1. A simple Node http server

```
const http = require('http');

const hostname = process.argv[2];
const port = process.argv[3];

const server = http.createServer((req, res) => {
  res.statusCode = 200;
  res.setHeader('Content-Type', 'text/plain');
  res.end('Hello World');
});

server.listen(port, hostname, () => {
  console.log(`Server running at http://${hostname}:${port}/`);
});
```

Save this file as `run-server.js`. Next, get your computer's IP address. On the Mac you can get this information using the Network Utility app that comes with Mac as shown in Figure 5. 4. [88]

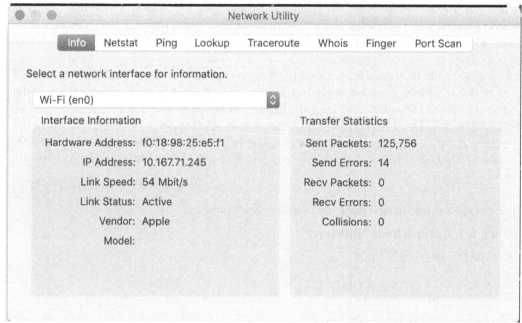

Figure 5. 4. The Network Utility app can be used to get the IP address of your computer

The IP address can also be had by running:

```
$ ifconfig | grep inet
```

You will get a multi-line output corresponding to all the network interfaces (wifi, ethernet etc.) attached to the host. For example, on my Mac I see following output when I run above command:

```
inet 127.0.0.1 netmask 0xff000000
inet6 ::1 prefixlen 128
inet6 fe80::1%lo0 prefixlen 64 scopeid 0x1
inet6 fe80::aede:48ff:fe00:1122%en5 prefixlen 64 scopeid 0x9
inet6 fe80::10fb:b507:84ae:ba22%en0 prefixlen 64 secured scopeid 0xb
inet 10.167.71.245 netmask 0xfffff800 broadcast 10.167.71.255
inet6 fe80::2cc5:1ff:fef6:1847%awdl0 prefixlen 64 scopeid 0xd
inet6 fe80::c789:88e8:68e3:3a1c%utun0 prefixlen 64 scopeid 0x13
```

The entries beginning with inet6 are IPv6 addresses. From above I can see the IPv4 address of my Mac is 10.167.71.245. In subsequent discussion you will replace 10.167.71.245 with the IP address in your case. Run the following command which will bind the server to 127.0.0.1:9000:

```
$ node run-server.js 127.0.0.1 9000
Server running at http://127.0.0.1:9000/
```

Next, verify the server is truly listening on 9000 by running lsof. On Mac this gives:

```
$ lsof -i:9000
COMMAND  PID  USER   FD   TYPE DEVICE           SIZE/OFF NODE NAME
node  8947 siddjain 13u  IPv4 0xe002f0ad8569ab5f  0t0  TCP localhost:cslistener (LISTEN)
```

You will get similar output on Linux. The LISTEN confirms a server is listening on the port. Next, test the connection by running nc in another terminal window:

```
$ nc -zv 127.0.0.1 9000
found 0 associations
found 1 connections:
     1: flags=82<CONNECTED,PREFERRED>
     outif lo0
     src 127.0.0.1 port 50620
     dst 127.0.0.1 port 9000
     rank info not available
     TCP aux info available

Connection to 127.0.0.1 port 9000 [tcp/cslistener] succeeded!
```

Try using the IP address instead:

```
$ nc -zv 10.167.71.245 9000
```

There is a long pause after which I get this output:

```
nc: connectx to 10.167.71.245 port 9000 (tcp) failed: Operation timed out
```

Now terminate the server and run it on 10.167.71.245:9000 instead replacing 10.167.71.245 with your IP address. Repeat the nc commands above. *This time the connection to* 10.167.71.245:9000 *will succeed but the connection to* 127.0.0.1:9000 *will fail*. Terminate the server once again and for the final time run it on 0.0.0.0:9000 instead. *Verify you are now able to connect using both localhost (*127.0.0.1*) as well as the* inet *address.*

Above also shows how to troubleshoot networking issues. When you are not able to connect to a server, run lsof on the server to verify if something is even listening on the port. After that check if there is any firewall blocking the port from clients and then run nc on the client to see what the problem is.

You can see a list of all open ports on Mac by running lsof or netstat. The lsof command to do so looks like following:

Listing 5. 2. List all open ports

```
$ lsof -i
```

You could use the same command on Linux, but its more convenient to use ss that comes installed with most distributions. ss is a replacement for netstat on Linux. netstat is available but deprecated in favor of ss on Linux:

Listing 5. 3. List open TCP ports (Linux)

```
$ ss -tpln
```

Above will filter the output and only show TCP ports (t) that are in listening mode (l). The same command for Mac becomes:

Listing 5. 4. List open TCP ports (Mac)

```
$ netstat -ln -p tcp
```

netstat, ss, lsof, nc, traceroute, ping, tcpdump, host are some tools you need to know to troubleshoot networking issues. We did not cover all of them. Use online resources for ones we could not cover.

Table 5. 1. Networking tools

Tool	Purpose
nc	open TCP connections, send UDP packets, listen on arbitrary TCP and UDP ports, do port scanning etc.
netstat, ss, lsof	port scanning, socket statistics
tcpdump	packet sniffing
traceroute	trace route to a destination
host	DNS lookups. convert names to IP addresses and vice-versa

Now that we are done with our networking primer, we can proceed to network installation.

5.2. Generate genesis block

We work from $/three-org-network in this section.

The genesis block will be generated by a utility known as **configtxgen**. Verify you have a configtx.yaml file under the $/three-org-network folder and that you have the configtxgen utility that comes with Fabric binaries in your PATH. Check you have the right version:

```
$ configtxgen --version
configtxgen:
 Version: 2.0.1
 Commit SHA: 1cfa5da98
 Go version: go1.13.4
 OS/Arch: darwin/amd64
```

To generate the genesis block, run

Listing 5. 5. Command to generate genesis block used to bootstrap the orderer

```
$ configtxgen -profile Genesis -outputBlock foo.block -channelID foo
```

You should see output that looks like following:

Listing 5. 6. Example output of running configtxgen **to generate a genesis block**

```
[common.tools.configtxgen] main -> INFO 001 Loading configuration
[common.tools.configtxgen.localconfig] completeInitialization -> INFO 002 Orderer.Addresses
unset, setting to [127.0.0.1:7050]
[common.tools.configtxgen.localconfig] completeInitialization -> INFO 003 orderer type:
etcdraft
[common.tools.configtxgen.localconfig] Load -> INFO 004 Loaded configuration:
/Users/siddjain/go/src/github.com/siddjain/phf/three-org-network/configtx.yaml
[common.tools.configtxgen] doOutputBlock -> INFO 005 Generating genesis block
[common.tools.configtxgen] doOutputBlock -> INFO 006 Writing genesis block
```

Verify you now have a file named foo.block on your system:

```
$ ls -al foo.block
-rw-r----- 1 siddjain  staff  40232 Apr 16 15:48 foo.block
```

- You may want to make a note of the channelID you used (foo in example above) when creating the genesis block since that is not saved in any file.
- If your configtx.yaml file is in a different directory than the directory from which configtxgen is executed, then you can set the **FABRIC_CFG_PATH** environment variable equal to the directory that contains configtx.yaml
- You might want to chmod 444 foo.block

What is the genesis block? And what does the code in configtx.yaml mean? The genesis block is used to initialize the ordering service. Among other things, it contains the public certificates we generated using cryptogen. *The genesis block contains the necessary information using which at runtime when someone makes a request to Fabric, it can determine which organization the caller belongs to and what privileges the caller has* - is the caller a user from Biotor, or an administrator, or is the call coming from a peer node of Biotor? Further once the identity of the caller is established, what privileges does this caller have? What actions can the caller perform? If we open configtx.yaml in a text editor, we can see following lines in it for the three organizations that point to each organization's MSP directory:

```
MSPDir: crypto-config/peerOrganizations/biotor.com/msp
MSPDir: crypto-config/peerOrganizations/xmed.com/msp
MSPDir: crypto-config/peerOrganizations/keypharmacy.com/msp
```

The files under these directories will be copied into the genesis block and will form the basis on which identity verification takes place in Fabric. It will be covered in more detail in Section 7.3.

In last chapter you conveniently ran `cryptogen` and it generated crypto material for all organizations and now you have access to identities of all organizations. In real-world you will only have access to your organization's crypto material and would need to collect crypto material of other organizations that is referenced in `configtx.yaml`. Note that there are no private keys under the MSP directories defined in `configtx.yaml` - they only contain public certificates. That is super-important.

It is super-important not to run `cryptogen` again once you have generated your genesis block and *used it to provision an orderer*. Doing so will overwrite all the identities and you don't want that. The new certificates will not trace back to the old CAs stored in the genesis block and Fabric will reject all requests. Debugging such errors is quite difficult and you will be wondering what's wrong with Fabric.

5.2.1. Global vs. Org-specific orderer addresses

The *genesis block (and by extension* `configtx.yaml`*) also contains what type of orderer to provision*. We can see it in this line:

```
OrdererType: etcdraft
```

And *it also contains the addresses peer nodes will use to connect to the orderer*. There are two ways the orderer addresses can be set. One is to set them under the `Orderer.Addresses` section in `configtx.yaml`. These are known as *global endpoints*. All peers will use the addresses defined here to connect to the orderer. A peer node tries one address. If that address fails, the peer node can try the next address and so-on in round-robin fashion. The approach we take in this book is to set *org-specific addresses* or endpoints i.e., we specify the orderer endpoints at the org level so that *each organization's peer connects to that organization's respective orderer.* This is done by specifying the address at the `Organizations.<ORG>.OrdererEndpoints` level in `configtx.yaml`. We can see it for example in this line in `configtx.yaml` for Biotor:

```
OrdererEndpoints:
  - localhost:7050
```

Version `2.0.1` of `configtxgen` has a somewhat undesirable feature that even if you leave the `Orderer.Addresses` section in `configtx.yaml` empty, it will automatically generate an address `127.0.0.1:7050` and add it to the global endpoints list. This is reflected in following line in Listing 5. 6:

```
[common.tools.configtxgen.localconfig] completeInitialization -> INFO 002 Orderer.Addresses
unset, setting to [127.0.0.1:7050]
```

5.2.2. Inspecting the genesis block

The `foo.block` file is binary encoded and you won't be able to view it in a text editor. Fabric provides us a convenient utility known as **configtxlator** to decode the genesis block. Let's use it.

Verify you have the right version of `configtxlator`:

```
$ configtxlator version
configtxlator:
 Version: 2.0.1
 Commit SHA: 1cfa5da98
 Go version: go1.13.4
 OS/Arch: darwin/amd64
```

Next, run:

```
$ configtxlator proto_decode --input ./foo.block --type common.Block
```

You should see a long JSON output with a wealth of information (git.io/JI3dW). In case of any issues, I recommend verifying you are using the correct version as the first step in your debugging process.

Saving the output of `configtxlator` to a file hasn't worked for me. It gives me this error:

```
$ configtxlator proto_decode --input ./foo.block --type common.Block > genesis.json
configtxlator: error: open /dev/stdout: permission denied, try --help
```

So you have to save the output to a file by other means. Once you have a `genesis.json`, you can inspect and manipulate it from Node.js using following code snippet or use an online viewer:

Listing 5. 7. Code to read a block and parse into a JavaScript object

```
const fs = require('fs');
var blob = fs.readFileSync('genesis.json');
var str = blob.toString();
var o = JSON.parse(str);
```

Here we can see for example that the global orderer endpoints are defined deep in:

```
> o.data.data[0].payload.data.config.channel_group.values.OrdererAddresses
{ mod_policy: '/Channel/Orderer/Admins',
  value: { addresses: [ '127.0.0.1:7050' ] },
  version: '0' }
```

and the org-specific addresses are defined in:

```
>
o.data.data[0].payload.data.config.channel_group.groups.Orderer.groups.Biotor.values.Endpoi
nts
{ mod_policy: 'Admins',
  value: { addresses: [ 'localhost:7050' ] },
  version: '0' }
```

and the type of orderer is defined in:

```
> o.data.data[0].payload.data.config.channel_group.groups.Orderer.values.ConsensusType
{ mod_policy: 'Admins',
  value:
   { metadata: { consenters: [Array], options: [Object] },
     state: 'STATE_NORMAL',
     type: 'etcdraft' },
  version: '0' }
```

Exercise 5.1

Search for `HashingAlgorithm` in the configuration contained in the genesis block. It specifies the hash function used by Fabric to compute a block's hash. What is it? Write it down.

Our next step is to provision the orderer. Before doing that, make a copy of `foo.block` - the genesis block - into the `orderer` subdirectory of each organization.

5.3. Provisioning the orderer

> We work from `$/three-org-network/biotor/orderer` in this section. The directory will change for other organizations.

We are now ready to provision an orderer. We will show how to provision the orderer for Biotor and provisioning orderers for XMed and KeyPharmacy will be left as exercises. The orderer uses the genesis block we created before so verify you have `foo.block` file on your system. You should have downloaded a copy of the `orderer` binary when you installed Fabric in Section A.8. Verify you have correct version of orderer on your system:

```
$ orderer version
orderer:
 Version: 2.0.1
 Commit SHA: 1cfa5da98
 Go version: go1.13.4
 OS/Arch: darwin/amd64
```

The next thing to verify is that you have an `orderer.yaml` file in the `$/three-org-network` directory which is used by the orderer to read config settings when it is launched. The orderer is run by executing the `orderer` command but before you do that, there are a number of settings you have to configure. There are several ways to do this. The settings can be configured in the `orderer.yaml` file. They can also be configured using *environment variables. The environment variables will override any settings in* `orderer.yaml`. There is no right or wrong method; you decide what works for you. In what follows we will explain the `orderer.yaml` file and show the changes you need to make to that file. Later we will explain how to override settings in `orderer.yaml` using environment variables.

Cd to `$/three-org-network/biotor/orderer`. Copy over `orderer.yaml` to this directory as well as `msp` and `tls` directories of `orderer0.biotor.com` from the `crypto-config` folder as shown below:

```
$ cp ../../orderer.yaml .
$ cp -R ../../crypto-config/peerOrganizations/biotor.com/peers/orderer0.biotor.com/tls .
$ cp -R ../../crypto-config/peerOrganizations/biotor.com/peers/orderer0.biotor.com/msp .
```

The msp directory will provide the identity of the orderer and the tls directory will provide cert and keys for TLS communication. We won't use the tls directory in this chapter but copy over the files so we'll have them when we need them. We will now make changes to yaml file in current directory. Check the file into source control when you are done with your changes.

5.3.1. Understanding orderer.yaml

Provisioning the orderer is all about understanding the orderer.yaml file and customizing it to your use-case. When the orderer is run, it expects an orderer.yaml under the directory given by FABRIC_CFG_PATH environment variable. *An error will be thrown if no* orderer.yaml *is found under* FABRIC_CFG_PATH. The orderer.yaml is a big file so let's understand it bit by bit. The whole file is divided into following top-level sections:

Table 5. 2. Top level sections in orderer.yaml

Section	Purpose
General	Controls general settings such as where will orderer listen for connections, what certs it will use for TLS etc.
FileLedger	Provides the location where orderer will store its data
Kafka	Don't bother
Debug	Provides two variables BroadcastTraceDir and DeliverTraceDir which can be used to turn on verbose tracing of broadcast and deliver requests to the orderer
Operations	configures the operations server endpoint for the orderer
Metrics	configures metrics collection for the orderer
Consensus	Provides two options WALDir and SnapDir used to set the directories for write ahead logs and snapshots. Used by Raft algorithm.

In what follows we will show the changes that you need to make to the orderer.yaml. The file in the repo does not have these changes and running the orderer will fail if you try to use the file as-is.

GENERAL **SETTINGS**

The General section is the one which is most verbose and requires the most amount of fiddling so let's start digging into it and make changes as follows.

```
ListenAddress: 0.0.0.0
ListenPort: 7050
```

The ListenAddress is the IP address where the orderer should listen to connections from peers and client applications. Setting it to 0.0.0.0 causes orderer to listen on all network interfaces

(WiFi, Ethernet etc.) on the machine. That way it is able to accept incoming connections from any computer. Setting it to 127.0.0.1 will cause it to refuse connections from remote machines. When you are running everything locally you could set it to 127.0.0.1 and things will still work, but in production you should set it to 0.0.0.0. The ListenPort is self-explanatory. A port is needed *in addition* to an IP address to form a complete endpoint where communication can take place and ListenPort provides just that. Next, we will disable TLS as shown below:

```
TLS:
    Enabled: false
    ClientAuthRequired: false
```

The TLS settings are used to secure communication with peers and client (web) applications using TLS. The TLS section is only applicable when the orderer is communicating with peers and client applications. *It does not apply when the orderer is communicating with other orderers. There is a different section in the config (*Cluster*) that controls TLS specific settings in that case.* We covered TLS in previous chapter. Enabling TLS is going to open up a whole can of worms and so for simplicity we will disable it for now. There is a separate chapter in the book that covers changes you need to make to enable TLS (Chapter 11). Note that disabling TLS just means that in worst case someone can view the messages exchanged between orderer and peer nodes or client applications. Even if they are able to do that, they cannot modify the messages in any way as everything is protected by digital signatures.

The next sub-section under General is Keepalive. Read the comments in the yaml file to understand what it means. This takes us to the Cluster sub-section and is an important one as it controls the settings that apply when the orderer is communicating with other orderers in Raft mode.

```
Cluster:
    SendBufferSize: 10
    ClientCertificate: tls/server.crt
    ClientPrivateKey: tls/server.key
    ListenPort: 7070
    ListenAddress: 0.0.0.0
    ServerCertificate: tls/server.crt
    ServerPrivateKey: tls/server.key
    RootCAs:
      - tls/ca.crt
```

Unlike the TLS section where the orderer only acts as a server, when the orderer is communicating with other orderers *it can behave both as a server and as a client* - that is the definition of a p2p network. The ClientCertificate and ClientPrivateKey are used to provide the certificate and key when orderer is acting as a client whereas the ServerCertificate and ServerPrivateKey provide the certificate and key when orderer is acting as a server and someone else has made a connection to it. We use the same cert and key (ClientCertificate = ServerCertificate and ClientCertificate = ServerPrivateKey) - because cryptogen does not generate separate keys and certs - but that is not necessary. The RootCAs applies when orderer is acting as a client. It will validate the server's certificate against the list of trusted authorities in RootCAs. *Note that the* *complete list of trusted CAs is the UNION of what is declared here AND the trusted CAs defined in the genesis block (*configtx.yaml*). Note that unlike the* TLS *section, there is no option to enable or disable TLS under* Cluster. *The reason is that TLS cannot be disabled in Raft mode. It is a requirement of Raft protocol.* And it is also for this reason that Fabric provides a separate ListenAddress and ListenPort under the Cluster section so that if one wants they can disable TLS with rest of the world. If the Cluster listen address and port are not set, they will fallback to the General listen address and port. And if TLS is disabled on the General address:port an error will be thrown as Raft communication cannot proceed without TLS. The SendBufferSize is set to 10 by default and we accept that setting as-is. You can ignore it for the most part. It is the maximum number of messages in the egress buffer if you must know. Consensus messages are dropped if the buffer is full causing transaction messages to wait until space is freed.

The next set of settings under the General section are the following:

```
BootstrapMethod: file
BootstrapFile: foo.block
LocalMSPDir: msp
LocalMSPID: BiotorMSP
```

The BootstrapMethod sets the method by which the genesis file required to bootstrap the orderer will be provided. A genesis block (the BootstrapFile) is needed to bootstrap the orderer but should not be required to *restart* an already bootstrapped orderer. This is because in that case the genesis block can be had simply by querying the bootstrapped system channel. However, v2.0.1 of Fabric has a bug (FAB-17774) whereby you need to provide the genesis block again even when restarting the orderer. When the bug is fixed, there should be no need to set BootstrapFile when restarting the orderer. And the BootstrapMethod should be set to none in that case. The orderer will run under the identity given by LocalMSPDir. Remember that although the orderer is a machine, it still has an identity just like a real life person. We generated this identity using cryptogen and its made up of the public cert in signcerts subfolder and private key in keystore subfolder of LocalMSPDir. *The* LocalMSPID *must match the MSP ID of orderer used in* configtx.yaml.

There are a few more settings in the General section. We do not cover them here and refer the reader to the yaml file for details. The defaults for those settings are good enough.

FILELEDGER **SETTINGS**

FileLedger is an important section and contains the location where the orderer will store its data. It contains just two settings. Set them as follows:

```
Location: orderer0.biotor.com
Prefix: hyperledger-fabric-ordererledger
```

Location contains the location (directory) where the orderer will store its data. The orderer will attempt to create the directory if it does not exist. If the directory already exists (for example, if you are re-starting the orderer from a previous run), the orderer will use what it finds in it. Prefix can be ignored for the most part. We accept the default setting of Prefix.

DEBUG **SETTINGS**

Debug section has two settings:

```
BroadcastTraceDir:
DeliverTraceDir:
```

BroadcastTraceDir when set causes each request to the Broadcast service to be written to a file in this directory. DeliverTraceDir when set causes each request to the Deliver service to be written to a file in this directory. These options are good for verbose tracing, performance profiling and debugging of the orderer.

CONSENSUS **SETTINGS**

The Consensus section contains just two settings. Set them as follows:

```
WALDir: orderer0.biotor.com/etcdraft/wal
SnapDir: orderer0.biotor.com/etcdraft/snapshot
```

The WALDir is used to provide the location of write-ahead logs and SnapDir is used to set the location of directory that stores snapshots of the etcd database. Write-ahead logs (WAL) and snapshots are used to restore a database and prevent corruption in case of crashes by providing checkpoints. Both WAL and snapshots are general features that come with a database and not something specific to Fabric.

OPERATIONS **SETTINGS**

The orderer runs an operations server. We will not cover its internals in the book. The only thing that matters to us is to set a distinct ListenAddress for the operations server where no one is listening. Do that as follows:

```
ListenAddress: 0.0.0.0:8443
```

The Operations section also has a TLS subsection. My advice is to disable TLS - also the default setting.

METRICS **SETTINGS**

The Metrics section is used to list a Provider (one of statsd, prometheus, or disabled) to which the orderer will emit metrics - telemetry data which can be visualized in a dashboard or graph using tools such as Grafana. The Provider is disabled by default and we will accept that:

```
Provider: disabled
```

Once you disable the provider, no metrics will be sent. We leave the exploration of Metrics as an advanced exercise for the reader. This finishes discussion of orderer.yaml.

In case you are wondering, to my knowledge *it is not possible to specify a different name for the* orderer.yaml *file.* Thus you cannot have a biotor-orderer.yaml that can be input to the orderer binary. The orderer binary will always look for a orderer.yaml under FABRIC_CFG_PATH. This is the reason why I asked to create a biotor folder under $/three-org-network so we can create different yaml files for different organizations by placing them under different directories. The reason for the constraint has to do with the fact that its hardcoded on the following line in the orderer: [89]

```
coreconfig.InitViper(config, "orderer")
```

There are several settings in orderer.yaml *that must match what is declared in* configtx.yaml. They are listed below in Table 5. 3 and must be checked for accuracy very carefully. Mismatches between the two and are common source of errors:

Table 5. 3. Table showing orderer settings and their corresponding section in configtx.yaml.

Orderer Setting	configtx.yaml
GENERAL listen address and port	Organizations.<Org>.OrdererEndpoints
CLUSTER listen address and port	Orderer.EtcdRaft.Consenters
CLUSTER TLS certificates	Orderer.EtcdRaft.Consenters
General.LocalMSPID	Organizations.<Org>.ID

Note that nowhere in orderer.yaml *did we specify what type of orderer to run - Solo, Kafka or Raft. That setting is contained in the genesis block which in turn gets it from* configtx.yaml.

5.3.2. Logging: FABRIC_LOGGING_SPEC

Fabric provides an env variable FABRIC_LOGGING_SPEC that can be used to change the verbosity of logging when you are running the orderer or peer. Possible values are DEBUG, INFO (default), WARNING, ERROR, PANIC and FATAL (all are case-insensitive) in decreasing order of verbosity. For example, setting FABRIC_LOGGING_SPEC to debug will give the most verbose logs. The output can be so verbose that you might have trouble finding what you are looking for. There is a fix for this problem. It is possible to *fine-tune and set the verbosity of logs coming from different Go packages to different levels.* Internally the way its handled is that Fabric uses the common/flogging package and different loggers are created for different Go packages (Go does not have classes). And the log level of each logger instance can be set independently of other instances. An example can help to understand. Say you set:

```
FABRIC_LOGGING_SPEC=msp,gossip=error:chaincode=info:warning
```

This will set the log-level of messages from msp and gossip packages to error. The log-level of chaincode package is set to info and for all other packages a log-level of warning will be used. This way one can just print the messages one is interested in, so make sure you understand the syntax and how to use it. The default value of FABRIC_LOGGING_SPEC if its left unset is info.

Warning: *Fabric uses different environment variables to control the logging for different components.* In this chapter we will only need to use the FABRIC_LOGGING_SPEC env variable but the table below summarizes the different env variables, what logging they control and alternative settings in config file when applicable.

Table 5. 4. Fabric uses different environment variables to control the logging of different components.

Env Variable	What it controls	Config file	Config setting
FABRIC_LOGGING_SPEC	peer, orderer	-	-
CORE_CHAINCODE_LOGGING_LEVEL	chaincode logs	core.yaml	chaincode.logging.level
HFC_LOGGING	Node.js client application (Section 8.10) and fabric-ca-client (Section 14.2)	default.json	hfc-logging
FABRIC_CA_SERVER_LOGLEVEL	fabric-ca-server (Chapter 13)	fabric-ca-server-config.yaml	loglevel
FABRIC_CA_CLIENT_LOGLEVEL	Command line fabric-ca-client (Section 14.1)	fabric-ca-client-config.yaml	loglevel

5.3.3. Overriding settings in orderer.yaml using Environment Variables

All the settings in orderer.yaml *can be overridden using environment variables.* This is a general pattern in Fabric and you will see this with other config files as well. To take an example the setting General.BootstrapMethod in the yaml file can be overridden using the ORDERER_GENERAL_BOOTSTRAPMETHOD environment variable. To get the environment variable corresponding to a setting:

1. Convert all characters to uppercase. Thus General.BootstrapMethod becomes GENERAL.BOOTSTRAPMETHOD
2. Replace periods (.) with underscores (_). Thus GENERAL.BOOTSTRAPMETHOD becomes GENERAL_BOOTSTRAPMETHOD
3. Add an ORDERER prefix with an underscore delimiter. Thus GENERAL_BOOTSTRAPMETHOD becomes ORDERER_GENERAL_BOOTSTRAPMETHOD.

The environment variables can be set *inline* or can be *exported* in accordance with standard Unix principles.

The FABRIC_CFG_PATH and FABRIC_LOGGING_SPEC environment variables cannot be set (i.e., have no counterpart) in the yaml file.

Listing 5. 8 shows how to run the orderer when you have configured everything in orderer.yaml:

Listing 5. 8. Command to run orderer. **Method 1 - all the orderer settings with exception of** FABRIC_CFG_PATH **are defined in** orderer.yaml.

```
$ orderer
```

Listing 5. 9 shows how to run the orderer using *inline* environment variables which would override any settings in orderer.yaml. The entire code in Listing 5. 9 is *one single command* and we have used ellipses (...) to indicate that we are skipping listing all the environment variables for brevity. Since we have quite a few environment variables, we break up the command into multiple lines using the \ character. Take care there should be no whitespace after \ otherwise you will get an error.

Listing 5. 9. Command to run orderer. **Method 2 - use inline environment variables to override default settings in** orderer.yaml.

```
$ FABRIC_CFG_PATH="$PWD" \
ORDERER_GENERAL_BOOTSTRAPFILE=foo.block \
...
orderer
```

And finally, Listing 5. 10 below shows how to run the orderer using *exported* environment variables. Like the inline environment variables, the exported environment variables override any settings in orderer.yaml. *The difference between inline and exported variables is that whereas inline variables are good only for the command in which they appear, when variables are exported they get set for the entire session.* That is, they will apply to all subsequent commands in that shell session. So they are a great way to set those variables which otherwise you will need to set again and again. But be aware of unintended consequences. Whereas the code in Listing 5. 9 was a single command, the code in Listing 5. 10 below is multiple commands. You could export all variables in a single command if you like using spaces e.g., export VAR2=A VAR2=B and so on.

Listing 5. 10. Command to run orderer. **Method 3 - use exported environment variables which will apply to entire session and override settings in** orderer.yaml.

```
$ export FABRIC_CFG_PATH="$PWD"
$ export ORDERER_GENERAL_BOOTSTRAPFILE=foo.block
...
$ orderer
```

You can create a shell script and check it in source control so that you don't have to type long commands on the command line and instead just execute the script which does everything. This is not a book on Unix programming but as another tip, if you export variables in a shell script, their scope will vary depending on how you run the script. For example, given a script run-orderer.sh, if it is run like:

```
$ ./run-orderer.sh
```

Any env variables exported in the script will lose their scope once the script finishes. But voila if you run it like:

```
$ . ./run-orderer.sh
```

Then the env variables exported in the script will persist to current session.

5.3.4. Deploying the orderer

Run the orderer now using any of the methods you like. You may get a prompt from the OS asking to give permission to the orderer to accept incoming connections. Do give it permissions otherwise it won't be able to accept messages from other nodes. If there are any runtime errors, the first thing to check is whether your file paths are correct.

A complete log of what you might see when you run the orderer can be found at git.io/JkzfL. Use it only as a general reference. The results you see are likely to be a bit different since the log is with mutual TLS enabled. The neat thing here is that we are running this orderer in Raft mode which is the recommended mode to use in production. Thus we leapfrog without having to bother with first running in Solo mode and later upgrading to Raft. Note this line in the log:

```
[orderer.commmon.multichannel] Initialize -> INFO 009 Starting system channel 'foo' with
genesis block hash e595028e5f0ee7a46ade5697a684ece8633bd59dff5ad63218680b9e5ee40dc6 and
orderer type etcdraft
```

It tells the orderer is running under etcdraft mode. You will also see some error messages:

```
[orderer.consensus.etcdraft] logSendFailure -> ERRO 022 Failed to send StepRequest to 2,
... Error while dialing dial tcp [::1]:7071: connect: connection refused" channel=foo
node=1
[orderer.consensus.etcdraft] logSendFailure -> ERRO 023 Failed to send StepRequest to 3,
... Error while dialing dial tcp [::1]:7072: connect: connection refused" channel=foo
node=1
```

This is because the orderers for XMed and KeyPharmacy are not yet running.

Let's make sure the Biotor orderer endpoint is working as expected and orderer is listening on it. Run below command from another terminal window:

```
$ lsof -iTCP:7050 -sTCP:LISTEN
COMMAND   PID   USER   FD   TYPE              DEVICE SIZE/OFF NODE NAME
orderer 28197 siddjain   7u  IPv6 0x9a8c450699731d01      0t0  TCP *:7050 (LISTEN)
```

Above command is for Mac. On Linux you can use netstat -tuplen or ss -tuplen instead of lsof. Next, verify you have following directory and file structure under $/three-org-network/biotor/orderer:

```
$ tree orderer0.Biotor.com/
orderer0.Biotor.com/
├────── chains
│       └───── foo
│              └────── blockfile_000000
├────── etcdraft
│       ├────── snapshot
│       │       └───── foo
│       └────── wal
│               └───── foo
│                      ├────── 0.tmp
│                      └────── 0000000000000000-0000000000000000.wal
└────── index
        ├────── 000001.log
        ├────── CURRENT
        ├────── LOCK
        ├────── LOG
        └────── MANIFEST-000000

8 directories, 8 files
```

Go ahead and deploy the orderers for XMed and KeyPharmacy making necessary changes to ports and directories. Take care that the `fileledger.location` are different for different orderers otherwise very bad things will happen if multiple orderers use the same directory for their data. Run `lsof -i | grep orderer` to see all the ports used by the orderers.

5.3.5. Understanding Config Parsing in Fabric

We have seen above how environment variables override the config. This is a general pattern with Fabric and is made possible using the `Viper` library that Fabric uses to parse config files. The Viper library supports two functions: `SetEnvPrefix` and `AutomaticEnv`. The `SetEnvPrefix` sets a prefix that is set to `ORDERER` for orderer and `CORE` for the peer in Fabric's source code as we can see below:

```
cmd/peer/main.go:31: viper.SetEnvPrefix(common.CmdRoot)
orderer/common/localconfig/config.go:288: config.SetEnvPrefix(Prefix)
```

The `AutomaticEnv` function does the overriding and is used below in the peer and orderer:

```
cmd/peer/main.go:32: viper.AutomaticEnv()
orderer/common/localconfig/config.go:289: config.AutomaticEnv()
```

It converts the keys in the config to uppercase inserting underscores (the default delimiter is . and the `SetEnvKeyReplacer` function is used to replace it with an underscore), adds the prefix and then checks if there is an environment variable defined with that name anytime a `viper.Get` request is made. The code that does this is in the `find` method of Viper (`Get` calls `find`):   [90]

```
if v.automaticEnvApplied {
    if val, ok := v.getEnv(v.mergeWithEnvPrefix(lcaseKey)); ok {
        return val
    }
```

Some Fabric commands also support command line flags. These are wired up in Viper using the BindPFlag function. *One gotcha with Viper - and thus with Fabric - is how there is a different syntax to declare arrays for env variables vs. flags.* For env variables you have to use space as delimiter and enclose everything in double quotes like so LR_FOO_BAR="a b c" whereas with flags you use comma as delimiter like so --foobar=a,b,c. The issue is documented online. [91]

Viper is a powerful library for config parsing and you can use it in your other projects written in Go. Below code shows how the orderer uses it to parse config. We have made slight adjustments to the original code to make it easier to read.

Listing 5. 11. Parsing orderer config using the Viper **library**

```
config := viper.New()                              ❶
coreconfig.InitViper(config, "orderer")            ❷
config.SetEnvPrefix("ORDERER")                      ❸
config.AutomaticEnv()                               ❹
replacer := strings.NewReplacer(".", "_")           ❺
config.SetEnvKeyReplacer(replacer)                 ❻
config.ReadInConfig()                              ❼
```

❶ A new instance of viper config is created

❷ The config is bound to the orderer file. This does not read the file.

❸ Here we set a prefix which is used when overriding config with environment variables. Note that the env prefix and the name of config file don't have to be the same. Fabric uses same string but this is a matter of choice not a necessity.

❹ This turns on overriding with environment variables

❺ A function is defined which replaces all periods in a string with underscores

❻ By default Viper delimits the keys it finds in config file with a period. This converts periods to underscores and enables us to use underscore as the delimiter for environment variables.

❼ This reads in the config file. Viper will try all supported extensions in following order: "json", "toml", "yaml", "yml", "properties", "props", "prop"

5.4. Provisioning CouchDB

Recall we have two choices of the state database we can use and that *all peer nodes must use the same database type and its not possible to change this later.* CouchDB is useful especially in development phase because of the UI it provides to view and inspect the world state.

We use Docker in this book to provision CouchDB. Because of this, first we have to create a Docker network before we can provision CouchDB. When you are running everything on your local computer, you can setup just one Docker network as we will do in Listing 5. 12 but remember in real-world each organization is likely to have their own *separate* Docker network. Thus Biotor will have a biotor_net, XMed will have a xmed_net and KeyPharmacy will have a keyp_net. CouchDB can be run without Docker as well but we don't cover that in the book.

5.4.1. Create Docker Network

Begin by creating an *attachable* Docker network using the default `bridge` driver. We give the network the name of `pharmanet`. This command can be run from anywhere:

Listing 5. 12. Creating an attachable network using default `bridge` driver

```
$ docker network create --attachable -d bridge pharmanet
```

You should see above command output a long string, something like:

```
c0d70c64a014356e634b6511bb551a44e7ce3badf172792adad5a44a64d1e27b
```

The long string is the network identifier. You should be able to see the network by running `docker network ls`.

5.4.2. Run CouchDB Container

> We work from **$/three-org-network/biotor/couchdb** in this section. The directory will change for other organizations.

To provision a CouchDB for Biotor, run following from **$/three-org-network/biotor/couchdb** (change the directory for different organizations):

Listing 5. 13. Command to spin up a CouchDB database running inside a Docker container

```
$ docker run -d \
-v "$PWD/couchdb.peer0.biotor.com:/opt/couchdb/data" \
-p 17055:5984 \
  env COUCHDB_USER= \
--env COUCHDB_PASSWORD= \
--name couchdb.peer0.biotor.com \
--network pharmanet \
couchdb:2.3.1
```

This will spin up a Docker container and run CouchDB inside it. The directory `$PWD/couchdb.peer0.biotor.com` will be created. Using the `.` character instead of `$PWD` gives error on Docker CE 19.03.4 (the version I have). *The double-quotes around* `$PWD` *are there to handle any spaces in* `$PWD` *which are otherwise interpreted by* `bash` *as beginning the next command line argument.* Here we are provisioning a CouchDB instance for use by the peer of Biotor. Hence the name `couchdb.peer0.biotor.com`. Remember each peer node maintains its own independent DB. Open your web browser and navigate to localhost:17055/_utils/. Verify you see CouchDB UI as shown in Figure 5. 5. [92]

Figure 5. 5. A brand new CouchDB instance. There are no databases created on a clean install of CouchDB.

It won't list any databases as none have been created yet. Verify that a directory `couchdb.peer0.biotor.com` has been created with following contents:

```
$ tree couchdb.peer0.biotor.com/
couchdb.peer0.biotor.com/
├────── _dbs.couch
├────── _nodes.couch
├────── _replicator.couch
└────── _users.couch

0 directories, 4 files
```

A list of running containers can be seen with `docker ps` command:

```
CONTAINER ID     IMAGE          COMMAND          CREATED        STATUS
PORTS                           NAMES
0fdf1a4946af     couchdb:2.3.1   "tini -- /docker-ent…"  42 minutes ago   Up 42
minutes      4369/tcp, 9100/tcp, 0.0.0.0:17055->5984/tcp   couchdb.peer0.biotor.com
```

To stop the container (e.g., when you are done for the day), run:

Listing 5. 14. Command to stop a running container

```
$ docker stop couchdb.peer0.biotor.com
```

To stop all containers with a single command, you can use:

Listing 5. 15. Command to stop all running containers

```
$ docker stop $(docker ps -q)
```

Use above with caution as it will stop all containers running on the host - not just the CouchDB containers.

To re-start the container next day, run:

Listing 5. 16. Command to restart a container

```
$ docker start couchdb.peer0.biotor.com
```

Pretty simple. You create a container and then just do `docker stop/start`. Do not run the command in Listing 5. 13 to re-start a container. That command is meant to be run once to provision a new container.

5.4.3. Inspecting the container and logs

Once you see Figure 5. 5, that means you have a successfully running container. You can also go one step further and verify ports are working by running the commands below. Refer Section 10.3 in case you run into any difficulties.

Listing 5. 17. Inspecting open ports inside a Docker container

```
$ docker exec -it couchdb.peer0.biotor.com /bin/bash    ❶
root@0fdf1a4946af:/# apt-get update                      ❷
root@0fdf1a4946af:/# apt-get install iproute2            ❸
root@0fdf1a4946af:/# ss -tupln                           ❹
Netid State     Recv-Q Send-Q Local Address:Port    Peer Address:Port
udp   UNCONN    0      0      127.0.0.11:36534          *:*
tcp   LISTEN    0      128    127.0.0.11:33433          *:*
tcp   LISTEN    0      128         *:5984               *:*
tcp   LISTEN    0      128         *:5986               *:*
root@0fdf1a4946af:/# exit                                ❺
```

❶ Log into the Docker container
❷ Update the package manager
❸ Install `iproute2` package
❹ Run `ss` to view open ports. Use `-tpln` to list only TCP ports that are in listen mode.
❺ Exit the container

For readers familiar with Docker, if you look at the logs by running `docker logs -f couchdb.peer0.biotor.com` you will see error messages like:

```
$ docker logs -f couchdb.peer0.biotor.com
[error] 2020-04-21T17:27:28.631645Z nonode@nohost emulator -------- Error in process
<0.2672.1> with exit value:
{database_does_not_exist,[{mem3_shards,load_shards_from_db,"_users",[{file,"src/mem3_shards
.erl"},{line,395}]}],...
```

Ignore them. These errors occur because the database is empty. A database will be created when we create a channel and the errors will go away then.

Go ahead and provision CouchDB for other orgs using Listing 5. 13 as a template and making necessary changes. *Take care not to use the same port (17055) or same directory as the one used by* `couchdb.peer0.biotor.com` *or there will be a problem.* Basically, you need to replace `biotor` with xmed or keypharmacy as the case may be and replace `17055` with some other ports. The `5984` port will stay as is - do not make any changes to it. It is an internal port within the container. Run `docker ps` and browse to `localhost:<port>/_utils/` replacing `<port>` with the appropriate ports to verify all 3 containers are successfully running.

5.5. Provisioning peer nodes

At this stage we have provisioned 3 orderer nodes and 3 CouchDB nodes. We are now ready to provision the peer nodes which is the final step in this chapter. As before we will show how to provision peer for Biotor and provisioning peers for XMed and KeyPharmacy will be left as exercises. Begin by verifying you have the `peer` binary on your system which you should have downloaded as part of the Fabric installation in Section A.8:

Listing 5. 18. Peer binary that comes with Fabric

```
$ peer version
peer:
 Version: 2.0.1
 Commit SHA: 1cfa5da98
 Go version: go1.13.4
 OS/Arch: darwin/amd64
 Chaincode:
  Base Docker Namespace: hyperledger
  Base Docker Label: org.hyperledger.fabric
  Docker Namespace: hyperledger
```

Verify you have a file named `core.yaml` under the `$/three-org-network` directory. Make a copy of this file under the `biotor/peer` directory. Next, let's understand the two modes a peer node can be run in.

5.5.1. Dev *vs.* Net *Mode*

There are two modes a peer node can be run in and they are known as the `dev` and `net` modes. The config setting which controls the mode is given by the `chaincode.mode` field in `core.yaml` and can be overridden using the corresponding `CORE_CHAINCODE_MODE` environment variable. The `chaincode.mode` is set to `net` in the `core.yaml` that ships with Fabric so that becomes the default mode of the peer. The factory installed `core.yaml` provides a good explanation of the two modes:

```
# There are 2 modes: "dev" and "net".
# In dev mode, user runs the chaincode after starting peer from
# command line on local machine.
# In net mode, peer will run chaincode in a docker container.
mode: net
```

The `net` mode is intended to be used in production. *During development phase of the project, I have found the* `dev` *mode to be invaluable because of following two reasons*:

• *The* `dev` *mode allows you to debug your chaincode in a debugger*

- *In the* dev *mode you do not have to re-install, approve and commit your chaincode with a new version and sequence number when you make changes to it*

If you are one of those rockstar developers who can write the complete smart contract in 1 commit and push to it production - good for you. For most of us, development of the smart contract will be an iterative process where we write something, test it, find bugs, make changes, want to deploy corrected code and so on until we get to the finished product. And that's where the power of dev mode comes in. Table 5. 5 further expands on the differences between the two modes.

Table 5. 5. Net **vs.** Dev **Mode**

Net **Mode**	Dev **Mode**
chaincode runs in a Docker container	chaincode does not have to run in a Docker container
peer needs access to Docker daemon (docker.sock) to create a container	Docker daemon is not involved
peer runs fabric-chaincode-node inside new container	developer runs fabric-chaincode-node manually
peer will automatically build a Docker image and launch a container when chaincode is installed and committed respectively	developer will take responsibility of instantiating the chaincode and registering it against a peer
chaincode needs to be re-installed and re-committed with a new version and sequence number when you make changes to it	no need to re-install and re-commit for changes to take effect
-	TLS must be disabled on the peer node
chaincode.mode=net	chaincode.mode=dev or --peer -chaincodedev=true when peer is started

Because of its advantages, we will run the peer nodes in dev mode in this chapter as I am sure you want to learn how to debug the chaincode and don't want to have to re-install and re-commit every time you make a tiny change to it. Before you get excited, I have some bad news. *The* dev *mode is broken in Fabric 2.0.1 (FAB-17584).* This goes back to the comment I made in Section 1.11.2 about the developer experience.

5.5.2. *Fixing* Dev *Mode*

The good news is that I can show you how to fix the dev mode. It can be done by applying the ~/fix-dev-mode.diff patch that comes with the book's code repo. This patch was created on top of v2.0.1 of Fabric so you need to sync to v2.0.1 to apply the patch. If you are using a newer version of Fabric, the patch won't apply and you have to make corresponding changes using ~/fix-dev-mode.diff as guideline. You can sync to v2.0.1 tag of the Fabric repo by running following command from the root directory of the master branch of Fabric repo:

```
$ git checkout tags/v2.0.1
```

If you get an error that says git cannot find the tag, run following command to fetch all tags from the remote repository:

```
$ git fetch --all --tags
```

After checking out `tags/v2.0.1`, you can simply apply the `$/fix-dev-mode.diff` patch that comes with the book's code repository like so:

```
$ git apply ~/phf/fix-dev-mode.diff
```

In above `~/phf` is where I have downloaded the patch. Substitute it with the correct directory as appropriate in your case. The full patch is about a 100 lines long and you can study it online but it consists of disabling *three* code paths when the peer is run in dev mode. These parts are explained below. In the *first* part, we guard the code in `/internal/peer/node/start.go:656` behind an `if` check so it will not execute in dev mode:

```
if !userRunsCC {
    go chaincodeCustodian.Work(buildRegistry, containerRouter, custodianLauncher)
}
```

In the *second* part, we introduce following code in `/core/chaincode/chaincode_support.go` on line 84:

```
if cs.UserRunsCC {
    return nil, errors.Errorf("peer running in DEV mode and no handler is registered for
%s", ccid)
}
```

And the *third* part consists of following changes in `/core/chaincode/lifecycle/lifecycle.go:554` where I have introduced the `if` check which is not there in original Fabric codebase:

```
if !userRunsCC {
    buildStatus, ok := ef.BuildRegistry.BuildStatus(packageID)
    ...
    if err := buildStatus.Err(); err != nil {
        ef.Resources.ChaincodeStore.Delete(packageID)
        return nil, errors.WithMessage(err, "could not build chaincode")
    }
}
```

After applying the patch, re-compile the `peer` binary using following command substituting the path as necessary:

```
$ go build -gcflags="all=-N -l" $GOPATH/src/github.com/hyperledger/fabric/cmd/peer
```

The `gcFlags` is optional. Setting it to `"all=-N -l"` will disable all compiler optimizations and generate a binary that can be used for debugging. The command will take a while to finish and at the end you should see following file on your system:

```
$ ls -al peer
-rwxr-xr-x  1 siddjain  staff  54282036 May 28 10:13 peer
```

Move this file to the directory where you have the factory installed peer. On my computer it is
~/hyperledger/bin. Make a backup of the original peer just in case:

```
$ mv ~/hyperledger/bin/peer ~/hyperledger/bin/peer_2.0.1
$ mv peer ~/hyperledger/bin/peer
```

You have now replaced the peer that came with Fabric with your own custom version in which the
dev mode will work. You can test the version:

```
$ peer version
peer:
 Version: latest
 Commit SHA: development build
 Go version: go1.13.3
 OS/Arch: darwin/amd64
 Chaincode:
  Base Docker Namespace: hyperledger
  Base Docker Label: org.hyperledger.fabric
  Docker Namespace: hyperledger
```

Compare it to the version in Listing 5. 18.

A hack I have discovered to make the dev mode work without having to build a
custom binary is to set CORE_PEER_CHAINCODEADDRESS to a random address like
1.2.3.4:3000. When you do this, the peer creates a Docker container - which it
should not do in the dev mode - but that container is not able to register against the
peer and the registration fails during the *commit phase* of the chaincode (Section
7.9.2). The container gets terminated. You will see a warning in the logs. You will
then be able to register a chaincode that you start manually and reap the benefits of
the dev mode.

5.5.3. Understanding core.yaml configuration file

We work from $/three-org-network/biotor/peer in this and the next section. The
directory will change for other organizations.

Just like provisioning the orderer is an exercise in understanding orderer.yaml, provisioning a
peer is an exercise in understanding core.yaml. When a peer starts it will look for a core.yaml
under FABRIC_CFG_PATH and will throw an error if no core.yaml is to be found. The core.yaml
file is even bigger than orderer.yaml. It consists of following top-level sections:

Table 5. 6. Top-level sections of core.yaml

Section	Purpose
peer	Contains a variety of settings related to listen address, port, TLS etc.
vm	Provides connection string to the Docker daemon that is needed when peer needs to spin up a chaincode container
chaincode	Sets the mode in which peer is running (dev vs. net) and provides various settings needed in the net mode such as what Docker image to use to build the chaincode.
ledger	Sets whether we are going to use LevelDB or CouchDB plus other settings
operations	address and port of operations server
metrics	If you want to emit metrics to statsd or prometheus

The operations and metrics section have same information as in orderer.yaml and have been covered before. Set the operations.listenaddress to 0.0.0.0:9443 and use a distinct operations.listenaddress for each peer otherwise you will get the bind: address already in use error. Disable metrics. The vm section - and most of chaincode as well - is only relevant when we run the peer in net mode so we will cover those later in the book. In what follows - just like we did for the orderer - we list the changes you need to make to the core.yaml in the repo before you try to run the peer. Running the peer with the core.yaml provided as-is will cause problems. Environment variables can be used to override the settings in core.yaml and we cover that later once we have explained core.yaml.

Similar to what we did for the orderer, change your directory to $/three-org-network/biotor/peer and copy following files and directories:

```
$ cp ../../core.yaml .
$ cp -R ../../crypto-config/peerOrganizations/biotor.com/peers/peer0.biotor.com/tls .
$ cp -R ../../crypto-config/peerOrganizations/biotor.com/peers/peer0.biotor.com/msp .
```

Then make following changes to core.yaml. Don't forget to check the file into source control when you are done.

PEER **SETTINGS**

The peer section begins with id and networkId variables:

```
id: peer0.biotor.com
networkId: dev
```

These variables have no effect in dev *mode.* When the peer is run in net mode, these variables are used in naming of the chaincode image and container. The chaincode image as well as container are given following name:

```
{networkId}-{id}-{chaincode-package-identifier}
```

You will see `chaincode-package-identifier` when you install the chaincode in Section 7.6. The `networkId` and `id` are thus used to provide a namespace to the chaincode image and container. As best practice, you could set the `networkId` to the id of the Docker network the peer is attached to (when the peer is running in a Docker container). That takes us to:

```
address: 127.0.0.1:8051
listenaddress: 0.0.0.0:8051
chaincodeListenAddress: 0.0.0.0:8052
chaincodeAddress:
addressAutoDetect: false
```

`address` is the address other peers *in the same organization* will use to connect to this peer. The peers *in other organizations* will use `gossip.externalEndpoint` which is under the `gossip` subsection. We don't have other peers in same organization so the value of `address` field will not matter. `listenaddress` is the address and port at which peer will listen for communication from other peers and applications *but not the chaincode*. `chaincodeAddress` is the address that the chaincode container will use to connect to the peer. In `dev` mode the peer does not launch any chaincode container so this becomes a don't care field. We will set it later on in the book when we run the peer in `net` mode. Setting `chaincodeAddress` to empty actually causes it to fallback on `chaincodeListenAddress`. `chaincodeListenAddress` is the address and port at which peer will listen for messages from chaincode. *The `peer` uses different endpoints to communicate with chaincode vs. rest of the world.* We use `0.0.0.0` for all listen addresses as that causes the peer to listen to all the network interfaces it can find on the machine. In the `gossip` section make following changes:

```
gossip:
  bootstrap: 127.0.0.1:8051
  endpoint: 127.0.0.1:8051
  externalEndpoint: 127.0.0.1:8051
```

`gossip.bootstrap` is a list of other peers *in the same organization* that this peer reaches out to at startup to initialize the gossip protocol. We don't have any other peer in same organization so this field will not matter. `gossip.endpoint` if set *overrides* `peer.address`. The `externalEndpoint` is quite important and is the address peers of *other organizations* will use to connect to this peer. *If this isn't set, the peer will not be known to other organizations.* We can see that `peer.address` (or `peer.gossip.endpoint`) and `peer.gossip.externalEndpoint` serve a complementary purpose. There are a ton of other settings in `gossip` subsection. Refer to comments in yaml file for details.

WHY ARE THERE TWO SETS OF ADDRESSES - A LISTEN ADDRESS AND A CONNECTION ADDRESS?

Notice that `core.yaml` defines two sets of addresses. For example, the `peer.address` (or `peer.gossip.endpoint`) tells other peers what address to use to connect to this peer (I call this the *connection address*) and `peer.listenAddress` defines the address where the peer actually listens for messages. It is natural to wonder why are there two sets of addresses? Isn't it a given that if the address used to connect is not the same as the address where the peer is listening, there will be a problem? Indeed for a local deployment you can set both to 127.0.0.1:8051 and everything will work. The answer to the question is not obvious until you consider a multi-node deployment where peers are running on different machines or a containerized deployment where peers are running on different containers. Given two peers A and B that run on two different machines or containers, A will listen on 0.0.0.0:8051 but when B has to make connection to A it has to use A's IP address or a name that is resolved to an IP address by DNS mapping. And that is why we have a different connection address. Also when TLS is enabled, it turns on *hostname validation* and *the connection address has to be listed in the* subjectAltNames *or* SAN *section of the server's TLS certificate or the two machines will not be able to establish a connection.* This is the most common problem when using TLS. The connection addresses in core.yaml are handed off to the discovery service and the gossip protocol who *advertise* them to all the nodes in the network. That's how other nodes *discover* this node.

WHY ARE THERE NO CONNECTION ADDRESSES DEFINED IN ORDERER.YAML?

Notice that unlike core.yaml, orderer.yaml does not define any connection addresses. How come? The answer is that the orderer's connection address is obtained from the genesis block which in turn gets it from configtx.yaml.

Let's come to the tls subsection. As with the orderer, we are going to disable all TLS for now - its unnecessary when you are running everything on localhost in dev mode. Actually, its more than that. TLS has to be disabled in dev mode according to Fabric docs. [93]

```
tls:
    enabled:  false
    clientAuthRequired: false
```

Next, make following changes in peer subsection:

```
fileSystemPath: peer0.biotor.com
mspConfigPath: msp
localMspId: BiotorMSP
```

fileSystemPath is a very important setting and gives the directory where peer will store all its data. It is set to /var/hyperledger/production by default in the standard core.yaml that comes with Fabric distribution. mspConfigPath is the directory containing the identity which the peer will run under. This identity is made up of the public cert in signcerts subfolder and private key in keystore subfolder of mspConfigPath. localMspId must match with what you declared in configtx.yaml. Make sure the discovery service is enabled (that is the default anyway):

```
discovery:
    enabled: true
```

The discovery service is used by clients to query information about peers, such as - which peers have joined a certain channel, what is the latest channel config, and most importantly - given a chaincode and a channel, what possible sets of peers satisfy the endorsement policy. There are many more settings under `peer` in `core.yaml`. Accept the defaults and refer to yaml file for details.

CHAINCODE **SETTINGS**

The only setting we will set under `chaincode` is:

```
mode: dev
```

This will make the peer run in `dev` mode. The rest of the settings under `chaincode` are don't care in `dev` mode.

LEDGER **SETTINGS**

Under the `ledger` subsection we will make following changes:

```
state:
    stateDatabase: CouchDB      ❶
    couchDBConfig:
        couchDBAddress: 127.0.0.1:17055
```

❶ As I learned the very, very hard way this string is case-sensitive so `couchdb` won't work

This configures the peer to use CouchDB for its key-value store. We use CouchDB so we can inspect the world state independently using a UI or CLI that comes with CouchDB. `couchDBAddress` provides the `address:port` where the CouchDB is running. *This should be different for peers of other organizations so take care otherwise all of them will connect to same CouchDB causing weird behavior at runtime.* There are many more settings under `ledger`. Refer to yaml for details and explore them at your pace.

Just like you cannot change the name of the file which the orderer reads at startup to load config settings, you cannot change the name of `core.yaml` which is used by peer to load config settings. `peer` binary will always look for a `core.yaml` (or other supported extensions) under `FABRIC_CFG_PATH`. It is hardcoded in:

```
internal/peer/common/common.go:99: err := config.InitViper(nil, cmdRoot) // cmdRoot is a
constant defined as "core"
```

> The meaning of variables in `core.yaml` changes depending on the context in which they are used. For example, when used in conjunction with `peer node start` as in this chapter, `peer.address` refers to address of the peer. But when used in other `peer` commands (we will see them in Chapter 7), `peer.address` refers to a target peer against which a request is to be executed. As another example in this chapter `peer.mspConfigPath` is used to provide the identity of the peer. But in Chapter 7 `peer.mspConfigPath` will be used to provide identity of the user or admin.

Just like we can use environment variables to override settings in `orderer.yaml`, we can do the same with `core.yaml`. To find the environment variable corresponding to a setting in `core.yaml`:

1. Convert all characters to uppercase. Thus `peer.address` becomes `PEER.ADDRESS`
2. Replace periods (`.`) with underscores (`_`). Thus `PEER.ADDRESS` becomes `PEER_ADDRESS`
3. Add a `CORE` prefix with an underscore delimiter. Thus `PEER_ADDRESS` becomes `CORE_PEER_ADDRESS`.

The logging of peer can be configured using the same `FABRIC_LOGGING_SPEC` variable that controls the logging of orderer.

5.5.4. Starting peer nodes

The command to start a peer node is `peer node start`. Run a peer node by executing following command from `$/three-org-network/biotor/peer`:

Listing 5. 19. Command to run peer node

```
$ peer node start
```

You might be prompted with a screen requesting permission for peer node to accept incoming connections. Please grant the permissions. When the peer has successfully started, you should see a message like following in the log (git.io/JkzfO)

```
[nodeCmd] serve -> INFO 019 Started peer with ID=[peer0.biotor.com], network ID=[dev],
address=[127.0.0.1:8051]
```

To verify peer node is running correctly check you have a directory on your system corresponding to `peer.fileSystemPath`. Next check that a directory named `ledgersData` is created under `peer.fileSystemPath`. And check `peer.listenAddress` is working as shown below:

```
$ lsof -iTCP:8051 -sTCP:LISTEN
COMMAND   PID     USER    FD  TYPE            DEVICE SIZE/OFF NODE NAME
peer      24423 siddjain  8u  IPv6 0xe4650e51527382cd     0t0  TCP *:8051 (LISTEN)
```

At this stage if you refresh the CouchDB URL (localhost:17055/_utils) you should see some databases created like the screenshot in Figure 5. 6.

Databases

Name	Size	# of Docs
_replicator	3.8 KB	1
_users	3.8 KB	1
fabric__internal	436 bytes	1

Figure 5. 6. CouchDB after peer node has been provisioned but no application channel is created. We can see a few databases are created at this stage.

Go ahead and provision the peer nodes for XMed and KeyPharmacy and adjusting the configuration variables as necessary. Please use distinct `peer.fileSystemPath` for each peer and take care to use distinct ports as well. For example, use ports 8053 (general listen port), 8054 (chaincode listen port), 9444 (operations listen port) for XMed and ports 8055, 8056, 9445 for KeyPharmacy. Run the other nodes in dev mode as well. Run `lsof -i | grep peer` to see all the ports in use by peer nodes.

Congratulations! You have provisioned a Fabric network - no small feat. Each organization is running 1 peer, 1 orderer and 1 CouchDB node. The peers form a p2p network and same goes for the orderer nodes.

5.5.5. Understanding the Internals

If you want to understand what goes on behind the scenes when a peer is started, stick a breakpoint in `internal/peer/node/start.go:180`: [94]

```
func serve(args []string) error {
    // currently the peer only works with the standard MSP
    // because in certain scenarios the MSP has to make sure
```

This function should serve as your entry point to debug any issues you encounter while starting the peer. It would be a good exercise to study this function.

Exercise 5.2

Write a script in your familiar programming language e.g., `one-click-installer.sh` or `one-click-installer.py` that does everything we covered in this chapter with click of a button. Bonus: For extra points, modify your script so that it takes input the number of organizations, their names and other info as may be required and provisions a network. *Hint*: your script will have to generate the `crypto-config.yaml` and `configtx.yaml` files. This is how IDEs such as the IBM Blockchain Extension for VS Code work. When you press a button, it runs a script in the background to do the work. The IBM extension can only provision a 1 org network. Your script will be much more powerful.

5.6. Shutting down and re-starting the network

To shutdown the network simply terminate the peers and orderers using `Ctrl-C` or the `kill` Unix command. The Docker containers are shut down by running `docker stop` as noted in Listing 5. 14. And to re-start the network, bring up the Docker containers by running `docker start` as noted in Listing 5. 16 and run the `orderer` and `peer node start` commands to bring up the orderer and peer nodes. The peer and orderer will pick up the data saved in `peer.fileSystemPath` and `orderer.FileLedger.Location` respectively and resume.

Table B.1 (Appendix B) summarizes some of the commands covered in this chapter used to provision a network.

Exercise 5.3

Write a script in your familiar programming language e.g., `shutdown.sh` to shutdown a network and a script `restart.sh` to restart a previously provisioned network.

5.7. Summary

- A genesis block is needed to bootstrap the orderer. It is generated by running `configtxgen` on a `configtx.yaml` file.
- The genesis block contains a wealth of information but it does not contain any private keys.
- The system channel that bootstraps the orderer resides solely on the ordering service and stores channel configuration transactions which are used to create and update application channels.
- The connection string used to connect to the orderer (i.e., its address) is stored in the genesis block. That is the address peer nodes will use to connect to the orderer. The genesis block in turn gets that address from `configtx.yaml`. It is recommended to use org-specific endpoints rather than global endpoints in `configtx.yaml`.
- The type of orderer to run (Solo, Kafka or Raft) is also configured in the genesis block.
- The `orderer` binary reads settings from `orderer.yaml` and stores its data under the directory given by `FileLedger.Location` in yaml file.
- The addresses and ports you set when running the orderer need to match with what is defined in the genesis block (and by extension `configtx.yaml`) otherwise there will be a problem.
- Run peer nodes in `dev` mode if you want to be able to debug the chaincode and not have to re-install and re-commit when you make changes to it.
- The `peer` binary reads settings from `core.yaml` and stores its data under the directory given by `peer.fileSystemPath` in the yaml file.
- Environment variables can be used to override the settings in `core.yaml` or `orderer.yaml`. Both these yaml files should exist under `FABRIC_CFG_PATH` or there will be an error while running the `orderer` or `peer`.
- Change the `FABRIC_LOGGING_SPEC` to control the level of verbosity you want in the peer and orderer logs.

5.8. Further Reading

- Read about `configtx.yaml` at hyperledger-fabric.readthedocs.io/en/release-2.2/create_channel/create_channel_config.html and hyperledger-fabric.readthedocs.io/en/release-2.0/configtx.html

[84] Note for nitpicky readers: You can consider these as 9 programs running on a single node if you want.

[85] I call such an artificial setup a *test, toy or development* network. All samples that come with official Fabric distribution provision test networks.

[86] Note for experts: we do not use IPv6 addresses in this book.

[87] From nodejs.org/en/docs/guides/getting-started-guide/

[88] For more on the Network Utility app, see support.apple.com/en-us/HT202790

[89] github.com/hyperledger/fabric/blob/v2.0.1/orderer/common/localconfig/config.go#L287

[90] github.com/spf13/viper/blob/master/viper.go#L1172

[91] github.com/spf13/viper/issues/380

[92] For readers familiar with Docker, a successful container log is shown in git.io/JI3dE

[93] hyperledger-fabric.readthedocs.io/en/release-1.4/peer-chaincode-devmode.html

[94] github.com/hyperledger/fabric/blob/v2.0.1/internal/peer/node/start.go#L180

Chapter 6. Debugging Fabric

This chapter covers:

• Debugging Fabric using `dlv` - Go command line debugger

Code for this chapter is under `$/debugging-fabric`

It is not unusual to run into errors while doing Fabric development. What sets apart the great from the merely good developer is the ability to debug and troubleshoot problems. In this chapter we will show how to debug the underlying Fabric code itself. Fabric is written in Go and Delve is Go's debugger. Most of the chapter will be about learning Delve and how to use it to debug Go code. We will show how to do this using the command line as well as the VS Code IDE. Readers already familiar with Go and Delve might just want to know the commands to debug the orderer and peer and those are given in Listing 6. 2 and Listing 6. 8. Before beginning make sure you have downloaded the Fabric repo and have Go and Delve installed as explained in Section A.7 and Section A.5. *All commands in this chapter are to be run from the* `$/debugging-fabric` *directory unless noted otherwise.* It should have following files in it:

```
$ git ls-files
configtx.yaml
core.yaml
crypto-config.yaml
orderer.yaml
```

Further, to see matching results and line numbers with the listings in this chapter, make sure you are synced to following tag in the Fabric repo:

```
commit 1cfa5da98dee4e66a098c993cc6a74705aae74eb (HEAD -> mybranch, tag: v2.0.1)
Author: David Enyeart <enyeart@us.ibm.com>
Date:   Wed Feb 26 14:20:39 2020 -0500

    Updates for fabric release v2.0.1

    Updates for release v2.0.1 including release notes and version
    reference updates.

    Signed-off-by: David Enyeart <enyeart@us.ibm.com>
```

Its okay if you have the custom changes we made in Section 5.5.1 to be able to run the peer in dev mode.

6.1. Debugging the orderer with the command line debugger `dlv`

Let's begin by showing you how to debug the Fabric orderer. In what follows we will try to mimic a debug session as it might happen in real-life. This will not only show how to use Delve but also how to go about troubleshooting and debugging an error in general. Begin by running the commands to create crypto material, genesis block and an orderer but this time executing the commands from the $/debugging-fabric directory. Make sure you have appropriately configured orderer.yaml or are using environment variables to provide the config settings.

```
$ cryptogen generate --config=./crypto-config.yaml
$ configtxgen -profile Genesis -outputBlock foo.block -channelID foo
$ orderer
```

This time you will get an error when you try to run the orderer. I have cheated slightly and am showing you the error you will get on v1.x of Fabric. In 2.0 the error message is more informative but we use the 1.x version to highlight the fact how difficult it can be sometimes to identify and debug what is causing a problem.

Listing 6. 1. Sample error while running orderer

```
[orderer.common.server] Main -> PANI 003 Failed validating bootstrap block: initializing
configtx manager failed: error converting config to map: illegal characters in key: [Group]
panic: Failed validating bootstrap block: initializing configtx manager failed: error
converting config to map: illegal characters in key: [Group]

goroutine 1 [running]:
github.com/hyperledger/fabric/vendor/go.uber.org/zap/zapcore.(*CheckedEntry).Write(0xc0000e
4dc0, 0x0, 0x0, 0x0)
    /__w/1/go/src/github.com/hyperledger/fabric/vendor/go.uber.org/zap/zapcore/entry.go:229
+0x546
github.com/hyperledger/fabric/vendor/go.uber.org/zap.(*SugaredLogger).log(0xc00011e248,
0x1d41204, 0x1bc291d, 0x25, 0xc000241a68, 0x1, 0x1, 0x0, 0x0, 0x0)
    /__w/1/go/src/github.com/hyperledger/fabric/vendor/go.uber.org/zap/sugar.go:234 +0x100
github.com/hyperledger/fabric/vendor/go.uber.org/zap.(*SugaredLogger).Panicf(...)
    /__w/1/go/src/github.com/hyperledger/fabric/vendor/go.uber.org/zap/sugar.go:159
github.com/hyperledger/fabric/common/flogging.(*FabricLogger).Panicf(...)
    /__w/1/go/src/github.com/hyperledger/fabric/common/flogging/zap.go:74
github.com/hyperledger/fabric/orderer/common/server.Main()
    /__w/1/go/src/github.com/hyperledger/fabric/orderer/common/server/main.go:130 +0x1327
main.main()
    /__w/1/go/src/github.com/hyperledger/fabric/cmd/orderer/main.go:15 +0x20
```

Good luck trying to debug this. You might have the urge to ask on Stack Overflow or Fabric mailing list but chances are no one will be able to help you out with an error as cryptic as above. Unfortunately errors like above are common in Fabric. *The first thing to do in situations such as these is to re-run with* FABRIC_LOGGING_SPEC=debug *which will print out more verbose logs.* Many times the verbose logs contain helpful clues to solve the problem. Sometimes we have to go one step further and need to get inside the Fabric codebase - put it under a knife so to speak. The Fabric codebase can be debugged using Delve - a debugger for the Go programming language. We will first show how to use the command line debugger dlv and later on we'll show how to integrate it with VS Code IDE for readers who would like to be able to debug from VS Code.

First, its a good idea to check the dlv version:

```
$ dlv version
Delve Debugger
Version: 1.3.2
Build: $Id: 569ccbd514fc47c8b4c521b142556867ec5e6917 $
```

Next, to debug the orderer using dlv, run following command:

Listing 6. 2. Command to debug orderer

```
$ dlv debug github.com/hyperledger/fabric/cmd/orderer --api-version=2 --log=true --
```

Above   assumes   the   Fabric   codebase   is   available   under
$GOPATH/src/github.com/hyperledger/fabric directory. Change the path to match the
location on your system. When above command is run, dlv will compile and begin debugging the
main package in the given directory. Conventionally this package is found in a file called main.go.
For   example,   in   above   case,   if   we   open   the   main.go   file   under
github.com/hyperledger/fabric/cmd/orderer we can see:

```
package main

import "github.com/hyperledger/fabric/orderer/common/server"

func main() {
        server.Main()
}
```

dlv debug will take some time to finish as its doing a lot of hard work. Once the compilation is
done, you should see output like below:

Listing 6. 3. Delve command prompt

```
info layer=debugger launching process with args: [/Users/siddjain/.../debugging-
fabric/__debug_bin]
error layer=debugger Error reading debug_info: concrete subprogram without address range at
0x31bd92
error layer=debugger Error reading debug_info: concrete subprogram without address range at
0x31dfbd
error layer=debugger Error reading debug_info: could not find abstract origin (0x33508e) of
inlined call at 0x334091
Type 'help' for list of commands.
(dlv)
```

Ignore the seemingly scary error messages in above. They come from cgo - the library Go uses to
interop with C code. The first thing I would like you to verify is that there is a binary by the name
of __debug_bin in the current directory. Do this from another terminal window:

```
$ ls -al orderer
-rwxr-xr-x  1 siddjain  staff  40254020 May  7 16:40 __debug_bin
```

This is the binary built by dlv as it compiles the main package and its path and name can be
changed by adding an --output flag in Listing 6. 2. *This binary will get auto-deleted by Delve*

when it exits the debug session. Make a copy of this binary as we'll use it later:

```
$ cp __debug_bin orderer
```

Coming back to Listing 6. 3, the debugger has now attached itself to the program, paused execution and waiting for us to tell it what to do next. You might get some prompt from dlv asking for elevated privileges - please grant them. The first step for us should be to insert some breakpoints in the code. This is done using the break command (b for short). Looking at the callstack in Listing 6. 1 we can see an error happened in fabric/orderer/common/server/main.go:130 and so we will insert a breakpoint there as follows:

Listing 6. 4. Setting a breakpoint using the file and the line-number

```
(dlv) break github.com/hyperledger/fabric/orderer/common/server/main.go:130
```

You will get some long output as you enter the command. It basically tells the debugger has inserted a breakpoint. Now we'll tell the debugger to continue execution by typing the shortcut c or the long form continue:

```
(dlv) c
```

There is some output and finally the debugger breaks when it encounters the breakpoint (line 130) as shown below:

Listing 6. 5. Breakpoint Hit

```
> github.com/hyperledger/fabric/orderer/common/server.Main() ...
    125:        var clusterType, reuseGrpcListener bool
    126:        var serversToUpdate []*comm.GRPCServer
    127:        if conf.General.BootstrapMethod == "file" {
    128:            bootstrapBlock := extractBootstrapBlock(conf)
    129:            if err := ValidateBootstrapBlock(bootstrapBlock, cryptoProvider); err !=
nil {
=> 130:                logger.Panicf("Failed validating bootstrap block: %v", err)
    131:            }
    132:            sysChanLastConfigBlock := extractSysChanLastConfig(lf, bootstrapBlock)
    133:            clusterBootBlock = selectClusterBootBlock(bootstrapBlock,
sysChanLastConfigBlock)
    134:
    135:            typ := consensusType(bootstrapBlock, cryptoProvider)
(dlv)
```

We can step through the code but it won't be much use as the problem that caused the exception has already past. We can see that it failed on line 129 in ValidateBootstrapBlock so that is where we should have set the breakpoint. On Linux, Delve supports a nifty command rewind that allows you to run backwards but since its not available on Mac or Windows, let's exit the orderer and re-run again. Type exit to exit:

```
(dlv) exit
```

Check that the __debug_bin *binary will get auto-deleted. That is why we made a copy of it.* Now when we want to re-run, we don't need to compile the binary again as that was already done. We'll use the dlv exec command instead of dlv debug and you'll see dlv will attach right away without any pause:

```
$ dlv exec ./orderer --api-version=2 --log=true --
info layer=debugger launching process with args: [./orderer]
...
(dlv)
```

Now let's set breakpoint in the function ValidateBootstrapBlock. We can do this by specifying the file and the line number as was done previously in Listing 6. 4 but its also possible to set a breakpoint by specifying the unambiguous function name:

```
(dlv) break ValidateBootstrapBlock
```

If the function were ambiguous we would use the package name to disambiguate it. Let the program run after setting the breakpoint and you should see it break at:

```
> github.com/hyperledger/fabric/orderer/common/server.ValidateBootstrapBlock() ...
    334:       return verifier
    335: }
    336:
    337: // ValidateBootstrapBlock returns whether this block can be used as a bootstrap
block.
    338: // A bootstrap block is a block of a system channel, and needs to have a
ConsortiumsConfig.
 => 339:  func ValidateBootstrapBlock(block *common.Block, bccsp bccsp.BCCSP) error {
    340:       if block == nil {
    341:           return errors.New("nil block")
    342:       }
    343:
    344:       if block.Data == nil || len(block.Data.Data) == 0 {
```

Perfect! Now we'd want to step through the code line by line. We can do that but it will take a while to find the exact spot where the error occurs. *Instead why not search the codebase for the error message that we see in the log?* We can do that using the git grep command to further isolate the location where the code fails. Cd to the Fabric repo and from there run:

```
$ git grep -n "initializing configtx manager failed"
common/channelconfig/bundle.go:212:    return nil, errors.Wrap(err, "initializing configtx
manager failed")
```

The -n switch also displays the line number. We see the line is wrapping an error. So the actual error has already happened by then. Let's try:

```
$ git grep -n "error converting config to map"
common/configtx/validator.go:118:    return nil, errors.Errorf("error converting config to
map: %s", err)
```

Voila! This time we found the source where the root error is coming from. Let's open this file (`common/configtx/validator.go`) in an editor. I can see following code:

```
configMap, err := mapConfig(config.ChannelGroup, namespace)
if err != nil {
    return nil, errors.Errorf("error converting config to map: %s", err)
}
```

So this is where the mischief is happening. We need to stick a breakpoint in the first line of above snippet. Do that:

```
(dlv) break common/configtx/validator.go:116
```

and let the program run. It should break at:

```
> github.com/hyperledger/fabric/common/configtx.NewValidatorImpl() ...
    111:
    112:        if err := ValidateChannelID(channelID); err != nil {
    113:            return nil, errors.Errorf("bad channel ID: %s", err)
    114:        }
    115:
=> 116:        *configMap, err := mapConfig(config.ChannelGroup, namespace)*
    117:        if err != nil {
    118:            return nil, errors.Errorf("error converting config to map: %s", err)
    119:        }
    120:
    121:        return &ValidatorImpl{
```

Now we can step into this function using the `step` command:

```
(dlv) step
2020-05-08T13:19:38-07:00 debug layer=debugger stepping
> github.com/hyperledger/fabric/common/configtx.mapConfig() ...
    27:        hackyFixNewModPolicy        = "Admins"
    28: )
    29:
    30: // mapConfig is intended to be called outside this file
    31: // it takes a ConfigGroup and generates a map of fqPath to comparables (or error on
invalid keys)
=> 32: func mapConfig(channelGroup *cb.ConfigGroup, rootGroupKey string)
(map[string]comparable, error) {
    33:        result := make(map[string]comparable)
    34:        if channelGroup != nil {
    35:            err := recurseConfig(result, []string{rootGroupKey}, channelGroup)
    36:            if err != nil {
    37:                return nil, err
```

We can now step through the code line by line using `next`:

```
(dlv) next
2020-05-08T13:20:36-07:00 debug layer=debugger nexting
> github.com/hyperledger/fabric/common/configtx.mapConfig() ...
    28: )
    29:
    30: // mapConfig is intended to be called outside this file
    31: // it takes a ConfigGroup and generates a map of fqPath to comparables (or error on
invalid keys)
    32: func mapConfig(channelGroup *cb.ConfigGroup, rootGroupKey string)
(map[string]comparable, error) {
=>  33:        result := make(map[string]comparable)
    34:        if channelGroup != nil {
    35:            err := recurseConfig(result, []string{rootGroupKey}, channelGroup)
    36:            if err != nil {
    37:                return nil, err
    38:            }
```

If we type `locals` it will show us all the local variables:

```
(dlv) locals
result = map[string]github.com/hyperledger/fabric/common/configtx.comparable nil
```

The `args` command can be used to inspect the arguments to the function:

```
(dlv) args
channelGroup = ("*github.com/hyperledger/fabric/vendor/github.com/hyperledger/fabric-
protos-go/common.ConfigGroup")(0xc0000e4f50)
rootGroupKey = "Channel"
~r2 = map[string]github.com/hyperledger/fabric/common/configtx.comparable nil
~r3 = error nil
```

The `print` command can be used to inspect a variable. For example, we can use it to inspect the `channelGroup`. It will show a long output which we omit for brevity.

```
(dlv) print channelGroup
```

We can drill down into a particular field of interest. This is shown below:

```
(dlv) print channelGroup.Groups["Consortiums"].Groups["PharmaLedger"].Groups["Key
Pharmacy"]
```

One problem you might run into is that print *truncates the output and limits the display of long strings to 64 characters or so.* To display more than 64 characters use the slice operation e.g., like print s[64:] which will print the next 64 characters in the string s. Another way to fix this problem is to set the max-string-len variable. Type config -list on the dlv command prompt:

```
(dlv) config -list
aliases                  map[]
substitute-path          []
max-string-len           <not defined>
max-array-values         <not defined>
max-variable-recurse     <not defined>
show-location-expr       false
source-list-line-color   34
debug-info-directories   [/usr/lib/debug/.build-id]
```

You can see by default `max-string-len` is not defined. You can define it like so:

```
(dlv) config max-string-len 1000
```

and this will set the display length of strings to 1000 characters. The `max-array-values` setting is also very helpful to print out long arrays.

We can move up or down the callstack by using the `down` and `up` commands respectively - yes its not a typo. For example, if you want to go to the function which called the current function you are in (i.e., moving down the stack), run:

```
(dlv) up
> github.com/hyperledger/fabric/common/configtx.recurseConfig() ...
Frame 2: /Users/.../fabric/common/configtx/validator.go:116 ...
    111:
    112:        if err := ValidateChannelID(channelID); err != nil {
    113:            return nil, errors.Errorf("bad channel ID: %s", err)
    114:        }
    115:
=> 116:        configMap, err := mapConfig(config.ChannelGroup, namespace)
    117:        if err != nil {
    118:            return nil, errors.Errorf("error converting config to map: %s", err)
    119:        }
    120:
    121:        return &ValidatorImpl{
```

The `down` command does the opposite of `up`. If you ever get lost as it happens to me after printing a bunch of variables, you can use the `list` command to quickly show you where the debugger is paused currently. The `breakpoints` command will list all the breakpoints. `dlv` automatically inserts following two breakpoints when it starts which causes it to automatically break on unhandled exceptions:

```
(dlv) breakpoints
Breakpoint runtime-fatal-throw at ... /usr/local/go/src/runtime/panic.go:820 (0)
Breakpoint unrecovered-panic at ... /usr/local/go/src/runtime/panic.go:847 (0)
    print runtime.curg._panic.arg
```

Use `clear n` to delete the n-th breakpoint. The `stack` command can be used to print the current callstack and the `frame n` command can be used to directly jump to the n-th frame in the stack. For example, to move your cursor to the top of the callstack you would run `frame 0`. The `stepout` method is used to step out of a function. It lets the program run until the topmost frame (frame 0) is no longer on the stack and will break when the frame is popped out of the stack. When debugging multi-threaded code, the threads command can be used to list all the threads and thread n can be used to switch to the n-th thread. Another useful command is funcs which will list all available functions. This will result in very long output and you can use funcs <regex> to filter the output. Only the functions matching the regular expression will be returned. Try them out. These are summarized in Section 6.5.

For most common tasks above is enough. You can check out Delve's complete command line reference online for more advanced stuff. [95]

Exercise 6.1

Fix the error in Listing 6. 1.

6.2. Debugging from VS Code

In this section we show how we can debug Fabric from VS Code IDE for readers who prefer that over the command line debugger. To do that, open Fabric repo in VS Code IDE. Create a file .vscode/launch.json under the repo and add following lines to it. You can change the port from 41305 to something else if you want. You can also change the name to anything else you like:

Listing 6. 6. Configuring VS Code to debug Fabric

```
{
    "version": "0.2.0",
    "configurations": [
        {
            "name": "Launch remote",
            "type": "go",
            "request": "attach",
            "mode": "remote",
            "port": 41305,
            "host": "127.0.0.1",
            "env": {}
        }
    ]
}
```

Also set some breakpoints. Next we need to run Delve in *headless* or *server* mode and specify a port where it will listen to connections from VS Code IDE. This is done by adding --headless=true --listen=127.0.0.1:41305 to the command in Listing 6. 2 so that it becomes:

Listing 6. 7. Running Delve in headless or server mode

```
$ dlv debug github.com/hyperledger/fabric/cmd/orderer --headless=true
--listen=127.0.0.1:41305 --api-version=2 --log=true --
```

You should see following message in the output:

```
API server listening at: 127.0.0.1:41305
```

This confirms that Delve is waiting for a client to attach. Now start debugging in VS Code IDE using the F5 shortcut or by clicking on the green RUN button (▷) and using the Launch remote configuration defined in Listing 6. 6. Voila! You should see the ribbon at the bottom of VS Code turn from blue to orange and IDE attach to the debugger! Below I am showing screenshot of VS Code IDE when a breakpoint is hit:

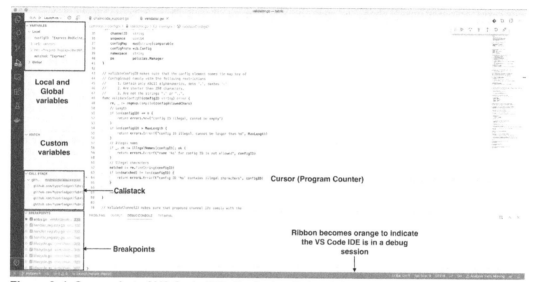

Figure 6. 1. Screenshot of VS Code IDE attached to Delve debugger

From here you can do all the usual stuff that you normally do with VS Code in debug mode. The panel on the left shows all the breakpoints, the callstack, the local and global variables and any variables you want to watch. There is a *Run* sub-menu in the menu bar on the top (the menu bar is not shown in Figure 6. 1) from where you can step over, into and out of a function as well as continue execution and toggle breakpoints (turn them on or off). Try it.

Refer to VS Code's online documentation for even more tips and tricks on how to use it for debugging. [96] It is a liberating experience once you are able to put the Fabric code under a knife. No more running to Stack Overflow or the Fabric mailing list to get answers to your questions. Happy debugging! You are welcome.

You may find that the VS Code IDE does not offer as much functionality when it comes to debugging Go code as it does when debugging C# or some other languages. For example, the *Debug Console* of VS Code is extremely handy as it allows one to inspect variables, evaluate complex expressions and even check the result of calling a function. But it does not work in Go as shown in Figure 6. 2:

PROBLEMS   OUTPUT   DEBUG CONSOLE   TERMINAL

```
ValidateChannelID(channelID)
Unable to eval expression: "function calls not allowed without using 'call'"
call ValidateChannelID(channelID)
Unable to eval expression: "1:6: expected 'EOF', found ValidateChannelID"
```

Figure 6. 2. Evaluating expressions (function calls) does not work in VS Code for Go code.

Some of this has to do with the IDE and some of it has to do with what Delve itself provides and can support. See Issue 2655 on vscode-go GitHub page and Section 6.3 for related discussion. [97] Also check the other issues on the GitHub page to see if a question you have has already been asked by someone else.

6.3. Limitations of Delve

As you get advanced with your debugging, there are some limitations you might run into using Delve. Often, one wants to evaluate a function during debugging i.e., one wants to check what would be the result of calling a function. The print command cannot be used to do that. It can only be used to inspect the values of variables sitting in the memory. Delve (1.3.2) has added a call command to its repertoire but its experimental, and comes with several additional limitations which make it all but useable: [98]

- only pointers to stack-allocated objects can be passed as argument.
- only some automatic type conversions are supported.
- functions can only be called on running goroutines that are not executing the runtime.
- the current goroutine needs to have at least 256 bytes of free space on the stack.
- functions can only be called when the goroutine is stopped at a safe point.
- calling a function will resume execution of all goroutines.
- only supported on Linux's native backend. [99]
- Delve is not able to disambiguate package names. As an example Fabric contains two identically named util packages under common/util/utils.go and core/chaincode/platforms/util/utils.go. And when one tries to call a function such as util.ComputeSHA256, Delve will randomly pick a util package and if the one it picks is not the correct package, you will get a Command failed: could not find symbol value error. [100]

6.4. Debugging the peer

The peer binary can be debugged the same way as the orderer. The command is as follows:

Listing 6. 8. Command to debug peer

```
$ dlv debug github.com/hyperledger/fabric/cmd/peer --api-version=2 --log=true -- node start
```

If you compare it to Listing 6. 2, you notice node start trailing the --. Anything after the last -- are construed as program arguments that are passed by dlv to the program it is debugging. In case of orderer we did not need any program arguments but the peer binary needs these arguments to spin up a peer node. You can again verify there is a main.go file under github.com/hyperledger/fabric/cmd/peer that has the main package which is the entry point to dlv when it runs.

Exercise 6.2: List the system chaincodes installed on a peer

When a peer node starts Fabric installs a couple of system chaincodes on the peer nodes. Get a list of these chaincodes by sticking a breakpoint under /core/chaincode/handler_registry.go:113 and starting a peer node.

```
// Register adds a chaincode handler to the registry.
// An error will be returned if a handler is already registered for the
// chaincode. An error will also be returned if the chaincode has not already
// been "launched", and unsolicited registration is not allowed.
func (r *HandlerRegistry) Register(h *Handler) error {
    r.mutex.Lock()
    defer r.mutex.Unlock()
...
```

6.5. Summary

• When faced with an error, run Fabric under a debugger instead of posting a question to StackOverflow or the Fabric mailing list.
• Use FABRIC_LOGGING_SPEC=debug to print out verbose logs and fine-tune the variable to filter out logs from Go packages that are not of interest.
• When an error happens, search the Fabric codebase for the error message using git grep -n to isolate and identify the location where the code is failing.
• Common dlv commands:
  ◦ break (b): set breakpoint
  ◦ breakpoints (bp): list breakpoints
  ◦ clear: delete breakpoint
  ◦ continue (c): continue execution
  ◦ exit: exit debugger. exit -c will detach the debugger but let the program run.
  ◦ print (p): inspect a variable
  ◦ args: print function arguments
  ◦ locals: print local variables
  ◦ list: show source code near current cursor
  ◦ next (n): step through the program line by line
  ◦ step (s): step into a function
  ◦ stepout (so): step out of a function
  ◦ stack: display current callstack
  ◦ up: move down the callstack
  ◦ down: move up the callstack
  ◦ frame: jump to a particular frame

- ◦ `threads`: list all the threads
  - ◦ `thread`: switch to a particular thread
  - ◦ `funcs`: list available functions
- Run `dlv debug` to compile and debug a package
- Run `dlv exec` to debug precompiled package
- Run `dlv` with `--headless=true` to debug from VS Code
- `dlv` does not support calling functions in the debugger

[95] github.com/go-delve/delve/tree/master/Documentation/cli

[96] code.visualstudio.com/docs/editor/debugging

[97] github.com/microsoft/vscode-go/issues/2655

[98] github.com/go-delve/delve/blob/v1.3.2/Documentation/cli/README.md#call

[99] I have tried it on Mac and got mixed results. Most of the time it will fail but in some cases it does work.

[100] github.com/go-delve/delve/issues/1910

Chapter 7. Provisioning a Channel and Installing the Chaincode

This chapter covers:

- Provisioning a channel and joining peer nodes to it
- Understanding identity verification in Fabric
- Installing smart contracts or chaincode
- Internals of chaincode installation and instantiation

> We work from `$/three-org-network/biotor/admin` directory in this chapter.

This chapter will continue the work we began in Chapter 5. We provisioned a network in that chapter but that does not finish the setup. This chapter covers the remaining steps before we can make requests and perform transactions. They are:

1. Create channel
2. Join peer nodes to the channel
3. Install chaincode on peer nodes
4. Approve and Commit chaincode on the channel. Also known as chaincode instantiation.

Let's dive in. We assume you have the orderer, peer and CouchDB nodes running that we setup in Chapter 5. *Only administrators are allowed to perform the steps 1-4 above and note these steps are a one-time setup and do not have to be repeated when restarting a network that was shutdown previously. All commands in this chapter will be run from the* `admin` *directory we created in Chapter 5 unless otherwise noted.* I will use Biotor admin for most of the commands but it could be admin of any organization.

7.1. Setting up the `admin` *environment*

We begin by noting that *the* `peer` *binary serves a dual purpose*. In Section 5.5 we used the `peer` binary to provision peer nodes using the `peer node start` command. In this chapter we use use `peer` but not pass the `node start` arguments to it. In that case, `peer` serves a completely different purpose and can be used to:

- create a channel
- join peer nodes to the channel
- install, instantiate or upgrade chaincode

This is what we will use it for in this chapter and for lack of a better word, I will sometimes refer to it as "client mode". [101] I think it would have been better if Fabric had released a separate binary for the client mode and named it something like `fabclient`. When we run `peer` binary in client mode, it will be running under the credentials of an admin user. So change your directory to `$/three-org-network/biotor/admin` and run following commands:

```
$ cp -R ../../crypto-config/peerOrganizations/biotor.com/users/Admin\@biotor.com/msp .
$ cp -R ../../crypto-config/peerOrganizations/biotor.com/users/Admin\@biotor.com/tls .
```

The msp directory contains identity of Biotor's admin and the tls directory will be used for TLS communication. We won't use TLS for now and have separate chapter that you should consult for TLS. We also need to create a core.yaml file under the admin folder. When we run the peer binary as a client most of the config settings we saw in Chapter 5 *don't apply and don't need to be set*. Indeed only the peer section is applicable and within the peer section too we only need a few settings. We list them below in Listing 7. 1:

Listing 7. 1. core.yaml **file when** peer **CLI is run as a client (i.e., user or administrator).**

```
peer:
    address: 127.0.0.1:8051
    mspConfigPath: msp
    localMspId: BiotorMSP
    localMspType: bccsp
    tls:
        enabled: false
        clientAuthRequired: false

    keepalive:
        ...
    client:
        ...
    BCCSP:
        ...
```

The explanation of Listing 7. 1 is as follows. address is used to specify the address of the server that the client will connect to. I will call this the ***target peer***. In Chapter 5 we ran Biotor's peer on 127.0.0.1:8051 so we will set the address equal to that. mspConfigPath contains the identity that will be used to bootstrap the peer client. localMspId has same meaning as before and is the MSP ID of the user's organization. Set localMspType to bccsp and don't bother about it. Copy the keepalive, client and BCCSP sections from the default core.yaml as-is into the new file.

7.2. Create channel

A flowchart of the steps required to create a channel is shown in Figure 7. 1. It can be thought of as consisting of two stages:

- Create a channel configuration transaction (channel.tx)
- Use it to create a channel

Figure 7. 1. Channel creation flowchart.

7.2.1. Generating channel configuration transaction

We work from $/three-org-network in this section.

The channel configuration transaction is a request to create a channel for your application that is processed by a special system chaincode. Thus it is a chaincode invocation request, similar to the requests you will make later in the book to exercise your chaincode. The only difference is that this request is processed by special system chaincode(s) that reside on the ordering service. Run:

Listing 7. 2. Command to generate channel configuration transaction which is used to create a channel.

```
$ FABRIC_CFG_PATH="$PWD" configtxgen -profile Channel -outputCreateChannelTx channel.tx
-channelID tracktrace
```

If all goes well you should see output that looks like:

```
[common.tools.configtxgen] main -> INFO 001 Loading configuration
[common.tools.configtxgen.localconfig] Load -> INFO 002 Loaded configuration:
/Users/siddjain/go/src/github.com/siddjain/phf/three-org-network/configtx.yaml
[common.tools.configtxgen] doOutputChannelCreateTx -> INFO 003 Generating new channel
configtx
[common.tools.configtxgen] doOutputChannelCreateTx -> INFO 004 Writing new channel tx
```

and you should have a small file channel.tx on your system

```
$ ls -al channel.tx
-rw-r----- 1 siddjain  staff  497 Apr 16 16:04 channel.tx
```

You might want to chmod 444 channel.tx.

* You may want to keep a note of the channelID you used (tracktrace in example above) since we have not saved it in any file.
* The channel ID used when creating the orderer genesis block (foo.block in Chapter 5) has to be *different* from the channel ID used when generating channel configuration transaction. If you use the same channel ID there won't be any error now, but when you try to create the channel there will be an extremely cryptic error. [102] The reason is that in our example foo is the *system channel* whereas tracktrace is the *application channel*.
* The *system channel* resides solely on the ordering service and stores channel configuration transactions which are used to create and update *application channels*.
* Keep the channel IDs simple. I'd suggest just using alphabets a-z. Do not use underscores. I once used underscores. There was no error at this stage, but later on at some point I got an error. [103] You can imagine that if it doesn't like underscores, then what other characters it may not like.

If you are curious, you can decode the channel.tx and see what's inside it by running:

```
$ configtxlator proto_decode --input channel.tx --type common.Envelope
```

Make a copy of channel.tx under the admin folder of each organization.

7.2.2. *Create channel using* peer channel create

Assuming you have channel.tx in the admin folder, run the peer channel create command as follows from Biotor admin's directory:

Listing 7. 3. Command to create a channel assuming orderer is running with no TLS

```
$ peer channel create -o localhost:7050 -c tracktrace -f channel.tx
```

The peer channel create command makes a request to the orderer to create a channel. It - and all peer commands - relies on the variables configured in core.yaml. *The request is being made on behalf of the* peer.localMspId *in* core.yaml *using the identity provided by the public cert in* peer.mspConfigPath. When the request reaches the orderer (localhost:7050), the orderer is able to verify that the caller is not only a member, but is an admin of Biotor using the crypto material that was used to bootstrap the orderer. How this is possible is explained in Section 7.3. If all goes well, you should see an output that ends with: [104]

```
2020-03-02 15:08:56.138 PST [cli.common] readBlock -> INFO 032 Received block: 0
```

It is possible that you might see some error messages. For example, I saw following messages in the orderer logs:

```
[common.deliver] deliverBlocks -> WARN 04d [channel: tracktrace] Rejecting deliver request
for [::1]:52044 because of consenter error
[common.deliver] deliverBlocks -> WARN 04f [channel: tracktrace] Rejecting deliver request
for [::1]:52045 because of consenter error
[common.deliver] deliverBlocks -> WARN 051 [channel: tracktrace] Rejecting deliver request
for [::1]:52046 because of consenter error
```

You might not even have anything running on the ports above. Then what is it complaining about? To understand these errors, we have to look at the internals. What happens is that the peer channel create command submits a request to create a channel and starts polling the orderer for the genesis block. The ports you are seeing in the errors above are the ports at which the peer channel create is listening for the genesis block from the orderer. It opens a new port when it receives an error. The errors happen because the orderer will reject the request for a genesis block until all the ordering nodes have to come to consensus about it - hence the consenter error. The errors will disappear once all the orderer nodes reach consensus. When that happens the genesis block will be delivered back to the peer CLI and you should see a file tracktrace.block in your directory.

```
-rw-r--r--  1 siddjain  staff  43052 May 14 11:38 tracktrace.block
```

The file can be decoded using configtxlator (git.io/JI3dM). You should compare it to the decoded genesis block in Section 5.2 using a JSON viewer. A comparison of the two can be seen in Table 7. 1.

Table 7. 1. Comparison of `foo.block` **and** `tracktrace.block`.

foo.block	tracktrace.block

They contain a lot of overlapping data but there are some notable differences as well which are important to understand and listed in Table 7. 2.

Table 7. 2. Differences between `foo.block` **and** `tracktrace.block`

foo.block	tracktrace.block
Used to bootstrap *system channel*	Used to bootstrap *application channel*
First block on the `foo` blockchain	First block on the `tracktrace` blockchain
Channel ID = `foo`	Channel ID = `tracktrace`
Not signed by anyone	Signed by the orderer

foo.block	tracktrace.block
Both blocks are genesis blocks but of different blockchains	
In both cases previous_hash is null which is the defining characteristic of a genesis block	
The foo channel resides solely on the ordering service	

You will see no change in CouchDB at this stage. Internally, the channel creation request is processed as any other request to update an application channel's configuration. When the orderer receives a config update for a channel which does not exist, the orderer assumes that this must be a channel creation request and creates the channel. Fabric docs provide a detailed summary of the process. [105]

If you inspect the biotor/orderer/orderer0.biotor.com directory, among other things you should see following directories:

```
$ find orderer0.biotor.com -name tracktrace
orderer0.biotor.com/etcdraft/snapshot/tracktrace
orderer0.biotor.com/etcdraft/wal/tracktrace
orderer0.biotor.com/chains/tracktrace
```

This confirms the tracktrace channel has been created.

7.3. Understanding identity verification in Fabric

Anyone can make a request using peer channel create to create a channel. How does the orderer know whether this is a legitimate request or not? The answer is that when a peer channel create - or any other channel administration request for that matter - is made, the caller also has to provide an X.509 certificate with the request which represents the identity of the caller. The orderer then verifies whether the caller has necessary privileges to create the channel. In case of channel creation, the necessary privilege is being an administrator. A conceptual flowchart of the process is given in Figure 7. 2. The gist of this section is that every Fabric request contains following:

- *message*: message contains what to do. e.g., create a channel or transfer $100 from Alice to Bob's account.
- *mspId*: The ID of the organization that the caller belongs to. This is an assertion made by the caller which is verified by the recipient (peer or orderer)
- *certificate*: Pubic certificate of the caller. The public cert is validated against the cacerts found in the genesis block under *mspId*
- *digital signature*: protects against hackers and spoof requests

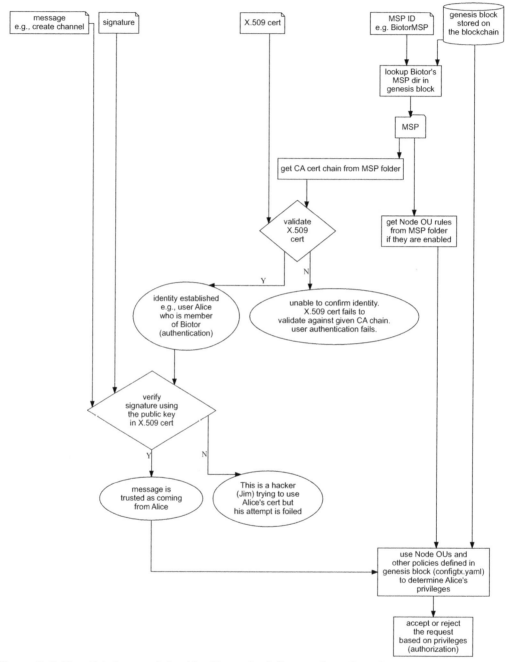

Figure 7. 2. How Fabric ascertains identity and privileges of a caller when a request arrives on a peer or orderer node. In addition to the message, the node receives an X.509 certificate, a digital signature and a MSP ID accompanying the request payload. The data stored in the genesis block plays a critical role in authenticating the user and determining user's

privileges.

When we bootstrapped the orderer we provided it a genesis block created from `configtx.yaml`. The MSP directory of every organization declared in `configtx.yaml` and shown in Table 7. 3 for reference is *copied* into this genesis block. You can verify this for yourself as an exercise by inspecting the decoded genesis block using the `configtxlator` tool.

Table 7. 3. Each organization's MSP is stored inside the genesis block used to bootstrap the orderer.

Organization	MSP Directory
Biotor	`crypto-config/peerOrganizations/biotor.com/msp`
XMed	`crypto-config/peerOrganizations/xmed.com/msp`
KeyPharmacy	`crypto-config/peerOrganizations/keypharmacy.com/msp`

7.3.1. Part One: Authentication

When the channel creation request is made (Listing 7. 3), the public certificate defined in `peer.mspConfigPath` setting in `core.yaml` is included with the request. The `peer` CLI looks for the certificate under a directory `signcerts` under `peer.mspConfigPath`. You can print out this certificate by running following command:

Listing 7. 4. Command to print out an X.509 certificate.

```
$ openssl x509 -in msp/signcerts/Admin\@biotor.com-cert.pem -text -noout
```

This will show a long output a truncated version of which is shown below:

Listing 7. 5. Public certificate of Biotor's admin user (truncated)

```
Certificate:
    Data:
        Version: 3 (0x2)
        Serial Number:
            8b:a6:d4:24:50:90:0b:d4:c9:38:7b:a2:0c:d4:4f:0c
    Signature Algorithm: ecdsa-with-SHA256
        Issuer: C=US, ST=California, L=San Francisco, O=biotor.com, CN=ca.biotor.com
        Validity
            Not Before: Apr 16 19:05:00 2020 GMT
            Not After : Apr 14 19:05:00 2030 GMT
        Subject: C=US, ST=California, L=San Francisco, OU=admin, CN=Admin@biotor.com
```

The thing to note here is that don't think if the output shows the Subject *as* Admin@biotor.com *or the* Issuer *as* ca.biotor.com *then the certificate really belongs to Biotor admin. This point cannot be overemphasized.* Anyone with sufficient skill can generate a X.509 certificate with whatever fields they want. *The key is to verify whether the certificate is signed by a trusted authority. That is what legitimizes the certificate.* How does the orderer do this? The orderer will get the trusted authority from the genesis block. We can mimic the same by accessing the `cacerts` folder under the MSP directory and we can verify whether the X.509 certificate is signed by the authority in `cacerts` folder by using the `openssl verify` command shown in Listing 7. 6 (from Biotor admin's directory):

Listing 7. 6. Verifying issuer and thus legitimacy of an X.509 certificate.

```
$ openssl verify -CAfile \
../../crypto-config/peerOrganizations/biotor.com/msp/cacerts/ca.biotor.com-cert.pem \
msp/signcerts/Admin\@biotor.com-cert.pem
```

This should give:

```
msp/signcerts/Admin@biotor.com-cert.pem: OK
```

We - or the orderer for that matter - have now verified that the public certificate accompanying the channel creation request is signed by a certificate authority of Biotor. The genesis block contains MSP directories of all the organizations. *How does the orderer know which organization's MSP directory to use to verify the public certificate?* The answer is that the channel creation request also has to tell the orderer which organization's MSP to use to validate the certificate. And this comes from the `peer.localMspId` setting (in `core.yaml`) when the request is made from the `peer` CLI. *That is the purpose of* `peer.localMspId` *when* `peer` *CLI is run in client mode.*

The orderer has now confirmed identity of the caller as someone from Biotor organization (authentication). But the game is not over. The orderer needs to now assert that this identity has admin privileges as only administrators are allowed to create a channel. How does it do that?

7.3.2. Part Two: Authorization

Summary: The policies defined in genesis block (which in turn gets them from `configtx.yaml`) together with Node OUs (if enabled) determine what a caller is allowed to do.

Fabric has *two* ways of determining if a caller has admin privileges. In earlier versions of Fabric, all administrators would need to have their public certificates stored in the genesis block. They are listed under the `admincerts` folder of the MSP directory. Fabric would then match the caller's cert to the admin certs to ascertain whether caller is an admin. This works, however as you can imagine it has the pitfall of knowing and declaring a-priori all the people who have admin privileges. To address this problem, later versions of Fabric introduced the concept of *Node OUs* - OU standing for Organizational Unit. The idea is to leverage *attribute based access control*. This is done as follows: in the X.509 certificate, we set `OU=admin`. You can verify this is the case in Listing 7. 5. And the presence of this attribute grants the caller admin privileges. This feature is not turned on by default and has to be enabled in the `config.yaml` file under the organization's MSP directory as shown below in Listing 7. 7:

Listing 7. 7. Biotor MSP's `config.yaml`

```
NodeOUs:
  Enable: true                                        ❶
  ClientOUIdentifier:
    Certificate: cacerts/ca.biotor.com-cert.pem       ❷
    OrganizationalUnitIdentifier: client              ❸
  PeerOUIdentifier:
    Certificate: cacerts/ca.biotor.com-cert.pem       ❹
    OrganizationalUnitIdentifier: peer                ❺
  AdminOUIdentifier:
    Certificate: cacerts/ca.biotor.com-cert.pem       ❻
    OrganizationalUnitIdentifier: admin               ❼
  OrdererOUIdentifier:
    Certificate: cacerts/ca.biotor.com-cert.pem       ❽
    OrganizationalUnitIdentifier: orderer             ❾
```

❶ Enabling NodeOUs simplifies identity management by turning on attribute based access control

❷ Certificate of the authority who has to sign and thereby endorse X.509 certs of Biotor's clients. Clients are users such as company employees or customers.

❸ The presence of client attribute in X.509 cert of caller will grant the privileges associated with client role to the caller

❹ Certificate of the authority who has to sign and thereby endorse X.509 certs of Biotor's peer nodes

❺ The presence of peer attribute in X.509 cert of caller will grant the privileges associated with peer role to the caller

❻ Certificate of the authority who has to sign and thereby endorse X.509 certs of Biotor's administrators

❼ The presence of admin attribute in X.509 cert of caller will grant the privileges associated with admin role to the caller

❽ Certificate of the authority who has to sign and thereby endorse X.509 certs of Biotor's orderer nodes

❾ The presence of orderer attribute in X.509 cert of caller will grant the privileges associated with orderer role to the caller

In Listing 7. 7 the same CA (`ca.biotor.com-cert.pem`) is used for issuing/verifying the certificates of clients, peer, orderers and administrators but this is not a requirement and one could use different CAs for different roles if one wishes to. It is possible to use different OU attributes than `client`, `peer`, `admin` and `orderer`. What we mean by this is that if let's say our yaml file was modified so that it had following section in it:

```
PeerOUIdentifier:
    Certificate: cacerts/ca.biotor.com-cert.pem
    OrganizationalUnitIdentifier: peach
```

Then we would need to put `OU=peach` in the X.509 certificate of a peer for it to be granted privileges associated with the peer role.

7.3.3. Protecting against spoof requests

Public certificates are not secrets. Indeed as reflected in the term they are meant to be public. What this means is that the public cert of Biotor's admin would be public knowledge and thus available to anyone. *So what prevents someone else by imposing as Biotor admin using their public cert?* The answer is nothing. So then the alert reader will notice that the whole discussion in this section crumbles down to nothing. What gives? The answer is that when the channel creation request is made, *the request will also be signed using the private key of Biotor's admin.* The peer CLI will pickup this key from the keystore directory under peer.mspConfigPath. This is one reason why we don't directly give path to the public cert in the channel creation command. We give path to a directory from where the peer CLI can pickup the public cert and also the private key used to sign the request. If an impostor tries to perform channel creation request using Biotor's public cert, they won't be able to sign the request using the corresponding private key as the private key will be kept a secret and never shared with anyone. The impostor could sign it with another private key but when the request reaches the orderer, the signature will fail to validate and the request will be rejected.

Exercise 7.1

Run channel creation command in Listing 7. 3 with modifications below. We use environment variables to override core.yaml settings. Note down what happens in each case and explain your findings:

* Use Biotor's credentials but set CORE_PEER_LOCALMSPID=XMedMSP.
* Use credentials of a non-admin user by setting CORE_PEER_MSPCONFIGPATH to msp folder of User1@biotor.com.
* Temporarily move the private key in keystore to some other folder.
* Use a different private key from the actual one.
* Temporarily move your crypto-config directory to some other place on your computer. Run the cryptogen utility once again to generate a new crypto-config and use that to create a channel.

7.4. Join peers to channel

After a channel has been created, the next step is for peer nodes to join this channel. This is analogous to users joining a chat room in WhatsApp. To join a channel, an admin of each peer's organization has to perform three steps:

1. Fetch the genesis block of the application channel.
2. (Recommended) Check the genesis block for correctness. Do the assorted policies, certificates, and other pieces of information match your expectations?
3. Join the channel using the block you fetched in Step 1.

We list the commands for Biotor and leave corresponding commands for the other orgs as exercise for the reader. Since this is a mock network in which you already have the tracktrace.block, you may wish to skip the first two steps and jump directly to Step 3 but remember in real-world

Steps 1 and 2 will need to be followed. The command to fetch the genesis block is as follows:

Listing 7. 8. Fetch genesis block from the orderer

```
$ peer channel fetch 0 0.block -o localhost:7050 -c tracktrace
```

Above assumes an orderer is running at `localhost:7050`. Verify received block is identical to `tracktrace.block`:

```
$ diff tracktrace.block 0.block
```

Next, as best practice, the admin would decode this using `configtxlator` and manually verify the contents look correct - the policies and certificates match expectations. Note that you are free to connect to any orderer in Listing 7. 8; there is no compulsion to connect to the orderer of your own organization.

Finally, to join the peer node to the channel, the administrator will run:

Listing 7. 9. Join peer node to a channel

```
$ peer channel join -b 0.block
```

When we run above command, the client will make a connection to the *target peer*. That peer then in turn connects to the orderer, but note that *it derives the connection information to connect to the orderer from the* `0.block` *passed to it. Note there is no orderer address specified in the command to join peer nodes to a channel.* The *target peer* must be accessible and listening for incoming connections. If you are getting connection errors, verify that the address you are using matches the `listenAddress` you used when starting the peer in Section 5.5.4. When you run the `peer channel join` command, you should see an output that resembles:

```
[channelCmd] InitCmdFactory -> INFO 001 Endorser and orderer connections initialized
[channelCmd] executeJoin -> INFO 002 Successfully submitted proposal to join channel
```

In the logs of peer node, you should see (git.io/JkPTc):

```
[gossip.election] beLeader -> INFO 036
0f11f4de225ecca713c2c67ea7ce3e10e796ba9510160d66da642930c45f1ccc : Becoming a leader
[gossip.service] func1 -> INFO 037 Elected as a leader, starting delivery service for
channel tracktrace
[deliveryClient] StartDeliverForChannel -> INFO 038 This peer will retrieve blocks from
ordering service and disseminate to other peers in the organization for channel tracktrace
[deliveryClient] RequestBlocks -> INFO 039 Starting deliver with block [1] for channel
tracktrace
```

This confirms the peer has indeed joined the `tracktrace` channel. In the present case the `tracktrace` channel is empty. We haven't yet performed any transactions and the blockchain does not contain any blocks. *But if the channel was non-empty, then the peer would start downloading blocks from the orderer and other peers via the gossip protocol.* This is how new organizations that join a consortium will be able to download a copy of existing blockchain and previous data.

You can use following command to list the channels a peer node has joined:

Listing 7. 10. List channels that a peer node has joined

```
$ peer channel list
```

Above should give an output that ends in

```
Channels peers has joined:
tracktrace
```

At this point you should be able to see the ledger data on the peer nodes (we show Biotor as example):

```
$ ls -al peer0.biotor.com/ledgersData/chains/chains/tracktrace/blockfile_000000
-rw-r----- 1 siddjain staff  43045 May 18 11:45
peer0.biotor.com/ledgersData/chains/chains/tracktrace/blockfile_000000
```

If you navigate to localhost:17055/_utils/#/_all_dbs you should be able to see a `tracktrace` db further confirming that peer has joined the channel:

Databases

Name	Size	# of Docs
_replicator	3.8 KB	1
_users	3.8 KB	1
fabric__internal	1.0 KB	1
tracktrace_	41.8 KB	2
tracktrace__lifecycle	33.2 KB	0

Figure 7. 3. Tracktrace **world db has been created in CouchDB**

You might see following warning in the peer logs:

```
[peer.orderers] Update -> WARN 01d Config defines both orderer org specific endpoints and
global endpoints, global endpoints will be ignored channel=tracktrace
```

Remember the discussion about global vs. org-specific orderer endpoints in Section 5.2.1? This is related to that. When both global as well as org-specific endpoints are defined in the config contained in the genesis block, Fabric will ignore the global endpoints and use the org-specific endpoints.

Go ahead and join peer nodes of the other organizations to the channel.

Finally we come to the point where we get to install the smart contract we wrote in Chapter 3. The process of chaincode installation and instantiation is where Fabric 2.0 departs from its predecessor 1.4 release. The new process roughly involves 4 steps:

1. Package the chaincode into a `tar` file.
2. Install the `tar` file onto the peer nodes. This not only copies over the code but also kicks off a Docker build when peer is running in `net` mode which is time consuming. In 1.x the installation step merely copied the code and so was very quick.
3. Organizations individually approve the chaincode. They provide consent at individual level that the chaincode is allowed to run on their peer nodes and set the endorsement policy individually. Version 1.x of Fabric did not allow for consent at individual level.
4. Once enough organizations have consented, the chaincode can be committed to the channel by an administrator of some org. If there is a mismatch in the endorsement policies, the commit will fail.

Steps 1-3 have to be done individually by all organizations. Step 4 has to be done by only one organization. Assuming the chaincode is being developed in a shared repo, it is a good idea to tag the commit to be used to package the chaincode in Step 1. [106] This will ensure all organizations sync to the same snapshot of the code and create identical `tar` packages and thus avoid errors downstream as a result of using different commits to build the individual chaincode packages. Alternatively the `tar` file itself can be published to the repo, and org admins can pull the `tar` file to make sure every one is using the same chaincode.

To understand the internals of the chaincode lifecycle, look at the `lifecycle` package in `/core/chaincode/lifecycle/scc.go` in the Fabric repo. [107] This file contains the functions which get executed on the peer node to process the chaincode install, approve, commit and other commands.

7.5. Package Chaincode

Begin by copying the smart contract you wrote in Chapter 3 to the `$/three-org-network` directory. A copy of the finished contract is stored in `$/your-first-contract` so we'll copy over that directory to a folder named `mycc`. Run below from `admin` folder:

```
$ cp -R ../../../your-first-contract mycc
$ tree mycc
mycc
├──── package-lock.json
├──── package.json
├──── src
│    ├──── asset-contract.ts
│    ├──── asset.ts
│    └──── index.ts
├──── tsconfig.json
└──── tslint.json

1 directory, 7 files
```

Next, *since our smart contract is written in TypeScript we need to convert it to JavaScript before packaging into a* `tar` *file. This step is very important and if you forget to do it, it won't make a difference in this chapter where we run the peer nodes in* `dev` *mode, but it will come to bite you when you run the peer nodes in* net *mode as you will do in production.* Cd to the mycc directory and install all dependencies:

```
$ cd mycc
$ npm install
```

Then build the TypeScript code:

```
$ npm run build
> first-contract@0.0.1 build /Users/siddjain/phf/code/three-org-network/mycc
> tsc
```

Verify you have a dist folder that has JavaScript code corresponding to the TypeScript files. We can now package the chaincode. Change your working directory back to admin folder and from there run the command to build a tar file: [108]

Listing 7. 11. Command to package source code into a tar file

```
$ peer lifecycle chaincode package mycc.tar.gz --path mycc --lang node --label mycc_1.0
```

We set the --path variable to point to the directory where the source code is stored. We set --lang equal to node as our chaincode is written in JavaScript. We also give a *label* to the chaincode package. Verify:

```
$ ls -al mycc.tar.gz
-rw-------  1 siddjain  staff  41075 May 18 16:45 mycc.tar.gz
```

Let's go one step further and crack open this tar file to see what's in it. To do this, create some temp directory and copy the tar file in it. From there run:

```
$ tar -xvf mycc.tar.gz
x metadata.json
x code.tar.gz
```

It outputs a metadata.json and another tar file. The metadata.json is simply:

Listing 7. 12. Metadata associated with chaincode

```
$ cat metadata.json
{"path":"mycc","type":"node","label":"mycc_1.0"}
```

Go ahead and untar code.tar.gz. *You should see all the source files but no* node_modules *that were generated as a result of running* npm install. That is one of the things the peer lifecycle chaincode package command does for us. *It automatically excludes any* node_modules *under* --path *in the tar file.* The node_modules will be re-installed when the package is built during the installation step.

7.6. *Install Chaincode*

After the chaincode has been packaged, we can install it onto the peer nodes. We give the command for Biotor and leave it as an exercise to install chaincode on peer nodes of other organizations. From the `admin` folder, run:

Listing 7. 13. Command to install chaincode on a peer

```
$ peer lifecycle chaincode install mycc.tar.gz
```

This command will take a while to finish if you are running the peer node in `net` mode because it builds a Docker image. In `dev` mode that does not happen provided you are using the `$/fix-dev-mode.diff` patch and the command shouldn't take long. In both cases, the command will install chaincode on the *target peer* and should finish with an output like below:

```
[cli.lifecycle.chaincode] submitInstallProposal -> INFO 001 Installed remotely:
response:<status:200 payload:...
[cli.lifecycle.chaincode] submitInstallProposal -> INFO 002 Chaincode code package
identifier: mycc_1.0:fe8dda253c0f6f49d79ceaff17ae9bbe21364f380312b60154cc38084056a44b
```

The chaincode package identifier will be used later on when we instantiate the chaincode manually in Chapter 8. In the peer logs I can see:

```
[lifecycle] InstallChaincode -> INFO 022 Successfully installed chaincode with package ID
'mycc_1.0:fe8dda253c0f6f49d79ceaff17ae9bbe21364f380312b60154cc38084056a44b'
[endorser] callChaincode -> INFO 023 finished chaincode: _lifecycle duration: 14443ms
channel= txID=7cdf1158
```

You have now installed chaincode on the Biotor peer. The chaincode gets installed under `<core.peer.filesystempath>/lifecycle/chaincodes` where the `core.peer.filesystempath` will come from `core.yaml` or environment variable. Verify you have following file in Biotor peer's directory where again I have truncated the complete filename:

```
$ ls -al peer0.biotor.com/lifecycle/chaincodes/*.gz
-rw------- 1 siddjain  staff  41075 May 19 11:26
peer0.biotor.com/lifecycle/chaincodes/mycc_1.0.fe8d...tar.gz
```

We can query the peer to get list of all installed chaincode as follows:

Listing 7. 14. Command to list all the chaincodes installed on the peer

```
$ peer lifecycle chaincode queryinstalled
```

This should return

```
Installed chaincodes on peer:
Package ID: mycc_1.0:fe8dda253c0f6f49d79ceaff17ae9bbe21364f380312b60154cc38084056a44b,
Label: mycc_1.0
```

Congrats! well done. Go ahead and install chaincode for other organizations.

For reference, Fabric 2.0 still supports the old way of installing chaincode that came with 1.x releases of Fabric. To do it the old way, we do not package the chaincode into a tar file and instead run the following command where I have omitted the environment variables for brevity:

Listing 7. 15. Command to install chaincode on a peer in Fabric 1.x

```
$ peer chaincode install -n mycc -v 1.0 -l node -p "$PWD/mycc"
```

This command will package the chaincode under $PWD/mycc into a deployment spec, sign it and install the chaincode on the target peer. The chaincode installed using the old method would get installed under <core.peer.filesystempath>/chaincodes. *Note that the only difference between the commands in Listing 7. 13 and Listing 7. 15 is the* lifecycle *keyword so be careful when running the* install *command!*

7.7. Approve Chaincode

After chaincode is installed, the peer organizations will approve it for usage individually. The command for Biotor looks like:

Listing 7. 16. Command to approve chaincode

```
$ peer lifecycle chaincode approveformyorg \
  -o localhost:7050 \
  --channelID tracktrace \
  --name mycc \
  --version 1.0 \
  --package-id mycc_1.0:fe8dda253c0f6f49d79ceaff17ae9bbe21364f380312b60154cc38084056a44b \
  --sequence 1 \
  --signature-policy "AND ('BiotorMSP.peer','XMedMSP.peer','KeyPharmacyMSP.peer')" \
  --waitForEvent
```

This command performs a system chaincode transaction. It first connects to the *target peer* in core.yaml, gets an endorsement and then submits the endorsement to an orderer. Now this approval will be recorded on the ledgers of all the organizations. Thus, all organizations know now that Biotor has approved the chaincode and also what signature policy has been approved. In summary, running the above command *authorizes* the mycc_1.0:fe8dda253c··· chaincode to be executed on Biotor. Each organization will do its own respective authorization.

In above *the package ID should match the ID of the package you installed on the peer. Note carefully that the* name *here does not have anything to do with the* mycc *used in the label of the chaincode in Listing 7. 12. The two are independent and you are free to choose whatever* name *you like.* The signature-policy is used to specify the endorsement policy. In above we require a sign off from all 3 organizations before a transaction can be committed to the ledger. If you do not set the signature-policy then Fabric will fallback to the endorsement policy defined in Application.Policies.Endorsement in the configtx.yaml that was used to generate the genesis block. The version is a number or value associated with a given chaincode package. If you upgrade the chaincode, you need to change your chaincode version as well. The sequence number is related to the number of times the chaincode has been defined. This value is an integer, and is used to keep track of chaincode upgrades. For example, when you first install and approve a chaincode definition, the sequence number will be 1. When you next upgrade the chaincode, the sequence number will be incremented to 2. The `--waitForEvent` flag causes the command to block until it receives a signal from the *target peer* notifying status of the approve request.

 As far as I can tell, both `version` and `sequence` seem to be doing the same thing which is keeping track of chaincode versions. Why have two fields then? I am not sure but I think the answer lies in the fact that the `sequence` number is an auto-incrementing integer - thus you are forced to increment it to 1, 2, 3 and so on as you commit new versions of the chaincode - whereas you can change the `version` freely to whatever you want.

The command will pause for a while and if all goes well, this command should give an output that resembles:

```
[cli.lifecycle.chaincode] setOrdererClient -> INFO 001 Retrieved channel (tracktrace)
orderer endpoint: 127.0.0.1:7050
[chaincodeCmd] ClientWait -> INFO 002 txid
[7cf3a32bbc18b1007bc07aed092f4eaa2849da7f7ce61615c5402f2815d0ea8c] committed with status
(VALID) at
```

The peer logs show:

```
[lifecycle] ApproveChaincodeDefinitionForOrg -> INFO 02e Successfully endorsed chaincode
approval with name 'mycc', package ID
'mycc_1.0:fe8dda253c0f6f49d79ceaff17ae9bbe21364f380312b60154cc38084056a44b', on channel
'tracktrace' with definition {sequence: 1, endorsement info: (version: '1.0', plugin:
'escc', init required: false), validation info: (plugin: 'vscc', policy:
'0a481210120e0803120208001202080112020802 1a0f120d0a0942696f746f724d535010031a0d120b0a07584d
65644d535010031a1412120a0e4b6579506861726d6163794d53501003'), collections: ()}
[lifecycle] update -> INFO 02d Chaincode with package ID
'mycc_1.0:fe8dda253c0f6f49d79ceaff17ae9bbe21364f380312b60154cc38084056a44b' now available
on channel tracktrace for chaincode definition mycc:1.0
[kvledger] CommitLegacy -> INFO 02e [tracktrace] Committed block [4] with 1 transaction(s)
in 221ms
```

One flag that is not used in Listing 7. 16 but worth mentioning is the `--init-required` flag. Fabric supports smart contracts to have an `Init` method used to initialize the contract. This method is only available when using the lower-level `fabric-shim` API to program the smart contracts. [109] In this book we use the higher-level `fabric-contract-api` to program the smart contracts. Anyway if you use the `fabric-shim` API and define the `Init` method, *by default it will get ignored*. You have to specify `--init-required` in Listing 7. 16 for the method to have any effect. If `--init-required` has been set when approving the chaincode definition, then Fabric will ensure that a single call to the `Init` method is made before any method in the smart contract is allowed to be invoked.

Go ahead and approve the chaincode for XMed but *do not approve it for KeyPharmacy*.

7.8. Commit Chaincode

The last step to make the chaincode usable is to commit it. Before we do that, Fabric provides us a checkcommitreadiness command that can be used to check which organizations have approved it. Run the command as follows:

Listing 7. 17. Command to check chaincode commit readiness

```
$ peer lifecycle chaincode checkcommitreadiness \
  --channelID tracktrace \
  --name mycc \
  --version 1.0 \
  --sequence 1 \
  --signature-policy "AND ('BiotorMSP.peer','XMedMSP.peer','KeyPharmacyMSP.peer')"
```

For information, note that above command could be run by a Biotor admin while targeting the peer of KeyPharmacy running on port 8055. That is possible. Assuming you approved the chaincode definition for XMed, this command should return:

```
Chaincode definition for chaincode 'mycc', version '1.0', sequence '1' on channel
'tracktrace' approval status by org:
BiotorMSP: true
KeyPharmacyMSP: false
XMedMSP: true
```

Above output is saying that Biotor and XMed have approved version 1.0 of mycc to be run on channel tracktrace subject to the endorsement policy in Listing 7. 17. *Note that* checkcommitreadiness *does not provide a boolean answer telling if the* commit *command will succeed. It checks which organizations have approved a chaincode definition subject to the given parameters.* checkcommitreadiness *will throw an error for a chaincode definition that has already been committed.* For example, if you commit the chaincode and re-run the command you will get:

```
Error: query failed with status: 500 - failed to invoke backing implementation of
'CheckCommitReadiness': requested sequence is 1, but new definition must be sequence 2
```

This is because the chaincode definition with sequence number 1 has already been committed so checking commit readiness does not make sense.

Let's see what happens now if we try to commit the chaincode. ***Only one organization has to commit the chaincode***. Do that by running following command:

Listing 7. 18. Command to commit chaincode

```
$ peer lifecycle chaincode commit \
-o localhost:7050 \
--channelID tracktrace \
--name mycc \
--version 1.0 \
--sequence 1 \
--signature-policy "AND ('BiotorMSP.peer','XMedMSP.peer','KeyPharmacyMSP.peer')" \
--peerAddresses localhost:8051 \
--peerAddresses localhost:8053 \
--waitForEvent
```

What do you expect will happen?

There are several interesting things that happen when above command is run. First, confirm you get a response that resembles below output:

```
[chaincodeCmd] ClientWait -> INFO 001 txid
[ce5b13496f1f3a37749a2400851bbbd273149cef2ed21ebbd028be76d65b303b] committed with status
(VALID) at localhost:8053
[chaincodeCmd] ClientWait -> INFO 002 txid
[ce5b13496f1f3a37749a2400851bbbd273149cef2ed21ebbd028be76d65b303b] committed with status
(VALID) at localhost:8051
```

Voila! This is telling that the commit was successful. This is because 2 out of 3 organizations have approved the chaincode definition and that is enough to satisfy the `Application.Policies.LifecycleEndorsement` policy we defined in our `configtx.yaml`.

```
LifecycleEndorsement:
    Type: ImplicitMeta
    Rule: "MAJORITY Endorsement"
```

Next look at the peer logs of Biotor or XMed. They should contain following info:

```
[lifecycle] CheckCommitReadiness -> INFO 03c Successfully checked commit readiness of
chaincode name 'mycc' on channel 'tracktrace' with definition {sequence: 1, endorsement
info: (version: '1.0', plugin: 'escc', init required: false), validation info: (plugin:
'vscc', policy:
[lifecycle] CommitChaincodeDefinition -> INFO 03d Successfully endorsed commit for
chaincode name 'mycc' on channel 'tracktrace' with definition {sequence: 1, endorsement
info: (version: '1.0', plugin: 'escc', init required: false), validation info: (plugin:
'vscc', policy:
[lifecycle] update -> INFO 043 Updating cached definition for chaincode 'mycc' on channel
'tracktrace'
[lifecycle] update -> INFO 044 Chaincode with package ID
'mycc_1.0:fe8dda253c0f6f49d79ceaff17ae9bbe21364f380312b60154cc38084056a44b' now available
on channel tracktrace for chaincode definition mycc:1.0
```

The last line confirms the chaincode is available to be used on the channel. Although we have committed the chaincode and it is ready to be used, if we try to perform any transactions they will fail because our endorsement policy requires a signature from all 3 organizations. So let's approve the chaincode from KeyPharmacy as well. We leave it as exercise for the reader.

 Note that the chaincode commit command (Listing 7. 18) does not require the package ID. This allows different organizations to run different variants of the chaincode. The only requirement is that the readwrite sets in response to chaincode invocation should match. We will see an example of this later on in the book in Chapter 12.

Table B.3 (Appendix B) summarizes channel and chaincode administration commands covered in this chapter and also lists the mapping between the chaincode CLI commands and corresponding functions that get executed in the lifecycle package in /core/chaincode/lifecycle/scc.go.

We are now ready to perform transactions on the network! As you can see it takes a fair amount of work just to provision a network and make the chaincode operational. This makes for a steep learning curve programming Fabric. It takes us 7 chapters before we can even begin to exercise the smart contracts. And this is after taking some shortcuts such as using cryptogen instead of Fabric CA to generate credentials.

7.9. Understanding Internals of Chaincode Installation and Instantiation

In this section we take a behind-the-scenes look at chaincode installation and commit. The knowledge here will be very helpful to troubleshoot chaincode problems when running peer in net mode. The TL;DR of this section is as follows:

• The chaincode install command results in a Docker image being built and the chaincode commit command results in a chaincode container being launched.
• Further, the Docker image gets built *synchronously* in response to chaincode install whereas the container gets launched or instantiated *asynchronously* in response to chaincode commit.

With the as-is version of Fabric v2.0.1, above happens irrespective of the mode the peer is run in. The $/fix-dev-mode.diff patch that comes with the book fixes Fabric so that above steps happen only when the peer is run in net mode and do not happen when peer is run in dev mode. That is the correct behavior. You should open the Fabric codebase in a text editor or VS Code to follow along the discussion in this section. You are also welcome to skip this section and come back to it later if/when you encounter problems running peer in net mode.

7.9.1. Install Phase

The install phase can be subdivided into two parts - part one when Docker image is built and part two when a task is enqueued in an *asynchronous task queue*.

PART ONE: BUILD DOCKER IMAGE

When you make a peer lifecycle chaincode install call as in Listing 7. 13 that call is processed by scc.go which is a system chaincode. From there it goes to lifecycle.go which triggers a Docker build in the InstallChaincode function as shown in following code:

Listing 7. 19. The `peer lifecycle chaincode install` **command causes a Docker image to be built by Fabric.**

```
buildStatus, ok := ef.BuildRegistry.BuildStatus(packageID)
if !ok {
    err := ef.ChaincodeBuilder.Build(packageID)
    buildStatus.Notify(err)
}
<-buildStatus.Done()
```

The `$/fix-dev-mode.diff` *patch guards above code in an* `if` *check so that it will execute only in* `net` *mode.* When `ef.ChaincodeBuilder.Build` is called, it will make its way to `dockercontroller.go` and from there to `platform.go` which does the hard work. For example, below is the method that generates the Dockerfile used to build the chaincode container:

Listing 7. 20. Code that generates Dockerfile of the chaincode container

```
func (p *Platform) GenerateDockerfile() (string, error) {
    167: var buf []string
    168:
=> 169:  buf = append(buf, "FROM "+util.GetDockerImageFromConfig("chaincode.node.runtime"))
❶
    170: buf = append(buf, "ADD binpackage.tar /usr/local/src")  ❷
    171:
    172: dockerFileContents := strings.Join(buf, "\n")
    173:
    174: return dockerFileContents, nil
```

❶ `chaincode.node.runtime` controls the base image used to build the chaincode container. We can change this setting in `core.yaml` or using the `CORE_CHAINCODE_NODE_RUNTIME` environment variable.

❷ `binpackage.tar` is nothing but our packaged chaincode which will get installed under `/usr/local/src` on the container.

A truncated callstack showing the chain of events and the files involved is as follows:

Table 7. 4. Callstack showing how `chaincode install` **is processed by Fabric.**

Function	Filename
Platform.GenerateDockerfile	/core/chaincode/platforms/node/platform.go:169
Registry.GenerateDockerfile	/core/chaincode/platforms/platforms.go:84
Registry.GenerateDockerBuild	/core/chaincode/platforms/platforms.go:168
Builder.GenerateDockerBuild	/core/chaincode/platforms/builder.go:21
DockerVM.Build	/core/container/dockercontroller/dockercontroller.go:194
Router.Build	/core/container/container.go:124
ExternalFunctions.InstallChaincode	/core/chaincode/lifecycle/lifecycle.go:556

Function	Filename
Invocation.InstallChaincode	/core/chaincode/lifecycle/scc.go:258

`dockercontroller.go` and `platform.go` are your goto classes to debug issues related to Docker build. If you print the `Dockerfile` in Listing 7. 20, you should see following:

```
FROM hyperledger/fabric-nodeenv:latest
ADD binpackage.tar /usr/local/src
LABEL org.hyperledger.fabric.chaincode.type="NODE" \
org.hyperledger.fabric.version="latest"
ENV CORE_CHAINCODE_BUILDLEVEL=latest
```

I have seen cases where the `chaincode install` command fails with following error:

```
Error: chaincode install failed with status: 500 - failed to invoke backing implementation
of 'InstallChaincode': could not build chaincode: docker build failed: docker image build
failed: docker build failed: Failed to pull hyperledger/fabric-nodeenv:latest: API error
(404): manifest for hyperledger/fabric-nodeenv:latest not found: manifest unknown: manifest
unknown
```

This is because it cannot find the `hyperledger/fabric-nodeenv:latest` image on DockerHub. Change the `chaincode.node.runtime` to a specific tag such as `hyperledger/fabric-nodeenv:2.1` to fix this error. The actual build happens on line 162 in `dockercontroller.go` and will take some time:

```
       156:          NetworkMode:  vm.NetworkMode,
       157:          InputStream:  reader,
       158:          OulputStream: outputbuf,
       159:      }
       160:
 => 161:      startTime := time.Now()
       162:      err = vm.Client.BuildImage(opts)
       163:
       164:      vm.BuildMetrics.ChaincodeImageBuildDuration.With(
       165:          "chaincode", ccid,
       166:          "success", strconv.FormatBool(err == nil),
```

In above, `opts.Name` gives the name of the image built. `ccid` gives the package ID. From here if you stick a breakpoint in `/core/chaincode/platforms/node/platform.go:188`:

```
   183: fi
   184: `
   185:
   186: func (p *Platform) DockerBuildOptions(path string) (util.DockerBuildOptions, error)
{
   187:     return util.DockerBuildOptions{
=> 188:         Image: util.GetDockerImageFromConfig("chaincode.node.runtime"),
   189:       Cmd:    buildScript,
   190:     }, nil
   191: }
```

You can then print out the `buildScript` which shows the code that will be executed to build the source code inside the container:

```
set -e
if [ -x /chaincode/build.sh ]; then
  /chaincode/build.sh
else
  cp -R /chaincode/input/src/. /chaincode/output && cd /chaincode/output && npm install
--production
fi
```

Once you get success from the `chaincode install` command, you can run the `docker image ls` command to see the image built by Fabric. Example is shown below:

```
$ docker image ls --format="{{.Repository}}"
dev-peer0.biotor.com-mycc_1.0-fe8dda253c0f6f49d79ceaff17ae9bbe21364f...
```

PART TWO: ENQUEUE TASK IN ASYNCHRONOUS TASK QUEUE

After a successful build, there is a call to the `NotifyInstalled` function in `custodian.go`:

```
   49: }
   50:
   51: func (cc *ChaincodeCustodian) NotifyInstalled(chaincodeID string) {
   52:     cc.mutex.Lock()
   53:     defer cc.mutex.Unlock()
=> 54:      cc.choreQueue = append(cc.choreQueue, &chaincodeChore{
   55:         chaincodeID: chaincodeID,
   56:     })
   57:     cc.cond.Signal()
   58: }
   59:
```

What this function does is to enqueue a task to the `choreQueue` task queue. A truncated callstack showing the chain of events that lead to this call is as follows:

Table 7. 5. Callstack showing the chain of events that leads to `NotifyInstalled` function call

Function	Filename
ChaincodeCustodian.NotifyInstalled	/core/chaincode/lifecycle/custodian.go:54

Function	Filename
Cache.handleChaincodeInstalledWhileLocked	/core/chaincode/lifecycle/cache.go:234
Cache.HandleChaincodeInstalled	/core/chaincode/lifecycle/cache.go:218
ExternalFunctions.InstallChaincode	/core/chaincode/lifecycle/lifecycle.go:566
Invocation.InstallChaincode	/core/chaincode/lifecycle/scc.go:258

The task is *asynchronously* processed by the Work function in custodian.go.

```
func (cc *ChaincodeCustodian) Work(buildRegistry *container.BuildRegistry, builder
ChaincodeBuilder, launcher ChaincodeLauncher) {
```

What this function does is spin up an infinite loop that keeps checking for any tasks in the choreQueue. As soon as it finds a task, it will dequeue it and start processing it. This is known as the *producer-consumer* pattern. The NotifyInstalled is the *producer* method and Work is the *consumer. The producer and consumer run on different threads or goroutines in case of Go.* A goroutine is a Go programming language construct that can be thought of as a lightweight thread. The Work method checks the registry of Docker images and if for some reason the chaincode image is not there in the registry - this should not happen as an image was already built earlier in Part One - it kicks off another build as shown in the code below:

```
buildStatus, ok := buildRegistry.BuildStatus(chore.chaincodeID)
if ok {
    logger.Debugf("skipping build of chaincode '%s' as it is already in progress",
chore.chaincodeID)
    continue
}
err := builder.Build(chore.chaincodeID)
```

7.9.2. Commit Phase

The chaincode commit command is processed by following function in /core/chaincode/lifecycle/scc.go:457:

```
func (i *Invocation) CommitChaincodeDefinition(input *lb.CommitChaincodeDefinitionArgs)
(proto.Message, error) {
```

and results in a call to NotifyInstalledAndRunnable in custodian.go:

```
    58: }
    59:
    60: func (cc *ChaincodeCustodian) NotifyInstalledAndRunnable(chaincodeID string) {
    61:     cc.mutex.Lock()
    62:     defer cc.mutex.Unlock()
=>  63:      cc.choreQueue = append(cc.choreQueue, &chaincodeChore{
    64:         chaincodeID: chaincodeID,
    65:         runnable:    true,
    66:     })
    67:     cc.cond.Signal()
    68: }
```

The only difference between the append *call in this function and* NotifyInstalled *is the presence of the* runnable: true *attribute.* Otherwise the two are identical and both enqueue a task which is processed asynchronously by the Work function. What the runnable: true attribute does is to tell Fabric to also *run* the chaincode container instead of just building the Docker image. The callstack showing the chain of events leading up to the function call above is shown below:

Table 7. 6. Callstack showing the chain of events that lead to NotifyInstalledAndRunnable **function call**

Function	Filename
ChaincodeCustodian.NotifyInstalledAndRunnable	/core/chaincode/lifecycle/custodian.go:63
Cache.update	/core/chaincode/lifecycle/cache.go:558
Cache.HandleStateUpdates	/core/chaincode/lifecycle/cache.go:303
LockBasedTxMgr.invokeNamespaceListeners	/core/ledger/kvledger/txmgmt/txmgr/lockbasedtxmgr/lockbased_txmgr.go:454
LockBasedTxMgr.ValidateAndPrepare	/core/ledger/kvledger/txmgmt/txmgr/lockbasedtxmgr/lockbased_txmgr.go:163
kvLedger.CommitLegacy	/core/ledger/kvledger/kv_ledger.go:442
closableLedger.CommitLegacy	<autogenerated>:1
LedgerCommitter.CommitLegacy	/core/committer/committer_impl.go:62
coordinator.StoreBlock	/gossip/privdata/coordinator.go:224
GossipStateProviderImpl.commitBlock	/gossip/state/state.go:785
GossipStateProviderImpl.deliverPayloads	/gossip/state/state.go:575

There is an important difference to notice if you compare above callstack to the callstack of the install command in Table 7. 5. It is this: whereas the call to NotifyInstalled *happens synchronously as a result of running* chaincode install *the call to* NotifyInstalledAndRunnable *happens asynchronously.* If it isn't clear, observe the InstallChaincode function at the bottom of the callstack in Table 7. 5. That is the function Fabric executes when it receives a chaincode install command. The corresponding function that is executed when a `chaincode commit` command is received is `CommitChaincodeDefinition` but *observe this function is not present in the callstack in* Table 7. 6. *That is why we say the call to* `NotifyInstalledAndRunnable` *happens asynchronously. This is why there is provision for a* `--waitForEvent` *flag in the* `chaincode commit` *command which makes the client wait for completion of the asynchronous call. There is a reason for this design.* The callstack in Table 7. 6 shows the peer calls `NotifyInstalledAndRunnable` *when it commits a block to its ledger. This design causes the same chain of events to also repeat when a peer node restarts and replays the commit history or when a peer node joins a channel on which chaincode was previously committed. In both cases, this causes previously committed chaincodes to be automatically launched again which is what we want.* The `Work` function is smart enough to check if the chaincode's Docker image has already been built previously and it even checks to see if the chaincode container is already running in which case it does nothing.

The function that does the launch is in `/core/chaincode/runtime_launcher.go` and shown below:

```
   66:           TLSConfig: tlsConfig,
   67:        }, nil
   68: }
   69:
   70: func (r *RuntimeLauncher) Launch(ccid string, streamHandler extcc.StreamHandler)
error {
=> 71:        var startFailCh chan error
   72:        var timeoutCh <-chan time.Time
   73:
   74:        startTime := time.Now()
   75:        launchState, alreadyStarted := r.Registry.Launching(ccid)
   76:        if !alreadyStarted {
```

and its callstack is as follows:

Table 7. 7. Callstack which leads to a chaincode container being launched

Function	Filename
RuntimeLauncher.Launch	/core/chaincode/runtime_launcher.go:71
custodianLauncherAdapter.Launch	/internal/peer/node/start.go:173
ChaincodeCustodian.Work	/core/chaincode/lifecycle/custodian.go:102

Phew! That was a lot! One last tip. The `Work` function is run in a goroutine in `internal/peer/node/start.go#L656`:

```
go chaincodeCustodian.Work(buildRegistry, containerRouter, custodianLauncher)
```

By wrapping this in a if statement in `$/fix-dev-mode.diff` we disable this function in the dev mode. This causes the work items in `choreQueue` to never be dequeued and no Docker related code ever executes. This is how we fix the broken dev mode of Fabric. Hopefully these insights make you feel like a pro in Fabric!

7.10. Summary

- Every channel has a respective blockchain associated with it. Channels are very much like chat rooms in WhatsApp.
- We use the `peer` CLI to create a channel and join peer nodes to it.
- The `peer` CLI is also used to package the smart contract, install it onto peer nodes, approve the chaincode definition and commit the chaincode onto a channel. These steps make the chaincode operational and ready to use.
- All the steps above have to be done by org administrators and are part of a one-time setup that does not have to be repeated when restarting a network.
- The genesis block contains the necessary information using which at runtime when someone makes a request to Fabric, it can determine which organization the caller belongs to and what privileges the caller has.
- There are plans to develop a `fabric-admin` Node.js package that would allow chaincode administration (things like chaincode install, approve, commit) to be done from a Node.js app but no progress on it has been made yet (FABN-1416). There is no plan to develop a Node.js package for channel administration yet (things like create channel, join peer nodes to a channel).
- The lifecycle chaincode is a special system (i.e., not user-defined) chaincode that is used to process the channel create, join and commit operations. Like any other chaincode, it has its own endorsement policy defined in `configtx.yaml`.
- Don't forget to compile the TypeScript code and convert it into JavaScript before packaging.
- Chaincode commit operation has to be done by only one organization.
- Any changes to the chaincode - be it changes to the JavaScript code or its manifest such as the endorsement policy - result in its `sequence` number getting incremented.

7.11. Further Reading

- Fabric policies are explained in hyperledger-fabric.readthedocs.io/en/release-2.0/policies.html

[101] I put this in double-quotes because the `peer` also acts a client in the p2p network of peers that we provisioned in Chapter 5.

[102] You can read more about it at github.com/bft-smart/fabric-orderingservice/issues/8

[103] `panic: Error creating channelconfig bundle: initializing configtx manager failed: bad channel ID: channel ID 'mychannel_genesis' contains illegal characters`

[104] If you get error messages, the very first thing to check is if the environment variables are taking effect or not.

[105] hyperledger-fabric.readthedocs.io/en/release-2.0/configtx.html#channel-creation

[106] You would use the `git tag` command for this.

[107] github.com/hyperledger/fabric/blob/v2.0.1/core/chaincode/lifecycle/scc.go

[108] For completeness we mention that the `chaincode package` command is the only command in this chapter that can be run by a non-admin. It does not connect to any peer or orderer.

[109] hyperledger.github.io/fabric-chaincode-node/release-2.0/api/fabric-shim.ChaincodeInterface.html

Chapter 8. Performing Transactions on the Network

This chapter covers:

- Making requests to the chaincode from command line and from Node.js
- Debugging the chaincode
- Upgrading the chaincode

> We will switch between multiple directories in this chapter. The `$/three-org-network/biotor/user` directory is used to perform chaincode requests from the command line. The `$/three-org-network/biotor/admin` directory will be used to register chaincode and update channel (set anchor peers). And we'll switch to `$/client-application` directory when we make chaincode requests from Node.js.

In Chapter 5 we provisioned our network and in Chapter 7 we provisioned the chaincode. Now its time to use it. In this chapter, we continue working in the `$/three-org-network` directory but we will now be running commands as a user so we'll switch to `$/three-org-network/biotor/user`. All commands are to be run from this directory unless otherwise noted.

Before we begin, let's do quick recap of the application we are building. We are building an application that can be used to track and trace products in a supply chain. We picked a pharmaceutical supply chain with three players - Biotor as drug manufacturer, XMed as distributor and KeyPharmacy as retailer. We have a very simple smart contract or chaincode that we wrote in Chapter 3 with just three functions - a method to *create* an asset which should only allow a manufacturer to create an asset, a method to *verify* ownership of the asset which any buyer will call before purchasing the asset and finally a method to *update* or transfer ownership of the asset. These are nothing but the Create, Read and Update operations expected out of a database. Maybe you have heard of the CRUD acronym which stands for Create, Read, Update, Delete and is commonly used when one talks of databases.

This chapter will introduce following 3 peer commands:

Table 8. 1. peer commands to make chaincode requests and update channel.

Command	Purpose	Orderer	Need administrator privileges
`peer chaincode invoke`	submit a transaction, write to the ledger and world db	✓	✗
`peer chaincode query`	read from the world db	✗	✗

Command	Purpose	Orderer	Need administrator privileges
`peer channel update`	update channel configuration	✓	✓

Before running the `peer` CLI commands of this chapter, we need to setup the environment for Biotor user. To do this we would repeat the steps in Section 7.1. The only difference is that the steps need to be repeated w.r.t. a user not the administrator. The complete setup can be done by simply running below commands from **$/three-org-network/biotor/user**:

Listing 8. 1. Setup Biotor user's environment

```
$ cp ../admin/core.yaml .
$ cp -R ../../crypto-config/peerOrganizations/biotor.com/users/User1\@biotor.com/msp .
$ cp -R ../../crypto-config/peerOrganizations/biotor.com/users/User1\@biotor.com/tls .
```

We can re-use the `core.yaml` of `admin` user as-is. And we copy over credentials of Biotor's user to respective directories.

8.1. Launch chaincode and attach VS Code Debugger

The chaincode has to be manually launched and registered against peers running in `dev` mode (`chaincode.mode=dev`). We do that in this section. *If we were not running our peers in* `dev` *mode, then we would skip this section.* Although we have installed the chaincode on the peer, we won't be using the installed tar package to run the chaincode. The command to launch the chaincode and register it with the peer is shown below for Biotor as example. We assume all node dependencies are installed and TypeScript code has been compiled to JavaScript before running following command from **$/three-org-network/biotor/admin/mycc** directory:

Listing 8. 2. Command to run chaincode

```
$ npm start -- --peer.address localhost:8052 --chaincode-id-name
mycc_1.0:fe8dda253c0f6f49d79ceaff17ae9bbe21364f380312b60154cc38084056a44b
```

`8052` is the port we used for `peer.chaincodeListenAddress` in Section 5.5.3. This is the port at which the peer is listening for connections from chaincode. *It is crucial that the* `chaincode-id-name` *should match the package id that you got when you installed the chaincode in Section 7.6.* The output of running the command is shown below where I have deleted some content for brevity:

```
> fabric-chaincode-node start "--peer.address" "localhost:8052" "--chaincode-id-name"
"mycc_1.0:fe8dda253c0f6f49d79ceaff17ae9bbe21364f380312b60154cc38084056a44b"

info [c-api:contracts-spi/bootstrap.js] No metadata file supplied in contract,
introspection will generate all the data
info [c-api:./lib/contract.js] Creating new Contract
info [c-api:./lib/contract.js] Creating new Contract "org.hyperledger.fabric"
info [c-api:lib/chaincode.js] Registering with peer localhost:8052 as chaincode
"mycc_1.0:fe8dda253c0f6f49d79ceaff17ae9bbe21364f380312b60154cc38084056a44b"
info [c-api:fabric-shim/cli]
Command succeeded

info [c-api:lib/handler.js] Successfully registered with peer node. State transferred to
"established"
info [c-api:lib/handler.js] Successfully established communication with peer node. State
transferred to "ready"
```

The last two lines confirm the chaincode has been successfully registered against the peer. If the chaincode registration fails, you will not see the last two messages. This terminal window should be now left open for the chaincode to keep running.

Next we can open the `mycc` folder in VS Code and define following debug configuration in `.vscode/launch.json`:

Listing 8. 3. VS Code configuration to debug JavaScript chaincode

```
{
    "type": "node",
    "request": "attach",
    "name": "Attach by Process ID",
    "processId": "${command:PickProcess}",
    "skipFiles": [
        "<node_internals>/**"
    ],
    "sourceMaps": true
}
```

This will allow us to debug the chaincode from VS Code. Press F5 in VS Code or Run (▷) using the configuration above. It should prompt you to select a process.

Pick the node.js process to attach to

node   /Users/sjain68/go/src/github.com/siddjain/phf-solutions/three-org-network/mycc/node_modul...
process id: 8960 (SIGUSR1)

Code Helper (Renderer) --inspect-port=0 /Applications/Visual Studio Code.app/Contents/Resourc...
process id: 10531, debug port: 0

Code Helper (Renderer) --inspect-port=0 /Applications/Visual Studio Code.app/Contents/Resourc...
process id: 9590, debug port: 0

Figure 8. 1. VS Code prompt to select which process you want to debug

Select the Node.js process and you should see the debugger attach as shown in the screenshot below:

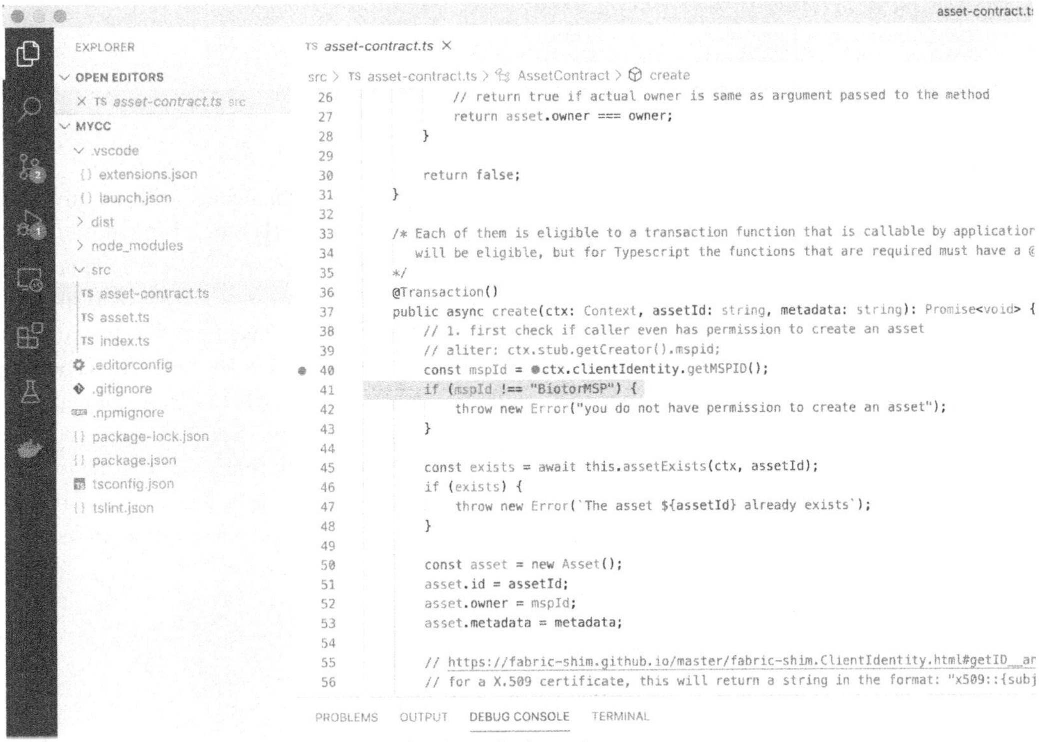

Figure 8. 2. VS Code Debugger attached to chaincode process

You should also see following output in the chaincode terminal window:

```
Debugger listening on ws://127.0.0.1:9229/ea9f9468-4e6e-4715-8af9-069892d42417
For help see https://nodejs.org/en/docs/inspector
Debugger attached.
```

Repeat the steps for the other peers running in `dev` mode modifying the `peer.address` in Listing 8. 2 as necessary.

We are now ready to submit transactions to the network. But first, go ahead and stick some breakpoints in VS Code in each of the methods in `mycc/src/asset-contract.ts`.

8.2. Creating Assets

Let's begin by creating a few assets in the system. This is done using the `peer chaincode invoke` command as follows. Execute it from `$/three-org-network/biotor/user` directory with identity of a Biotor user (not an admin):

Listing 8. 4. Create asset in the system

```
$ peer chaincode invoke -C tracktrace -n mycc -c '{"Args":["create","00000","Sample Drug
1"]}' -o localhost:7050 \
--peerAddresses localhost:8051 \
--peerAddresses localhost:8053 \
--peerAddresses localhost:8055
```

What's going on here?

This is the first time we are using a non-admin identity. The chaincode will be invoked independently and in parallel on the peers running at `localhost:8051` (Biotor), `localhost:8053` (XMed), `localhost:8055` (Key Pharmacy). *The name `mycc` used in Listing 8. 4 needs to match the name used in the chaincode definition of the approve command in Section 7.7.* The results of chaincode invocation will be collected back and compared to check all peers have endorsed (i.e., signed off) on the result and that results are the same across the peers On success, the responses will be packaged into a transaction that will be submitted to the orderer running at `localhost:7050`. Finally the transaction will get committed on the peers. Recall Figure 1. 3. The peers will check the endorsement policy is satisfied before committing the transaction. If endorsement policy is not satisfied, the transaction is still committed but a flag is set to reflect failure of endorsement policy. This is just a technical detail and for all practical purposes its as if the transaction never occurred.

Voila! you should see VS Code debugger break as shown in Figure 8. 3!

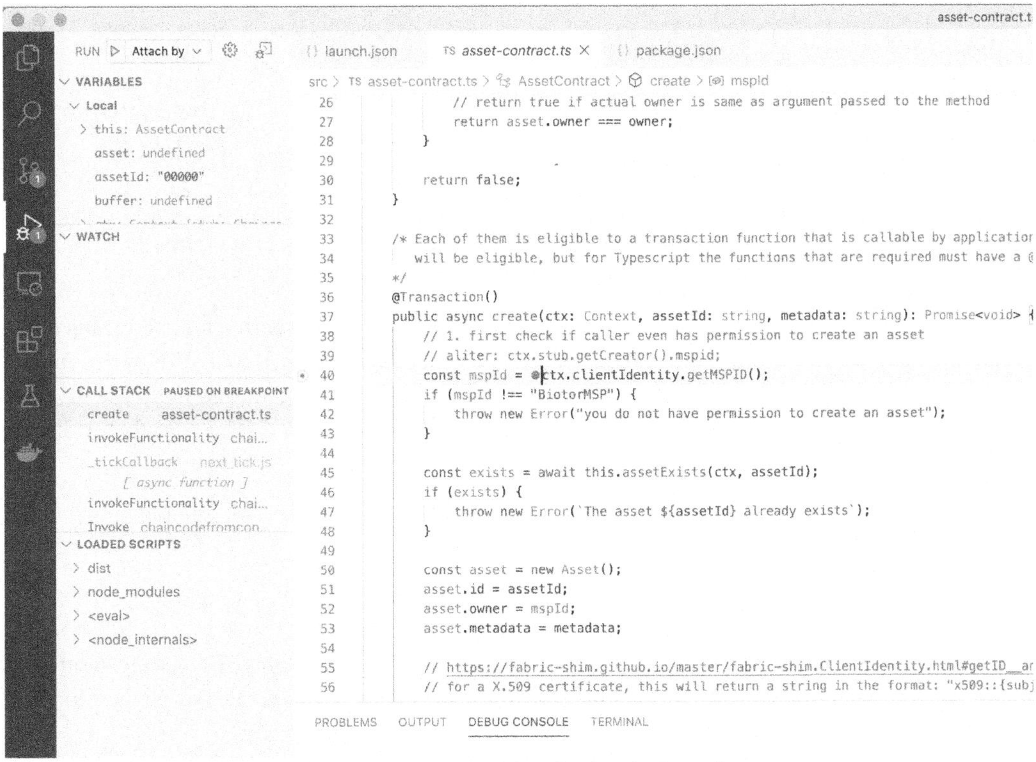

Figure 8. 3. VS Code debugger paused at breakpoint in chaincode

Did you realize that the debugger is attached to a Node.js process (and Node.js does not know anything about TypeScript) but is still breaking in TypeScript code and allowing you to debug TypeScript? That is neat. How is this possible? The secret to this is the sourceMap file(s) found under the dist folder where the TypeScript compiler outputs the compiled code. The TypeScript compiler is instructed to output these files by setting "sourceMap": true under compilerOptions in tsconfig.json.

Let the debugger continue and you should see following output from the peer chaincode invoke command:

```
[chaincodeCmd] chaincodeInvokeOrQuery -> INFO 001 Chaincode invoke successful. result:
status:200
```

The chaincode window will show:

```
info [c-api:lib/handler.js] [tracktrace-c0971143] Calling chaincode Invoke() succeeded.
Sending COMPLETED message back to peer
```

and peer logs should show:

```
[couchdb] CreateDatabaseIfNotExist -> INFO 025 Created state database tracktrace_mycc
[endorser] callChaincode -> INFO 026 finished chaincode: mycc duration: 20806ms
channel=tracktrace txID=5ce53ed8
[gossip.privdata] StoreBlock -> INFO 028 [tracktrace] Received block [5] from buffer
[committer.txvalidator] Validate -> INFO 029 [tracktrace] Validated block [5] in 7ms
[gossip.privdata] prepareBlockPvtdata -> INFO 02a Successfully fetched all eligible
collection private write sets for block [5] channel=tracktrace
[kvledger] CommitLegacy -> INFO 02b [tracktrace] Committed block [5] with 1 transaction(s)
in 161ms (state_validation=4ms block_and_pvtdata_commit=35ms state_commit=110ms)
commitHash=[2de022c229b79e2f12fcb0ab90e9d1bb7e6f9694571a0707ed42621d351e0f8f]
```

These logs are quite instructive. Since this is the first transaction we are performing, it results in the creation of the world state db tracktrace_mycc. The next line is telling it took 20.8 sec to run the smart contract. The long time is because I paused the code in the debugger. Next there is a message informing when the peer receives a new block containing the transaction. The peer then validates the block and commits it to its copy of the ledger.

Go ahead and create 10 assets. As you are creating the assets, tail the following file under $/three-org-network/biotor/peer directory:

```
$ tail -f peer0.biotor.com/ledgersData/chains/chains/tracktrace/blockfile_000000
```

Above file is storing the blocks on the peer's ledger. You should see this file getting written as assets are created in the system. We will call this the blockfile. Throughout this chapter monitor this file as you are running peer chaincode invoke and query commands.

In the CouchDB viewer (localhost:17055/_utils), you should see a tracktrace_mycc database.

Databases

Name	Size	# of Docs
_replicator	3.8 KB	1
_users	3.8 KB	1
fabric__internal	1.0 KB	1
tracktrace_	42.9 KB	2
tracktrace__lifecycle	2.2 KB	5
tracktrace__lifecycle$$h_implicit_org_$biotor$msp	2.9 KB	6
tracktrace__lifecycle$$h_implicit_org_keypharmacy$m$s$p	2.9 KB	6
tracktrace__lifecycle$$h_implicit_org_$x$med$m$s$p	2.9 KB	6
tracktrace__lifecycle$$p_implicit_org_$biotor$msp	2.8 KB	6
tracktrace_lscc	33.2 KB	0
tracktrace_mycc	1.9 KB	4

Figure 8. 4. CouchDB showing the world state db `tracktrace_mycc`

You can also inspect CouchDB from the command line as follows:

Listing 8. 5. Get list of all databases in CouchDB from the command line

```
$ curl -X GET http://localhost:17055/_all_dbs
["_replicator","_users","fabric__internal","tracktrace_","tracktrace__lifecycle","tracktrac
e__lifecycle$$h_implicit_org_$biotor$m$s$p","tracktrace__lifecycle$$h_implicit_org_$key$pha
rmacy$m$s$p","tracktrace__lifecycle$$h_implicit_org_$x$med$m$s$p","tracktrace__lifecycle$$p
_implicit_org_$biotor$m$s$p","tracktrace_lscc","tracktrace_mycc"]
```

If you click on `tracktrace_mycc` in the CouchDB viewer, you should see the records you have created (select the `Table` view):

	_id	createdBy	lastModifiedBy	metadata	owner
	00000	x509::/C=US/ST=California/L=San Fra...	x509::/C=US/ST=California/L=San Fra...	Sample Drug 1	BiotorMSP
	00001	x509::/C=US/ST=California/L=San Fra...	x509::/C=US/ST=California/L=San Fra...	Sample Drug 2	BiotorMSP
	00002	x509::/C=US/ST=California/L=San Fra...	x509::/C=US/ST=California/L=San Fra...	Sample Drug 3	BiotorMSP
	00003	x509::/C=US/ST=California/L=San Fra...	x509::/C=US/ST=California/L=San Fra...	Sample Drug 4	BiotorMSP

Figure 8. 5. Examples of some assets and their owners.

To do the same from the command line, run:

Listing 8. 6. Get list of records in the world state db from CouchDB

```
$ curl -X GET http://localhost:17055/tracktrace_mycc/_all_docs?include_docs=true
```

This should return an output that resembles below where I am just showing one record for brevity:

```
{"total_rows":4,"offset":0,"rows":[
{"id":"00000","key":"00000","value":{"rev":"1-
29d461d1488288060922e4ab07d14f72"},"doc":{"_id":"00000","_rev":"1-
29d461d1488288060922e4ab07d14f72","createdBy":"x509::/C=US/ST=California/L=San
Francisco/OU=client/CN=User1@biotor.com::/C=US/ST=California/L=San
Francisco/O=biotor.com/CN=ca.biotor.com","id":"00000","lastModifiedBy":"x509::/C=US/ST=Cali
fornia/L=San Francisco/OU=client/CN=User1@biotor.com::/C=US/ST=California/L=San
Francisco/O=biotor.com/CN=ca.biotor.com","metadata":"Sample Drug
1","owner":"BiotorMSP","~version":"CgMBBQA="}},
```

If we were using LevelDB for the world state, we wouldn't be able to inspect the world state like we did above with CouchDB. That is CouchDB's main advantage over LevelDB.

Exercise 8.1

Try creating an asset with the identity of a user belonging to a org other than Biotor (e.g., use XMed) and verify the system only allows users of Biotor to create an asset. This is by design.

Exercise 8.2

Verify that if you invoke the chaincode on only one node then chaincode invocation succeeds but there is an error when the peers try to commit the transaction:

```
[vscc] Validate -> ERRO 0a1 VSCC error: stateBasedValidator.Validate failed, err validation
of endorsement policy for chaincode mycc in tx 14:0 failed: signature set did not satisfy
policy
```

Explain this error.

Exercise 8.3

Invoke the chaincode but set the `CORE_PEER_LOCALMSPID` to an incorrect ID. For example, invoke using the credentials of a Biotor's user but set `CORE_PEER_LOCALMSPID` to XMedMSP. Verify there is an error.

```
Error: error endorsing query: rpc error: code = Unknown desc = access denied: channel
[tracktrace] creator org [XMedMSP] - proposal response: <nil>
```

In peer logs you should see:

```
[protoutils] ValidateProposalMessage -> WARN 03d channel [tracktrace]: MSP error: the
supplied identity is not valid: x509: certificate signed by unknown authority
```

The value in `CORE_PEER_LOCALMSPID` is an assertion made by the caller and that assertion is verified on the peer nodes. In above we are using Biotor's credentials but asserting that we belong to Express Medicinals. Fabric will catch this discrepancy.

8.3. Updating Assets

Let us now transfer ownership of an asset to another organization. Run following command as a Biotor user (i.e., from $/three-org-network/biotor/user directory):

Listing 8. 7. Transferring asset ownership to another organization

```
$ peer chaincode invoke -C tracktrace -n mycc -c '{"Args":["update","00000","XMedMSP"]}' -o
localhost:7050 \
--peerAddresses localhost:8051 \
--peerAddresses localhost:8053 \
--peerAddresses localhost:8055
```

If all goes well, you should see output ending in

```
[chaincodeCmd] chaincodeInvokeOrQuery -> INFO 065 Chaincode invoke successful. result:
status:200
```

In CouchDB viewer, verify that XMed is the new owner of the asset. We can also do verification using the verify endpoint in next section.

Exercise 8.4

Verify you are not able to transfer ownership of an asset that you do not own.

Exercise 8.5

The update method in its current form does not have any checks on the organization the asset is being transferred to i.e., one could easily transfer it to an organization that does not even exist. Fix the method so that it will complain if the caller tries to transfer asset to an invalid organization.

8.4. Verify Assets

Let's use the verify endpoint to verify owner of asset denoted by 00000. You can run below command as a user of any organization.

Listing 8. 8. The peer chaincode query **command**

```
$ peer chaincode query -C tracktrace -n mycc -c '{"Args":["verify","00000","XMedMSP"]}' \
--peerAddresses localhost:8051
```

Note that we are using peer chaincode query and not peer chaincode invoke. The query command can be used when the chaincode only reads data and does not perform any writes. Methods which perform only read operations are decorated with @Transaction(false) attribute in the TypeScript code:

```
@Transaction(false)
@Returns('boolean')
public async verify(ctx: Context, assetId: string, owner: string): Promise<boolean>
```

The query *command does not result in any new transactions being committed to the ledger.* Since we will not be writing any transaction, there is no need to specify the orderer endpoint when calling peer chaincode query. *The* query *command only works against a single peer.* So we need to specify only one --peerAddress or could just use the peer.address configured in core.yaml. The query command will execute against the world db of that peer. You can run multiple queries targeting different peers to confirm the result is the same across peers. For example, you might want to confirm that your peer node is giving same answer as the peer node of another org.

You should see a single line output when the above command is executed:

```
true
```

Exercise 8.6

Go ahead and try the command on other peer nodes keeping an eye on the blockfile. Is there any change to the blockfile as you run the peer chaincode query command? You can also invoke the verify endpoint by making a peer chaincode invoke call instead of peer chaincode query. Try doing that. Is there any change to the blockfile in this case? Explain your findings.

8.5. Upgrading the chaincode

Add a new method to asset-contract.ts which will return all the assets owned by the caller:

Listing 8. 9. Method to get all assets belonging to an organization

```
@Transaction(false)
public async getAssets(ctx: Context): Promise<Asset[]> {
}
```

Use the getStateByRange method which will return a StateQueryIterator and put it in a for loop to iterate over the collection. After you have implemented the method, follow below steps to make it functional:

1. Terminate the chaincode (use Ctrl+C)
2. Build the chaincode again by running npm run build. This is necessary to generate new JavaScript code from TypeScript.
3. Launch the chaincode again by re-running the npm start command (Listing 8. 2)

That's it! *If you were running peer nodes in* net *mode, you have to re-install the chaincode giving it a new version and re-commit for changes to take effect.* So the steps from Section 7.5 to Section 7.8 have to be repeated with a new version and sequence number. This can be very time consuming. Imagine having to do this with every tiny change you make to the chaincode. And trust me there will be many little changes you'll want to make while you are developing the smart contracts as you fix bugs etc. In dev mode, we can make changes to the chaincode *without having to re-install and re-commit the chaincode.* This feature is very useful and almost a godsend for rapid prototyping and write-test-iterate cycle (test driven development). Test the new method as follows:

Listing 8. 10. Get all the assets belonging to an organization

```
$ peer chaincode query -C tracktrace -n mycc -c '{"Args":["getAssets"]}' \
--peerAddresses localhost:8051
```

8.6. Out of band changes to the world state db

Open a new chrome window and navigate to localhost:17055/_utils which should open the CouchDB viewer. Navigate to the tracktrace_mycc database which corresponds to our smart contract. Now change some record. For example, you can change owner of drug with id 00000 from XMedMSP to KeyPharmacyMSP. See the screenshot below for illustration:

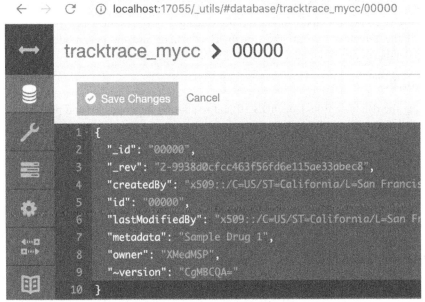

Figure 8. 6. Making out-of-band changes to the world state db

Click on Save Changes to save your changes. We call this an "out-of-band" change since we are making changes bypassing the chaincode and normal transaction flow of Fabric. *Notice there is nothing stopping you from doing this.* Is there any change to the blockfile as you do this? Now invoke the verify endpoint and pass it KeyPharmacyMSP for the owner argument. What value do you see returned? What did you expect?

Terminate the peer node, re-start it, and make the call to the verify endpoint again. What value do you see returned? Do you get back the same result?

This exercise shows that nothing prevents you from making out-of-band changes to the world db. We touched upon this in Section 2.7. If we had used LevelDB instead of CouchDB, making such changes is more difficult but perhaps not impossible for the determined hacker. [110] These out of band changes change the world state, but leave the ledger unchanged as you can verify by inspecting the blockfile.

Fabric consensus is not some magical algorithm that will take whatever change you make and replicate it on all the peer nodes. The truth could not be far from it. This is not a system like a cloud drive where you make whatever changes you want to a shared document and all copies update with those changes. Moral of the story is not to make out of band changes to the database (or even the blockchain) or you just end up shooting yourself in the foot. Other peer nodes will not update with your changes.

Now that we have shot ourselves in the foot, is there any way to recover from it? The answer is yes. To do that, terminate the peer node and the CouchDB container it is using. After that, delete the contents of the couchdb.peer0.biotor.com directory. We used this directory in Section 5.4.2 to store the CouchDB data. Note that you have to delete the contents of the directory, not the directory itself. To be safe you can backup the directory if you want. Once you have deleted the contents of the directory, re-start the CouchDB container and the peer node. You will see the CouchDB databases are rebuilt and your out of band changes are lost.

Exercise 8.7

Try deleting the database from CouchDB UI and re-starting the container and peer node. Does that rebuild the db?

8.7. Understanding the Internals of Chaincode Launch and Registration

What is really going on when we run npm start in Listing 8. 2? As we mentioned in Section 3.3.4, if you open package.json, you will see that npm start is really an alias or shorthand for fabric-chaincode-node start. What is fabric-chaincode-node itself? We can see below that it is itself an alias or symlink for cli.js:

```
$ ls -al node_modules/.bin/fabric-chaincode-node
lrwxr-xr-x  1 siddjain  staff  21 May 22 10:40 node_modules/.bin/fabric-chaincode-node ->
../fabric-shim/cli.js
```

You can also run the chaincode by using following command from the terminal:

Listing 8. 11. Alternate way to run the chaincode

```
$ ./node_modules/fabric-shim/cli.js start --peer.address localhost:8052 --chaincode-id-name
mycc_1.0:fe8dda253c0f6f49d79ceaff17ae9bbe21364f380312b60154cc38084056a44b
```

You may be wondering, cli.js is a plain text JavaScript file. How can it execute something? The answer lies in the very first line of the file. If you open the file in a text-editor you will see following line:

Listing 8. 12. The shebang line in cli.js

```
#!/usr/bin/env node
```

This line serves the same purpose as the `#!/bin/bash` line you see in shell scripts. It is known as the *shebang* line in Unix. [1111] In case of shell scripts, the shebang line tells the shell to pass the file to the `bash` interpreter located at `/bin/bash`. It is the `bash` interpreter which then actually executes the shell script. The same thing happens for `cli.js`. When we run `./cli.js` on the command line in Listing 8. 11, what is actually happening is that

```
$ /usr/bin/env node cli.js
```

is being run under the covers. You might think why do we need the `/usr/bin/env` prefix? Couldn't we just write `#!node cli.js` in Listing 8. 12? Its a good question and the answer is that *Unix requires the absolute path of the interpreter to be specified on the shebang line.* You can thus replace `#!/usr/bin/env node` with `#!/path/to/node` and that will work but the path to node will be different on different systems. If the authors of `cli.js` had used `#!/path/to/node` in the shebang line, it would not run on a lot of machines! The `/usr/bin/env` is a hack to work around this problem. The absolute path of `env` utility is the same on all modern unix systems. The real purpose of the `env` command is to execute another command with a modified environment, adding or removing specified environment variables before running the command. In our case, it just executes `node` with an unchanged environment, which is all we need.

Moving on, the `start` argument passed to `cli.js` in Listing 8. 11 is wired to this function in `fabric-shim/lib/cmds/startCommand.js`:

```
exports.handler = function (argv) {
    const Bootstrap = require('../contract-spi/bootstrap');
    return argv.thePromise = Bootstrap.bootstrap();
};
```

This takes us to following method in `fabric-shim/lib/contract-spi/bootstrap.js`:

```
static async bootstrap() {
    const opts = StartCommand.getArgs(yargs);
    const {contracts, serializers, title, version} = this.getInfoFromContract(opts['module-
path']);
    const fileMetadata = await Bootstrap.getMetadata(opts['module-path']);
    Bootstrap.register(contracts, serializers, fileMetadata, title, version);
}
```

and finally to:

```
static register(contracts, serializers, fileMetadata, title, version) {
    const chaincode = new ChaincodeFromContract(contracts, serializers, fileMetadata,
title, version);

    // say hello to the peer
    shim.start(chaincode);
}
```

If you keep tracing the code, you will get to following line in `fabric-shim/lib/chaincode.js`:

```
client.chat({
    type: fabprotos.protos.ChaincodeMessage.Type.REGISTER,
    payload: fabprotos.protos.ChaincodeID.encode(chaincodeID).finish()
});
```

which is where the chaincode tries to connect to the peer and register itself.

8.8. Other ways of debugging chaincode

In Section 8.1 we showed how to debug the chaincode from VS Code by attaching the VS Code
IDE to the running process. This will allow you to debug the chaincode *past the point* when its
successfully registered against the peer, but what if you want to debug some problem you are
facing during the *bootstrap phase* when the chaincode tries to register itself to the peer? How to do
that? There are two ways to do so which are described below.

8.8.1. Using the command-line debugger that comes with Node.js

Node.js comes with a built-in debugger that can be run using `inspect` command from the `mycc`
chaincode directory:

```
$ node inspect ./node_modules/fabric-shim/cli.js start --peer.address localhost:8052
--chaincode-id-name
mycc_1.0:fe8dda253c0f6f49d79ceaff17ae9bbe21364f380312b60154cc38084056a44b
< Debugger listening on ws://127.0.0.1:9229/0ef38b63-991f-4979-a86a-28b4aebc8dfb
< For help, see: https://nodejs.org/en/docs/inspector
< Debugger attached.
Break on start in node_modules/fabric-shim/cli.js:2
  1 #!/usr/bin/env node
> 2 const version = 'v' + require('./package.json').version;
  3 const Logger = require('./lib/logger');
  4
debug>
```

After this, you can set a breakpoint like so:

```
debug> setBreakpoint('bootstrap.js', 38);
Warning: script 'bootstrap.js' was not loaded yet.
```

and let it continue:

```
debug> c
```

it should break at the following:

```
break in node_modules/fabric-shim/lib/contract-spi/bootstrap.js:38
  36
  37          // say hello to the peer
>38          shim.start(chaincode);
  39      }
  40
debug>
```

From here you can print out the callstack:

```
debug> bt
#0 register node_modules/fabric-shim/lib/contract-spi/bootstrap.js:38:8
#1 bootstrap node_modules/fabric-shim/lib/contract-spi/bootstrap.js:49:18
```

Refer online for the complete command line API. [112]

8.8.2. *Using* Launch via NPM *configuration in VS Code*

Open package.json and add following code in it under the scripts section:

```
"debug": "CORE_CHAINCODE_LOGGING_LEVEL=debug node --inspect-brk=9229 node_modules/fabric-shim/cli.js start"
```

The CORE_CHAINCODE_LOGGING_LEVEL=debug is a flag we use to get more verbose logging output to help in debugging. Then open /.vscode/launch.json and add following config to it:

```
{
    "type": "node",
    "request": "launch",
    "name": "Launch via NPM",
    "runtimeExecutable": "npm",
    "runtimeArgs": [
        "run-script",
        "debug",
    ],
    "args": ["--", "--peer.address", "localhost:8052", "--chaincode-id-name",
"mycc_1.0:fe8dda253c0f6f49d79ceaff17ae9bbe21364f380312b60154cc38084056a44b"],
    "port": 9229,
    "skipFiles": [
        "<node_internals>/**"
    ],
    "console": "integratedTerminal",
    "sourceMaps": true
}
```

Now press F5 in VS Code, sit back and relax. Figure 8. 7 shows screenshot of debugging with Launch Via NPM configuration:

Figure 8. 7. Debugging chaincode from VS Code using a Launch via NPM **configuration**

8.9. Understanding the Internals of Chaincode Invocation

When the peer chaincode invoke or peer chaincode query commands are run, they lead to following function calls getting executed on the peer node (git.io/JI3dF).

Table 8. 2. Callstack behind chaincode invocation

Function	Filename
RuntimeLauncher.Launch	/core/chaincode/runtime_launcher.go:71
ChaincodeSupport.Launch	/core/chaincode/chaincode_support.go:84

Function	Filename
ChaincodeSupport.Invoke	/core/chaincode/chaincode_support.go:197
ChaincodeSupport.Execute	/core/chaincode/chaincode_support.go:155
SupportImpl.Execute	/core/endorser/support.go:126
Endorser.callChaincode	/core/endorser/endorser.go:114
Endorser.SimulateProposal	/core/endorser/endorser.go:173

The gRPC server on the peer node listens for the commands and forwards the invoke or query call to /core/endorser/endorser.go. From there, the peer then looks up the chaincode handler as there can be multiple chaincodes running on the peer, and then calls the chaincode passing it the invocation parameters. This is done via another gRPC call. The peer gets back the result and finally sends it back to the client. This is known as the endorsement phase. The second part of the change we made to fix the dev mode in Section 5.5.1 is to throw an error if the peer is running in dev mode and if no chaincode handler can be found. If we don't throw an error, the peer will try to build a Docker image and launch a Docker container for the chaincode.

Let's see how well you understand Fabric. We have seen the chaincode makes get/put calls to update the world state key-value store. *Pop Quiz: Do you think the chaincode connects directly to the world state db? The answer is no. The* getState, putState *calls we make in the chaincode cause requests to be sent to the chaincode's peer to get or update the world state db. The chaincode does not talk directly to the world state db.* The getState, putState and pretty much all other calls to interact with the world state are defined on the ChaincodeStub class and get forwarded to ChaincodeSupportClient which then forwards them onto the peer. You can find the relevant source code in the fabric-chaincode-node repository. [113]

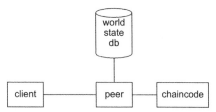

(a) Endorsement Phase. Put calls to world state db won't have any effect until changes are committed. Ledger is not involved.

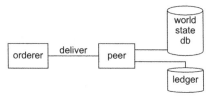

(b) Commit Phase. Peer verifies endorsement policy and readwrite set. Chaincode is not involved.

Figure 8. 8. Understanding internals of chaincode invocation.

Figure 8. 8 shows a diagram of endorsement vs commit phases. *The* `chaincode` `invoke` *call results in both phases being executed whereas the* `chaincode` `query` *call only results in endorsement or simulation phase being executed.* The `putState` calls during the simulation phase have no effect on the ledger or the world state db until the simulation results are committed. They only change the writeset of the simulation. During the commit phase the peer will either dequeue block from the orderer using the `deliver` API or get it through the gossip protocol. Then for each transaction in the block, the peer will carefully check if all the stakeholders defined in the endorsement policy have signed off on the transaction. This is necessary but not sufficient. What if the the ledger or world state db has changed since the time the simulation run was executed? The peer will reject the changes in that case. [114] The ledger might be storing vast volumes of data and it would be foolish to reject changes if any part of the ledger has changed. For example, the transaction might want to update asset with ID 999. The peer only needs to check that that particular asset has not changed. Its okay if some other asset that was untouched by the transaction and that had no bearing on our decision to update 999 has changed in the meanwhile. That is why the output of the simulation is a *readwrite* set. The *readset* contains values that were read (or touched) and the *writeset* contains the changes that should be made. Continuing our example the readset might consist of asset IDs 999, 1000, 1001 and the writeset might consist of just 999. The simulation touches IDs 1000, 1001 but only writes to 999.

Exercise 8.8

Try calling a method such as `create` that makes `put` calls on the world state db using `peer` `chaincode` `query`. What do think should happen? What do you observe? Explain your findings.

8.10. Using `fabric-network` *to perform transactions*

So far in this chapter we have shown how to use the `peer` CLI to invoke or query the chaincode. That works but eventually we would want to perform transactions using a web application or a mobile app written in a language like JavaScript or Java. Let's see how to do that in this section. The first step is to set ***anchor peers*** of our network - something we have not done so far. Anchor peers act as *gateway* nodes of an organization. The peers in Org A will connect to the anchor peer(s) of Org B to communicate with the peers of Org B. Thus, anchor peers are critical to cross-organization communication. Without them, no cross-org communication can take place. Not setting the anchor peers did not present any problem with `peer` CLI because we were manually specifying all the peer addresses but we'll need to set up the anchor peers when using `fabric-network` library to perform transactions.

8.10.1. Update Anchor Peers

We will switch to `$/three-org-network/biotor/admin` in this section as only an administrator can perform a channel update.

The anchor peers are defined in `configtx.yaml` under `Organizations[<org-name>].AnchorPeers`. For example, below is the definition for Biotor:

```
AnchorPeers:
# AnchorPeers defines the location of peers which can be used
# for cross org gossip communication.  Note, this value is only
# encoded in the genesis block in the Application section context
- Host: localhost
  Port: 8051
```

The first step is to generate a transaction that would update the anchor peer. Do that by running following command from $/three-org-network:

```
$ configtxgen -profile Channel -outputAnchorPeersUpdate biotor-anchors.tx -channelID
tracktrace -asOrg Biotor
```

You should have a file `biotor-anchors.tx` on your system. It is in protobuf format and can be decoded by running:

```
$ configtxlator proto_decode --input biotor-anchors.tx --type common.Envelope
```

It will give a long output in which you should see following:

```
"values": {
    "AnchorPeers": {
        "mod_policy": "Admins",
        "value": {
            "anchor_peers": [
                {
                    "host": "localhost",
                    "port": 8051
                }
            ]
        },
        "version": "0"
    },
```

Next, we perform a `channel update` transaction to update the anchor peer. Technically, its not an update since we are setting the anchor peers for the first time. Change your directory to $/three-org-network/biotor/admin and then run the command below:

```
$ peer channel update -o localhost:7050 -c tracktrace -f ../../biotor-anchors.tx
```

Voila! on the other peer nodes you will see following message in the logs:

```
[gossip.channel] reportMembershipChanges -> INFO 037 [[tracktrace] Membership view has
changed. peers went online:  [[127.0.0.1:8051 ]] , current view:  [[127.0.0.1:8051 ]]]
```

Go ahead and set the anchor peers for the other organizations. As you set the anchor peer of XMed, you will see following message in peer logs:

```
[gossip.channel] reportMembershipChanges -> INFO 04d [[tracktrace] Membership view has
changed. peers went online:  [[127.0.0.1:8055 ]] , current view:  [[127.0.0.1:8055 ]
[127.0.0.1:8051 ]]]
```

and when the anchor peer for KeyPharmacy is set, you should see following messages:

```
[gossip.channel] reportMembershipChanges -> INFO 04d [[tracktrace] Membership view has
changed. peers went online:  [[127.0.0.1:8055 ]] , current view:  [[127.0.0.1:8055 ]
[127.0.0.1:8051 ]]]
[gossip.gossip] JoinChan -> INFO 056 Joining gossip network of channel tracktrace with 3
organizations
[gossip.gossip] learnAnchorPeers -> INFO 057 Learning about the configured anchor peers of
XMedMSP for channel tracktrace : [{localhost 8053}]
[gossip.gossip] learnAnchorPeers -> INFO 058 Learning about the configured anchor peers of
KeyPharmacyMSP for channel tracktrace : [{localhost 8055}]
[gossip.gossip] learnAnchorPeers -> INFO 059 Learning about the configured anchor peers of
BiotorMSP for channel tracktrace : [{localhost 8051}]
```

Well done. *One question that arises is that why does Fabric not set the anchor peers as part of the* channel create *transaction?* After all they are defined in configtx.yaml and so could be used when creating the channel. I am not exactly sure but I think the answer is that the channel create is done by one organization, whereas above process allows each organization to set their anchor peers independently. Biotor organization should not be able to set the anchor peers of XMed for example. It is possible - and maybe Fabric will do this in some later version - that just like committing the chaincode now requires endorsement from sufficient stakeholders, similarly creating a channel could also be done when enough signatures are present to satisfy a policy. And maybe then anchor peers could be set at time of channel creation itself.

After the anchor peers have been set for the first time, *any further changes to them will have to be done through the updating channel configuration process which we will cover in the next chapter.* For reference, if you try updating the anchors repeating the steps above, you will get this error:

```
Error: got unexpected status: BAD_REQUEST -- error applying config update to existing
channel 'tracktrace': error authorizing update: error validating ReadSet: proposed update
requires that key [Group]  /Channel/Application/Biotor be at version 0, but it is currently
at version 1
```

We can now move on to the next step.

8.10.2. *Install* fabric-network

fabric-network is the package that enables us to make chaincode requests from a Node.js app. Begin by changing to the $/client-application directory. You should see a package.json with following dependencies in it:

```
"dependencies": {
    "fabric-network": "~2.1.0",
    "js-yaml": "3.14.0"
}
```

The js-yaml is there to parse yaml files. Install the dependencies by running npm i.

fabric-network uses the grpc library. This is a *Node Add-On*. Node Add-On are packages that talk to native C/C++ code. Installing grpc will trigger the C/C++ compiler on your machine. Refer to online help if you run into any issues. For your information, fabric-shim - the package used to run Node.js chaincode - also relies on grpc but version 2.1.2 of fabric-shim uses a pure JavaScript library for grpc and so we don't run into C/C++ issues with fabric-shim. The grpc package is scheduled to be deprecated in April 2021 and will no longer receive any updates after that. Hopefully fabric-network will transition to using grpc-js before that.

8.10.3. fabric-network *and* fabric-common *packages*

fabric-network depends on fabric-common. Most of the code and classes actually reside in fabric-common. fabric-network adds the Gateway, Wallet and a few other classes. The Gateway class provides a gateway to the classes in fabric-common without having to explicitly construct them. For advanced scenarios we can always create the low-level classes in fabric-common directly. Table 8.3 shows the important classes in fabric-network and fabric-common packages. We will be using some of these as we progress in the book.

Table 8. 3. Most used classes and interfaces in fabric-network **and** fabric-common.

fabric-network	fabric-common
• Gateway • Network • Wallet • Wallets • IdentityProviderRegistry • HsmX509Provider • TxEventHandler • Checkpointer	• Client • CryptoSuite • SigningIdentity • BlockDecoder • Channel • DiscoveryHandler • DiscoveryService • EventListener • EventService • ServiceEndpoint • ServiceHandler

8.10.4. Create Identity Wallet

When we made chaincode invoke/query calls using the peer CLI we set the peer.mspConfigPath variable to provide the identity of the person making the calls. fabric-network takes the identity of the user from something known as a Wallet. Below is a code snippet that shows how to create a Wallet and store an identity in it.

Listing 8. 13. Storing Fabric identity in a wallet

```
const wallet = await Wallets.newFileSystemWallet('wallet'); ❶

const certificate =
    fs.readFileSync(process.env.PUBLIC_CERT).toString();     ❷
const privateKey =
    fs.readFileSync(process.env.PRIVATE_KEY).toString();     ❷

const username = process.env.USER_NAME;                      ❸

const identity = {
    credentials: {
        certificate,
        privateKey
    },
    mspId: process.env.MSP_ID,                               ❹
    type: 'X.509'
}

await wallet.put(username, identity);                        ❺
```

❶ A FileSystemWallet stores data on the local filesystem. Fabric supports a few other wallet types of which HSM (Hardware Security Module) is the most secure.

❷ Read public cert and private key from the paths given by env variables passed to the script

❸ We can assign any username we want to be associated with the X.509 identity

❹ Set the organization this identity belongs to. This cannot be arbitrary. It should be the same organization that issued the certificate otherwise you will get error when you try to make requests on behalf of this user.

❺ Store the X.509 identity in a Fabric wallet. The username acts as a key to retrieve this identity from the wallet.

The `identity` consists of the user's public-private key pair plus the MSP ID of the organization the user belongs to. Each `identity` is assigned a label which is a free form string that can be anything you wish. This label is then used when we want to load the identity from the `Wallet`. We can store the identity of Biotor's user by running the `addToWallet.sh` script provided in the code repository:

```
$ ./addToWallet.sh
done
```

After running the script you should have a `wallet` directory on your system with a file `Alice.id` in it - `Alice` is the label we used for the identity. If you open the file, you can see it simply contains the `identity` in JSON format. I have truncated the public cert and private key for brevity:

```
$ cat wallet/Alice.id
{"credentials":{"certificate":"-----BEGIN CERTIFICATE-----\nMIICGDCCA6Yt9P\n-----END
CERTIFICATE-----\n","privateKey":"-----BEGIN PRIVATE KEY-----\nMIGHAgEAMBMGByqGljm\n-----
END PRIVATE KEY-----\n"},"mspId":"BiotorMSP","type":"X.509","version":1}
```

> The logging of `fabric-network` package - or `fabric-common` to be more accurate - is controlled by the **HFC_LOGGING** environment variable or `hfc-logging` setting in a `default.json` config file. [115] Set the variable to `HFC_LOGGING='{"debug":"console","info":"console","warn":"console","error":"console"}'` to turn on debug logging. The `console` directs log output to the console. You can also specify a filename if you want to log to a file instead of logging to `console`.

8.10.5. The `connection.yaml` *file*

By now you have seen a large part of programming Fabric has to do with configuration files. The `fabric-network` library is no different. We give it a config file that contains all the details of the Fabric network plus many other configurable options. The simplest and shortest file that will do for us is given below:

Listing 8. 14. The `yaml` **file that contains network details**

```
name: any-name-you-like
version: 1.0.0
client:                          ❶
  organization: Biotor           ❷
  connection:
    timeout:
      peer:
        endorser: '300'          ❸
organizations:
  Biotor:
    mspid: BiotorMSP
    peers:
    - peer0.Biotor.com           ❹
peers:
  peer0.Biotor.com:
    url: grpc://localhost:8051   ❺
```

❶ Used to configure the `Client` in `fabric-common` package

❷ The organization this client belongs to. The organization must appear under `organizations` section.

❸ Timeout in seconds after which client will abort when it submits a chaincode invocation request to an endorsing peer. Thus it is the time client will give the peer to execute the chaincode.

❹ List of peers in this organization. They are further described under `peers` section.

❺ The connection address. This will change when the peer is running on a remote machine in a production environment.

This file is stored as `Biotor-connection.yaml` in the repo. Please refer to online documentation for details on more settings that can be configured in this file. [116]

8.10.6. Perform Transactions

We can now create an asset by running following Node.js script:

Listing 8. 15. Performing a `create` **transaction using the** `fabric-network` **library**

```
let connectionProfile = yaml.safeLoad(
    fs.readFileSync('Biotor-connection.yaml', 'utf8'));        ❶

let connectionOptions = {                                      ❷
    identity: userName,
    wallet: wallet,
    discovery: { enabled: true, asLocalhost: false }           ❸
};

await gateway.connect(connectionProfile, connectionOptions);   ❹
const network = await gateway.getNetwork('tracktrace');        ❺
const contract = await network.getContract('mycc');            ❻
const result = await contract.submitTransaction(               ❼
                    'create', '00009', 'Sample Drug 10');
```

❶ Load connection profile which will be used to initialize a gateway
❷ Set the identity we will use to perform transactions
❸ Use Fabric's discovery service to automatically discover other nodes in the network. `asLocalhost` replaces all hostnames returned by the discovery service with `localhost`.
❹ Connect to gateway using application specified parameters
❺ Access tracktrace channel
❻ Access mycc contract
❼ Perform transaction to create an asset in the system

We start off by loading a connection profile that is stored in `Biotor-connection.yaml`. It contains the address of the peer to connect to. After that we set the identity and wallet we want to use and then open a connection to the network using `gateway.connect`. The Gateway class serves as the gateway to a Fabric network. This is followed by selecting the `tracktrace` channel and `mycc` chaincode on this channel. Finally we submit a transaction. You should compare the code above to Listing 8. 4 where we invoked chaincode using the `peer` CLI.

I don't know if you have noticed this or not, but the neat thing using `fabric-network` to make chaincode requests vs. the `peer` CLI is that we only specified the address of one peer in our connection profile which is stored in `Biotor-connection.yaml`. Don't forget that to commit the transaction, we need to get endorsement from all 3 organizations and then the endorsements need to be packaged and submitted to the orderer. How does `fabric-network` know the addresses of other peer nodes and the ordering service? `fabric-network` automatically discovers those addresses using the Fabric `discovery` service which is set to `enabled` in Listing 8. 15. This is where the *anchor peers* in Section 8.10.1 come in. If we hadn't set the anchor peers, there would be an error when submitting the transaction.

The `asLocalhost` option to the discovery service in Listing 8. 15 replaces all hostnames returned by the discovery service with `localhost`. For example, if the discovery service discovers a peer with the hostname `peer0.xmed.com` - this will happen when we containerize the peers in Chapter 10 - the `asLocalhost` will replace the hostname with `localhost`. This in turn will cause the Node.js application to connect to `localhost` instead of `peer0.xmed.com` which might be useful if the peer is indeed running locally and if there is no DNS mapping set to map `peer0.xmed.com` to the local computer. In present case the option will have no effect as the peers and orderers are already running on `localhost`. So it doesn't matter whether you set it to `true` or `false`. You will not need this option later on as well when we containerize the network because we will setup a DNS mapping in the `/etc/hosts` file so that `peer0.xmed.com` is resolved to the local IP address but I mention the option for completeness and as the docs are not clear as to what it does.

The code in Listing 8. 15 is saved as `create-asset.js` in the repo. Run it as follows:

```
$ node create-asset.js
```

Using `fabric-network` to make chaincode calls is handy when the arguments to your smart contract are objects instead of simple strings. The `peer` CLI can be used but the syntax gets complicated when you have to write a serialized object on the command line.

The **submitTransaction** in Listing 8. 15 is equivalent of `peer chaincode invoke`. `fabric-network` also provides us with an **evaluateTransaction** method which is the equivalent of `peer chaincode query`. You can test it by running following script which will query for all assets belonging to Biotor organization:

```
$ node get-assets.js
```

This assumes you have implemented the `getAssets` function in Listing 8. 9. If you haven't here is a cheat sheet:

```
@Transaction(false)
public async getAssets(ctx: Context): Promise<Asset[]> {
    const assets: Asset[] = [];
    const mspId = ctx.clientIdentity.getMSPID();
    const promiseOfIterator = ctx.stub.getStateByRange('', '');
    for await (const res of promiseOfIterator) {
        const asset = JSON.parse(res.value.toString()) as Asset;
        if (asset.owner === mspId) {
            assets.push(asset);
        }
    }
    return assets;
}
```

Exercise 8.9

A batch or lot of a drug can easily have hundreds of individual units in it. A unit is the smallest quantity that an end customer can purchase from a pharmacy or drug store. Calling `create` and `update` for each unit as a batch is created by a manufacturer or sold between wholesalers can present performance challenges. How would you optimize the smart contract so that it is performant while at the same time not losing visibility at the level of an individual unit?

8.11. Summary

* Use `CORE_CHAINCODE_LOGGING_LEVEL` to control the verbosity of the chaincode logs.
* `sourceMaps` allow us to debug TypeScript code from VS Code debugger even though the program being debugged (`node`) does not know anything about TypeScript.
* `peer chaincode invoke` leads to new records being written onto the ledger whereas the `query` call only results in data being read from the ledger.
* Fabric consensus does not prevent you from making out of band changes to CouchDB. But any such changes will not propagate to other nodes.
* The chaincode gets auto-terminated when its peer node is shutdown.
* The chaincode never talks directly to the world state db. All interaction between chaincode and world state db is mediated via the chaincode's peer.
* The `fabric-network` library allows us to invoke and query chaincode from a Node.js app instead of using the `peer` CLI. It uses a wallet in which it stores public certs and private keys of users.
* Fabric discovery service allows peers to discover other peers in the Fabric network and engage in gossip communication.
* Anchor peers act as gateway nodes of an organization and are the point of contact for cross-org communication and service discovery.
* Use `HFC_LOGGING` to control the verbosity of `fabric-network` package used by your client application.

8.12. Further Reading

* Familiarize yourself with service discovery. hyperledger-fabric.readthedocs.io/en/release-2.2/discovery-overview.html
* Read `fabric-network` tutorials. hyperledger.github.io/fabric-sdk-node/release-2.2/module-fabric-network.html
* Familiarize yourself with event handling. hyperledger.github.io/fabric-sdk-node/release-2.2/tutorial-transaction-commit-events.html
* Read source code of the internal `TransactionEventHandler` of `fabric-network` package (`lib/impl/event/transactioneventhandler.js`). This should help you in writing your own custom `TxEventHandler`.

[110] I haven't tried it myself but it would be a good challenge exercise to change the world state in LevelDB out-of-band.
[111] en.wikipedia.org/wiki/Shebang_(Unix)
[112] nodejs.org/docs/latest-v12.x/api/debugger.html
[113] github.com/hyperledger/fabric-chaincode-node/tree/v2.1.2/libraries/fabric-shim/lib
[114] In `git` world this is known as a merge conflict.
[115] github.com/hyperledger/fabric-sdk-node/blob/v2.2.2/fabric-common/lib/Utils.js#L152
[116] hyperledger.github.io/fabric-sdk-node/release-2.2/tutorial-grpc-settings.html

Chapter 9. Updating channel configuration

This chapter covers:

• Updating a channel's configuration

> You continue working from the `$/three-org-directory` in this chapter. You will need to switch to `user` or `admin` subdirectories depending on whether you want to run commands as a user or administrator.

As your usage of Fabric increases, it is a given that you will run into situations where you would want to make changes to a channel's configuration. For example, adding an organization to the network or updating the orderer and anchor peer addresses require changing the channel's configuration. We will perform a change to orderer and anchor peer addresses in this chapter as prep work for the next chapter. Why? Because in the next chapter we will Dockerize the network we have developed until now. What does it mean? It means simply that all the peers and orderers will run inside Docker containers. Each peer or orderer will get its dedicated container. To the peer or orderer, this container will appear to be its computer or host as if its living in a virtual reality. It will be unaware of the fact that other peers and orderers are also running on the same machine. *In fact, they don't have to be running on the same machine*. It does not matter. The other containers will always appear as different machines. We show this visually in Figure 9. 1.

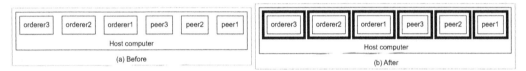

Figure 9. 1. Effect of Dockerizing our three org network (a) Before: peers and orderers can reach other using localhost (b) After: Each peer or orderer runs in its own container that acts like a virtual machine and is represented by a thick line. Peers and orderers have to use container names to communicate with each other. If a peer or orderer uses localhost, it will be looped back to its own container.

A consequence of this will be that ***all the addresses we have been using to communicate amongst the nodes will change***. Throughout our journey so far every address has been of the form `localhost:<port>`. The `localhost` will need to be substituted with the Docker container name as we Dockerize the network since in the Docker world `localhost` would map to the container itself. Recall from Section 5.2 that in `configtx.yaml` we defined the orderer address as following to take the example of Biotor:

```
OrdererEndpoints:
  - localhost:7050
```

This address gets stored in the genesis block and that is how the peer nodes know how to reach the orderer when they join a channel. The address above works for now but won't work when the orderer is running inside a Docker container. So we can either create a brand new channel using a new `configtx.yaml` but imagine if you have lot of transaction data. You don't want to lose all that data as you migrate to Docker. You just want to be able to update the orderer addresses of the current channel to `orderer0.biotor.com:7050` where `orderer0.biotor.com` would be the name of the Docker container that is running Biotor's orderer. And similarly for XMed and KeyPharmacy. *This is the problem statement we set out to solve in this chapter. In practice, avoid using* `localhost` *at all to begin with in your* `configtx.yaml`. I purposely made that "mistake" to illustrate the process of updating channel configuration.

Let's see how to do this. There are many steps required and Fabric itself calls it a convoluted process but at a high level it works as follows where for convenience I have listed names of files we will create in this chapter so you can refer back if you are lost at any point:

1. Fetch the latest channel configuration as a protobuf (`config_block.pb`)
2. Decode it to human readable JSON (`config_block.json`)
3. Strip away headers, signature and metadata (`config_data.json`)
4. Make the changes you want (`modified_config_data.json`)
5. Convert it back to a protobuf format (`modified_config_data.pb`)
6. Compute the delta between stripped config and the modified config (`delta_update.pb`)
7. Wrap the delta in an envelope and add back header to it (`config_update_in_envelope.pb`)
8. Sign the changes (this is where policies come in and dictate who all need to sign)
9. Commit the new configuration to the channel (`peer channel update`)

Blockchain being an append-only ledger, we cannot make changes to the genesis block. We can only append a block with updated configuration. When peer nodes receive the updated config, they will update the addresses they are using to connect to the orderer. *This means that until they process the block containing the updated config, peer nodes inside a container will not be able to connect to the orderer. The astute reader might be wondering if peer nodes can't connect to orderer, how will they receive the block with updated config in the first place?* The answer is that we will commit the updated config to each peer's ledger in this chapter and then *port* this ledger to the containerized peers in the next chapter so that when they boot up they don't start with an empty ledger and get the updated addresses from the copy of the ledger stored locally.

Begin by pretending to be a Biotor admin or user and download latest configuration block:

Listing 9. 1. Get latest configuration block as a protobuf file.

```
$ peer channel fetch config config_block.pb -o localhost:7050 -c tracktrace
```

Above command will connect to the orderer at `localhost:7050` to fetch the latest config block - *there is no connection made to any peer.* It should output:

```
[channelCmd] fetch -> INFO 003 Retrieving last config block: 0
```

and you should see something like:

```
$ ls -al config_block.pb
-rw-r--r-- 1 siddjain  staff  43052 Jun  1 14:57 config_block.pb
```

config_block.pb should be identical to the tracktrace.block:

```
$ diff tracktrace.block config_block.pb
```

Decode the config block to human readable JSON using configtxlator and save it in a file named config_block.json. Note that redirecting output of configtxlator to a file does not work - at least not for me. You will have to save to file by manual copy and paste. You can verify the JSON you get against git.io/Jk8T0.

Listing 9. 2. Decode protobuf to human readable JSON.

```
$ configtxlator proto_decode --input config_block.pb --type common.Block
```

Next strip away headers, metadata and creator signatures from the JSON:

Listing 9. 3. Strip headers, signatures and metadata from config block.

```
$ cat config_block.json | jq .data.data[0].payload.data.config > config_data.json
```

Convert config_data.json to protobuf as we'll need it later to compute the delta of the changes:

Listing 9. 4. Convert JSON back to protobuf.

```
$ configtxlator proto_encode --input ./config_data.json --type common.Config --output config_data.pb
```

Next, run the following Node.js script which is going to update the orderer endpoints and replace localhost with name of corresponding Docker container in which the orderer will run:

Listing 9. 5. Node.js script to update orderer addresses to respective containers.

```
var fs = require('fs');
var blob = fs.readFileSync('config_data.json');
var str = blob.toString();
var o = JSON.parse(str);
var groups = o.channel_group.groups.Orderer.groups;
var consenters =
    o.channel_group.groups.Orderer.values.ConsensusType.value.metadata.consenters;
groups["Biotor"].values.Endpoints.value["addresses"] =
    ["orderer0.biotor.com:7050"];                                       ❶
groups["ExpressMedicinals"].values.Endpoints.value["addresses"] =
    ["orderer0.xmed.com:7051"];                                         ❷
groups["KeyPharmacy"].values.Endpoints.value["addresses"] =
    ["orderer0.keypharmacy.com:7052"];                                  ❸
consenters[0].host = 'orderer0.biotor.com';                             ❹
consenters[1].host = 'orderer0.xmed.com';                               ❹
consenters[2].host = 'orderer0.keypharmacy.com';                       ❹
fs.writeFileSync('modified_config_data.json', JSON.stringify(o, null, 2));  ❺
```

❶ We assume that Biotor's orderer will be running in a container named orderer0.biotor.com and listening at port 7050 inside this container. We will see how to do this in next chapter.

❷ We assume that XMed's orderer will be running in a container named orderer0.xmed.com and listening at port 7051 inside this container

❸ We assume that KeyPharmacy's orderer will be running in a container named `orderer0.keypharmacy.com` and listening at port 7052 inside this container

❹ We also need to update orderer addresses over here

❺ Save updated addresses

You should see a file `modified_config_data.json` after running the script. Encode it to protobuf:

Listing 9. 6. Convert JSON to protobuf.

```
$ configtxlator proto_encode --input ./modified_config_data.json --type common.Config
--output modified_config_data.pb
```

Tip: If you do not strip way the header in Listing 9. 3, there is this error when we try to encode `modified_config_block.json` to protobuf:

```
configtxlator: error: Error decoding: error decoding input: *common.Config: unknown field
"header" in common.Config
```

Calculate delta between original and modified config:

Listing 9. 7. Calculate delta between the original and modified config.

```
$ configtxlator compute_update --channel_id tracktrace --original config_data.pb --updated
modified_config_data.pb --output delta_update.pb
```

Verify:

Listing 9. 8. Decode the config update into human readable JSON.

```
$ configtxlator proto_decode --input delta_update.pb --type common.ConfigUpdate
```

You should see a long output with updated orderer addresses (see git.io/Jk8fY for reference). An excerpt from the full output is shown below:

Listing 9. 9. Updated orderer endpoint for Biotor

```
"Endpoints": {
    "mod_policy": "Admins",
    "value": {
        "addresses": [
            "orderer0.biotor.com:7050"
        ]
    },
    "version": "1"
}
```

Note the version has been updated to 1. Save the full output as `config_update.json`. Next we need to wrap this in an envelope and add a header as shown below:

Listing 9. 10. Add back header and envelope to the config update.

```
$ echo '{"payload":{"header":{"channel_header":{"channel_id":"tracktrace",
"type":2}},"data":{"config_update":'$(cat config_update.json)'}}}' | jq . >
config_update_in_envelope.json
```

Convert to protobuf:

Listing 9. 11. Convert config update into protobuf format.

```
$ configtxlator proto_encode --input config_update_in_envelope.json --type common.Envelope
--output config_update_in_envelope.pb
```

As we are updating a channel's configuration, there are certain policies to be satisfied. Let's explain them. From Listing 9. 9 observe that there is a mod_policy of Admins that applies when changing the orderer Endpoints. The general syntax is:

```
"X": {
    "mod_policy": "Y",
```

which means *to change* X *you need to satisfy* Y. The Admins policy is itself defined in o.channel_group.groups.Application.groups.Biotor.policies.Admins where o is the config_data object of Listing 9. 5. The policy is shown below in Listing 9. 12:

Listing 9. 12. Example of how a policy is defined in Channel's Configuration

```
"Admins": {                                     ❶
    "mod_policy": "Admins",                     ❶
    "policy": {
      "type": 1,
      "value": {
        "identities": [
          {
            "principal": {
              "msp_identifier": "BiotorMSP",
              "role": "ADMIN"
            },
            "principal_classification": "ROLE"
          }
        ],
        "rule": {
          "n_out_of": {                         ❷
            "n": 1,                             ❸
            "rules": [
              {
                "signed_by": 0                  ❹
              }
            ]
          }
        },
        "version": 0
      }
    },
  "version": "0"
}
```

❶ To change Admins policy, one needs to satisfy the Admins policy itself

❷ This is saying that n out of m rules should be satisfied for this policy to be satisfied

❸ n=1 so at least 1 rule out of all the rules should be satisfied for overall policy to be satisfied

❹ `0` is an index into the `identities` array and this rule is therefore saying that the 0-th identity should sign off on the change

The opening lines can be confusing but they are saying that to change `Admins` policy, one needs to satisfy the `Admins` policy itself in accordance with the syntax we have seen earlier. The policy can be very hard to understand from the output above but this is what it is saying. We need to satisfy `n=1` rule out of all the rules in the `rules` array. Since the array contains only 1 item in it, the `n=1` does not make much of a difference. Next the rule we need to satisfy is `signed_by: 0`. The `0` is an index into the `identities` array. So we need signature from `identities[0]`. And `identities[0]` as you can see is a user who belongs to `BiotorMSP` and has the `ADMIN` role associated with them. So in plain English this is saying we need to get a signature from `BiotorMSP` administrator. You can cross check that the same policy is specified in `configtx.yaml` under `Organizations.Biotor.Policies.Admins` as:

```
Admins:
    Type: Signature
    Rule: "OR('BiotorMSP.admin')"
```

Indeed `configtx.yaml` is the place from where the policy originates and makes its way to the config block as we saw in Section 5.2. You will see similar policies specified that control who can make changes to orderer addresses of XMed and KeyPharmacy.

We are not done yet. There is another place where we change the orderer addresses and that is at the level of consenters in Listing 9. 5. To see what `mod_policy` applies at this level, we look at `o.channel_group.groups.Orderer.values.ConsensusType.mod_policy` which turns out to be `Admins`. Again `Admins` is just a pointer or a reference. Now we need to lookup what `Admins` really is which is done as follows:

```
> o.channel_group.groups.Orderer.policies.Admins
{
  mod_policy: 'Admins',
  policy: { type: 3, value: { rule: 'MAJORITY', sub_policy: 'Admins' } },
  version: '0'
}
```

Phew! This itself is making a reference to a `sub_policy`. Hopefully by now you have some pointers on how to follow the trail. We can instead jump to `configtx.yaml` and see the policy over there under `Orderer.Policies.Admins`:

Listing 9. 13. Example of `ImplicitMeta` **Policy**

```
Admins:
    Type: ImplicitMeta
    Rule: "MAJORITY Admins"
```

You can see this policy is of type `ImplicitMeta` and that translates to a `sub_policy` in the config block. The Orderer is made up of the organizations declared in `Profiles.Genesis.Orderer.Organizations` in `configtx.yaml`. The `ImplicitMeta` policy is saying that a majority of the Admins policy of those organizations should be satisfied. So now we need to evaluate the Admins policy of each of the orgs and test if a majority of the sub-policies is satisfied. I know its too much to take in.

Ultimately when we consider all the policies we have to satisfy, we come to the conclusion that we need signature from every organization's admin. So let's do that. Run following command with identity of Biotor admin:

Listing 9. 14. Signing off on a channel update transaction.

```
$ peer channel signconfigtx -f config_update_in_envelope.pb
```

and then repeat the command with XMed and KeyPharmacy's credentials. Note that here you are conveniently able to assume any organization's credentials but in practice *in the real-world, one admin will sign and then pass on the protobuf file for another admin to sign and so on*. You can decode the config_update_in_envelope.pb by running following command and verify the signatures are in place:

Listing 9. 15. Decoding an envelope block into JSON to verify it has required signatures.

```
$ configtxlator proto_decode --input config_update_in_envelope.pb --type common.Envelope
```

 The peer channel signconfigtx command is sensitive to the output filename. If you change the filename, the signature will become invalid and you will get error when you run peer channel update.

Finally we need to update the channel using credentials of an admin. Before we do that, we have a problem. You might have already realized it. The update we are making is going to change the orderer addresses. The update itself will succeed but *as soon as the peer and orderer nodes get the new addresses the network is going to break down as we don't have anything running at* orderer0.biotor.com, orderer0.xmed.com *and* orderer0.keypharmacy.com. To fix it, modify the local DNS on your system by editing the **/etc/hosts** file (editing the file will require root privileges) and map the hostnames above to the localhost as shown below:

```
127.0.0.1 orderer0.biotor.com
127.0.0.1 orderer0.xmed.com
127.0.0.1 orderer0.keypharmacy.com
```

What this does is setup a local DNS mapping so any request to orderer0.biotor.com (and others) is resolved to 127.0.0.1. Now run the update command as an *administrator* of any organization:

Listing 9. 16. Update channel configuration.

```
$ peer channel update -f config_update_in_envelope.pb -o localhost:7050 -c tracktrace
```

If all goes well, you should see following output from above command:

```
[channelCmd] InitCmdFactory -> INFO 001 Endorser and orderer connections initialized
[channelCmd] update -> INFO 002 Successfully submitted channel update
```

In orderer logs you should see something like following (the block number is likely to be different as you would have committed a different number of transactions than I have on my network):

```
[orderer.consensus.etcdraft] run -> INFO 06a Received config transaction, pause accepting
transaction till it is committed channel=tracktrace node=1
[orderer.consensus.etcdraft] writeBlock -> INFO 06d Writing block [31] (Raft index: 44) to
ledger channel=tracktrace node=1
```

And then verify the block gets committed on each peer by inspecting their logs:

```
[gossip.privdata] StoreBlock -> INFO 02c [tracktrace] Received block [31] from buffer
[committer.txvalidator] Validate -> INFO 035 [tracktrace] Validated block [31] in 22ms
[gossip.privdata] prepareBlockPvtdata -> INFO 037 Successfully fetched all eligible
collection private write sets for block [31] channel=tracktrace
[kvledger] CommitLegacy -> INFO 038 [tracktrace] Committed block [31] with 1 transaction(s)
in 145ms commitHash=[8f844c6640dc494f94b92167b130dcf2203765435f6904858f88f1b7a54759cb]
```

You are all set! That was a lot but now you know how to update a channel configuration - an essential skill you need to possess to master Fabric. Table B.5 (Appendix B) summarizes the commands we used in this chapter. In addition we used jq to strip away headers and add them back in as needed.

Remember in real-world the config update would need to be exchanged securely and out of band between various parties in order to get their signatures.

Exercise 9.1

Fetch the latest config and verify the orderer addresses are updated in that.

Exercise 9.2

Go ahead and update the anchor peer addresses of all 3 organizations from localhost to peer0.biotor.com, peer0.xmed.com and peer0.keypharmacy.com respectively. Also edit your /etc/hosts appropriately. You will have to run 3 peer channel update commands - one command per organization. Each organization will update its own anchor peers independently of others.

9.1. Summary

- There are certain policies to be met before a channel's configuration can be updated. These policies are defined in configtx.yaml and appear as mod_policy in the channel's config stored on the blockchain.
- ImplicitMeta policies in configtx.yaml appear as sub_policy in the channel's configuration.
- Adding an organization to a channel, updating orderer or anchor peer addresses are some operations that require updating the channel's configuration.
- Modifying a channel's configuration is danger zone because if you break down the network as a result, there is no way to recover from a bad config as far as I know. [117]

[117] lists.hyperledger.org/g/fabric/topic/74634907#8441

Chapter 10. Dockerizing the Three-Org Network

This chapter covers:

- What is Docker and how to use it?
- Dockerizing (containerizing) the application in previous chapter
- Running peer nodes in `net` mode
- Migrating the ledger and data of previous chapter

You continue working from `$/three-org-network` in this chapter.

This chapter has two main objectives: containerize the network of previous chapter and switch peer nodes to `net` mode. In addition we will show in this chapter how to re-use or migrate the entire corpus of data of previous chapters so that we don't start with an empty ledger and do not have to re-do all the transactions we committed in previous chapters.

A large part of this chapter is going to be all about Docker. The goal of this chapter is to equip the reader with a solid knowledge of Docker which will pave the way to transition to a more production-like environment. This will also help you in understanding the official Fabric samples as all of them use Docker. This chapter will put everything together as far as Docker is concerned. It is aimed at killing two birds with one stone - it will show how to Dockerize the three-org network of previous chapters and explain Docker as well in the process. There are entire books on Docker so it is not possible for me to cover everything about Docker in one chapter. The hope is that this chapter will give the reader basic information and familiarity of Docker - a crash course if you will - needed in order to be productive with Fabric.

10.1. Docker Basics

Let's begin with a quick-fire round of Docker.

10.1.1. What is Docker and why does it matter?

Wikipedia gives us a good description of Docker: "Docker is a set of platform as a service products that use OS-level virtualization to deliver software in packages called containers. Containers are isolated from one another and bundle their own software, libraries and configuration files; they can communicate with each other through well-defined channels. All containers are run by a single operating-system kernel and are thus more lightweight than virtual machines." [118] In the next sections we will unpack what all of the above means through hands-on examples rather than formal definitions and abstract language. Docker comes in two flavors - the *Community Edition (CE)* which is free and the *Enterprise Edition (EE)*.

There are many reasons why Docker has become very popular and is increasingly used in the world of DevOps. *First* and foremost its just like a virtual machine (VM) albeit more lightweight.

Just like a VM, it provides an isolated and self-contained environment in which your application can run without interference from other apps. You could argue that Docker is used to run VMs inside VMs! [119] *Second* when you are using Docker to deploy your application, there is no need to install anything on the target server other than Docker itself. When the application is deployed, Docker automatically pulls in all required dependencies in a sandboxed environment. *Third*, in old days sometimes a text file used to be handed off to DevOps which would contain instructions for deployment. With Docker we don't need this anymore. Docker image contains a blueprint of all instructions needed to be followed to perform a deployment by an automated agent. *Fourth*, Docker containers are extremely fast to boot. And Docker is also a godsend for horizontally scaling services and rolling out incremental upgrades without service disruption.

10.1.2. Docker vs. Moby

This section can be skipped by readers who don't know or have not heard of Moby. For others, you might be confused as to what is the difference between Docker and Moby. Is Docker now Moby? The company that makes Docker has open-sourced many components of it to the Moby project which are now developed in an open-source manner. It is completely analogous to how Android is both an open-source project [120] and Google's Android is based on the code from that open-source project. [121] Sometimes the open-source project is known as Android Open Source Project (or AOSP) to distinguish it from Google's Android. Amazon's FireOS is also based on Android Open Source Project (AOSP). Moby will enable companies and organizations to assemble specialized container systems (such as Docker itself) without having to reinvent the wheel and there is a separate term to distinguish the open source project from the company that makes Docker. Docker Inc. hoped that people would use Moby when they are talking about the generic containerization platform and the Docker word would be reserved for the platform which Docker Inc. makes. But that has not happened and many people still use the word Docker when in fact they are referring to the open-source project. Docker Inc. was itself acquired by Mirantis in 2019.

10.1.3. Installing Docker

This was covered in Section A.6. You should already have Docker installed on your computer by the time you are at this chapter in the book. Once Docker is installed run `docker info` to get information about Docker.

10.1.4. Docker Components

At a high level Docker is a client-server application made up of:

* A server with a long-running daemon process **dockerd**.
* APIs which specify interfaces that programs can use to talk to and instruct the Docker daemon.
* A command line interface (CLI) client **docker**.

That is why in Listing A.1 there is a client section and a server section. When we use commands such as `docker create` and `docker run` (we have seen some examples in previous chapters), we are using the client. This client talks to a server - the `dockerd` daemon - through a set of well-defined APIs to create and run containers. The Docker daemon or server runs as a Unix domain socket (a `sock` file) and can be found under `/var/run/docker.sock` by default on Mac and Linux.

If you are familiar with MySQL, it is completely analogous. There is a server or daemon in MySQL by the name of `mysqld` and `mysql` CLI is the client that talks to this server. We use the client or CLI to log in to MySQL server and create tables, perform queries etc.

In the early days, all of the server side code of Docker was bundled into one application - the Docker daemon or `dockerd`. But now some of the functionality has been outsourced to other components in the spirit of breaking apart a monolithic application. These other components are **containerd** and **runc**. They thus become the dependencies of Docker daemon. `containerd` manages the containers life cycle. It also takes care of pushing and pulling images. And it uses `runc` to run containers. `runc` is a command line client for running applications packaged in the OCI (Open Container Initiative) format.

10.1.5. Images, Containers, Host and Services - the building blocks of Docker

We have used some of these terms in previous chapters. Let us now define or at least understand them more precisely. An *image* is a template (much like a class in Java) using which a *container* (much like an object) is instantiated. The machine or computer (could be real or virtual) on which the container runs is known as the *host*. A host can host multiple containers as we illustrated visually in Figure 9. 1. A list of all containers can be obtained by running `docker ps` on the host. A *service* is useful when we want to scale an application *horizontally* - this refers to making multiple replicas of an application so that you have more instances which can serve incoming requests. If we have N replicas then we can process N times more requests per second than otherwise. A service is a collection of identical containers all deriving from the same image. We will not need to use services in this chapter.

We first used Docker in this book in Section 5.4 to provision CouchDB. A modified version of the command is reproduced below for convenience:

```
$ docker run -d --name couchdb.peer0.biotor.com couchdb:2.3.1
```

In this command, `couchdb:2.3.1` is the name of the image that will be used to create a container which will be named `couchdb.peer0.biotor.com`. Docker will automatically download the image if it does not exist on the local machine. Figure 10. 1 shows the life cycle of a container.

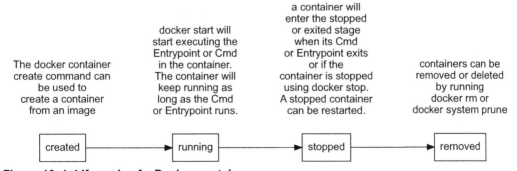

Figure 10. 1. Life cycle of a Docker container.

10.1.6. Single vs. Multi-Node and Single vs. Multi-Network Deployment

Docker can be run in two modes - *swarm* and *non-swarm*. By default, it runs in non-swarm mode which is okay for deploying standalone containers on a *single* machine. The swarm mode comes in handy when you want to deploy containers across *multiple* machines and when you want to add *service orchestration* on top of this. Service orchestration automatically creates new containers when old ones die for any reason. This avoids service disruption without you having to do anything about it. It is also the key to rolling out software upgrades. As new containers are being built Docker will automatically redirect their traffic temporarily to other containers and restore the traffic once the new containers are built without the service incurring any downtime. Add to this phased rollouts - the ability to rollout an upgrade to 10% of the machines today, 20% of the machines tomorrow and so on until you get to 100% rollout based on a pre-determined schedule.

The instructions for single vs. multi-node deployment remain the same except for setting up the swarm mode and running commands on respective machines. In a realistic setup each organization could be maintaining its own multi-node Docker network; so there could be *three separate swarms* hosted in three separate cloud providers or data centers. Do this as an exercise or better yet form a team of three developers who mimic the three orgs and setup their networks independently.

A frugal but practical (MVP) real-world setup is possible where each organization runs all their services on a single node utilizing a *bridge* network. We have a single-node single-network setup at level of each individual organization but when the whole consortium is considered there will be three bridge networks. Each network could be hosted in separate data center. Docker swarm is needed only when you want to setup a network spanning multiple nodes.

For advanced readers who want to take up the multi-node challenge where the orderers and peers will be running on different hosts, first you will need to get a network of machines up and running in Azure, AWS or your own data center. The instructions for this are outside the scope of this book. Next, ensure that following ports are available and not blocked by any firewall. [122]

- TCP port 2377 for cluster management communications
- TCP and UDP port 7946 for communication among nodes
- UDP port 4789 for overlay network traffic

On some systems, these ports are open by default. After that you need to initialize a Swarm on a master node. Do that by running following command:

```
$ docker swarm init
```

Example output is shown below:

```
Swarm initialized: current node (2fezvjh1myjk9kwnjhm5wxf5n) is now a manager.

To add a worker to this swarm, run the following command:

    docker swarm join --token SWMTKN-1-5uo8pmh7h7n5uym2h7yb9hsps3bk25303t5s56yds24ui3wveb-
9y2y31vix727qfp1rej8e7rll 10.67.220.46:2377

To add a manager to this swarm, run 'docker swarm join-token manager' and follow the
instructions.
```

Now join all other nodes to this swarm as manager or workers. For example, to join a node as a worker, run:

```
$ docker swarm join --token SWMTKN-1-4xq2y6eams5lm7eu15ghjkdmsu5tdx2erolko5glziwbaw9qh7-
b9wmzhqkwxolbgj8mfaxe4r08 10.67.220.41:2377
```

After that you will need to create an ***overlay*** network by running following command:

```
$ docker network create -d overlay --attachable biotor_net
```

Adding the `--opt encrypted` flag to the `network create` command turns on *IPsec (Internet Protocol Security)* and automatically encrypts all traffic between containers. This encryption imposes a non-negligible performance penalty and using TLS (Chapter 11) might be better instead. Experiment and decide what works best for you! IPsec operates at Layer 3 (packet) while TLS operates at Layer 4 (transport) of the network stack.

In a realistic setup, there could be a `biotor_net` managed by Biotor, a `xmed_net` managed by XMed and a `keyp_net` managed by Key Pharmacy and all three do not even need to be in same data center or cloud provider.

After this point, the subsequent steps are the same whether doing a single or multi-node deployment except that the `docker` commands in the upcoming sections need to be run on respective nodes and that you will need to have necessary bootstrap data such as certs and keys available on the machines. You also need to watch out for connection addresses (explained in next section).

Troubleshooting: If you are having connectivity issues between hosts in swarm mode check that ports 2377, 7946 and 4789 are not blocked using the `ss` or `netcat` utility. In my setup I can see following output (filtered to show only the Docker ports):

```
$ ss -tupln
Netid  State    Recv-Q Send-Q    Local Address:Port   Peer Address:Port
udp    UNCONN   0      0         *:4789               *:*
udp    UNCONN   0      0         [::]:7946            [::]:*
tcp    LISTEN   0      128       [::]:2377            [::]:*
tcp    LISTEN   0      128       [::]:7946            [::]:*
```

The `ss` command helps you to test if someone is even listening at the ports and the `nc` command helps you to test there is no firewall blocking the ports. The `ss` would be run on server and `nc` on the client.

10.1.7. How Containerization affects Connection Addresses

In a network, depending on whether the client and server are running in a Docker container, there can be four possibilities covered in Table 10. 1 and useful to keep in the back of your mind.

Table 10. 1. Effect of containerization on the address a client uses to communicate with a server. The boolean variable in table below is true if client or server is containerized.

Client	Server	Notes
✖	✖	Client uses `server-ip:server-port` to connect to the server. `localhost` works if both client and server are on same machine.
✖	✔	*Port publishing* is necessary for client to be able to connect to server. We saw example of this when we connected to CouchDB from peer in earlier chapters.
✔	✖	A chaincode container connecting to a peer that is not containerized. The client will use public or private IP of the server.
✔	✔	There are two sub-possibilities here. If both client and server are on *same* Docker network, then the client can use container name to connect to the server and Docker will handle routing. Port publishing is not necessary. If client and server are on *different* networks then port publishing is necessary and client will connect to the host of the target container. The host will then forward the message to the container (that is what port publishing does).

The connection address we use in our Node.js application (`Biotor-connection.yaml` file in Section 8.10.5) will change after we containerize the network. If the Node.js app is not containerized then row #2 of the table above applies when it has to make connection to the peers and orderers.

Similarly, if you have a multi-network setup where each organization maintains their own *separate* Docker network as is likely to be the case in production, a peer of Biotor cannot connect to peer container of XMed directly using the container name. It will connect to the host computer and vice-versa. All peer and orderer addresses in config files and genesis block have to set or updated keeping that in mind.

10.2. Provision orderer using Docker

> We work from `$/three-org-network/biotor/orderer` in this section. The directory will change for different organizations.

With the basics out of our way, let's see how we can provision the three org network except this time we will run the peers, orderer and chaincode in Docker containers. That is the goal of this chapter. At this stage the `orderer` directory should already be having `foo.block` and `orderer.yaml` from previous chapters. It should also contain a `orderer0.biotor.com` directory which contains data from previous chapters. *We will use this directory to bootstrap our orderer so that it doesn't start from scratch but instead picks up the state from previous chapters!* Verify you still have the `pharmanet` network we created in Section 5.4.1 or the `biotor_net`. Truncated output showing `pharmanet` network exists is shown below:

Listing 10. 1. Check `pharmanet` **exists**

```
$ docker network ls
NETWORK ID          NAME                                    DRIVER          SCOPE
c0d70c64a014        pharmanet                               bridge          local
```

We are ready to run the orderer using Docker.

10.2.1. Script to Dockerize the orderer

You can run the orderer in a container by executing the script in Listing 10. 2 from the `orderer` folder.

Listing 10. 2. Script used to provision a Docker container that runs Fabric orderer. There are 3 stages. Stage 1: create container. Stage 2: copy files into container. Stage 3: run container.

```
#!/bin/bash
CONTAINER_NAME=orderer0.biotor.com
DATA_DIR=orderer0.biotor.com
FILELEDGER_LOCATION=/var/hyperledger/production
WORKDIR=/home

docker container create \                                                     ❶
--name $CONTAINER_NAME \                                                       ❷
--network pharmanet \                                                          ❸
-p 7050:7050 \                                                                 ❹
--volume "$PWD/$DATA_DIR:$FILELEDGER_LOCATION" \                               ❺
--workdir $WORKDIR \                                                           ❻
--log-opt max-file=3 \                                                         ❼
--log-opt max-size=10m \                                                       ❼
--env FABRIC_CFG_PATH=$WORKDIR \                                               ❽
--env ORDERER_FILELEDGER_LOCATION=$FILELEDGER_LOCATION \                       ❾
--env ORDERER_CONSENSUS_WALDIR=$FILELEDGER_LOCATION/etcdraft/wal \             ❿
--env ORDERER_CONSENSUS_SNAPDIR=$FILELEDGER_LOCATION/etcdraft/snapshot \       ❿
hyperledger/fabric-orderer:2.0.1 \                                            ⓫
orderer                                                                        ⓬

docker cp foo.block $CONTAINER_NAME:$WORKDIR                                   ⓭
docker cp msp $CONTAINER_NAME:$WORKDIR                                         ⓭
docker cp tls $CONTAINER_NAME:$WORKDIR                                         ⓭
docker cp orderer.yaml $CONTAINER_NAME:$WORKDIR                                ⓭

docker start $CONTAINER_NAME                                                   ⓮
```

❶ Create the container

❷ Give a name to the container

❸ Attach it to the `pharmanet` network. Replace `pharmanet` with your network name as the case may be.

❹ Publish container port 7050 to host port 7050

❺ Setup a bind mount so we don't lose data when container is deleted

❻ Set the working directory

❼ Retain 3 latest log files where each log file is 10MB. This way logs are bounded and cannot eat up entire disk.

❽ Set directory where `orderer` will search for `orderer.yaml`

❾ Override the `Fileledger.Location` in `orderer.yaml` with environment variable. The reason for this is that we now need to specify a location w.r.t. the container's filesystem.

❿ Override other locations in `orderer.yaml` so they are valid file paths expressed w.r.t. container's filesystem.

⓫ The Docker image from which container will be instantiated

⓬ Command to start orderer

⓭ Copy necessary files and directories into the container.

⓮ Start the container

The code in Listing 10. 2 illustrates many Docker concepts such as *volumes, port publishing, log rotation* and *copying files* between host and container. If you look at it closely, you can see it is divided into *three stages*. In the *first stage*, we create a Docker container using the `docker container create` command. In the *second stage*, we copy over some files to the container using the `docker cp` command. And in the *third* and final stage, we start the container using `docker start` command. This is when the container starts running. We use some bash variables in the script which will help you in re-using it for other organizations.

The container is given a name which is `orderer0.biotor.com`. It is joined to the `pharmanet` network. A container has to join or attach to a network to be able to communicate with other containers on the same network. The `-p` flag is used for *port publishing. What this does is that if a request comes to a port on the host machine, it will be forwarded to a port on the container.* This allows those clients to be able to connect to the container who are not joined to the Docker network but can connect to the host on which the container is running. This is how an orderer of Biotor can connect to an orderer of XMed even though they may not be on the same network. The syntax of the ports following the -p flag is `host-port:container-port`. In Listing 10. 2 we used the same number `7050` for both host and container ports but that is not a requirement. *The* `container-port` *must match the* `General.ListenPort` *declared in* `orderer.yaml` *file.*

Next we come to the `--volume` flag which is explained in following subsection.

DOCKER VOLUMES AND BIND MOUNTS

The `--volume` flag is used to setup a Docker volume. *The purpose of a Docker volume is to persist data.*

One big gotcha for newbies coming to Docker is that when a container is deleted, *all the data stored inside the container is deleted as well!* unless you map it to a volume. Volumes and other persistent data is stored under **/var/lib/docker** by default on Linux. This directory can be changed by using the **--data-root** flag when Docker daemon (`dockerd`) is started. On Linux systems - I have tested this on RHEL - you would need to edit

`/lib/systemd/system/docker.service`   and   add   `--data-root`   to   the `ExecStart=/usr/bin/dockerd` command in the file.

Just like ice-cream, Docker volumes come in many flavors: *host volumes (also known as bind mounts), anonymous volumes and named volumes.* [123] The term host volume is used less and less these days and they are instead referred to as bind mounts and some authors don't even categorize them as volumes. The difference between these three types of volumes is as follows: a *bind mount* specifies the location on the host where the data will be persisted whereas this location is not specified and automatically inferred by Docker for *anonymous* and *named volumes*. On Linux, the location is given by `/var/lib/docker/volumes` by default. Named volumes are given a name by the user whereas anonymous volumes get an autogenerated name.

In Listing 10. 2 we are using the `--volume` (or just `-v`) flag to setup a *bind mount*. The first argument to the flag is a location on the host's filesystem and the second argument is a location on the container's filesystem. The bind mount will now *mirror* these two locations or directories and the host directory will retain the data even when the container is deleted; in Docker parlance we usually talk of removing containers rather than deleting them but its the same thing. Although the main purpose of a volume or bind mount is to persist data, it has another equally important use-case which is to *inject data into a container*. We can see this in action in Listing 10. 2 where we set the location on the host to `$PWD/$DATA_DIR` which is the path where the data of Biotor's orderer is stored from previous chapters. This will cause the data from previous runs to be injected into our container at `/var/hyperledger/production` and prevent the orderer from starting from scratch. *It will pick up all the data we had from previous runs.*

- You may run into errors if you try to use relative paths in bind mounts. For example, the version of Docker I am using (`19.03.4`) does not support it. I get an error if I try to use a relative path. It looks like a changeset has been made to add support for relative paths to bind mounts but not sure in what release it will be available. [124]
- Please do not do fancy stuff like trying to mount a *symbolic link*. It will not work. [125]

As a tip, you can also create a bind mount using the `--mount` flag instead of `--volume`. Named or anonymous volumes are more powerful than bind mounts because by using an appropriate driver, we can set them up so that the data can be stored on remote hosts and thus *they provide a mechanism by which you can share data between containers on different hosts.* You can't do that with a bind mount. This is one reason why some authors and even latest Docker documentation prefers to keep bind mounts separate and not categorize them as volumes. There is one important difference between using `--volume` vs. `--mount` to create a bind mount and that is this: *in case of* `--volume` *if the location on the host does not exist, it is created as a directory whereas* `--mount` *will throw an error.*

Named volumes are given a name using the `docker volume create` command so that we can reference them later. This is illustrated below:

Listing 10. 3. Creating and using a named volume

```
$ docker volume create my_awesome_vol
$ docker run -v my_awesome_vol:/path/in/container ...
```

An anonymous volume is created when you use the -v flag and leave the host directory as empty and only specify the directory on the container like so:

Listing 10. 4. Creating and using an anonymous volume

```
$ docker run -v /path/in/container ...
```

Anonymous volumes get automatically deleted when the associated container is deleted *if the container is run with the --rm switch.* [126] *So use the combination of --rm switch and anonymous volumes with care because in that case your data will not be persisted when the container is deleted.* One thing you cannot do with volumes is mounting subdirectories. For example, say you have a volume named my_awesome_vol you cannot mount my_awesome_vol/foo to path/in/container and my_awesome_vol/bar to another/path/in/container. You will have to create two distinct named volumes or do other hacks. [127]

When a volume exists and is no longer connected to any containers, it's called a *dangling volume*. Dangling volumes are expected since the whole point of using a volume is to persist data when a container is deleted. A list of all dangling volumes can be obtained by running:

```
$ docker volume ls -f dangling=true
```

As you work with Docker, over time you will create many dangling volumes and will eventually want to do a clean up. You can do that by running:

```
$ docker volume prune
```

This will remove all dangling volumes. *Use it with caution!* If there are some volumes that should be preserved, create a text file containing the volumes that should be deleted and remove them using following command:

```
$ docker volume rm $(cat unwanted-volumes.txt)
```

The **--workdir** flag sets the working directory within the container. When the container is started, it executes a startup command. The command will be run from the --workdir. The **--log-opt** flags are used to setup *log rotation* and prevent the logs from growing infinitely. The settings in Listing 10. 2 ensure that the container will have a maximum of 3 log files (--log-opt max-file=3) no larger than 10 megabytes each (--log-opt max-size=10m). [128] When the logs become larger than 30MB Docker will prune the logs so that only the most recent 30MB of data is retained.

The **--env** *flag is used to inject environment variables into the container and to override the file paths in* orderer.yaml. The file paths in the orderer.yaml from previous chapters are w.r.t. your machine. When you run the orderer inside a container, it uses the container's filesystem.

Remember the container is like a VM. So its very important to change the file paths otherwise you'll get file not found errors. We can either draft a separate `orderer.yaml` for use with Docker, or as shown here, we can use environment variables to override the settings in `orderer.yaml`.

`hyperledger/fabric-orderer:2.0.1` tells Docker what image it should use to run the container. Docker downloads the image on the fly if it doesn't already exist on the host. This is one of the nice things about Docker and part of its value proposition. You literally don't have to install anything. Docker will download the image and the image and will have all the required dependencies in it.

We use `docker cp` to copy the genesis block (`foo.block`), `orderer.yaml`, `msp` and `tls` directories of the orderer into the container prior to starting it. Finally `docker start` starts the container. Its amazing how quickly Docker can start a container. There is virtually no wait time. The `docker run` command can be thought of as a `docker create` followed by an immediate `docker start`. *It does not leave you any room to do intermediate tasks such as copying files with* `docker cp`.

The `fabric-orderer` Docker image comes pre-installed with a default `orderer.yaml` located at `/etc/hyperledger/fabric`. If we had forgotten to set `FABRIC_CFG_PATH` in Listing 10. 2, it would have read settings from this file instead of the correct `orderer.yaml`. The default value of `FABRIC_CFG_PATH` is `/etc/hyperledger/fabric` inside the container. Take care to not forget setting `FABRIC_CFG_PATH` to path of your `orderer.yaml` (or you can overwrite the `orderer.yaml` in `/etc/hyperledger/fabric` with your version).

 It is not possible to make any sort of config changes to a container after it has been created or started. For example, you can't publish new ports, change port numbers, add new environment variables, change verbosity of logs etc. The only thing you can do is to rename the container.

10.2.2. Running the script to provision Docker container

Save the code in Listing 10. 2 in a `.sh` file (shell script), make it executable (`chmod +x`), and then run it from the command line. You should get an output like following:

```
$ ./run-biotor-orderer.sh
199a1ff417c57189c0c95cbd0a52a36b117c9b019623493cb7b5a1e86750ddb8
orderer0.biotor.com
```

Run `docker ps` to see list of containers:

```
$ docker ps
CONTAINER ID      IMAGE                               COMMAND      CREATED
STATUS            PORTS                  NAMES
199a1ff417c5      hyperledger/fabric-orderer:2.0.1    "orderer"    30 seconds ago
Up 28 seconds     0.0.0.0:7050->7050/tcp orderer0.biotor.com
```

Next inspect the logs by running:

```
$ docker logs -f orderer0.biotor.com
```

Following lines in the log are instructive to note (full log can be found at git.io/Jk0vD):

Listing 10. 5. Excerpt of Docker logs of `orderer0.biotor.com`

```
[orderer.common.server] extractSysChanLastConfig -> INFO 003 Not bootstrapping because of 2
existing channels ❶
[orderer.common.cluster] loadVerifier -> INFO 007 Loaded verifier for channel foo from
config block at index 1 ❷
[orderer.common.cluster] loadVerifier -> INFO 008 Loaded verifier for channel tracktrace
from config block at index 47 ❸
[orderer.common.server] Main -> INFO 009 Not bootstrapping because of existing channels
[orderer.consensus.etcdraft] createOrReadWAL -> INFO 00b Found WAL data at path
'/var/hyperledger/production/etcdraft/wal/foo', replaying it channel=foo node=1 ❹
[orderer.commmon.multichannel] Initialize -> INFO 00c Starting system channel 'foo' with
genesis block hash c9fd969605a9158289065b71a7ed5367e4ddbb3c1fad83f55c0c8409641c8f12 and
orderer type etcdraft ❺
[orderer.common.server] Main -> INFO 02c Starting orderer:
 Version: 2.0.1
 Commit SHA: 1cfa5da
 Go version: go1.13.4
 OS/Arch: linux/amd64
[orderer.common.server] Main -> INFO 02d Starting cluster listener on [::]:7070
[orderer.common.server] Main -> INFO 02f Beginning to serve requests ❻
```

❶ This line confirms that the orderer is not bootstrapping from scratch but is instead picking up the data we created in previous chapters

❷ Orderer recognizes the `foo` system channel we created in previous chapters

❸ Orderer recognizes the `tracktrace` application channel created earlier

❹ Orderer picks up the WAL directory of `foo` channel

❺ This line shows we are running in `etcdraft` mode

❻ This confirms successful initialization

Lines 1-4 are super-important and confirm that the orderer has picked up the channels we created in previous chapters - there was a system channel `foo` that was created and an application channel `tracktrace`. Thus the orderer is not starting from scratch - our work in previous chapters is not lost. Both `foo` and `tracktrace` channels are under `$DATA_DIR/chains`:

```
$ ls orderer0.biotor.com/chains
foo     tracktrace
```

> If the orderer is not picking up the channels, run it under a debugger and stick a breakpoint in the function `extractSysChanLastConfig` in file `/fabric/orderer/common/server/main.go`. By the way this is how you can map a log message (for example in Listing 10. 5) to where it occurs in the Fabric codebase.

Go ahead and provision the orderer for the other organizations.

Exercise 10.1

When you create a bind mount, there are four possibilities that can happen depending on whether the locations on the host and container already exist or not. They are shown in following table:

Host Directory	Container Directory	Result
does not exist	does not exist	
does not exist	exists	
exists	does not exist	
exists	exists	

Fill out the table above with what happens in each case. The last case is particularly to be watchful of because both locations exist and may have different data. How will the bind mount mirror the data between the two locations?

10.3. From Zero to Hero with Docker

This section will cover a range of Docker topics and is your baptism to Docker. We provide a cheat sheet in Table B.7 of most common commands that you can refer later on.

10.3.1. Container Basics

Once the orderer is running, you can log into the container by simply running:

Listing 10. 6. Logging into a Docker container

```
$ docker exec -it orderer0.biotor.com /bin/ash
```

The above command is telling Docker to run `/bin/ash` in `orderer0.biotor.com`. The `-it` flag tells Docker to run the command in *interactive mode*. The *interactive mode* attaches a terminal to the container. `ash` is a shell like `bash`. It stands for Almquist shell. It is more lightweight than `bash`. The alpine image from which Fabric images descend does not have `bash` installed in it. Note that other users that can access the host can also log into the container. Docker does not ask for any password. Verify that when you log in, the directory that you are in matches the working directory in Listing 10. 2:

```
/home #
```

From here you can do normal stuff that you can do from any other command line. Take a look at the directory where the orderer stores its data:

```
/home # ls -al /var/hyperledger/production
total 4
drwxr-xr-x    5 root     root           160 May 14 18:38 .
drwxr-xr-x    3 root     root          4096 Jun 16 23:23 ..
drwxr-xr-x    4 root     root           128 May 14 18:38 chains
drwxr-xr-x    4 root     root           128 May 14 18:38 etcdraft
drwxr-xr-x   10 root     root           320 Jun 19 22:38 index
```

Log out of the container by running:

```
/home# exit
```

It is possible to run commands against the container without logging into an interactive shell like so to give an example (note the absence of -it flags):

```
$ docker exec orderer0.biotor.com cat /etc/hyperledger/fabric/orderer.yaml
```

which should print out `orderer.yaml` stored in the container at `/etc/hyperledger/fabric`. To see a list of all running containers, run:

```
$ docker ps
```

The `ps` command accepts various flags to filter the output. [129] For example, to see just container names:

```
$ docker ps --format "{{.Names}}"
```

To stop a container run `docker stop` and to start it run `docker start`. If the container does not exist, `docker start` will give an error.

10.3.2. Inspecting Logs

Backend developers routinely rely on logs to do troubleshooting or debugging. Logs are sacrosanct. The logs of a container can be inspected by running (to give an example):

```
$ docker logs -f orderer0.biotor.com
```

Above will tail the logs and pause (instead of exiting) when no more log messages are available. To store the logs in a text file run:

```
$ docker logs orderer0.biotor.com >& log.txt
```

The ampersand (&) is necessary. The >& symbol is an operator that copies the output of the first file descriptor and redirects to the output of the second file descriptor. To grep the logs (e.g., to search for errors) run:

```
$ docker logs orderer0.biotor.com 2>&1 | grep -i "erro"
```

The reason for the funny syntax is that as you will see, Docker writes the logs to `stderr` (standard error). The 1 denotes standard output (`stdout`). The 2 denotes standard error (`stderr`). So 2>&1 copies `stderr` and redirects (or pastes) to `stdout`. That can then be piped to `grep`.

Note that the logs of a container can be accessed even after the container has terminated (exited) but not removed (deleted).

10.3.3. Where are the Logs?

To get the location of the logs of our orderer run:

```
$ docker inspect orderer0.biotor.com
```

This should give a long output full of useful information (git.io/Jk0fA). Among other things it shows following where I have truncated the long filename for brevity:

```
"LogPath": "/var/lib/docker/containers/52bd060e80/52bd060e80-json.log",
```

So this is where the log is being stored. The only catch is that if you are on Mac, you won't find this directory (/var/lib/docker) on your machine. The reason is that on the Mac, Docker spins up a tiny Linux VM and it is this VM which hosts the containers! And the file path is w.r.t. this VM. The steps to access the Linux VM are arcane and not well documented but are as follows. With newer versions of Docker and MacOS the steps could change, so don't be surprised if you run into some issues. I have tested these on Mojave and Docker 19.03.4.

ACCESSING LINUX VM ON THE MAC

Verify you have a file /dev/ttys000:

```
$ ls -al /dev/ttys000
crw--w---- 1 siddjain tty 16,  0 Feb  6 09:04 /dev/ttys000
```

Note the special file type c. It stands for *character device file*. Terminals are classic example of this file type. In this case /dev/ttys000 is the terminal of the Linux VM running inside the Mac.

To log into this terminal, run:

```
$ screen /dev/ttys000
```

Your entire terminal will become completely blank. Don't panic. Just press ENTER without typing any command. This logs you in and should give you a docker-desktop prompt as follows:

```
docker-desktop:~#
```

Now try looking for /var/lib/docker:

```
docker-desktop:~# ls -al /var/lib/docker
total 168
drwx--x--x   15 root     root      4096 Feb  6 17:05 .
drwxr-xr-x   10 root     root      4096 Oct 28 16:20 ..
drwx------    2 root     root      4096 Sep 19  2018 builder
drwx------    4 root     root      4096 Sep 19  2018 buildkit
drwx------    3 root     root      4096 Sep 19  2018 containerd
drwx------   35 root     root      4096 Feb  6 23:40 containers
drwx------    3 root     root      4096 Sep 19  2018 image
drwxr-x---    3 root     root      4096 Sep 19  2018 network
drwx------  391 root     root     49152 Feb  6 23:40 overlay2
drwx------    4 root     root      4096 Sep 19  2018 plugins
drwx------    2 root     root      4096 Feb  6 17:05 runtimes
drwx------    2 root     root      4096 Sep 19  2018 swarm
drwx------    2 root     root      4096 Feb  6 17:05 tmp
drwx------    2 root     root      4096 Sep 19  2018 trust
drwx------  490 root     root     61440 Feb  6 23:40 volumes
```

Voila! Look for the log file:

```
docker-desktop:~# ls -al /var/lib/docker/containers/52bd060e80/52bd060e80-json.log
-rw-r-----    1 root      root         970154 Jun 19 23:05
/var/lib/docker/containers/52bd060e80/52bd060e80-json.log
```

You can do usual stuff with this file now. For example, try tailing the file:

Listing 10. 7. Docker logs using the `json-file` **driver**

```
docker-desktop:~# tail /var/lib/docker/containers/52bd060e80/52bd060e80-json.log
{"log":"\u001b[34m2020-06-19 22:43:03.947 UTC [orderer.consensus.etcdraft]
becomePreCandidate -\u003e INFO 1b6\u001b[0m 1 became pre-candidate at term 19
channel=tracktrace node=1\n","stream":"stderr","time":"2020-06-19T22:43:03.94850478Z"}
{"log":"\u001b[34m2020-06-19 22:43:03.947 UTC [orderer.consensus.etcdraft] poll -\u003e
INFO 1b7\u001b[0m 1 received MsgPreVoteResp from 1 at term 19 channel=tracktrace
node=1\n","stream":"stderr","time":"2020-06-19T22:43:03.9487315622"}
```

We can see the orderer logs! Note that it is logging to `stderr`. When you are ready to quit or exit the session, press `Ctrl+a` followed by `:quit`. Just like `vi` has special control sequences, `screen` uses `Ctrl+a` to get into a command mode and the `:quit` tells it to quit. [130] If used successfully you should see:

```
$ screen /dev/ttys000
[screen is terminating]
```

An alternate command you might run into to log in to the Linux VM is

```
$ screen ~/Library/Containers/com.docker.docker/Data/vms/0/tty
```

The `~/Library/Containers/com.docker.docker/Data/vms/0/tty` file is actually a symlink to `/dev/ttys000`:

```
$ ls -al ~/Library/Containers/com.docker.docker/Data/vms/0/tty
lrwxr-xr-x 1 siddjain  staff 12 Feb  6 09:04
/Users/siddjain/Library/Containers/com.docker.docker/Data/vms/0/tty -> /dev/ttys000
```

10.3.4. Log Drivers

By default Docker stores the logs as JSON formatted strings. This setting can actually be seen in the `LogConfig` when you run `docker inspect` on the container. For example, the output of `docker inspect orderer0.biotor.com` will show:

```
"LogConfig": {
    "Type": "json-file",
    "Config": {
        "max-file": "3",
        "max-size": "10m"
    }
}
```

We can get just the driver name (`LogConfig.Type`) from the long output of `docker inspect` `orderer0.biotor.com` by running:

```
$ docker inspect -f '{{.HostConfig.LogConfig.Type}}' orderer0.biotor.com
```

which should give a single line output of

```
json-file
```

The `-f` followed by `{{···}}` is a general syntax to *format* the output of a Docker command. Some commands like `ps` for example take a *filter* also given by `-f`. Use `--format` to format in that case. *Do not confuse format with filter. The two are different!* Use `--filter` to filter and `--format` to format.

There are many other log drivers that Docker supports besides `json-file`. [131] The log driver can be changed by using the `--log-driver` flag when creating a container.

10.3.5. Inspecting an image

It is possible to inspect a Docker image (e.g., the `fabric-orderer` image) by running:

```
$ docker inspect hyperledger/fabric-orderer:2.0.1
```

It has lot of interesting information in it (git.io/JI3FJ). For example, note following lines under the `Config` section:

Listing 10. 8. Inspecting `fabric-orderer` **image**

```
"Env": [              ❶
    "PATH=/usr/local/sbin:/usr/local/bin:/usr/sbin:/usr/bin:/sbin:/bin",
    "FABRIC_CFG_PATH=/etc/hyperledger/fabric"
],
"Cmd": [              ❷
    "orderer"
],
"Image": "sha256:a2399d44d1d14bd95915cb0bdf4d659e2d6c28d8af87acc3fd1b29013162e86e", ❸
"Volumes": {          ❹
    "/etc/hyperledger/fabric": {},
    "/var/hyperledger": {}
},
"WorkingDir": "",
"Entrypoint": null,
```

❶ Define environment variables. `FABRIC_CFG_PATH` is necessary to define as the orderer will look for an `orderer.yaml` under `FABRIC_CFG_PATH`.

❷ Set the command to be executed when container is run or started

❸ The SHA fingerprint of the image

❹ Define anonymous volumes

To get details beyond what `docker inspect` provides you, there is a tool called `dive` [132] that can be installed on the Mac by running:

```
$ brew install dive
```

Once installed, you simply give it an image name like so:

```
$ dive hyperledger/fabric-orderer:2.0.1
```

and it will show details of the image. Explaining this tool is beyond the scope of this book; refer to its GitHub page for details.

10.3.6. Cmd *vs.* Entrypoint

What does a container do when it is started? It starts executing the Cmd or Entrypoint defined in the image (refer Listing 10. 8) unless those values are overridden by the user. We can *override* the Cmd hardcoded in the image by specifying an argument *after* the image name when starting the container as done in Listing 10. 2. In Listing 10. 2 it did not make any difference since the hardcoded Cmd in the image is also orderer. There is another field called Entrypoint which does the same thing as Cmd. It can also be overridden but requires the use of the **--entrypoint** flag. E.g.,

```
$ docker run --entrypoint orderer hyperledger/fabric-orderer:2.0.1
```

Note that in this case the override comes ***before*** the image name (in case of Cmd the override comes ***after*** the image name). *If there are two fields which do the same thing then what happens if both are specified? When both an* Entrypoint *and* Cmd *are specified, the* Cmd *string(s) are appended to the* Entrypoint *in order to generate the full command to be executed when container is run. So in a sense the* Entrypoint *triumphs over the* Cmd. A possible use-case when you might use both Entrypoint and Cmd is when you intend the command to execute when container is started to be fixed (and given by Entrypoint) but the command requires some arguments (given by Cmd) that will be provided by user when container is started.   [133]

The Cmd *or* Entrypoint *is typically supposed to be a command that will run forever such as starting a server that will keep listening for requests forever. If the* Cmd *or* Entrypoint *exits then so does the Docker container. This puts the container in exited or terminated state. It still exists but is no longer running.* You can check this by running docker ps -a -f name=<container-name> which will show the container as exited. *If the container is run with the* --rm *flag then it will get auto-deleted when it exits. In that case the container name will not show up if you run* docker ps -a command.

   Do not run multiple services inside a container. A container is intended to run only one service. That service may fork into multiple processes. That is okay, but to get the most benefit out of Docker, avoid one container being responsible for multiple aspects of your overall application.   [134]

10.3.7. Debugging containers that crash on startup

Sometimes (or rather definitely at some point as your Docker usage increases) you will run into issues when a container immediately crashes on startup. Running docker ps will show the container has exited or it might not even show the container in the listing - use docker ps -a in that case to list all running as well as stopped containers. If the container is removed, then its logs will also be lost. How do you debug such a scenario? We have seen that all a container does when its started is to execute the Cmd or Entrypoint. If the Cmd or Entrypoint crashes, it will also crash the container. So we want to be able to get inside the container *before* the Cmd or Entrypoint starts running and monitor the execution of the Cmd or Entrypoint. Take the case of the fabric-orderer. When the container starts, it will start executing the orderer binary. But for the orderer binary to work it expects a proper orderer.yaml file, a proper MSP directory and so on. We would like to make sure these exist and are as expected. How can we do this? We have already seen in Section 10.3.6 that the Cmd or Entrypoint can be overridden by specifying a different value on the command line. A common newbie mistake is to specify /bin/bash or /bin/ash for the Cmd or Entrypoint with the expectation that this would allow you to log into the container so that you can do ad-hoc tasks such as verifying the orderer.yaml or MSP directory for errors before starting the orderer. For example:

```
$ docker run --name corvette hyperledger/fabric-orderer:2.0.1 /bin/ash
```

This won't work and the new container will immediately exit as we can see below:

```
$ docker ps -a --filter "name=corvette"
CONTAINER ID  IMAGE                              COMMAND      CREATED         STATUS
bd97736fed80  hyperledger/fabric-orderer:2.0.1   "/bin/bash"  52 seconds ago  Exited (0) 51
seconds ago
```

If you try to see the logs, they will be empty:

```
$ docker logs corvette
```

This is because the Cmd immediately exited. The solution is to use a Cmd that runs forever. **tail -f** provides such a command. It prints a file and *hangs* when it reaches the end of file (EOF) waiting for new data to be written to the file. We can use it like tail -f /dev/null as example. You can replace /dev/null with any other filename (but make sure the file exists). **/dev/null** is the *null device* in Unix. It immediately discards whatever is written to it. Combined with tail -f its just a way to contrive a Cmd that waits forever. The full command is shown below:

```
$ docker run -d hyperledger/fabric-orderer:2.0.1 tail -f /dev/null
3c3c520514ad0b7e9938980cb4b7ba1340697d450414437f92b8788663328331
```

Now you will be able to log into the container and perform debug tasks like inspecting orderer.yaml or verify the MSP directory is setup correctly before starting the orderer manually. In above we use the **-d** flag to run the container in *detached* mode - otherwise the terminal will get attached to the container. If you are using docker create and docker start you won't need the -d flag.

10.3.8. The Dockerfile

Docker images are created from a file conventionally known as the `Dockerfile`. We can see the `Dockerfile` for the orderer below in Listing 10. 9:   [135]

Listing 10. 9. `Dockerfile` **for** `hyperledger/fabric-orderer:2.0.1`

```
ARG GO_VER
ARG ALPINE_VER
FROM alpine:${ALPINE_VER} as base     ❶
RUN apk add --no-cache tzdata         ❷

FROM golang:${GO_VER}-alpine${ALPINE_VER} as golang
RUN apk add --no-cache \              ❸
    gcc \
    musl-dev \
    git \
    bash \
    make;
ADD . $GOPATH/src/github.com/hyperledger/fabric
WORKDIR $GOPATH/src/github.com/hyperledger/fabric

FROM golang as orderer
ARG GO_TAGS
RUN make orderer GO_TAGS=${GO_TAGS} ❹

FROM base
ENV FABRIC_CFG_PATH /etc/hyperledger/fabric
VOLUME /etc/hyperledger/fabric       ❺
VOLUME /var/hyperledger
COPY --from=orderer /go/src/github.com/hyperledger/fabric/build/bin /usr/local/bin  ❻
COPY --from=orderer /go/src/github.com/hyperledger/fabric/sampleconfig/msp
${FABRIC_CFG_PATH}/msp
COPY --from=orderer /go/src/github.com/hyperledger/fabric/sampleconfig/orderer.yaml
${FABRIC_CFG_PATH}
COPY --from=orderer /go/src/github.com/hyperledger/fabric/sampleconfig/configtx.yaml
${FABRIC_CFG_PATH}
EXPOSE 7050                           ❼
CMD ["orderer"]                       ❽
```

❶ FROM instruction is used to extend another Docker image in much the same way as classes can be inherited and extended in Java

❷ RUN instruction is used to run shell commands. Here we use `apk` - alpine package manager - to install `tzdata` package (time zone database)

❸ Install C/C++ compiler toolchain

❹ Build the `orderer` binary from the source code

❺ Create an anonymous volume

❻ Copy the `orderer` binary into the current layer

❼ The EXPOSE instruction informs Docker that the container listens on the specified network ports at runtime. EXPOSE does not make the ports of the container accessible to the host.

❽ Setup the command to be executed when a `fabric-orderer` container is run

A common confusion is the purpose of the EXPOSE command or instruction in Listing 10. 9. It acts just like a code comment. Beyond that it does not serve any purpose and is completely optional. In particular it does not publish any ports to the host. That is done by the publish (-p) flag or command when creating a container as shown in Listing 10. 2.

The Dockerfile for an image cannot be had by running docker image inspect or even the dive utility. You have to find it by some other means - mostly searching on the web and finding the actual source code. The interesting thing to note from Listing 10. 9 is that *Docker images build on top of each other just like classes in Java or C# can be extended or inherited.* This makes for a powerful ecosystem where images can be re-used as building blocks. The fabric-orderer:2.0.1 image itself builds upon alpine .alpine *is a very popular base image containing a super lightweight Linux distribution. The other base image that is commonly encountered with Docker is* debian. *Fabric 2.0 images are all* alpine *based. Fabric 1.x images were based on* debian. [136]

Although you cannot see the Dockerfile of an image, there is a command **docker history** that can be used to gain some information about how an image was created and reverse engineer it to some extent. Try running the command as follows on the fabric-orderer image and compare what it gives to the actual Dockerfile:

```
$ docker history --format "{{.CreatedBy}}" --no-trunc hyperledger/fabric-orderer:2.0.1
```

10.3.9. Installing Packages

Debian and Alpine use different package managers. The Debian package manager is apt-get whereas Alpine package manager is apk. The command to install packages in Debian looks like

```
$ apt-get install package1 package2
```

whereas the same command to install it in Alpine looks like:

```
$ apk add package1 package2
```

We can see examples of its usage in Listing 10. 9. A common task is to install the familiar bash shell in an alpine based container. It can be done like so:

```
$ apk add --no-cache bash
```

The --no-cache is an optional flag that tells the package manager not to cache the installed package. By default the apk package manager caches installed packages under /var/cache/apk. In most cases this is of no use as containers are single-serving friends and by avoiding caching them, the container size is kept small. [137]

10.3.10. Building, Downloading and Listing Images

Assuming you have a Dockerfile, an image can be built using following command:

```
$ docker image build -t foo/bar:1.2.3 .
```

This will read the Dockerfile in current directory and build an image out of it. The image will be given name of foo/bar (foo acts as a namespace to avoid conflict with another image that is also named bar such as from another vendor) and tagged 1.2.3.

There is one other way an image can be built. Sometimes you start working with a container and in course of your work install packages or do other setup related tasks. And then you want to preserve a snapshot for use later. Run the docker commit command to build an image from the container like so:

```
$ docker commit container-name image-name
```

This command should be used only for development/prototyping and you should always create a Dockerfile for use in production and check it into source control. docker commit will not generate any Dockerfile for you.

Images are downloaded by default from hub.docker.com using the docker pull command and multiple images with different tags can exist side-by-side on a machine. For example, you can download versions 1.3 and 1.4 of fabric-orderer by running commands below:

```
$ docker pull hyperledger/fabric-orderer:1.3.0
$ docker pull hyperledger/fabric-orderer:1.4.4
```

You can get a list of images on your machine by running (you guessed it!):

```
$ docker image ls
```

10.4. Provision peer using Docker in net mode

We work from $/three-org-network/biotor/peer in this section. The directory will change for different organizations.

Let us now continue to provisioning of the peer nodes. We have already provisioned the orderer in a Docker container. After provisioning the orderer, start the CouchDB containers we created in previous chapters. To run the peer inside a Docker container, change to the peer directory, and make a copy of core.yaml (call the copy docker.yaml). Then make following changes to docker.yaml. Don't forget to check the file into source control when you are done. First of all we will need to change all connection addresses to use container-name:container-port. A multi-network setup will use host-name:host-port. We also need to change the fileSystemPath to a file path expressed w.r.t. the container's filesystem. All these changes are made under the peer section as follows:

```
peer:
    address: peer0.biotor.com:8051
    chaincodeAddress: peer0.biotor.com:8052
    gossip:
        bootstrap: peer0.biotor.com:8051
        endpoint: peer0.biotor.com:8051
        externalEndpoint: peer0.biotor.com:8051
    fileSystemPath: /var/hyperledger/production
```

Assuming for a moment that all peers will run on same host in a single-node single-network setup, when you have to make the changes for another organization, normally you just need to replace peer0.biotor.com with container name of the other organization. The ports need not be changed. Thus its possible for all organizations to use container ports 8051 and 8052. The container name provides the disambiguation when the full IP address + port is considered since different containers will have different underlying IP addresses. When the ports are published to the single host (as in Listing 10. 10 later in this section), you will need to ensure there is no conflict on the host as there can't be many container ports mapped to same port on the host. In our case there is one caveat: we defined anchor peers in Ex 9.2 with certain ports e.g., anchor peer of XMed was defined as running on peer0.xmed.com:8053. Because of this, you'll have to change ports accordingly.

Confirm peer.localMspId is set to BiotorMSP. Next, we need to change the address we use to connect to CouchDB. It will become:

```
ledger:
  state:
    couchDBConfig:
        couchDBAddress: couchdb.peer0.biotor.com:5984
```

where 5984 is the Docker port at which CouchDB is running (it was set in Section 5.4.2). After this we will edit the chaincode section as follows:

```
chaincode:
    mode: net
    node:
        runtime: hyperledger/fabric-nodeenv:2.1
```

We set the chaincode.mode to net to run peer in net mode. chaincode.node.runtime sets the base Docker image that will be used to build the chaincode image. Being able to set the base image is pretty neat because it *decouples the version of* hyperledger/fabric-peer *from the version of the* fabric-shim *and Node.js. Thus you can keep on using v2.0.1 of* hyperledger/fabric-peer *but take advantage of new versions of* fabric-shim *and Node.js.* If you do not edit the chaincode.node.runtime, the default settings will resolve to hyperledger/fabric-nodeenv:latest and I have seen it fail sometimes as there is no latest image available on DockerHub. Edit the vm section like so:

```
vm:
    endpoint: unix:///host/var/run/docker.sock
    docker:
        hostConfig:
            NetworkMode: pharmanet
```

Replace `pharmanet` with name of your network as the case maybe. In the `net` mode, the peer creates and launches the chaincode container and it needs access to the Docker daemon to be able to do so. **`vm.endpoint`** tells the peer where the Docker daemon is located. The path given by `vm.endpoint` is w.r.t. to the container's filesystem. In reality the Docker daemon is located on the host and we will setup a bind mount in Listing 10. 10 in order for the path given by `vm.endpoint` to resolve to the real `sock` file on the host machine. When the peer node creates the chaincode container, the chaincode container will be attached to whatever network is given by `vm.docker.hostConfig.NetworkMode`. So we should set this variable to the same network that the peer node is attached to, otherwise the peer and chaincode container won't be able to communicate. The default value of `vm.docker.hostConfig.NetworkMode` in the `core.yaml` that comes factory-installed with Fabric is `host`.

The `host` mode is a special mode in which the container uses the networking provided by the host and it actually behaves *as if it was not containerized at all as far as networking is concerned (refer Table 10. 1)*. The container's network stack is not isolated from the host and the container shares the host's networking namespace. The container does not get its own distinct IP-address allocated. *Port publishing does not have any effect in* `host` *mode and produces a warning instead. The* `host` *mode only works on Linux hosts, and is not supported on Mac or Windows.*

Now the peer can be provisioned inside a Docker container with following script:

Listing 10. 10. Running peer node inside a Docker container. There are 3 stages. Stage 1: create container. Stage 2: copy files into container. Stage 3: run container.

```
#!/bin/bash
docker container create \
  --name peer0.biotor.com \
  --network pharmanet \
  --volume "$PWD/peer0.biotor.com":/var/hyperledger/production \    ❶
  --volume /var/run/:/host/var/run/ \                               ❷
  -p 8051:8051 \                                                    ❸
  -p 8052:8052 \                                                    ❸
  -p 9443:9443 \                                                    ❸
  --workdir /home \
  --log-opt max-file=3 \
  --log-opt max-size=10m \
  --env FABRIC_CFG_PATH=/home \
  --env FABRIC_LOGGING_SPEC=info \
  --env GODEBUG=netdns=go \                                         ❹
  hyperledger/fabric-peer:2.0.1 \
  peer node start                                                   ❺

docker cp msp peer0.biotor.com:/home                               ❻
docker cp tls peer0.biotor.com:/home                               ❻
docker cp docker.yaml peer0.biotor.com:/home/core.yaml            ❻

docker start peer0.biotor.com                                      ❼
```

❶ use a bind mount to port or inject the data from previous chapters into the Docker container

❷ use a bind mount to make the Docker daemon on /var/run/ on the host accessible to the peer container

❸ setup port publishing so that a non-Docker client can communicate with the peer. The host port must be available and not already in use.

❹ used to prevent SIGSEGV: segmentation violation error caused by cgo based DNS resolver.

❺ command to run inside the container when its started

❻ copy necessary files and directories. Note that we rename docker.yaml to core.yaml inside the container.

❼ start the container

The structure of Listing 10. 10 is similar to Listing 10. 2 and is divided into 3 stages. In first stage, we create a container. In second stage, we copy over the msp, tls directories and the docker.yaml file to the container. In the third stage, we start the container. It is assumed that the pharmanet network is setup and is attachable. CouchDB should be running in a Docker container named couchdb.peer0.biotor.com and listening at port 5984 in the container. We did this in the section on provisioning CouchDB (Section 5.4) in earlier chapters. Change the name and port if they are different in your case. There are two bind mounts we setup. The first bind mount $PWD/peer0.biotor.com:/var/hyperledger/production is to *inject the already existing data* from previous chapters so that *the peer node does not start with an empty ledger*. The second bind mount /var/run/:/host/var/run/ is to make the Docker daemon on the host accessible to the peer running inside the Docker container. Verify you have the Docker daemon running on the host and that docker.sock file is under /var/run directory of the host. If the Docker daemon is located in a different directory, then substitute that directory for /var/run in Listing 10. 10. The GODEBUG=netdns=go environment variable changes the default library that the peer uses for DNS resolution. Without it, you will run into a SIGSEGV: segmentation violation error when the peer is run in a distributed (multi-node) environment. There are two choices for netdns - go and cgo. The go resolver sends DNS requests directly to the servers listed in /etc/resolv.conf whereas the cgo-based resolver calls C library routines such as getaddrinfo and getnameinfo for DNS name resolution. [138]

When you run the Biotor peer in net mode, it will auto-magically create a chaincode container and register it against the peer. You can see the chaincode container if you run docker ps.

```
$ docker ps --format="{{.Names}}"
dev-peer0.biotor.com-mycc_1.0-fe8dda253c0f6f49d79ceaff17ae9bbe213...
```

Of course, this does assume the chaincode was installed, approved and committed on the peer as we did in Chapter 7. This is the definition of net mode. If you do not see the chaincode container, then you have a problem. Refer Section 10.5 for some troubleshooting tips.

Go ahead and provision Docker containers for the other organizations using above as a guide. Look at the logs and verify things are working properly (e.g., git.io/Jk0cG). Verify all chaincode containers are automatically started without you having to do anything about it.

Once in a while I have seen the error below when starting a peer node:

```
[gossip.comm] authenticateRemotePeer -> ERRO 023 Failed verifying signature from
172.18.0.9:8053 : Could not acquire policy manager for channel tracktrace
```

As far as I can tell, this is a bug in Fabric (FAB-17035).

Exercise 10.2

Verify you can make requests to the Dockerized network and perform transactions like you did in Chapter 8. Verify all the data created in Chapter 8 is persisted and is not lost.

10.5. Troubleshooting a chaincode container that won't start

Sometimes you might run into an issue when chaincode container does not auto-start in net mode. What makes it worse is that you might not be able to see any container logs to debug what happened. In case you run into this, use below as a guide to troubleshooting:

* Run the peer node with FABRIC_LOGGING_SPEC=dockercontroller,chaincode=debug:info and closely monitor the output from the dockercontroller and chaincode packages.
* Did you install, approve and commit the chaincode?
* Check paths to docker.sock are correctly setup and that Docker daemon is running on the host

- If the `docker.sock` is under `/var/run` on the host, take care not to mount it to `/var/run` on the peer since that would overwrite what normally goes under `/var/run` of the peer. That's why in the examples we mount it to `/host/var/run`.
- Is `vm.endpoint` correctly set to resolve to `docker.sock`?
- Is `vm.hostConfig.NetworkMode` set to the same network to which the peer node is attached? The chaincode container needs to be on the same network as the peer node otherwise it won't be able to connect to it. You can get this network by inspecting the peer container using `docker container inspect <container-name>`.
- Did you set the `peer.chaincodeAddress` correctly in `core.yaml`?
- When you installed chaincode did you build it if it was written in TypeScript? Fabric does not build TypeScript when it creates the chaincode container image. It only installs the node dependencies listed in `package.json` while building the chaincode image. I have been bit by this a few times. If this is the problem, you need to install a new version of the chaincode and upgrade it to newer version.
- Is the chaincode image getting built? You can check this by running `docker image ls`. It should have a name that is `{networkId}-{id}-{chaincode-package-identifier}`.
- Manually create a container from the chaincode image. Attach it to the same network as the peer. Start the container and log into it. Do you see the Node.js smart contract under `/usr/local/src`?
- Verify the chaincode container can connect to `peer.chaincodeAddress` using `netcat`. We saw example of using `netcat` in Section 5.1.
- Cd to the chaincode directory (`/usr/local/src`) and manually run the chaincode. Does it run successfully?
- If you are still unable to fix the problem, run the peer under a debugger without Docker and stick some breakpoints in `core/container/dockercontroller/dockercontroller.go`. You might want to debug below functions.

```
// Build is responsible for building an image if it does not already exist.
func (vm *DockerVM) Build(ccid string, metadata *persistence.ChaincodePackageMetadata,
codePackage io.Reader) (container.Instance, error) {

// Start starts a container using a previously created docker image
func (vm *DockerVM) Start(ccid string, ccType string, peerConnection
*ccintf.PeerConnection) error {
```

The `Start` function also creates the container if one doesn't exist already. The actual act of starting the container is done by following call inside the function:

```
err = vm.Client.StartContainer(containerName, nil)
```

In above `vm.Client` is nothing but the connection to the Docker daemon (`docker.sock`). Above will start the container and run `npm start` from the chaincode directory (`/usr/local/src`) inside the container. If there is an unhandled exception while running `npm start` the exception terminates the container and *Fabric removes (deletes) the container taking away any opportunity you have to inspect the logs.* That is why sometimes when the container fails to start, the peer log messages show container exited but if you run `docker ps -a` it won't show the container as it gets removed immediately. *Set breakpoints in the code so you can inspect the container before Fabric deletes it.*

10.6. Stopping and Re-starting the Network

To stop or shutdown the Docker containers, simply run (caution: this will shutdown all running containers so you may get more than what you bargained for):

```
$ docker stop $(docker ps -q)
```

The `docker stop` command sends the `SIGTERM` signal to the process running inside the container, and after a default grace period of 10s a `SIGKILL` is sent. `SIGTERM` and `SIGKILL` are standard interrupts in Unix. `SIGTERM` is a request for the process to shutdown whereas `SIGKILL` kills the process immediately. `SIGTERM` signal can be handled, ignored and blocked but `SIGKILL` cannot be handled or blocked. To re-start the nodes, simply run:

```
$ docker start couchdb.peer0.biotor.com \
couchdb.peer0.xmed.com \
couchdb.peer0.keypharmacy.com \
peer0.biotor.com \
peer0.xmed.com \
peer0.keypharmacy.com \
orderer0.biotor.com \
orderer0.xmed.com \
orderer0.keypharmacy.com
```

Do not `docker start` *the chaincode containers yourself. In* `net` *mode, the containers are supposed to be automatically started by the peer.*

Its a beautiful system when it works. In fact once its setup, it is so easy to shutdown and restart that one forgets all the labor required to create it. This chapter is quite an achievement because not only did we Dockerize the network, but we also ported all our data to the containers and we can now run the network with or without Docker.

Exercise 10.3

Whether the peer is run in `net` mode and whether the peer is run inside a Docker container are two *independent* boolean variables. Previous chapters showed how to run the peer when both are `false` and in this chapter we saw how to run the peer when both are `true`. But other combinations are possible. This exercise asks you to run the peer in `net` mode without using Docker - you may very well need to do this at some point to debug a chaincode container that does not start. The trick will be setting the `peer.chaincodeAddress` - the address chaincode container will use to connect to the peer. *Hint:* you will need to use the IP address of the computer; you can get this address by running `ifconfig | grep inet`. To complete the exercise also run peer in `dev` mode but inside Docker container.

10.7. *Using Docker Compose to provision a network*

In this chapter we have shown how to spin up Docker containers using the most fundamental docker create and docker start commands. The samples that come with Fabric use a different method to create Docker containers so let's go over it in this section. Fabric samples use the **docker-compose** CLI to bring up a network. In this method, we write a yaml file - known as Docker Compose file - which contains the configuration of all the containers, volumes and networks that we want to create and run. This file is then input to docker-compose - a CLI which creates all the resources defined in the yaml file. To help you in understanding the Fabric samples, let's analyze an excerpt of a docker compose file below. [139] Notice it is split into services, networks and volumes sections.

Listing 10. 11. Excerpt of a docker compose file

```
version: '2'                          ❶

volumes:                              ❷
  orderer2.example.com:
  orderer3.example.com:
  orderer4.example.com:
  orderer5.example.com:

networks:                             ❸
  byfn:

services:                             ❹

  orderer2.example.com:               ❺
    extends:                          ❻
      file: base/peer-base.yaml
      service: orderer-base
    environment:                      ❼
      - ORDERER_GENERAL_LISTENPORT=8050
    container_name: orderer2.example.com  ❽
    networks:                         ❾
      - byfn
    volumes:
      - ./channel-artifacts/foo.block:/var/hyperledger/orderer/orderer.foo.block ❿
      - ./crypto-
config/ordererOrganizations/example.com/orderers/orderer2.example.com/msp:/var/hyperledger/
orderer/msp
      - ./crypto-
config/ordererOrganizations/example.com/orderers/orderer2.example.com/tls/:/var/hyperledger
/orderer/tls
      - orderer2.example.com:/var/hyperledger/production/orderer ⓫
    ports:
      - 8050:8050                     ⓬
```

❶ define the version of docker compose file. Latest version is '3.8'.

❷ list the named volumes you want to create.

❸ list the networks you want to create. There are many network options that can be specified for each network.

❹ list the docker services you want to create and run.

❺ service identifier. this is not the container name.

❻ the `extends` keyword is removed and no longer supported in version 3.x. It allows you to extend another compose file.

❼ list all the environment variables you want to inject into the container here.

❽ the name of the container

❾ the networks the container will attach itself to

❿ a bind mount

⓫ a volume mount

⓬ publish ports

A compose file can thus be used to build a complete specification of the network you want to provision. We can also setup dependencies between containers using the **depends_on** keyword. For example, if we want to provision a CouchDB container before its corresponding peer container, we would add a `depends_on` keyword under the peer's configuration.

The `networks` section allows you to set various networking related options such as what driver to use. If you have the network already setup, you can use the **external** keyword to indicate the network was setup outside the compose file and `docker-compose` will not attempt to create it. This is shown below:

Listing 10. 12. The external keyword is used to tell docker-compose **that the resource has been created externally.**

```
networks:
  default:
    external:
      name: my-pre-existing-network
```

With this, `docker-compose` will look for a network called `my-pre-existing-network` and connect your app's containers to it. An error will be thrown if the external network cannot be found. A `projectname` is automatically assigned to a compose file based on the name of the directory it lives in. You can override the project name with either the `--project-name` flag or the `COMPOSE_PROJECT_NAME` environment variable when you run the `docker-compose` command. If no `networks` are defined in the compose file, `docker-compose` will automatically create a default network named `<projectname>_default`. The `external` keyword can also be used with `volumes` in a similar manner to tell `docker-compose` not to create a volume when you have already created it externally by some other means.

The **image** tag is used to define the Docker image from which a container should be instantiated. For example:

```
services:
  my_awesome_db:
    image: postgres
```

Sometimes you will come across code that looks like this:

```
services:
  web:
    build: .
```

The **build** tag instructs docker-compose to build the Dockerfile in the given directory and use the resulting image. working_dir is used to set the working directory of the container.

Once you have a compose file, it can be run using the docker-compose command. *docker-compose does not come with Docker CE installation and has to be installed separately.* Refer to online documentation for details. [140] On Linux I was able to install it with just two commands:

```
$ sudo curl -L "https://github.com/docker/compose/releases/download/1.26.0/docker-compose-
$(uname -s)-$(uname -m)" -o /usr/local/bin/docker-compose
$ sudo chmod +x /usr/local/bin/docker-compose
```

Above downloads the precompiled binary of version 1.26 of docker-compose on Linux and makes it executable. Once you have installed docker-compose, you can run it like so:

```
$ docker-compose up -d
```

This will run Docker in detached mode and bring up all the containers, networks and volumes declared in the compose file. By default it will look for a file named docker-compose.yml or docker-compose.yaml in the current directory. The filename can be changed using the -f flag. To see what is currently running you can run the familiar docker ps or you can also use:

```
$ docker-compose ps
```

To shutdown - but not delete - the running containers, run:

```
$ docker-compose stop
```

To tear down everything and delete the containers entirely, use the down command. Passing the --volumes flag will also remove any named volumes you created. So use with caution. Example below:

```
$ docker-compose down --volumes
```

For a list of all the commands, run docker-compose --help.

A detailed discussion of all the features in the Compose file is outside the scope of this chapter and I would refer the reader to online documentation. I did not use a compose file in this chapter because I wanted to illustrate the most basic and fundamental method of creating and running containers. The advantage of using docker-compose is that the entire configuration of the whole network is in one yaml file and not spread across multiple files.

One issue that I have run into with Compose is that what if there is a partial success - some of the containers are started and others fail. With docker commands I can focus on the containers which failed, whereas with Compose I have to unnecessarily shutdown working containers and start them again. It increases the development time. Turns out there is a `--no-recreate` flag that can be used with the `up` command to get the desired behavior. One nifty feature with the `docker` commands was that we are able to `docker cp` files into the container before starting it. Can we do that with `docker-compose`? Fortunately we can. Run `docker-compose up` with the `--no-start` flag which will just create the containers but not start them. Then you can `docker cp` the files into the containers and run `docker-compose up --no-recreate` to start the containers. Fabric samples extensively use (or abuse if you will) bind mounts to copy files into the container. Docker's value proposition was around providing an isolated sandboxed runtime environment. By setting up bind mounts the environment is not sandboxed and isolated from outside world. The downside of using `docker cp` is that all the code is not in one yaml file now.

`docker-compose` can create and deploy multiple instances of a Docker image - this is known as horizontally scaling an application. To use this feature you would run the `up` command with the `--scale` flag specifying the service name and number of replicas you want to create. Example below:

```
$ docker-compose up -d --scale my_service=5
```

There are several gotchas to be aware of when scaling services in above manner. The *first* is that if you scale a service, do not specify `container_name` in the compose file since the containers need distinct names. *Second*, do not publish any ports because otherwise there will be a clash and you will get a `port is already allocated` error. *Third*, you can use bind mounts and volumes but be very careful of doing a many to one mapping where multiple container directories are mapped to same directory on the host. Are you getting the desired behavior from bind mounts?

I used to think that `docker-compose` *is a command that internally translates the Compose file into* `docker` *commands (e.g.,* `docker container create` *and so on) and then runs them but that is not the way it works. It talks to the Docker daemon directly and there is no intermediate step of converting the yaml file into* `docker` *commands. Note that there is a difference between the* `docker-compose` *command and a Docker Compose file. The Compose file defines a syntax. That Compose file can also be given as input to the* `docker stack` *command which is used to deploy and orchestrate services across many machines in swarm mode. The* `docker-compose` *CLI is limited to deploying containers on one host and does not do any service orchestration. If you come* across a compose file with the **deploy** section in it under a `service` then that's a clue that the Compose file is meant to be run with `docker stack` not `docker-compose`. What do we mean by service orchestration? Say you run a service with 5 replicas. What if one replica dies? `docker stack` will automatically bring up and instantiate another replica and this is an example of service orchestration. `docker-compose` does none of that.

Table 10. 2 shows a taxonomy of Docker commands in increasing order of power in what they can do.

Table 10. 2. Taxonomy of docker commands ranging from most basic to most advanced.

Command	Notes
docker create/start/run	the most fundamental way to create and run individual Docker containers
docker-compose	a separate CLI tool - *not part of Docker installation* - that can be used to run containers on a *single* host
docker service	can be used to deploy and orchestrate a service across *multiple* nodes in swarm mode
docker stack	the ultimate. can be used to deploy and manage a multi-service application across many nodes in swarm mode

Some online docs say that docker-compose can be used against a swarm instance and can run your apps across multiple hosts. [141] Unfortunately, that documentation is wrong. You can run docker-compose against a swarm but you will get following message:

```
WARNING: The Docker Engine you're using is running in swarm mode.
Compose does not use swarm mode to deploy services to multiple nodes in a swarm. All
containers will be scheduled on the current node.
To deploy your application across the swarm, use `docker stack deploy`.
```

One big advantage of deploying containers using the docker commands as we have done in this chapter vs. using docker-compose as done by Fabric samples is that with our method the code is portable when you want to run the containers in swarm mode across multiple machines. We just run the same commands but on the respective machines. docker-compose cannot deploy to multiple nodes.

Exercise 10.4

Write a docker-compose.yaml file that can be used to Dockerize the 3-org network with docker-compose. Better yet, write a file that can be used with docker service or docker stack.

10.8. Summary

- The docker run command can be thought of as a docker create followed by an immediate docker start. It does not leave you any room to do intermediate tasks such as copying files with docker cp.
- There are (mainly) two types of Docker networks: *bridge* and *overlay*. A *bridge* requires all containers to run on the *same* host. An *overlay* network removes this restriction but requires Docker to be run in *swarm* mode. It is possible to create an overlay without using a swarm but it is just an academic exercise not worth the effort.
- Volumes or bind mounts can be used to persist data even after a container is removed.
- Use docker inspect command to inspect a container, image or any other Docker object.
- The Entrypoint or Cmd define what command is executed when a container is started. If both are set Cmd becomes an argument to the Entrypoint. When the Entrypoint or Cmd exits, so does the container.

- Docker images are created from a `Dockerfile`. The `Dockerfile` itself is lost in the image but the `docker history` command can be used to get some information on how an image was created.
- Multiple Docker images with different tags can be downloaded and can exist side-by-side on the host.
- Always setup log rotation when creating a Docker container to prevent the logs from growing infinite in size.
- It is not possible to make any changes to a container's config other than renaming it after the container has been created.
- `docker-compose` is a tool that can deploy containers on a *single* host from a yaml config file. It does not do any service orchestration and has to be installed separately.

10.9. Further Reading

- Docker Secrets: docs.docker.com/engine/swarm/secrets/

[118] en.wikipedia.org/wiki/Docker_(software)

[119] The adventurous reader can even run Docker inside Docker. See stackoverflow.com/questions/27879713/is-it-ok-to-run-docker-from-inside-docker. This is not recommended and I just mention it for information sake.

[120] source.android.com/

[121] another apt analogy is Chrome - Google's web browser - and Chromium - the open source project from which it is derived.

[122] docs.docker.com/engine/swarm/swarm-tutorial/#open-protocols-and-ports-between-the-hosts

[123] success.docker.com/article/different-types-of-volumes

[124] github.com/docker/cli/pull/1273

[125] stackoverflow.com/a/40322275/147530

[126] docs.docker.com/storage/volumes/#remove-anonymous-volumes

[127] github.com/moby/moby/issues/32582

[128] docs.docker.com/config/containers/logging/json-file/

[129] refer docs.docker.com/engine/reference/commandline/ps for more information

[130] Press `Ctrl+a` followed by `?` to see a list of all screen key bindings.

[131] a list of supported log drivers can be found in docs.docker.com/config/containers/logging/configure/

[132] github.com/wagoodman/dive

[133] A good article on `Entrypoint` vs. `Cmd` is available at www.ctl.io/developers/blog/post/dockerfile-entrypoint-vs-cmd/

[134] More on this at docs.docker.com/config/containers/multi-service_container/

[135] github.com/hyperledger/fabric/blob/v2.0.1/images/orderer/Dockerfile

[136] A comparison of `debian` vs. `alpine` can be found at nickjanetakis.com/blog/benchmarking-debian-vs-alpine-as-a-base-docker-image

[137] stackoverflow.com/a/49119046/147530

[138] Read more about it at: medium.com/@Alibaba_Cloud/hyperledger-fabric-deployment-on-alibaba-cloud-environment-sigsegv-problem-analysis-and-solutions-9a708313f1a4

[139] the code is borrowed from github.com/hyperledger/fabric-samples/blob/v2.0.1/first-network/docker-compose-etcdraft2.yaml

[140] docs.docker.com/compose/install/

[141] docs.docker.com/compose/production/

Chapter 11. Securing Communications with TLS

This chapter covers what you need to do to turn on TLS in Fabric. We covered TLS in Section 4.6. Please review that section before moving forward. Whether or not you want to use TLS in your application will be a personal choice depending on your risk tolerance. You will find it does sometimes create lot of complexity and headaches when things are not configured properly. This chapter will make use of the `tls` folder you copied under `orderer` and `peer` subdirectories of `three-org-network` but never used earlier in the book.

11.1. Provisioning peers and orderers with TLS

In this section, we describe the changes that need to be made to `orderer.yaml` and `core.yaml`.

11.1.1. Changes to `orderer.yaml`

In order to turn on TLS on the orderer, the `orderer.yaml` has to be modified like so:

Listing 11. 1. Turning on TLS on the orderer

```
TLS:
    Enabled: true                    ❶
    PrivateKey: tls/server.key
    Certificate: tls/server.crt
    RootCAs:
      - tls/ca.crt
    ClientAuthRequired: true         ❷
    ClientRootCAs:
      - tls/ca.crt
```

❶ Turns on one-way TLS
❷ Turns on two-way or mutual TLS

Recall the TLS section is only applicable when the orderer is communicating with "rest of the world". *It does not apply when the orderer is communicating with other orderers.* TLS.Enabled: true turns basic *one-way* TLS on when the orderer will send down its TLS certificate to a client (the client could be a peer or a web application) but will not authenticate the client in turn i.e., it will allow any client to connect to it. Setting TLS.ClientAuthRequired to true *in addition* to TLS.Enabled: true will turn on *two-way* or *mutual* authentication where the orderer will also authenticate a client before allowing it to connect - this will prevent any random client from making a connection; only whitelisted clients will be able to connect to the orderer.

The PrivateKey and Certificate are used to provide the private key and public certificate of the orderer. Make sure the files exist and edit the paths if you have the key and cert stored somewhere else. The RootCAs is an array. Usually you only need one element in this array and that should store the complete certificate chain of the CA(s) who issued the certificate in Certificate variable. When in doubt, use the openssl verify command to verify that the certificate in

Certificate validates against the CA in RootCAs. For example:

```
$ openssl verify -CAfile ca.crt server.crt
server.crt: OK
```

Verifying the certificate on the server is not enough. The client must have the CA under RootCAs in its list of trusted CAs otherwise it will reject the certificate from the server (orderer). The ClientRootCAs is applicable only when ClientAuthRequired: true. ClientRootCAs is an array which will contain the certificates of CAs against which the orderer will validate the client certificate. The RootCAs and ClientRootCAs need not be the same - hence the provision of two different variables.

11.1.2. Changes to core.yaml

To turn on TLS on peers, edit core.yaml like so:

Listing 11. 2. Turning on TLS on the peer

```
tls:
    enabled:  true
    clientAuthRequired: true    ❶
    cert:
        file: tls/server.crt
    key:
        file: tls/server.key
    rootcert:
        file: tls/ca.crt
    clientRootCAs:
        files:
           - tls/ca.crt
    clientKey:                  ❷
        file: tls/server.key
    clientCert:                 ❷
        file: tls/server.crt
```

❶ peer will only allow clients who are endorsed by the CAs in clientRootCAs to connect to it

❷ The certificate and key to use when this peer is acting as a client. For example, when it connects to another peer or an orderer.

The meanings of various fields should be known by now and they mirror TLS settings in the orderer. rootcert is cert of CA that issued cert.file and clientRootCAs are the list of trusted CAs against which a client's certificate will be validated. We use same CA for both rootcert and clientRootCAs but that is not necessary. We also use same cert and key for both server and client mode but again that is not necessary and due to the fact that cryptogen does not generate a separate client cert and key.

 Note that you can run peers with TLS on even though CouchDB is not running with any TLS. This is because in the peer-CouchDB relationship, the peer is a client and CouchDB is the server. If it was the other way round, there would have been a problem.

11.2. Performing channel and chaincode administration with TLS

This section describes changes to the peer CLI in Chapter 7. The first thing you need to do is copy over TLS CA certs of other organizations as these will be needed to establish TLS connection to peers of other organizations. From the biotor/admin folder:

```
$ mkdir tls/cacerts
$ cp tls/ca.crt tls/cacerts/biotor-ca.crt
$ cp ../../xmed/tls/ca.crt tls/cacerts/xmed-ca.crt
$ cp ../../keypharmacy/tls/ca.crt tls/cacerts/keypharmacy-ca.crt
```

Perform similar steps for all other organizations. After that we will configure peer.tls in core.yaml as follows:

Listing 11. 3. Configuring TLS on peer client CLI

```
peer:
    tls:
        enabled: true                  ❶
        clientAuthRequired: true       ❷
        rootcert:
            file: tls/ca.crt
        clientRootCAs:
            files:
                - tls/ca.crt
        clientKey:
            file: tls/client.key
        clientCert:
            file: tls/client.crt
```

❶ Set to true if TLS is enabled on the server that the CLI will connect to

❷ Set to true if client authentication is enabled on the server that the CLI will connect to

The peer.tls section contains TLS pertinent settings when peer CLI is communicating with a peer. The TLS settings when peer CLI is communicating with an orderer are set elsewhere. Please keep this in mind. If the server (given by peer.address in core.yaml) is running with one-way TLS you will set tls.enabled to true. If the server is running with two-way mutual TLS you need to set both tls.enabled and tls.clientAuthRequired to true. tls.rootcert is the CA cert against which client will validate certificate sent by server. tls.clientRootCAs contains the cert of the CA who issued client's TLS certificate. And finally tls.clientKey and tls.clientCert contain the client's key and certificate that are used only when mutual TLS is enabled on the server.

The TLS settings when the peer client connects to an orderer are set on the command line using following flags:

Table 11. 1. Command line flags controlling TLS settings when peer client connects to an orderer.

Flag	Purpose
`--tls`	must be set if orderer has TLS enabled
`--clientauth`	must be set if orderer has mutual TLS enabled (a.k.a. client authentication)
`--cafile`	used to provide the CA cert against which server's certificate will be validated
`--certfile`	used to provide client cert (only applicable in case of mutual TLS)
`--keyfile`	used to provide client key (only applicable in case of mutual TLS)
`--ordererTLSHostnameOverride`	overrides the hostname used to validate the orderer. Very useful if the `subjectAltName` (SAN) section in orderer's certificate does not have the name or IP that you are using to connect to the orderer.

Thus, if the orderer was running with one-way TLS the command to create a channel would be modified as follows:

Listing 11. 4. Command to create a channel assuming orderer is running with one-way TLS

```
$ peer channel create -o orderer0.biotor.com:7050 -c tracktrace -f channel.tx --tls
--cafile tls/ca.crt
```

The `--tls` switch is used to indicate that the orderer is running with TLS on and causes the client to perform a TLS handshake. The `--cafile` contains the certificate of the CA against which the orderer's certificate would be validated. If the orderer was running with two-way mutual TLS you would use:

Listing 11. 5. Command to create a channel assuming orderer is running with two-way mutual TLS

```
$ peer channel create -o orderer0.biotor.com:7050 -c tracktrace -f channel.tx --tls
--cafile tls/ca.crt --clientauth --certfile tls/client.crt --keyfile tls/client.key
```

Here the `--certfile` and `--keyfile` are used to provide the certificate and key the client will use to authenticate itself to the server. What if the `subjectAltName` (SAN) section of the orderer's certificate does not contain `orderer0.biotor.com` (the address being used to connect to the orderer)? The client will reject the certificate. `--ordererTLSHostnameOverride` is a way to get around this problem. *Set `--ordererTLSHostnameOverride` equal to any name or IP address that appears in the SAN section and the client will accept the certificate.* Call it a hack if you will. All channel and chaincode administration commands that require peer to connect to orderer would need to be updated to use `--tls` and `--clientauth` as well.

The commands in Chapter 7 where the peer CLI connects to more than one peer will need to use a **`--tlsRootCertFiles`** command-line flag. For example, the chaincode commit command would become as follows:

```
peer lifecycle chaincode commit \
   -o orderer0.biotor.com:7050 \
   --channelID tracktrace \
   --name mycc \
   --version 1.0 \
   --sequence 1 \
   --signature-policy "AND ('BiotorMSP.peer','XMedMSP.peer','KeyPharmacyMSP.peer')" \
   --peerAddresses peer0.biotor.com:8051 \
   --peerAddresses peer0.xmed.com:8053 \
   --peerAddresses peer0.keypharmacy.com:8055 \
   --tlsRootCertFiles tls/cacerts/biotor-ca.crt \
   --tlsRootCertFiles tls/cacerts/xmed-ca.crt \
   --tlsRootCertFiles tls/cacerts/keypharmacy-ca.crt \
   --tls \
   --cafile tls/ca.crt \
   --clientauth \
   --certfile tls/client.crt \
   --keyfile tls/client.key \
   --waitForEvent
```

There is a 1:1 mapping and correspondence between `--peerAddresses` and `--tlsRootCertFiles`. The order also matters. Thus `tls/cacerts/biotor-ca.crt` is matched and associated with `peer0.biotor.com`.

11.3. Node.js Application

The Node.js application of Section 8.10 will need to be modified as follows.

11.3.1. Populate wallet with an Identity to be used for TLS client authentication

Create an identity in the wallet that will provide TLS cert and key for client authentication. We can do that by running (from `$/client-application`):

```
$ USER_NAME=Alice.Tls \
PUBLIC_CERT=${PWD}/../three-org-network/crypto-
config/peerOrganizations/biotor.com/users/User1\@biotor.com/tls/client.crt \
PRIVATE_KEY=${PWD}/../three-org-network/crypto-
config/peerOrganizations/biotor.com/users/User1\@biotor.com/tls/client.key \
MSP_ID=BiotorMSP \
node addToWallet.js
```

Verify the `wallet` folder now has a `Alice.Tls.id` file in it. Substitute the paths in `PUBLIC_CERT` and `PRIVATE_KEY` if needed.

11.3.2. Configure `connection.yaml` file to use TLS

Create a `tls` folder under `$client-application` and copy over the `tls/cacerts` from `biotor/admin` to this folder. Then make following changes to the `Biotor-connection.yaml` file. Its better to create a separate yaml file to be used in TLS mode.

Listing 11. 6. Changes to `connection.yaml` **to use TLS**

```
peers:
  peer0.Biotor.com:
    url: grpcs://peer0.biotor.com:8051  ❶
    grpcOptions:
      # ssl-target-name-override:       ❷
    tlsCACerts:
      path: tls/biotor-ca.crt            ❸
```

❶ We use `grpcs` instead of `grpc`

❷ This is an optional field and can be used to override the hostname used for hostname validation

❸ Certificate of the CA against which server will be validated

11.3.3. Changes to application code

Finally in the Node.js code we need to add `clientTlsIdentity` to the `connectionOptions` that are passed to the `Gateway` class. Do this only if server has client authentication turned on.

```
let connectionOptions = {
    identity: 'Alice',
    clientTlsIdentity: 'Alice.Tls',
    wallet: wallet,
    discovery: { enabled: true }
};
```

That's it! You should now be able to run the Node.js app. Use the `HFC_LOGGING` variable to output debug logs if you run into any issues. Below are sample messages (git.io/Jkuwq):

```
[ServiceEndpoint]: waitForReady - Successfully connected to remote gRPC server
peer0.xmed.com:8053 url:grpcs://peer0.xmed.com:8053
[Endorser]: sendProposal[peer0.keypharmacy.com:8055] - Received proposal response from peer
"grpcs://peer0.keypharmacy.com:8055": status - 200
[Endorser]: sendProposal[peer0.biotor.com:8051] - Received proposal response from peer
"grpcs://peer0.biotor.com:8051": status - 200
[Endorser]: sendProposal[peer0.xmed.com:8053] - Received proposal response from peer
"grpcs://peer0.xmed.com:8053": status - 200
[DiscoveryHandler]: commit - Successfully sent transaction to the committer
orderer0.keypharmacy.com:7052
[Transaction]: submit[create] - commit response {"status":"SUCCESS","info":""}
```

The interesting thing to note here is that we never specified the TLS CA certs of XMed and KeyPharmacy in Listing 11. 6. And also we never added the TLS CA certs of XMed and KeyPharmacy to the `clientRootCAs` in Listing 11. 2. The server-side can be explained because maybe Fabric gets the TLS CA certs of other organizations from the genesis block. But not having to provide the TLS CA certs in Listing 11. 6 is interesting. This concludes the chapter.

Chapter 12. Handling Data Privacy

This chapter covers:

- Implications of storing data on the blockchain
- Ways to protect data stored on the blockchain

Code for this chapter is in `$/data-privacy-lesson`

At this point in the book, we have written our smart contract, deployed it onto a network, performed transactions on it and also containerized the network. Let us now take a pause and look at a snapshot of transactions as shown in Figure 12. 1.

		id		createdBy		lastModifiedBy	metadata		owner
☐	🗐	00000		x509::/C=US/ST=California/L=San Fra...	x509::/C=US/ST=California/L=San Fra...	Sample Drug 1		XMedMSP
☐	🗐	00001		x509::/C=US/ST=California/L=San Fra...	x509::/C=US/ST=California/L=San Fra...	Sample Drug 2		BiotorMSP
☐	🗐	00002		x509::/C=US/ST=California/L=San Fra...	x509::/C=US/ST=California/L=San Fra...	Sample Drug 3		BiotorMSP
☐	🗐	00003		x509::/C=US/ST=California/L=San Fra...	x509::/C=US/ST=California/L=San Fra...	Sample Drug 4		BiotorMSP
☐	🗐	00004		x509::/C=US/ST=California/L=San Fra...	x509::/C=US/ST=California/L=San Fra...	Sample Drug 5		BiotorMSP
☐	🗐	00005		x509::/C=US/ST=California/L=San Fra...	x509::/C=US/ST=California/L=San Fra...	Sample Drug 6		BiotorMSP
☐	🗐	00006		x509::/C=US/ST=California/L=San Fra...	x509::/C=US/ST=California/L=San Fra...	Sample Drug 7		BiotorMSP
☐	🗐	00007		x509::/C=US/ST=California/L=San Fra...	x509::/C=US/ST=California/L=San Fra...	Sample Drug 8		BiotorMSP
☐	🗐	00008		x509::/C=US/ST=California/L=San Fra...	x509::/C=US/ST=California/L=San Fra...	Sample Drug 9		BiotorMSP
☐	🗐	00009		x509::/C=US/ST=California/L=San Fra...	x509::/C=US/ST=California/L=San Fra...	Sample Drug 10		BiotorMSP
☐	🗐	00010		x509::/C=US/ST=California/L=San Fra...	x509::/C=US/ST=California/L=San Fra...	Sample Drug 11		BiotorMSP

Figure 12. 1. A snapshot of the world state data stored in CouchDB

Do you see anything wrong in Figure 12. 1? Well it is this. *Anyone can easily calculate the manufacturing volume of a drug.* As an exercise write a CouchDB query that returns the number of records where metadata equals Sample Drug 1. To take a real-world case, imagine Sample Drug 1 was Lipitor - a blockbuster drug manufactured by Pfizer to control cholesterol. If Pfizer was participating in the consortium and storing their data on the blockchain, its competitors could mine the data and calculate how much quantity of Lipitor - or any other drug for that matter - Pfizer was producing per month or year. Data like this is usually deemed *business intelligence* and companies safeguard it and do not want it to be known to their competitors. This is just one example of the implications of storing data on the blockchain but enough to set off alarms and lead us to the topic of data privacy. Let us see how to fix this issue in this chapter. Put your hacker hat on as you read this chapter.

12.1. Ways of Inspecting the Ledger

The data in Fabric blockchain is stored under `${peer.fileSystemPath}/ledgersData/chains/chains` where `${peer.fileSystemPath}` is given in core.yaml. It is binary encoded and there is no convenient utility like cat that can print out the ledger contents in any intelligible form to a human. The world state is separate from the blockchain but derived from it and comes in two forms - LevelDB (default) or CouchDB.

When I was new to Fabric I thought I could store the data in LevelDB instead of CouchDB and that would fix the issue of data privacy because LevelDB does not come with any standalone CLI or GUI. In other words it is not queryable outside Fabric, that is why it is known as an embedded database. But that does not solve the problem. The data on the blockchain can still be inspected even if you use LevelDB. For example, we can use a combination of peer channel fetch and configtxlator commands to inspect the ledger. A sample script showing how to do that is provided in Listing 12. 1:

Listing 12. 1. Script to fetch a block and decode it

```bash
#!/bin/bash
peer channel fetch $1 $1.block -o orderer0.biotor.com:7050 -c tracktrace    ❶
configtxlator proto_decode --input $1.block --type common.Block             ❷
```

❶ Fetch block from the orderer. $1 returns the first argument passed to the script.
❷ Decode from protobuf to JSON format

You would run this script from Biotor's admin or user directory. Save above script as get-block.sh and then execute it modifying the orderer address as necessary and passing it the block number to be fetched. For example:

```
$ ./get-block.sh 10
```

This will print out a long JSON output showing all the details stored in a block. Try it. The lesson is that *using LevelDB does not protect the data from being mined or viewable*. It makes it harder to do so (just try parsing out the output you get from Listing 12. 1) since one cannot use CouchDB API to query the data but cannot stop it.

You can also print the blocks from Node.js using the script in Listing 12. 2 passing in an instance of the Network object. We saw how to create an instance of Network in Section 8.10.6.

Listing 12. 2. TypeScript function to get block by its number using the qscc system chaincode.

```typescript
const { BlockDecoder } = require('fabric-common');

async function queryBlock(network: Network, blockNum: number) {
    const channelName = network.getChannel().name;
    const contract = network.getContract('qscc');      ❶
    const resultByte = await contract.evaluateTransaction(
        'GetBlockByNumber',                             ❷
        channelName,                                    ❸
        String(blockNum)                                ❹
    );
    return BlockDecoder.decode(resultByte);             ❺
}
```

❶ qscc is the system chaincode or smart contract used to query blocks

❷ GetBlockByNumber function can be used to fetch block by its number

❸ The channel that we want to fetch blocks from

❹ The block number we want to fetch

❺ Convert protobuf encoded bytes to JavaScript object

The script above is not 1:1 compatible with Listing 12. 1. There is some additional processing you will have to do to the result from Listing 12. 2 to get it in the form that is returned from Listing 12. 1 that is left as an exercise for the reader.

You can even use Blockchain Explorer (github.com/hyperledger/blockchain-explorer) which as its name suggests provides a graphical user interface to inspect the data on the ledger. A screenshot of Blockchain Explorer is shown in Figure 12. 2.

Figure 12. 2. Using Blockchain Explorer to inspect the ledger.

Explaining it will require a separate chapter. Since the topic of this chapter is data privacy we leave running Explorer as an exercise for the reader. Refer to $/blockchain-explorer in the book's code repository for help and instructions on how to get started.

12.2. Using Fingerprints to Protect Data Privacy

Fabric, in its official documentation, provides us with two main tools to achieve data privacy - channels and private data collections. Channels as we know are just blockchains. The idea is to create multiple blockchains to limit data sharing just like one creates a group of friends and another group of close friends or family members in Facebook to limit what data is shared with whom. We will come to private data collections later. I want to illustrate a general pattern on how we can achieve data privacy without using any of these features and which is applicable to any blockchain not just Fabric. The idea itself is well-known in the industry and not a secret. It is simply this - *instead of storing the confidential data on the blockchain, we store a fingerprint of that data. The fingerprint should be verifiable and random enough so that the confidential data cannot be unmasked from the fingerprint.* Let's see how to do it in our present case.

The confidential data in our case is the owner of the asset. Instead of storing the owner of an asset in plain text, we will mask it behind a random hash known as a fingerprint and store the fingerprint on the blockchain. The idea is illustrated in Figure 12. 3. The hash should be a secure cryptographic hash. We use the double SHA256 hash in this chapter.

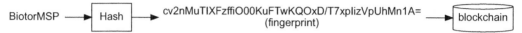

Figure 12. 3. Protecting confidential data by storing a fingerprint of it on the blockchain and how *not* to do it.

So now the owner field in Figure 12. 1 will store a hash instead of BiotorMSP in clear text. Astute readers will notice a bug in this method which is that one can simply use the hash to lookup the true owner. If we already know a-priori the list of possible values the owner field can take, we can a-priori compute a lookup table of (owner, hash) and use it to reverse engineer the owner. The lookup table itself is shown in Table 12. 1 for the present problem.

Table 12. 1. Precomputed lookup table that can be used to reverse engineer the owner from the hash

Owner	Hash
BiotorMSP	cv2nMuTIXFzffiO00KuFTwKQOxD/T7xpIizVpUhMn1A=
XMedMSP	kkRU3kFrLyQNgWQ4FcHuyACgfZbQXKDPr+VP01y9/54=
KeyPharmacyMSP	70M2W3zp0rvRBWtXNE8lOaixw4wSsPEV7/bh3ld339Q=

This is known as a *dictionary attack*. Looks like we haven't accomplished anything. *The problem is that our hash or fingerprint is not random enough so that the confidential data cannot be unmasked from it.* That condition is violated.

To fix the issue, we mix a *salt* with the owner field *prior* to hashing it. This is illustrated in Figure 12. 4.

Figure 12. 4. Correct way of using fingerprints to protect confidential data. The salt acts like a key or password to unlock the fingerprint and is not stored on the blockchain.

The actual mechanics of mixing the *salt* are as follows. The owner field is converted into a byte array. The salt is also converted into a byte array. The salt could be a random string of bytes or it could be non-random but the idea is to keep it secret. It is like a *password* or *key*. The two byte arrays are concatenated together - it doesn't matter which one comes first as long as you stick to a convention - and the concatenated byte array is input to the hash function. *The salt is never stored on the blockchain and a different salt will be used per transaction.* Now the owner field in Figure 12. 1 will appear completely random and unpredictable. *There is no way to reverse engineer the owner from the fingerprint.* Listing 12. 3 shows `create` method of the resulting smart contract.

Listing 12. 3. `create` **method of revised smart contract to protect identity of true owner of the asset.**

```
@Transaction()
public async create(ctx: Context, assetId: string, fingerprint: string): Promise<void> {
    // aliter: ctx.stub.getCreator().mspid;
    const mspId = ctx.clientIdentity.getMSPID();
    if (mspId !== "BiotorMSP") {
        throw new Error("you do not have permission to create an asset");
    }

    const exists = await this.assetExists(ctx, assetId);
    if (exists) {
        throw new Error(`The asset ${assetId} already exists`);
    }

    const buffer = Buffer.from(fingerprint);
    await ctx.stub.putState(assetId, buffer);
}
```

Note that Biotor will have to store a lookup table of (`assetId, salt`) off-chain in a private database otherwise it itself will run into trouble when proving later on that it owns an asset. This will become clear in a moment when we look at the `update` method. At first glance the new `create` method is not all that different from what we had in Section 3.4.1. In fact they are practically identical. The difference is that whereas in Section 3.4.1 we store all the metadata corresponding to an asset in clear text on the blockchain, in Listing 12. 3 we will only store fingerprint of the owner on the blockchain. You may be feeling confused and cheated as to how have we protected the identity of the true owner in Listing 12. 3 when it contains code to verify the call is coming from BiotorMSP. *The answer is that the code is running like a black-box. The assumption is no one can peek inside the black-box while the code is running. For example, no one is able to run it under a debugger and inspect the internals. We can only see the result of the run in the form of data that gets stored on the blockchain which we went over in Section 12.1 or data that is returned from the function call.* Make sure you understand this point. *As per the design requirements of the problem itself, the smart contract should be able to authorize the caller but once the function call has completed no one inspecting the ledger should be able to infer who was the owner of the asset.*

Let us now see how to transfer an asset from one owner to another. The modified `update` method is shown below in Listing 12. 4.

Listing 12. 4. Modified update **method that preserves data privacy of asset's owner.**

```
@Transaction()
public async update(ctx: Context, assetId: string, newFingerprint: string): Promise<void> {
    const buffer = await ctx.stub.getState(assetId);
    if (buffer && buffer.length > 0) {
        const oldFingerprint = buffer.toString();
        const mspId = ctx.clientIdentity.getMSPID();
        const transientMap = ctx.stub.getTransient();          ❶
        const key = transientMap.get("key");                    ❷
        const saltedMsp =
            Buffer.concat([key, Buffer.from(mspId)]);           ❸
        const digest = hash256(saltedMsp).toString("base64");   ❹
        if (digest === oldFingerprint) {                        ❺
            await ctx.stub.putState(assetId, Buffer.from(newFingerprint));
        } else {
            throw new Error("You do not have permission to modify this asset");
        }
    } else {
        throw new Error(`The asset ${assetId} does not exist`);
    }
}
```

❶ getTransient is used to get *transient data* passed to the function or smart contract. *Transient data* (unlike function arguments) is never recorded onto the blockchain in any form.

❷ This is the salt that was used to generate the old fingerprint. Only true owner will know this salt.

❸ Mix the salt with the MSP of the caller.

❹ Compute hash of the salted MSP. Refer Listing 12. 5 for implementation of hash256.

❺ Test if the computed hash matches the hash stored on the blockchain.

Let's run through an example. Suppose Biotor wants to transfer an asset to XMed. It will request XMed to provide it the new fingerprint of the asset. This communication and exchange takes place off-chain out-of-band. Then a person or agent belonging to Biotor invokes the function in Listing 12. 4 passing the salt corresponding to the asset in question which only Biotor knows. *The salt is not passed as part of function arguments but it is passed as **transient data***. The reason is that function arguments (assetId and newFingerprint in Listing 12. 4) get recorded onto the blockchain so if the *salt* were passed as function argument, it would get recorded onto the blockchain and a hacker could use it to compromise data privacy. *Transient data is never recorded onto the blockchain*. It is queried inside a smart contract using the ctx.stub.getTransient() call. The update function then mixes the *salt* with the MSP of the caller, hashes it and compares the result to the fingerprint stored on the blockchain. *The salt acts like a key or password that is used to unlock the fingerprint*. Only true owner of the asset knows this key. Once the fingerprint is unlocked, validation has passed and the asset can be transferred over to the new owner.

The hash256 used in Listing 12. 4 is a function that computes double SHA256 of its input. Listing 12. 5 shows implementation of hash256 and is borrowed from bitcoinjs-lib.

Listing 12. 5. Functions to compute SHA256 and double SHA256 hashes using native `crypto` **library of Node.js.**

```
import * as crypto from 'crypto';

export function sha256(data: Buffer): Buffer {
    return crypto.createHash('sha256').update(data).digest();
}

export function hash256(data: Buffer): Buffer {
    return sha256(sha256(data));
}
```

Before XMed makes the purchase from Biotor, it would also want to verify that Biotor is the legitimate owner of the asset. After all, that is the purpose of our blockchain! To prevent counterfeiting by verifying the legitimate owner of the drug. There are several ways of doing this. One is as follows. We could expose a method `getFingerprint(assetId: string)` to query the fingerprint stored on the blockchain. XMed could call this function to get the fingerprint. And it will get the salt to unlock the fingerprint off-chain and out-of-band from Biotor and run the hash to verify Biotor is indeed the true owner. This is shown in Figure 12. 5.

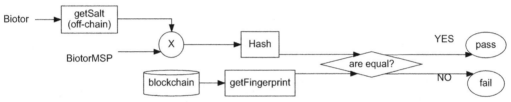

Figure 12. 5. Verifying owner of an asset. In above Biotor is claiming to be the owner. Substitute Biotor for purported owner.

Another method is shown below in Listing 12. 6.

Listing 12. 6. `verify` **function to prove ownership of an asset.**

```
public async verify(ctx: Context, assetId: string, email: string): Promise<void> {
    const oldFingerprint = this.getFingerprint(assetId);        ❶
    const digest = this.computeDigest(ctx);                     ❷
    if (digest === oldFingerprint) {
        await pass(assetId, email);                            ❸
    } else {
        await fail(assetId, email);                            ❹
    }
}
```

❶ Get the fingerprint stored on the blockchain corresponding to given asset.
❷ Compute the digest as illustrated in Listing 12. 4.
❸ Send notification to buyer confirming caller is owner of the asset.
❹ Send notification to buyer that validation has failed.

An agent belonging to Biotor will call this method passing it email address of XMed and the salt required to prove ownership. The method will verify Biotor is registered owner repeating the logic we have discussed previously in Listing 12. 4 and depending on whether the validation succeeds or fails, it will notify XMed of the outcome. The difference between this and Figure 12. 5 is that *in this case, the salt is never disclosed to XMed*. This is nothing but an example of zero-knowledge proof (ZKP) in action. Biotor has proved it owns the asset without giving away the secret itself. You can substitute email notification with any other form of notification you choose and add appropriate controls so recipient can verify the incoming message is genuine.

Exercise 12.1

Consider following code to compute the digest in which the salt or key is *never mixed* with MSP ID of the caller:

```
private computeDigest(ctx: Context): string {
    const transientMap = ctx.stub.getTransient();
    const key = transientMap.get("key");
    return hash256(key).toString("base64");
}
```

The reasoning is that since a cryptographic hash cannot be reverse engineered, if the caller knows the pre-image of the fingerprint stored on the blockchain, that fingerprint could only have come from the caller and thus the caller has demonstrated ownership of the asset. Would you use this function to compute the digest? Why or why not? *Hint:* Do not use this method.

12.2.1. Mutable and Immutable data

In general when you consider your application, there will be some confidential data that will change in response to transactions such as ownership of the asset. But there is likely to be some data which will be immutable. For example, in case of drug supply chain when an asset changes hands, the contents of the drug, its expiry date, date of manufacturing, who manufactured the drug etc. do not change. And a buyer should be able to verify that information prior to purchase. To address this there are two sets of fingerprints you should store. One for the mutable data which changes as we saw earlier and another one which does not change and is frozen and permanent. In case of drugs, there is something known as a *SGTIN - Serialized Global Trade Item Number.* The SGTIN together with the Expiry Date and Lot Number is encoded into a *GS1 Data Matrix.* GS1 stands for Global Standards organization - an organization like IEEE which develops standards. The Data Matrix is like a scannable QR code using which one can lookup all sorts of details about a product from a database. In case of drugs this database is the GDSN - Global Data Synchronization Network. The GS1 Data Matrix is example of an immutable data and an immutable fingerprint of the Data Matrix could be stored on the blockchain when the product is created by the manufacturer.

Summarizing, this is the general recipe. Divide the data to be stored onto the blockchain into confidential and non-confidential categories. The non-confidential data can be stored as-is. Divide the confidential data into two classes - immutable and mutable and store fingerprints of the two on the blockchain. The fingerprint of the immutable data will never change. The fingerprint of the mutable or dynamic data will change as its ownership or other changeable attributes change. The actual data is stored off-chain and exchanged out-of-band between businesses. And businesses can hash the data and verify the hash against the fingerprint on the blockchain to ensure it is correct.

12.2.2. What blockchain cannot solve

Remember the data stored on the blockchain is a digital representation of a physical asset. Blockchain cannot store the physical asset itself - drugs in our example. What if this digital representation is wrong? What we mean is that what if someone puts the wrong drug in a bottle labelled for something else or steals a Data Matrix from a package and affixes it to a counterfeit drug? Blockchain cannot solve that. This is the last-mile problem. To solve this one has to use tamper-evident packaging.

This is one reason why an ideal application of blockchain is finance because the asset there is purely digital. Other electronic assets such as e-books, mp3s, videos etc. also qualify.

12.3. An Inconvenient Truth

All the discussion we've had in Section 12.2 relies on the fact that all the consortium participants are running the same version of the chaincode. *In real-world if you are Biotor, you won't know what code XMed has deployed on their peer node.* Perhaps they deployed following smart contract:

Listing 12. 7. Modified smart contract in which sensitive information is compromised.

```
@Transaction()
public async update(ctx: Context, assetId: string, newFingerprint: string): Promise<void> {
    const oldFingerprint = this.getFingerprint(assetId);
    const digest = this.computeDigest(ctx);
    if (digest === oldFingerprint) {
        console.log(`${assetId} belongs to ${mspId}`);          ❶
        await ctx.stub.putState(assetId, Buffer.from(newFingerprint));
    } else {
        throw new Error("You do not have permission to modify this asset");
    }
}
```

❶ Log sensitive information!

Similarly they could have inserted log statements in the `create` method as well. Fabric actually allows this. Its release notes for 2.0 proudly claim that: [142]

> **Chaincode packages do not need to be identical across channel members** *Organizations can extend a chaincode for their own use case, for example to perform different validations in the interest of their organization. As long as the required number of organizations endorse chaincode transactions with matching results, the transaction will be validated and committed to the ledger. This also allows organizations to individually roll out minor fixes on their own schedules without requiring the entire network to proceed in lock-step.*
>
> — What's new in Hyperledger Fabric v2.0

In my opinion this is more of a bug and a security vulnerability that I will demonstrate in just a second rather than a useful feature. To get on with our demonstration there are two different smart contracts under $/data-privacy-lesson. There is a folder named biotor-smart-contract and another folder named `xmed-smart-contract` which contains identical code except for a log statement in the `update` method. As an exercise you could create a third folder `keypharmacy-smart-contract` in which you insert log statement(s) in the `create` method as well. Anyway, go ahead and build, package and install the smart contracts on the respective peers using the steps described in Chapter 7. Label the chaincode `privacy` and set version as `1.0` during installation. *You will notice that as you install the smart contracts, you will get different package IDs.* Next, approve and commit the smart contract. Note that the package ID is not needed during the commit step and there is no error. *The peers are now running different versions of the chaincode.*

Let us now create some assets in the system. For this use the Node.js application in `$/data-privacy-lesson/client-application` written in TypeScript. Build the application by running `npm run build`. Copy over the wallet you created in Section 8.10.4 into `$/data-privacy-lesson/client-application`. Then run following command to create assets from the `$/data-privacy-lesson/client-application` directory:

```
$ node dist/create-asset.js
```

The code that creates assets can be found in `$/data-privacy-lesson/client-application/src/create-asset.ts` and similar to what we saw in Section 8.10.6. Running above command will create 7 assets with following (`assetId`, `fingerprint`) shown in Table 12. 2:

Table 12. 2. Table of assets and their fingerprints.

assetId	fingerprint
f4c0cea8-9a93-42c3-a722-e8cce1993d6a	BcPHswkTXhRt5DtdOyTifs0C9WsLoP79VGrIlVG6Izc=
10b26499-59d5-4af9-8436-8c14b2d97acc	uewBV1A7o8JnBuluUAjwQYa53unXYerSoyNCzQeY0lw=
fb58b6c7-2aba-4b54-98db-976c4483b596	52qs0QZBYmMpSke3teZ2zpQmmhT+M7nJc/oompQa/6w=
2e5ccd11-378e-48e9-8909-c4bff1a3c3c2	1Ur0AFGKL9WApYplOADq0Zt/qMqObtaKdBlvJwIVqP4=
c2243d78-74ed-492a-bacc-a5ca3f54abeb	+JYznSeisydefWfMgIIP66iSau1UmHF47V2Xzqj/Z7o=
74a60a2c-bcdc-4ca9-9b73-a1c1d8284b27	tOoACKY21H+DBv6yc1cJBFhTQLALij0z1KafrCOI+1U=
6ef8ab91-a69a-40d1-8b7f-8412559c219b	fvjO8D+DZgm1DxgKou4kBjOmw41IKNalZvAPj33CFRs=

If you open CouchDB viewer, it should show something like Figure 12. 6:

_attachments ▾	_id ▾	~version ▾
☐ 🖹 { "valueBytes": { "content_type": "application/octet-stream", "revpo...	10b26499-59d5-4af9-8436-8c14b2d97aee	CgMBOgA=
☐ 🖹 { "valueBytes": { "content_type": "application/octet-stream", "revpo...	2e5ccd11-378e-48e9-8909-c4bff1a3c3c2	CgMBPAA=
☐ 🖹 { "valueBytes": { "content_type": "application/octet-stream", "revpo...	6ef8ab91-a69a-40d1-8b7f-8412559c219b	CgMBPwA=
☐ 🖹 { "valueBytes": { "content_type": "application/octet-stream", "revpo...	74a60a2c-bcdc-4ca9-9b73-a1c1d8284b27	CgMBPgA=
☐ 🖹 { "valueBytes": { "content_type": "application/octet-stream", "revpo...	c2243d78-74ed-492a-bacc-a5ca3f54abeb	CgMBPQA=
☐ 🖹 { "valueBytes": { "content_type": "application/octet-stream", "revpo...	f4c0cea8-9a93-42c3-a722-e8cce1993d6a	CgMBQAA=
☐ 🖹 { "valueBytes": { "content_type": "application/octet-stream", "revpo...	fb58b6c7-2aba-4b54-98db-976c4483b596	CgMBOwA=

Figure 12. 6. CouchDB viewer showing created assets.

There are three things to note here. *First*, the `assetId` is an opaque string using which no information can be gained about the asset. *Second*, the owner of the asset is the same for all 7 assets but we use a different fingerprint each time. This goes back to what we said earlier about using a different salt per transaction so that it is impossible to reverse engineer the owner from the fingerprint. Of course, in our mock application we only have one drug manufacturer so its no secret who the manufacturer of any asset is but in real-world we will have multiple manufacturers participating in the consortium. The *third* thing to note is to compare Figure 12. 6 with Figure 12. 1. Note that whereas Figure 12. 1 showed structured information, in Figure 12. 6 the entire data payload is stored as an attachment. Why? Because we did not JSON encode the data before storing it in CouchDB. I did this purely for illustration.

You can now see you cannot transfer an asset easily. You need to know the key to unlock the fingerprint which is not obvious. Try running following command:

Listing 12. 8. Update an asset from the client application

```
$ node dist/transfer-asset.js f4c0cea8-9a93-42c3-a722-e8cce1993d6a "old mac donald"
"X/H/d9eHcZBapRWKBRV409HIYB9WoI5+eI2n0bWSJ+E="
```

If all goes well, you should see success and your asset's fingerprint should change. In above `old mac donald` is the secret key or salt to unlock the fingerprint of asset whose id is `f4c0cea8-9a93-42c3-a722-e8cce1993d6a`. *Biotor will keep this a secret and only it will know this.* And as we can see here, the salt need not necessarily be a random string. `X/H/d9eHcZBapRWKBRV409HIYB9WoI5+eI2n0bWSJ+E=` is the new fingerprint which Biotor will get from the buyer. Biotor will update the fingerprint to whatever the buyer tells them to. Later on, we will come across P2PKH transaction of Bitcoin in Chapter 16 which works in a similar way. The client code to update or transfer the asset can be found in `transfer-asset.ts`. Much of the code is similar what we have seen earlier (so I don't repeat it here) except for setting of the transient data from a client application before making a call to the smart contract. The listing below shows how that is done using the `setTransient` method on the `Transaction` object.

Listing 12. 9. Code showing how to use transient data in a client application

```
const tx = contract.createTransaction("update");
tx.setTransient({
    "key": Buffer.from(key)
});
const result = await tx.submit(assetId, newFingerprint);
```

The bummer in all this is the appearance of following line in output of XMed's chaincode as you execute `transfer-asset.js` script:

```
f4c0cea8-9a93-42c3-a722-e8cce1993d6a belongs to BiotorMSP
```

This way XMed can easily compromise an otherwise secure system all thanks to Fabric's feature of allowing different organizations to run variants of the chaincode. Note that the asset is immediately transferred to someone else after the log message says it belongs to BiotorMSP in the very next line of code in Listing 12. 7.

Exercise 12.2

Modify Fabric so it would not allow organizations to run different variants of the chaincode. Use fingerprints (checksums) to ensure that chaincode package is identical across peers.

12.4. Exploring contents of a Block

Let us take a moment to put our hacker hat on and phish for information stored inside a block on Fabric. Use the script in Listing 12. 1 to fetch the block corresponding to the update transaction you performed in Listing 12. 8 and save the results to a file. Then load this file and parse the contents into a JavaScript object `o`. Refer Section 5.2.2 on how to do that in case you have forgotten. [143]

Let's start with following:

Listing 12. 10. Get name of chaincode that was invoked

```
>
o.data.data[0].payload.data.actions[0].payload.action.proposal_response_payload.extension.r
esults.ns_rwset[1].namespace
'privacy'
```

Above returns the name of the chaincode that was invoked. I named the chaincode in this chapter as `privacy` when I packaged and deployed it onto the network. Next look at:

Listing 12. 11. Inspecting readwrite set of a transaction

```
>
o.data.data[0].payload.data.actions[0].payload.action.proposal_response_payload.extension.r
esults.ns_rwset[1].rwset
{
  metadata_writes: [],
  range_queries_info: [],
  reads: [
    { key: 'f4c0cea8-9a93-42c3-a722-e8cce1993d6a',    ❶
      version: [Object] }                             ❷
  ],
  writes: [
    {
      is_delete: false,
      key: 'f4c0cea8-9a93-42c3-a722-e8cce1993d6a',
      value: 'WC9IL2Q5ZUhjWkJhcFJXS0JSVjQwOUhJWUI5V29JNStlSTJuMGJXU0orRT0='  ❸
    }
  ]
}
```

❶ Id of the asset we updated

❷ Fabric uses a `version` to keep track of changes to a key just like Git. When a key's value changes its version is updated. The history of changes is preserved.

❸ Base-64 encoded fingerprint

Above returns the readwrite set. From Listing 12. 8 we can see that we changed the fingerprint to X/H/d9eHcZBapRWKBRV409HIYB9WoI5+eI2n0bWSJ+E= which does not seem to match what we have in Listing 12. 11. This is because that string gets base64 encoded when its stored as shown below:

```
> s='X/H/d9eHcZBapRWKBRV409HIYB9WoI5+eI2n0bWSJ+E='
'X/H/d9eHcZBapRWKBRV409HIYB9WoI5+eI2n0bWSJ+E='
> Buffer.from(s).toString("base64")
'WC9IL2Q5ZUhjWkJhcFJXS0JSVjQwOUhJWUI5V29JNStlSTJuMGJXU0orRT0='
```

The other important thing to look at is the `chaincode_proposal_payload`:

Listing 12. 12. The `chaincode_proposal_payload` contains what method was called with what arguments

```
> o.data.data[0].payload.data.actions[0].payload.chaincode_proposal_payload
{
    "TransientMap": {},                          ❶
    "input": {
        "chaincode_spec": {
            "chaincode_id": {
                "name": "privacy",              ❷
                "path": "",
                "version": ""
            },
            "input": {
                "args": [
                    "dXBkYXRl",                  ❸
                    "ZjRjMGNlYTgtOWE5My00MmMzLWE3MjItZThjY2UxOTkzZDZh",       ❹
                    "WC9IL2Q5ZUhjWkJhcFJXS0JSVjQwOUhJWUI5V29JNStlSTJuMGJXU0orRT0="   ❺
                ],
                "decorations": {},
                "is_init": false
            },
            "timeout": 0,
            "type": "GOLANG"                     ❻
        }
    }
}
```

❶ Transient data never gets persisted on the blockchain so `TransientMap` will always be empty
❷ Name of the chaincode
❸ Base-64 encoded update method that was invoked
❹ Base-64 encoded assetId
❺ Base-64 encoded new fingerprint
❻ Seems like a bug as our chaincode is clearly not written in Go

The first thing to note is that the salt `old mac donald` in Listing 12. 8 never gets stored on the blockchain since it was passed as transient data. If we had passed it as function arguments, it would get recorded on the blockchain. The `args` in Listing 12. 12 may seem unintelligible because they are base-64 encoded. Let's decode them:

```
$ echo dXBkYXRl | base64 --decode
update
$ echo ZjRjMGNlYTgtOWE5My00MmMzLWE3MjItZThjY2UxOTkzZDZh | base64 --decode
f4c0cea8-9a93-42c3-a722-e8cce1993d6a
$ echo WC9IL2Q5ZUhjWkJhcFJXS0JSVjQwOUhJWUI5V29JNStlSTJuMGJXU0orRT0= | base64 --decode
X/H/d9eHcZBapRWKBRV409HIYB9WoI5+eI2n0bWSJ+E=
```

One can also see who performed the transaction:

```
> o.data.data[0].payload.data.actions[0].header.creator.mspid
'BiotorMSP'
```

Unfortunately, this compromises the data privacy of our application somewhat because an adversary can now use above to calculate for example how many `create` transactions a particular manufacturer is performing. That would give their total manufacturing volume. However, note that this will be aggregated over all their products and so the manufacturing volume of a particular drug is still protected. [144]

Exercise 12.3

This section in combination with Section 12.1 has shown how a hacker can inspect and mine the data on the ledger to gain business intelligence. *What if we could modify Fabric so this is not possible? What if the only access to data on the ledger was through the smart contract?* In that case we could continue with our original smart contract developed in Chapter 3. Modify Fabric to make this possible. *Hint*: Disable the Query System Chaincode (QSCC) and ensure only Fabric can read and decode the data on the ledger. How will you protect against someone running different version of Fabric that does not have this modification?

12.5. Epilogue

This is one of the most interesting, albeit difficult, chapters in this book, and one that comes with an anticlimax. I had originally planned this to be the final chapter of the book in the spirit of saving the best for the last but then I didn't want the reader to feel cheated by the book when he or she is done with it. *In many respects data privacy is the Achilles' heel of blockchain. Blockchain is all about sharing data whereas data privacy is about protecting data - two opposing requirements if you will.* Nowhere is the tension more palpable than when considering data privacy. This is where the rubber hits the road and you graduate from building toy apps to building a real-world application. It reminds me of the following slide I saw in a talk by Daniel Hardman in Hyperledger Global Forum 2020. [145]

Getting wiser about blockchain

Blockchain is awesome! Global source of truth. Store everything there.
Performance and scaling issues. How can we offload?
Data on blockchain is dangerous; must be encrypted.
Some stuff never belongs there.
Regulatory compliance and GDPR...
So many decentralize fails...

Figure 12. 7. Getting wiser about blockchain. Reproduced with permission from Daniel Hardman. Design Patterns for Decentralization, Hyperledger Global Forum 2020.

In this chapter we discussed ways - actually just one way - of handling data privacy on the blockchain. *The basic idea is to store a fingerprint of the confidential data on the blockchain rather than the data itself.* The actual data is stored off-chain in a separate database. It certainly takes some of the charm of blockchain away because now you have to maintain a separate database and also engage in off-chain out-of-band transactions on top of that. And so we wonder why are we using blockchain at all? Blockchain still brings value to the table as it provides indisputable record of ownership and provenance and we saw that in this chapter.

You might have noticed we never discussed Private Data Collections. There was no need. *Private Data Collections (PDC)* is a feature of Fabric whereby data can be shared selectively between participants. The designated participants will be able see the data whereas all others will see a hash of the data on the blockchain. For example, Biotor could create a PDC with only itself as the member. It could then store the salt in the PDC. The salt would only be visible to Biotor. All others will see an opaque unintelligible string. This way Biotor won't need a separate database to store the salt. Other organizations could do the same for their secrets. The smart contract API provides getPrivateData, putPrivateData and getPrivateDataHash methods to manage PDC. [146] When putPrivateData is called it will store the data in a private datastore on the peers that are part of the collection. And a hash of the data will be stored on all peers whether they are part of collection or not. The getPrivateData call will succeed only on those peers that are part of the collection. As an exercise you can try rewriting the smart contract in this chapter using PDC. PDCs have limited value when there is only one organization in the collection but when you have data that needs to be selectively shared between multiple organizations PDCs might be useful. Equivalently you could just create a separate channel which is effectively nothing but a separate blockchain and store the confidential data there just like we create a separate group of close friends and family members on Facebook with whom we feel comfortable sharing more intimate posts. With PDC a hash of the data serves as kind of a proof of its existence to others and may be useful for auditing purposes in some applications.

We conclude this chapter with a quote from David Brin (the quote was not made in the context of blockchain by the way):

When it comes to privacy and accountability, people always demand the former for themselves and the latter for everyone else.

— David Brin

12.6. Summary

- The concept of data privacy is at odds with the fundamental premise of blockchain which is about sharing data and establishing an auditable record of transactions.
- The issue of data privacy does not arise in permissionless blockchains because the identity of participants is unknown.
- Data privacy in permissioned blockchains is achieved by storing only a verifiable fingerprint of data on the blockchain. The actual data is stored off-chain. Unfortunately this has the side-effect of having to maintain additional databases and engaging in out-of-band transactions. Blockchain often becomes a small part of the overall solution, not the solution itself.
- It is important to use transient data when making function calls if you do not want a copy of that data to be recorded onto the blockchain.
- The as-is version of Fabric contains a security vulnerability where you cannot guarantee that all organizations are running the same version of the smart contract. This vulnerability can be easily exploited to log and record confidential data and compromise data privacy even if you are using transient data and fingerprints.
- The best way to handle data privacy is to modify Fabric to fix the security vulnerability and so that the only access to data is through the smart contract. That way no one can mine the ledger and use it for purposes other than what was agreed to in the smart contract. As a consequence you may have to sacrifice some of the auditability that comes with full access to the blockchain otherwise.

12.7. Further Reading

- Fabric docs on Private Data Collections. hyperledger-fabric.readthedocs.io/en/release-2.0/private-data/private-data.html
- KC Tam's article on PDC: medium.com/@kctheservant/private-data-and-transient-data-in-hyperledger-fabric-46b5258f391e

[142] hyperledger-fabric.readthedocs.io/en/release-2.0/whatsnew.html
[143] The full transcript of the block can be seen at git.io/Jkzvx
[144] This, of course, discounting the security vulnerability we have seen earlier.
[145] A video of the talk is available at www.youtube.com/watch?v=JDrdgk1L-ww
[146] hyperledger.github.io/fabric-chaincode-node/release-2.1/api/fabric-shim.ChaincodeStub.html

Chapter 13. Running the Fabric CA Server

This chapter covers:

- Running Fabric CA server with a sqlite3 backend database
- Using openssl to generate certificates used to bootstrap a Fabric CA server

Code for this chapter is in $/fabric-ca-lesson

In this chapter we will see how to use Fabric CA to issue identities instead of the cryptogen tool we used in Chapter 4. We will show how to use Fabric CA taking Biotor as example. The process will be the same for other organizations. We will create 3 CAs:

- the root CA for Biotor. We will give this a friendly name of *Mickey*.
- a CA used for issuing TLS server certs. We'll call this *Donald*.
- a CA used for issuing TLS client certs. We'll call this *Goofy*.

Mickey will issue Donald and Goofy their certificates. We will then use these CAs to get certificates for Biotor's members - user, admin, peer and orderer. Mickey will issue the ID certs and Donald and Goofy will issue TLS certs. We create 3 different CAs for illustration. In practice, there could be a single CA issuing both ID as well as TLS certs. In fact as we have seen in Chapter 4, by adding both the Digital Signature and Key Encipherment key usages, the same cert can be used both as ID cert as well as TLS cert. We will demonstrate all these variations in this chapter. It would be a good idea to refresh your memory of Section 4.5 before working through this chapter. This chapter will cover provisioning the fabric-ca-server and next chapter will cover using the fabric-ca-client.

How many CAs should you run? In this chapter we provision three CAs to illustrate a complex setup and cover advanced usage of fabric-ca-server. But do you need to do the same? Not necessarily. In theory you just need one CA server. Fabric's official recommendation is to use two CAs - one for ID certs and one for TLS certs. [147] As we have given a metaphor earlier in the book, think of the CA as Director of HR and the TLS CA as Director of IT in an organization. HR issues identities whereas IT issues communication equipment.

13.1. Fabric CA 101

In this section we cover the architecture and concepts behind Fabric CA. Similar to MySQL, Fabric CA is made up of a server which runs forever and waits for incoming requests - we call this fabric-ca-server - and there are clients (a command line client and Node.js client) which can be used to make requests against the server. Fabric CA is written in Go and you can find its source code at github.com/hyperledger/fabric-ca. We use version 1.4.6 of Fabric CA in the book which is tagged as v1.4.6 in the repository. The repository contains following packages from its online documentation (reproduced under terms of CC license):

- cmd/fabric-ca-server contains the main for the fabric-ca-server command.
- cmd/fabric-ca-client contains the main for the fabric-ca-client command.
- lib contains most of the code. a) server.go contains the main Server object, which is configured by serverconfig.go. b) client.go contains the main Client object, which is configured by clientconfig.go.
- util/csp.go contains the Crypto Service Provider implementation.
- lib/dbutil contains database utility functions.
- lib/ldap contains LDAP client code.
- lib/spi contains Service Provider Interface code for the user registry.
- lib/tls contains TLS related code for server and client.

Basically, Fabric CA relies heavily on the crypto, crypto/ecdsa, crypto/rsa, crypto/tls, crypto/x509 Go packages to do most of the crypto work. All these packages can be browsed at golang.org/search?q=crypto. These packages are used extensively in main Fabric as well to sign messages and validate certs, verify digital signatures etc. In addition, Fabric CA uses **cloudflare/cfssl** library developed by CloudFlare to issue certificates. cfssl is a CA in its own right and even comes with a HTTP based server so adventurous readers might want to check it out as replacement for Fabric CA. [148]

In addition to the command line client, Fabric provides a Node.js client (also named fabric-ca-client) for Fabric CA whose source code can be found under github.com/hyperledger/fabric-sdk-node and that can be installed from the official NPM repository at www.npmjs.com/package/fabric-ca-client. We will use version 2.2.2 of this client.

Fabric CA can be used as a general purpose CA in a non-Fabric project. The CA server takes a yaml config file as input known as fabric-ca-server-config.yaml similar to peer and orderer binaries. Sample config is available for preview at $/sample-configs/fabric-ca-server-config.yaml. One difference is that in case of fabric-ca-server this file is optional (at least as of v1.4.6). *If you do not provide a config file, a default config is auto-generated.* [149] As was mentioned in Section 2.2 there are two steps involved in order to use Fabric CA to issue a X.509 certificate: register which creates an account for a user in a database and enroll which actually issues an X.509 certificate to a registered user. *User registration is a prerequisite for enrollment.* fabric-ca-client *is used to perform these two steps.*

fabric-ca-server maintains two databases - a database of registered users which it uses to authenticate requests coming to it. The register call creates an entry in this database. The other database stores certificates issued to users plus other auxiliary data. The enroll call creates entries in this database. We will call these two databases *registry DB* and *certificate DB*. The *certificate DB* can be one of MySQL, Postgres or SQLite3. The *registry DB* adds LDAP to these three choices. There are two modes in which Fabric CA Server can be run:

- Both *certificate* and *registry* use the *same* MySQL, Postgres or SQLite3 instance. In this case there is only one database and thus there is no distinction between *registry* and *certificate* DB.

This is the mode in which we run `fabric-ca-server` in this chapter and further we will use SQLite3.

- The *registry DB* is implemented using LDAP and is separate from the *certificate DB*. We show how to implement this in Section 15.5. *In this mode the* `register` *endpoint is not used. Users are registered into the system by other means.* In fact, this mode exists precisely to serve the scenario when you already have a LDAP server in which your users are registered and so there is no need to register them again in a MySQL, Postgres or SQLite3 database.

SQLite3 is a simple but powerful database. The most important difference in relation to MySQL or Postgres is that whereas MySQL or Postgres come with a server that can be used to serve requests from a remote client, SQLite3 does not come with any server. This means that both `fabric-ca-server` and SQLite3 database file have to be on the same machine i.e., *sqlite3 is a local database without any support for a remote connection protocol.* SQLite3 also locks the entire database and *only supports one writer at a time.*

Before you begin the exercises in this chapter, check you have the correct version of `fabric-ca-server` on your system (the OS/Arch will be different on different OSes):

```
$ fabric-ca-server version
fabric-ca-server:
 Version: 1.4.6
 Go version: go1.13.4
 OS/Arch: darwin/amd64
```

You can download precompiled binaries for your OS from `github.com/hyperledger/fabric-ca/releases`. I put the binaries in the same folder where I have `peer` and `orderer`. As usual Docker images for Fabric CA are available at `hub.docker.com/r/hyperledger/fabric-ca`. We will run Fabric CA without Docker in this chapter but by now you have enough knowledge to run it in a container.

Fabric CA server can be started quite simply by running following command in an empty directory. Try it if you like:

Listing 13. 1. Command to start `fabric-ca-server`. **The** `-b` **option has no effect if a** `fabric-ca-server-config.yaml` **already exists in the search path. Edit the** `registry.identities` **section in the yaml file in that case.**

```
$ fabric-ca-server start -b mickey:mickeypw
```

In above the `-b` switch is used to provide username and password of the bootstrap user who will have admin privileges over the CA. *Fabric CA always requires a bootstrap user to start when not using LDAP.* Fabric CA server also needs its own X.509 identity for bootstrap. This is a chicken-end-egg problem because the very reason we are using a CA server is to generate identities. How can we generate its own identity? The answer is that this identity is *auto-generated* if not provided. The auto-generated identity is saved as `ca-cert.pem` and will have attributes like `C=US`, `ST=North Carolina`, `O=Hyperledger`, `OU=Fabric`, `CN=fabric-ca-server` which you may not like and would want to customize with name of your organization to make it appear more professional. If TLS is enabled with the `tls.enabled` setting, `fabric-ca-server` will also auto-generate a `tls-cert.pem` (if not provided with a TLS cert) but it may not have desired SANs and Common Name in it.

Our setup of Mickey, Donald and Goofy will have *two* stages. In the *first* stage, we will generate necessary certificates and keys used to bootstrap these CAs themselves. The bootstrap stage can be skipped if you are willing to work with the auto-generated certificates. And in the *second* stage, we will provision the CAs using the certs and keys from bootstrap stage.

13.2. Generating Bootstrap Certificates

The bootstrap stage involves following steps:

- a self-signed certificate is generated which will form Mickey's identity
- Mickey issues identities to Donald and Goofy
- Donald issues TLS certificates to all three including himself. Remember it is best practice to turn on TLS when running Fabric CA server.
- Goofy issues a TLS client cert which will be needed when making requests from `fabric-ca-client` if client authentication is enabled on Fabric CA server.

After this, all three Fabric CA servers can be started. Now there are at least two ways I can think of to generate the bootstrap certs. *Method 1* would use the `fabric-ca-server` itself. Instead we will demonstrate how to generate the certs using *Method 2* - the `openssl` tool. The reason I choose this method is because I feel it will be simpler and faster to do it this way. It also demonstrates the `openssl` tool itself. *Method 1* is sure to overwhelm the reader and will be left as a challenge exercise. In fact there is a clever *Method 3*. *We can use the credentials generated by* `cryptogen` *earlier to bootstrap the Fabric CAs - that way none of our work will be lost.* We can continue using the existing network and new users can register into the system and get X.509 credentials from Fabric CA. We can use the public cert and private key in `$/three-org-network/crypto-config/peerOrganizations/biotor.com/ca` for Mickey's identity and the `tlsca` folder under `biotor.com` can provide the identity of Donald. This will accomplish the first two steps in our list. There are some caveats - the `tlsca` cert (Donald) generated by `cryptogen` is self-signed. It is not issued by the `ca` (Mickey). It is not necessary that Mickey issues cert to Donald. `cryptogen` also does not generate a separate CA for TLS client certs - its not necessary to do so. We will do it to illustrate some nuances which we can't if we use a single CA for both server and client certs. Note that we can simply run the `cryptogen` tool once more to get a new `tlsca` and use that for Goofy.

Anyway let's come back to *Method 2*. Begin by opening a terminal session in the `$/fabric-ca-lesson/biotor/bootstrap` directory. You should find following files in it:

```
$ git ls-files
client_tls.cnf
donald_tls.cnf
goofy_tls.cnf
ica.cnf
mickey_tls.cnf
rca.cnf
signing.cnf
```

Go ahead and create three subdirectories - mickey, donald and goofy. Next create a folder newcerts and an empty file index.txt in each of these subdirectories.

 A word of advice as we move through this chapter: start making a secure backup of the keys and certs you are generating or chmod the files to read-only to avoid accidental modifications.

13.2.1. Are you really using OpenSSL when you run openssl?

openssl is a Swiss army knife useful for a variety of crypto tasks. We have used this utility earlier to inspect X.509 certificates. We can also use it to generate X.509 certificates. Before we begin, a word of caution. The openssl on Mac is different from the openssl that comes with Linux! On my Mac I see following when I run openssl:

```
$ openssl version
LibreSSL 2.6.5
```

whereas on a Linux box I get:

```
$ openssl version
OpenSSL 1.0.2k-fips  26 Jan 2017
```

LibreSSL is intended to be a drop-in replacement for OpenSSL that's why they have named their CLI openssl itself. The LibreSSL project was launched in the aftermath of the discovery of the *Heartbleed* security vulnerability in OpenSSL. According to Wikipedia, the OpenBSD team audited the codebase and decided it was necessary to fork OpenSSL to remove dangerous code. [150] I won't take any sides as to which is better, but just want you to be aware of the difference since the same command that works on Mac may not work as-is on Linux or vice-versa as the two CLIs are not strictly 1:1 compatible. The OpenSSL CLI has its source code at github.com/openssl/openssl whereas LibreSSL is to be found at github.com/libressl-portable/portable. From its online documentation, LibreSSL is API compatible with OpenSSL 1.0.1, but does not yet include all new APIs from OpenSSL 1.0.2 and later. As if the dichotomy between LibreSSL and OpenSSL was not enough, there is even a third command line tool that you may come across for X.509 certificate management - certtool.

13.2.2. Generate self-signed certificate for Root CA (Mickey)

Cd into the mickey subdirectory and from there run:

Listing 13. 2. Generate self-signed certificate and ECC key pair based on `prime256v1` **elliptic curve.**

```
$ openssl req -new -x509 -nodes -newkey ec:<(openssl ecparam -name prime256v1) -keyout
mickey_ca_key.pem -out mickey_ca_cert.pem -days 3650 -config ../rca.cnf
```

Above command creates an ECC private key `mickey_ca_key.pem` (based on `prime256v1` curve) and a self-signed X.509 certificate `mickey_ca_cert.pem` using the settings in `rca.cnf`. `fabric-ca-server` *only accepts certs with ECC keys and ECDSA algorithm* so its important you only use ECDSA keys and not something like RSA in above. You will be asked to enter certain information. Example is shown below:

```
Generating a 256 bit EC private key
writing new private key to 'mickey_ca_key.pem'

You are about to be asked to enter information that will be incorporated
into your certificate request.
What you are about to enter is what is called a Distinguished Name or a DN.
There are quite a few fields but you can leave some blank
For some fields there will be a default value,
If you enter '.', the field will be left blank.

Country Name (2 letter code) []:US
State or Province Name (full name) []:WA
Locality Name (eg, city) []:Bellevue
Organization Name (eg, company) []:Biotor
Organizational Unit Name (eg, section) []:HR
Common Name (eg, fully qualified host name) []:Mickey Mouse (Director of HR)
Email Address []:
```

Feel free to change and customize the fields to what you prefer to get a professional looking certificate for your company. `rca.cnf` is an important file and contains the settings of the X.509 cert. You can inspect the full file in a text editor. The most important section of the file is shown below in Listing 13. 3.

Listing 13. 3. Settings of Biotor's Root CA from `rca.cnf`.

```
[ v3_ca ]
keyUsage=critical,keyCertSign,cRLSign
basicConstraints=critical,CA:true,pathlen:1
```

As covered previously in Section 4.5.3 the minimum requirement for a CA cert is presence of `keyCertSign` bit which indicates that the public key in this cert can be used to sign and thus issue X.509 certs. We also need to set `CA:true` under `basicConstraints` which are always marked as `critical` without exception. We set the `pathlen` to be 1 since Mickey is going to issue CA certs to Donald and Goofy.

13.2.3. Mickey issues ID certs to Donald and Goofy

Now that we have a CA in the form of Mickey, we will see how we can use it to issue certs to Donald and Goofy. A non-self signed certificate creation involves two steps. The client (Donald for example) generates what is known as a *Certificate Signing Request* or *CSR*. Think of this as a piece of paper where the client makes come claims. This CSR is submitted to the CA. The CA reviews the CSR and signs off on it endorsing and legitimizing it. This transforms the CSR into a certificate.

Cd into `donald` directory and from there run:

Listing 13. 4. Step 1: Generating a CSR based on ECC key with `prime256v1` curve.

```
$ openssl req -nodes -newkey ec:<(openssl ecparam -name prime256v1) -keyout
donald_ca_key.pem -days 365 -out donald_ca.csr -config ../ica.cnf -extensions 'v3_ca'
```

The above command generates a ECC private key and an associated CSR using the settings in `ica.cnf`. You can see the command looks very similar to Listing 13. 2 with some differences. The `ica.cnf` file which contains the settings for Donald's cert is virtually identical to `rca.cnf`. The only difference is that we set `pathlen:0`. This means Donald will not be able to issue any CA certs. This is shown below:

Listing 13. 5. Settings for Biotor's TLSCA from `ica.cnf`. The `pathlen` is set to 0 meaning this CA won't be able to create any more CAs.

```
[ v3_ca ]
keyUsage=critical,keyCertSign,cRLSign
basicConstraints=critical,CA:true,pathlen:0
```

When you run the command, you will be asked to provide some information. Example is shown below:

```
Generating a 256 bit EC private key
writing new private key to 'donald_ca_key.pem'
...

Country Name (2 letter code) []:US
State or Province Name (full name) []:WA
Locality Name (eg, city) []:Bellevue
Organization Name (eg, company) []:Biotor
Organizational Unit Name (eg, section) []:IT
Common Name (eg, fully qualified host name) []:Donald Duck (Director of IT)
Email Address []:

Please enter the following 'extra' attributes
to be sent with your certificate request
A challenge password []:donald
```

Enter the details as you like. These are the claims Donald is making. You can also enter a password if you like. Entering the password is optional and it actually does not make any difference. The CSR can be printed by running following command:

Listing 13. 6. Command to print out a CSR.

```
$ openssl req -noout -text -in donald_ca.csr
```

It should give output like below:

Listing 13. 7. A certificate request. It contains the public key, requested extensions and subject metadata. A CA then signs this request to turn it into a certificate.

```
Certificate Request:
    Data:
        Version: 0 (0x0)
        Subject: C=US, ST=WA, L=Bellevue, O=Biotor, OU=IT, CN=Donald Duck (Director of IT)
        Subject Public Key Info:
            Public Key Algorithm: id-ecPublicKey
                Public-Key: (256 bit)
                pub:
                    04:0d:30:e5:54:b7:dd:57:6f:06:2c:f9:32:96:ba:
                    66:1e:28:9f:6b:87:2b:fd:03:53:73:2f:de:6b:57:
                    f4:6b:c6:63:4b:7c:ea:d1:7e:a4:7a:06:a1:93:f9:
                    a0:38:87:f5:21:3a:e9:24:e9:a1:bc:d5:81:88:00:
                    c5:22:06:69:90
                ASN1 OID: prime256v1
                NIST CURVE: P-256
        Attributes:
            challengePassword        :unable to print attribute
        Requested Extensions:
            X509v3 Key Usage: critical
                Certificate Sign, CRL Sign
            X509v3 Basic Constraints: critical
                CA:TRUE, pathlen:0
            X509v3 Subject Key Identifier:
                04:6E:EE:6B:B1:F6:83:72:1C:8A:22:A3:F6:59:D1:F3:40:6E:2B:0B
    Signature Algorithm: ecdsa-with-SHA256
         30:45:02:21:00:ef:fc:95:e8:a2:7b:98:46:21:a7:0e:e9:44:
         0c:7f:c8:4d:2f:9c:14:16:b3:a9:a2:3f:97:5c:03:d1:eb:b0:
         59:02:20:16:a3:d3:9d:66:c5:2d:9d:a5:bd:11:71:6c:b1:2f:
         10:0e:e8:6e:5c:7c:8c:1b:a8:3d:c1:eb:f3:0d:6f:7e:78
```

Now Donald will submit the CSR for signing by Mickey just like a student submits their dissertation for signing by their professor. Let's do it. Cd into mickey folder and from there run:

Listing 13. 8. Step 2: CSR is submitted to CA for signing.

```
$ openssl ca -config ../signing.cnf -cert mickey_ca_cert.pem -keyfile mickey_ca_key.pem
-extensions v3_ca -create_serial -out ../donald/donald_ca_cert.pem -notext -infiles
../donald/donald_ca.csr
```

In above, Mickey is using his credentials (mickey_ca_cert.pem and mickey_ca_key.pem) to sign on Donald's CSR (donald_ca.csr). The signing.cnf is an important file containing config settings used by the CA at time of signing. You can refer to online repository for full file contents. An excerpt is shown in Listing 13. 9.

Listing 13. 9. CA settings from `signing.cnf`

```
dir             = .                      ❶
database        = $dir/index.txt         ❷
new_certs_dir   = $dir/newcerts          ❸
serial          = $dir/serial            ❹
rand_serial     = yes                    ❺
RANDFILE        = $dir/private/.rand      ❻
```

❶ set dir equal to current directory

❷ index.txt will serve as a database of issued certificates

❸ a copy of issued certificate will be stored in this directory

❹ this file will simply contain the serial number of the next certificate to be issued. The serial number gets incremented when a cert is issued.

❺ the yes option generates a random starting serial number

❻ An optional file that can be used to provide random number seed. Not used in our example.

When you run the `openssl` command, you should see output like below and prompted to sign the certificate:

```
Using configuration from ../signing.cnf
Check that the request matches the signature
Signature ok
Certificate Details:
        Serial Number: 15922489301182766853 (0xdcf80ba890f4df05)
        Validity
            Not Before: Sep  2 17:21:53 2020 GMT
            Not After : Sep  2 17:21:53 2021 GMT
        Subject:
            countryName              = US
            stateOrProvinceName      = WA
            organizationName         = Biotor
            organizationalUnitName   = IT
            commonName               = Donald Duck (Director of IT)
        X509v3 extensions:
            X509v3 Authority Key Identifier:
                keyid:D4:62:F3:9A:36:AD:99:68:91:07:42:95:17:47:71:13:41:E9:15:E4

            X509v3 Key Usage: critical
                Certificate Sign, CRL Sign
            X509v3 Basic Constraints: critical
                CA:TRUE, pathlen:0
            X509v3 Subject Key Identifier:
                04:6E:EE:6B:B1:F6:83:72:1C:8A:22:A3:F6:59:D1:F3:40:6E:2B:0B
Certificate is to be certified until Sep  2 17:21:53 2021 GMT (365 days)
Sign the certificate? [y/n]:y


1 out of 1 certificate requests certified, commit? [y/n]y
Write out database with 1 new entries
Data Base Updated
```

There are several interesting things to note now. Begin by verifying you have a file donald_ca_cert.pem in donald directory. Print out the certificate and verify its correctness. The certificate should say Issuer: C=US, ST=WA, L=Bellevue, O=Biotor, OU=HR, CN=Mickey Mouse (Director of HR) and Subject: C=US, ST=WA, O=Biotor, OU=IT, CN=Donald Duck (Director of IT). Next print out the index.txt file. It should contain following:

```
V   2109021721532   DCF80BA890F4DF05    unknown /C=US/ST=WA/O=Biotor/OU=IT/CN=Donald Duck
(Director of IT)
```

The letter V is a code. 2109021721532 is the certificate expiry. Cross-check it with the value in donald_ca_cert.pem. DCF80BA890F4DF05 is the serial number of the certificate. Again cross-check it. And the last column has the metadata of the certificate's subject. A copy of donald_ca_cert.pem will be found in the newcerts folder under mickey directory. Verify it. And you will see a file named serial under mickey directory. If you print it out, it should simply contain

```
DCF80BA890F4DF06
```

which will be the serial number of the next certificate issued by Mickey.

You now have Donald's certificate. Repeat the steps and get a CA certificate for Goofy.

13.2.4. Donald issues TLS certs for all three

Let's see how Donald issues a TLS cert to Mickey. Begin by changing your directory to mickey and from there run:

Listing 13. 10. Generating a CSR based on 2048 bit RSA key.

```
$ openssl req  nodes  newkey rsa:2048  keyout mickey_tls_key.pem -days 365 -out
mickey_tls.csr -config ../mickey_tls.cnf -extensions 'v3_req'
```

The above command generates a 2048 bit RSA private key mickey_tls_key.pem and an associated CSR mickey_tls.csr using the settings in mickey_tls.cnf. We have used a RSA key to illustrate that *the TLS cert does not need to use ECC key*. The cnf file contains important settings some of which are shown below:

Listing 13. 11. TLS settings from mickey_tls.cnf

```
[v3_req]
keyUsage = critical,keyEncipherment          ❶
extendedKeyUsage = serverAuth, clientAuth    ❷
basicConstraints=critical,CA:false           ❸
subjectAltName=@alt_names                     ❹

[ alt_names ]                                 ❺
DNS.1=localhost
DNS.2=biotor.com
DNS.3=mickey.biotor.com
```

❶ keyEncipherment indicates that the public key in the cert can be used to encrypt another key. This is what makes a X.509 certificate a TLS certificate.

❷ serverAuth means the certificate can be used for server hostname validation. clientAuth means this certificate can be used for client authentication.

❸ this is not a CA cert so we must set CA:false

❹ The subjectAltName (SAN) section of a TLS certificate lists all the DNS names by which the server can be reached. In production one would remove localhost from the list.

❺ Use this section to list all DNS names of the server

We have three different TLS cnf files for mickey, donald and goofy under the bootstrap directory. All of them are identical except for the SAN section since the different servers will naturally have distinct addresses. We request a certificate with both serverAuth and clientAuth. In this chapter only the serverAuth property will be used. But if we want to connect Fabric CA to a LDAP server, the Fabric CA becomes a client of the LDAP server. If the LDAP server has client authentication turned on then the clientAuth permission will come in handy. When you run the openssl command, you will be asked to provide some information as we have seen before. Enter the details as you like. Print out the CSR as we have seen before. Next, sign it by changing to donald directory and from there running:

Listing 13. 12. Sign request for a TLS certificate.

```
$ openssl ca -config ../signing.cnf -cert donald_ca_cert.pem -keyfile donald_ca_key.pem
-extensions v3_ca -create_serial -out ../mickey/mickey_tls_cert.pem -notext -infiles
../mickey/mickey_tls.csr
```

In above, we are using Donald's credentials to sign a request. This will again prompt you for acknowledgment before signing. Verify the generated certificate mickey_tls_cert.pem has necessary attributes in it.

Repeat the process to generate TLS certs for Donald and Goofy.

13.2.5. Understanding ECC and RSA keys

Let us take a closer look at an ECC key inside an X.509 certificate. An example is shown below:

Listing 13. 13. Example ECC key

```
Subject Public Key Info:
    Public Key Algorithm: id-ecPublicKey
        Public-Key: (256 bit)
        pub:
            04:60:08:20:2e:5b:be:40:66:71:2e:fa:56:7d:1a:
            95:30:40:8d:8f:fe:52:19:a5:27:1a:f1:13:b1:12:
            45:dc:1d:1a:90:e0:4f:95:92:3d:58:8c:39:66:22:
            5f:06:a3:ae:d6:00:9a:5b:75:50:69:8d:c4:73:cb:
            8a:ba:de:58:e6
```

id-ecPublicKey indicates that the ECC public key can be used with any signature algorithm. Other options are: id-ecDH to indicate that the public key can only be used with Elliptic Curve Diffie-Hellman algorithm and id-ecMQV to restrict key usage to the Elliptic Curve Menezes-Qu-Vanstone key agreement algorithm. We only encounter the ECDSA algorithm in this book and for this reason you will only see id-ecPublicKey in the X.509 certificates. Next you will see that the public key is marked as 256 bit or equivalently 32 bytes but if you add up the octets under the pub section which contains the actual key, you get 15*4+5=65 bytes. What gives? The answer is that the first byte is used to indicate whether we are using the compressed or uncompressed representation. The uncompressed form is indicated by 0x04 and the compressed form is indicated by either 0x02 or 0x03. Any other value is illegal. That leaves us with 65-1=64 bytes which is twice of expected 32 bytes. The explanation is that the ECC key is nothing but a 2D point on an elliptic curve. This point has a *X* coordinate and a *Y* coordinate. The uncompressed form which is what we see in Listing 13. 13 first lists the *X* component followed by the *Y* component. Each component is encoded as 32 bytes. [151] So in total the key is made up of 64 bytes even though the X.509 cert will say 256 bit.

Let us now come to a RSA based X.509 certificate. An example with a 2048 bit (or equivalently 256 bytes) key from `mickey_tls_cert.pem` is shown below:

Listing 13. 14. Example RSA key

```
Subject Public Key Info:
    Public Key Algorithm: rsaEncryption
        Public-Key: (2048 bit)
        Modulus:
            00:c5:8b:4c:5e:88:d2:eb:c1:5e:fe:0d:b7:84:33:
            67:07:7a:58:29:07:91:04:a8:3e:75:09:b9:30:78:
            b7:7e:ac:5e:5e:1a:21:ca:a3:8c:8b:a1:c1:9a:01:
            77:9b:b1:47:37:f5:dc:61:0f:39:cd:d4:a4:e5:e6:
            7e:90:c3:74:2f:3c:ff:53:1a:61:e3:87:b9:69:72:
            93:ff:b5:c0:d6:f4:7d:45:16:5b:19:f3:2d:c3:47:
            52:7d:b1:d2:42:57:aa:90:62:ae:6d:87:07:8e:a7:
            51:fd:73:e3:56:79:aa:f3:20:e7:b6:46:2c:0d:09:
            fc:bb:9d:8a:a4:12:13:d5:42:1e:8b:5f:09:01:a6:
            3c:f7:f8:40:eb:9e:d6:6a:97:c8:4d:c9:9e:f0:ea:
            4b:fd:65:13:3f:1b:72:35:52:19:13:b5:02:ea:04:
            1b:84:5d:59:56:da:cd:61:1c:d2:7e:46:e0:88:89:
            0e:1a:2b:fe:6a:90:a0:e0:c1:05:ec:09:30:f7:b6:
            13:e2:77:ce:ae:ae:da:b0:80:58:35:a5:6b:18:9d:
            80:1a:bd:44:e3:ea:58:9a:f6:b7:84:cf:9c:bd:66:
            4a:6f:14:a4:32:1f:58:2a:71:9a:cc:67:4a:42:55:
            57:b0:19:6c:46:c6:27:be:5f:88:01:75:f6:96:97:
            af:9f
        Exponent: 65537 (0x10001)
```

An RSA public key is made up of the *modulus* plus the *exponent*. The leading 0x00 in the public key in Listing 13. 14 is to be ignored. If you count the remaining octets you will see that they add up to 256 bytes. The exponent is usually 65537. The ECC key is thus 4 times shorter than RSA key and that is one of the advantages of using ECC keys.

13.2.6. Extracting public key from X.509 certificate

Given a X.509 certificate, you can extract the public key from it by running:

Listing 13. 15. Extract public key from X.509 certificate.

```
$ openssl x509 -in cert.pem -pubkey -noout
```

This command works for both ECC as well as RSA certificates. If you run this command on
`mickey_tls_cert.pem` you should see something like following:

Listing 13. 16. RSA public key output by `openssl` **in Base64 format.**

```
-----BEGIN PUBLIC KEY-----
MIIBIjANBgkqhkiG9w0BAQEFAAOCAQ8AMIIBCgKCAQEAxYtMXojS68Fe/g23hDNn
B3pYKQeRBKg+dQm5MHi3fqxeXhohyqOMi6HBmgF3m7FHN/XcYQ85zdSk5eZ+kMN0
Lzz/Uxph44e5aXKT/7XA1vR9RRZbGfMtw0dSfbHSQleqkGKubYcHjqdR/XPjVnmq
8yDntkYsDQn8u52KpBIT1UIei18JAaY89/hA657WapfITcme80pL/WUTPxtyNVIZ
E7UC6gQbhF1ZVtrNYRzSfkbgiIkOGiv+apCg4MEF7Akw97YT4nfOrq7asIBYNaVr
GJ2AGr1E4+pYmva3hM+cvWZKbxSkMh9YKnGazGdKQlVXsBlsRsYnvl+IAXX2lpev
nwIDAQAB
-----END PUBLIC KEY-----
```

The key is printed in base64 format. It can be converted into hexadecimal format by first saving the
base64 string (MIIB···AQAB) in a temporary file `base64.txt` and then running:

Listing 13. 17. Converting Base64 string into hexadecimal. On Linux you have to use `-d`
instead of `-D`.

```
$ cat base64.txt | base64 -D | od -t x1 -An
```

Sample output is shown below:

Listing 13. 18. Result of converting Base64 encoded public key into hexadecimal

```
30  82  01  22  30  0d  06  09  2a  86  48  86  f7  0d  01  01
01  05  00  03  82  01  0f  00  30  82  01  0a  02  82  01  01
00  c5  8b  4c  5e  88  d2  eb  c1  5e  fe  0d  b7  84  33  67
07  7a  58  29  07  91  04  a8  3e  75  09  b9  30  78  b7  7e
ac  5e  5e  1a  21  ca  a3  8c  8b  a1  c1  9a  01  77  9b  b1
47  37  f5  dc  61  0f  39  cd  d4  a4  e5  e6  7e  90  c3  74
2f  3c  ff  53  1a  61  e3  87  b9  69  72  93  ff  b5  c0  d6
f4  7d  45  16  5b  19  f3  2d  c3  47  52  7d  b1  d2  42  57
aa  90  62  ae  6d  87  07  8e  a7  51  fd  73  e3  56  79  aa
f3  20  e7  b6  46  2c  0d  09  fc  bb  9d  8a  a4  12  13  d5
42  1e  8b  5f  09  01  a6  3c  f7  f8  40  eb  9e  d6  6a  97
c8  4d  c9  9e  f0  ea  4b  fd  65  13  3f  1b  72  35  52  19
13  b5  02  ea  04  1b  84  5d  59  56  da  cd  61  1c  d2  7e
46  e0  88  89  0e  1a  2b  fe  6a  90  a0  e0  c1  05  ec  09
30  f7  b6  13  e2  77  ce  ae  ae  da  b0  80  58  35  a5  6b
18  9d  80  1a  bd  44  e3  ea  58  9a  f6  b7  84  cf  9c  bd
66  4a  6f  14  a4  32  1f  58  2a  71  9a  cc  67  4a  42  55
57  b0  19  6c  46  c6  27  be  5f  88  01  75  f6  96  97  af
9f  02  03  01  00  01
```

At first glance the output in Listing 13. 18 does not match the key in Listing 13. 14. On closer
inspection it does. To see how, skip the first 32 bytes in Listing 13. 18. Verify the next 256 bytes in
Listing 13. 18 are the same as the modulus in Listing 13. 14. And then verify the last 3 bytes in

Listing 13. 14 namely `0x010001` is nothing but the exponent in Listing 13. 14. The extra stuff you see in Listing 13. 18 that is not present in Listing 13. 14 has to do with how `openssl` formats its output and not part of the public key. [152]

13.2.7. Verifying key pairs

It is possible to derive the RSA public key from the private key. Do that by running following command:

Listing 13. 19. Deriving RSA public key from private key.

```
$ openssl rsa -in mickey_tls_key.pem -pubout
```

The corresponding command for a ECC key is as follows:

Listing 13. 20. Deriving ECC public key from private key.

```
$ openssl ec -in mickey_ca_key.pem -pubout
```

You can now compare the results to the public keys stored in the respective X.509 certificates. This way one can tell if a public and private key pair match or not.

> The public key can be derived from the private key but not vice-versa. That is why its called asymmetric cryptography.

13.2.8. Goofy issues a TLS client cert

Let us now come back to the final step in generating the bootstrap certificates. Let us use Goofy to issue a TLS client certificate which will come in handy if the `fabric-ca-server` is run with `clientauth` enabled. To do this we pretty much repeat the steps that we did to generate the TLS certs of Mickey, Donald and Goofy except that we create a `client` directory under `bootstrap` folder. From this directory we will run following command to generate a CSR:

```
$ openssl req -nodes -newkey rsa:2048 -keyout client_tls_key.pem -days 365 -out
client_tls.csr -config ../client_tls.cnf -extensions 'v3_req'
```

Above command will use the settings in `client_tls.cnf`. If you open the file, among other things you will see it has `clientAuth` enabled and nothing else. This is shown below:

Listing 13. 21. Settings to generate a TLS client certificate.

```
[v3_req]
extendedKeyUsage = clientAuth
basicConstraints=critical,CA:false
```

As you run the command you will be prompted for information. Enter the details as you like. You can enter anything for the `Common Name (CN)` but do not leave it empty. Once you have the CSR, change to `goofy` directory and from there run following command which will sign the CSR and transform it into a certificate:

```
$ openssl ca -config ../signing.cnf -cert goofy_ca_cert.pem -keyfile goofy_ca_key.pem
-extensions v3_ca -create_serial -out ../client/client_tls_cert.pem -notext -infiles
../client/client_tls.csr
```

Verify the generated cert has required attributes and Goofy's signature on it.

This completes stage 1 - generation of bootstrap certs - and we are now ready to move to stage 2 which is using the bootstrap certs to provision the CAs. Before we do that a word of caution. It is okay to use openssl to obtain certificates necessary for one-time setup tasks like what we did just now but do not use openssl as a replacement for Fabric CA server itself! That is not its indented purpose. Its online documentation has following warnings among others: [153]

* The ca command is quirky and at times downright unfriendly.
* The ca utility was originally meant as an example of how to do things in a CA. It was not supposed to be used as a full blown CA itself: nevertheless some people are using it for this purpose.
* The ca command is effectively a single user command: no locking is done on the various files and attempts to run more than one ca command on the same database can have unpredictable results.

Exercise 13.1

Write a script to automate the generation of all the bootstrap certificates and keys. You can even use CloudFlare's cfssl utility instead of openssl to generate bootstrap certs.

A summary of openssl commands is given in Table B.6 (Appendix B) for reference later on.

13.3. *Customizing* fabric-ca-server-config.yaml

Now that we have the bootstrap certs, we can provision the CAs. Before doing that, make a secure backup of the certificates and keys in case they get accidentally modified. I recommend freezing the bootstrap folder and using a separate folder from which to provision the CAs. To do that create a folder mickey under $fabric-ca-lesson/biotor from where we will run Mickey CA and a folder client from where we will run fabric-ca-client.

Next, to provision the CA server corresponding to Mickey (Biotor's Root CA) change to mickey directory and copy Mickey's certs and keys from the bootstrap/mickey folder. After this, copy the sample fabric-ca-server-config.yaml from $/sample-configs to the directory. We will make several changes to it. When fabric-ca-server starts it looks for a fabric-ca-server-config.yaml in the search path. *The name of the file is fixed and cannot be changed* similar to what we have seen with core.yaml and orderer.yaml. In case of peer and orderer the search path is given by FABRIC_CFG_PATH. This variable has no effect in case of fabric-ca-server. fabric-ca-server tries to get the search path by inspecting three environment variables in following order: first it will check FABRIC_CA_SERVER_HOME followed by FABRIC_CA_HOME and CA_CFG_PATH in that order. If none of the env variables is set, then the present directory i.e., the directory from where the command is run is chosen as the search path. [154] *If no* fabric-ca-

`server-config.yaml` *is found in the search path, one is auto-generated*. This is in contrast to `peer` and `orderer` which throw an error if they cannot find their config file.

 `FABRIC_CA_SERVER_HOME`, `FABRIC_CA_HOME`, or `CA_CFG_PATH` are also used to resolve full path of any files with relative paths in `fabric-ca-server-config.yaml`. So if you have a file `foo.txt` in the current directory but `FABRIC_CA_HOME` is set to some other path, then `fabric-ca-server` will complain with file not found error if you don't specify the full path in config file.

The `fabric-ca-server-config.yaml` file contains a wealth of settings. We will modify some of them and explain their purpose along the way. As before, it is not necessary to make changes to the config file. One can use environment variables to *override* the settings in the config. *Every setting in the config maps to an environment variable with* `FABRIC_CA_SERVER` *as prefix and underscores delimiting the config keys.* So for example instead of changing the `port` in the config, one can instead set the `FABRIC_CA_SERVER_PORT` environment variable. The choice is up to you. There is no right or wrong way. You choose what works for you. In what follows, we will describe the settings as if they were being set in the config.

13.3.1. *Set* `version`, `port` *and* `loglevel`

Set the **version** in config to `1.4.6` or lower. The `version` is used to indicate the version of `fabric-ca-server` that this file can be run with. It should be less than or equal to the version of the `fabric-ca-server` you are using otherwise you will get an error. [155] The **port** defines the port at which the `fabric-ca-server` will listen for connections and is set to `7054` by default. Port `7054` has been used by the orderer in previous chapters so I changed it to `6000`. Unlike the peer and orderer, `fabric-ca-server` does not expose any setting to control the listen address. It is hardcoded to `0.0.0.0` within the server and is an appropriate choice. The `debug` flag controls whether to turn on debugging or not. Instead of using the `debug` flag you might want to set **loglevel** variable instead. `debug` is a boolean flag which can only be true or false whereas `loglevel` is more powerful and can be set to one of following values resulting in increasing order of log verbosity: `fatal`, `critical`, `warning`, `info` and `debug`. *Note that if you are using* `loglevel` *you should not set* `debug` *to* `true` *(even if* `loglevel` *is* `debug`*) or you will get an error.* `fabric-ca-server` even supports a command line `--loglevel` option for setting the log level.

13.3.2. Configuring TLS

Next, we come to the **tls** section in the config which we modify as follows:

Listing 13. 22. TLS settings of server

```
tls:
  enabled: true                               ❶
  certfile: mickey_tls_cert.pem               ❷
  keyfile: mickey_tls_key.pem                 ❸
  clientauth:
    type: requireandverifyclientcert ❹
    certfiles: goofy_ca_cert.pem              ❺
```

❶ For demonstration, we turn on TLS. It is recommended to turn on TLS with fabric-ca-server since passwords are sent to it.

❷ The TLS server cert that will be sent to a client. It must have keyEncipherment bit set and serverAuth permission enabled.

❸ The private key corresponding to the certificate.

❹ We turn on client authentication for demonstration.

❺ The client's certificate will be validated against goofy_ca_cert.pem i.e., the server will check the certificate is signed off by Goofy. Also the client cert must have clientAuth permission set.

fabric-ca-server supports varying levels of client authentication dictated by the tls.clientauth.type setting in yaml file. These options are listed in Table 13. 1 and actually come from the Go crypto/tls package that Fabric relies upon for TLS. [156] Practically speaking, none of them are interesting except for NoClientCert and RequireAndVerifyClientCert and you might as well ignore the rest.

Table 13. 1. Different levels of client authentication supported by fabric-ca-server **and** crypto/tls **Go package.**

Level	Meaning
NoClientCert	client authentication is completely disabled.
RequestClientCert	server will request a client TLS certificate but do nothing beyond that. client authentication is effectively disabled.
RequireAnyClientCert	server will accept any client TLS certificate i.e., it can be signed by any CA but a cert does need to be provided by the client to be able to connect.
VerifyClientCertIfGiven	if a client certificate is provided to the server, the server will check that it is issued by a trusted CA and only then allow client to connect. A clever client can skip providing any certificate at all to bypass client authentication.
RequireAndVerifyClientCert	server will only allow client to connect if it presents a client cert that is signed by a trusted authority. This is what we conventionally expect from client authentication.

Since we set client authentication to requireandverifyclientcert, we now also need to provide listed of trusted CAs for client certs. This is done via the tls.clientauth.certfiles setting that is set to goofy_ca_cert.pem. This is because in our demonstration setup Goofy is the one who is trusted to issue client TLS certs. So the TLS cert from a client has to be checked against Goofy for validation. You will thus need to copy goofy_ca_cert.pem from the bootstrap/goofy folder into the mickey directory.

13.3.3. *Configuring* ca

After this, we come to the **ca** section in the config that contains Fabric CA server's identity.

```
ca:
    name: mickey-mouse          ❶
    keyfile: mickey_ca_key.pem  ❷
    certfile: mickey_ca_cert.pem ❸
    chainfile:                  ❹
```

❶ Friendly name of fabric-ca-server

❷ The private key of the fabric-ca-server. This is the server's identity.

❸ The X.509 cert containing the public key. This cert must have Basic Constraints: true, certSign bit set and CA:TRUE. It is also recommended to have crlSign bit set to be able to revoke certificates.

❹ If you are not using a self-signed certificate, then you need to provide the complete chain of issuers starting from the least privileged and ending with the self-signed root CA or trust anchor.

Since we use a self-signed certificate (`mickey_ca_cert.pem` is issued by Mickey himself), we do not need to provide any `chainfile`. If we were not using a self-signed certificate, we would need to provide a file that has the PEM encoded certificates of the chain *starting with the* ca.certfile *and ending with the root CA*. These certs are simply *concatenated* in the chain file. *You will need this for Donald and Goofy*.

13.3.4. *Affiliations*

The purpose of **affiliations** section is to predefine a list of possible affiliations that can appear as OU attributes in the user's X.509 certificate. This is useful if you will be using *Attribute Based Access Control (ABAC)*. For example, we can define a whitelist of following affiliations:

Listing 13. 23. Affiliations appear as OUs in the X.509 certificate of the user.

```
affiliations:
    biotor:
        - HR
        - IT
        - Procurement
        - Supply Chain
        - Pharma
```

At time of user registration (Section 14.1.2), we can specify a user's affiliation (e.g., biotor.HR). Then when that user is issued a certificate, their affiliation will appear in the certificate as OU=biotor, OU=HR. It is not necessary to use the affiliations section and you may find that the type field is sufficient for the attribute based access control you are trying to achieve. The type field inserts one OU in the cert. If you want more OUs then affiliations is the way to achieve that. Fabric docs state that affiliations are *case sensitive* except for the non-leaf affiliations which are always stored in lower case. So you cannot use Biotor with a capital B in example above as its a non-leaf affiliation.

What happens if you try to use an affiliation that is not in the whitelist (e.g., biotor.Medical Devices)? fabric-ca-server will respond with an error when the registration request is made (msg: Failed to get Affiliation: sql: no rows in result set). To get around this, fortunately it is possible to add, modify or even remove affiliations dynamically (i.e., after the server has been started) using the fabric-ca-client affiliation command. Not anyone can do this. Only users with hf.AffiliationMgr: true privilege (Listing 13. 25) are able to do so and their own affiliation must be hierarchically above the affiliation being updated.

13.3.5. Configuring the registry

The next section of interest in the config file is the **registry** section. *The* registry *section is applicable only when* fabric-ca-server *is not using LDAP for its database (*ldap.enabled: false*)* and contains a list of users that are *auto-registered* in the database of registered users when the fabric-ca-server starts. These are known as bootstrap users. We have to provide at least one bootstrap user. Since these users are *auto-registered* they don't require any registration step from fabric-ca-client.

Listing 13. 24. The registry section provides a list of users who are auto-registered in the database.

```
registry:
  maxenrollments: -1     ❶

  identities:            ❷
    - name: mickey       ❸
      pass: mickeypw      ❹
      type: client       ❺
```

❶ The maximum number of times a password/secret can be reused for enrollment
❷ List of users who will be auto-registered in the database
❸ username. It is recommended to keep this different from the ca.name to avoid confusion.
❹ password of the user. change it as per your needs.
❺ This string will appear as OU=client in the X.509 certificate of the user. Fabric supports following types: client, peer, orderer, member and admin with client being the default.

Enrollment is the process of obtaining an X.509 cert from fabric-ca-server. The same user can be enrolled multiple times - the user will get a new cert with each enrollment. The maxenrollments setting controls the maximum number of times a user can re-enroll without having to change their password. -1 is used to indicate no limit. *Take care not to check in a config file having any production passwords into source control.*

SETTINGS CONTROLLING REGISTRAR PRIVILEGES

fabric-ca-server requires a *registrar* to register new users before they can be issued any certificates. *The registrar needs to be registered and enrolled itself before it can begin registering other users.* The bootstrap user can serve as the registrar. A user who can act as a registrar must have certain attributes associated with their profile. These are defined in Listing 13. 25. The configuration in Listing 13. 25 form the most "powerful" settings in the sense the registrar with these settings can do pretty much whatever they want when it comes to registering new users.

Listing 13. 25. Attributes that control a registrar's powers.

```
registry:
    ...
    identities:
        - name: mickey
          pass: mickeypw
          type: client
          affiliation: ""                          ❶
          attrs:
              hf.Registrar.Roles: "*"              ❷
              hf.Registrar.DelegateRoles: "*"      ❸
              hf.Revoker: true                     ❹
              hf.IntermediateCA: true              ❺
              hf.GenCRL: true                      ❻
              hf.Registrar.Attributes: "*"         ❼
              hf.AffiliationMgr: true              ❽
```

❶ This will allow `mickey` to be able to specify any affiliation for the users it registers.

❷ This will allow `mickey` to specify whatever `type` he wishes for the users it registers.

❸ This will allow `mickey` to specify whatever `hf.Registrar.Roles` he wishes for the users it registers.

❹ This will allow `mickey` to be able to revoke certificates.

❺ This allows `mickey` to register as an intermediate CA. In present case this is not applicable but plays a role when you want to spin up an intermediate CA.

❻ This allows `mickey` to generate a certificate revocation list (CRL).

❼ This allows `mickey` to be able to add whatever attributes he wants to the profile of users he is registering.

❽ This allows `mickey` to be able to make changes to the affiliations configuration of the fabric-ca-server dynamically.

Fabric places many controls and checks on the registrar when it comes to registering new users. For example, if Mickey's own affiliation were `biotor.hr`, he can register a user with affiliation `biotor.hr.director` but he cannot register a user with affiliation `biotor.it`. A "`.`" is used to indicate *root affiliation*. A registrar with root affiliation can specify any affiliation for the user it is registering. *If there is no affiliation provided when a user is registered, the user is given the affiliation of the registrar - this equals the most privileged affiliation the registrar can bestow on the user.* The empty string in Listing 13. 25 against `affiliation` indicates no affiliation and in case of bootstrap users it actually functions the same way as root affiliation.

The `hf.Registrar.Roles` controls what `type` a registrar can specify for the user. Putting it another way it controls what types of users a registrar can register. A registrar can only specify a `type` that is listed in `hf.Registrar.Roles`. *For example, if the* `hf.Registrar.Roles` *was* `client,peer,orderer` *then Mickey cannot register a user of type* `admin` *into the database.* The * character serves as a wildcard to mean Mickey can specify whatever he wants for the `type` attribute of a user. The `hf.Registrar.DelegateRoles` controls what `hf.Registrar.Roles` can be specified for the user. For example, if hf.Registrar.DelegateRoles was client,peer then when Mickey registers a user, he cannot set the user's hf.Registrar.Roles to be orderer,admin. The hf.Registrar.Attributes controls what attributes the registrar can set for the users it registers. For example, if hf.Registrar.Attributes was empty then Mickey cannot add any attributes to the profile of users its registering - thus it will not be able to create child registrars because at minimum a registrar needs the hf.Registrar.Roles attribute with at least some type. The hf.AffiliationMgr: true allows Mickey to be able to make runtime modifications to the affiliations config section of fabric-ca-server.

The different attributes are summarized in Table 13. 2.

Table 13. 2. Summary of attributes controlling a registrar's powers. From hyperledger-fabric-ca.readthedocs.io/en/latest/users-guide.html. Reproduced under terms of CC license.

Name	Type	Description
hf.Registrar.Roles	List	The types of users a registrar can register
hf.Registrar.DelegateRoles	List	List of roles that the registrar is allowed to give to a registree for its 'hf.Registrar.Roles' attribute
hf.Registrar.Attributes	List	List of attributes that registrar is allowed to register
hf.GenCRL	Boolean	A user with this permission can generate a certificate revocation list
hf.Revoker	Boolean	A user with this permission can revoke an identity and/or certificates
hf.AffiliationMgr	Boolean	A user with this permission can dynamically modify the affiliations config section of the fabric-ca-server
hf.IntermediateCA	Boolean	A user with this permission is able to enroll as an intermediate CA

The attributes listed under the attrs *section are not stored in the X.509 certificate of the user. They are stored as part of user's profile in the database.* Also the registrar with appropriate privileges can specify arbitrary attributes for the users in addition to the hf attributes. For example, Mickey can register a user and add an attribute foo with value bar to the user's profile. If you want this attribute to be recorded and listed in the X.509 certificate of the user, it can be done using the **ecert** keyword (Section 14.1.2).

13.3.6. Configuring the Certificate DB

We now come to the **db** section of the config file shown below for reference. The db section applies whether or not LDAP is disabled and governs the *certificate DB*. The default settings are good enough for us. The type of database fabric-ca-server uses is controlled by the db.type setting which is set to sqlite3 by default. The name of the database is controlled by db.datasource setting.

Listing 13. 26. Fabric CA server database settings.

```
db:
  type: sqlite3              ❶
  datasource: fabric-ca-server.db  ❷
  tls:                       ❸
      enabled: false         ❹
      certfiles:             ❺
      client:                ❻
        certfile:
        keyfile:
```

❶ `fabric-ca-server` supports SQLite3, Postgres, and MySQL for the `db.type`.

❷ name of the database

❸ TLS section has no effect in case of SQLite3

❹ Whether TLS is enabled on the MySQL or Postgres server

❺ The list of trusted CAs against which MySQL or Postgres TLS cert will be validated

❻ The cert and key to use for client authentication. This will be needed only if clientauth is enabled on MySQL or Postgres.

The `ldap` section in the config file can be ignored as we don't use LDAP in this chapter. This takes us to signing profiles.

13.3.7. Signing profiles

After this we come to the **signing** section in the config which is particularly important. When we used `openssl` in Section 13.2, we set the key usages in the CSR. But this is not how Fabric CA - or rather `cfssl`, the dependency it uses - works. With `cfssl` one predefines a set of profiles on the server and the client chooses one of those profiles when it submits a signing request. `cfssl` will then automatically insert the key usages corresponding to that profile in the X.509 certificate it issues to the client. Fabric CA supports *three* profiles - a **default** profile which is declared under `signing.default` and a **ca** and **tls** profile which are declared under `signing.profiles`. The three profile names are *reserved* and cannot be changed but we can customize the key usages under those profiles. The profiles that come with the default config file are shown below:

Listing 13. 27. Signing section can contain three profiles with user-defined key usages.
`fabric-ca-client` **specifies the profile it wants at time of enrollment and corresponding key usages will be inserted in the X.509 certificate issued to the client (user).**

```
signing:
    default:
      usage:
        - digital signature        ❶
      expiry: 8760h
    profiles:
      ca:
        usage:
          - cert sign
          - crl sign
        expiry: 43800h
        caconstraint:
          isca: true
          maxpathlen: 0
      tls:
        usage:
          - signing              ❶
          - key encipherment
          - server auth
          - client auth
          - key agreement
        expiry: 8760h
```

❶ Both `digital signature` and `signing` mean the same thing

The meanings of different key usages has been covered earlier in Section 4.5. The `default` profile is used whenever a profile is not explicitly specified in the request made by `fabric-ca-client`. Note that the `default` profile comes under the `signing` section, not under `signing.profiles` section. The `default` profile is typically used to obtain certificates of users, admins, peer and orderer. The `ca` profile is used to issue a CA certificate which can be used for bootstrapping another `fabric-ca-server` and the `tls` profile is used for TLS certs. In fact, since the `tls` profile has the `signing` bit set, we could use the cert obtained using this profile *as the TLS as well as the ID cert*. The `key agreement` usage defined in the default config file is not a requirement for TLS. *Note that you can enter whatever key usages you want under the three profiles.* For example, you could use the `ca` profile to issue TLS server cert and `tls` to issue TLS client certs while the `default` profile could be used for ID certs as shown below for demonstration:

Listing 13. 28. Example of customizing signing profiles.

```
signing:
    default:
        usage:
            - digital signature
        expiry: 8760h
    profiles:
      ca:
        usage:
            - key encipherment
            - server auth
        expiry: 8760h
      tls:
        usage:
            - client auth
        expiry: 8760h
```

It is not possible to declare new signing profiles. You can but you will get an error when you try to use that profile at time of enrollment. The reason for this has to do with an X.509 extension that needs to be enabled. `fabric-ca-server` enables this extension for the three profiles but won't do it for other profiles. As an exercise you can try modifying `fabric-ca-server` to add support for more profiles. *Hint*: modify the `initConfig` function in `lib/ca.go`
. [157]

 The certificate expiry is configured on the server. It is not something the client can choose. Thus the client cannot tell the server to issue a certificate that expires after 100 years.

13.3.8. Configuring self-generated certificate

The **csr** section in the config controls the creation of the root CA certificate and is not applicable for us since we provide a bootstrap cert to the CA. If however, you were relying on the `fabric-ca-server` to self-generate its identity, then this section becomes important. For example, you might want to edit it as follows:

Listing 13. 29. The csr section controls the attributes of the self-generated bootstrap certificate of fabric-ca-server. It is not applicable when the user provides provides a bootstrap certificate to fabric-ca-server.

```
csr:
    cn: mickey                    ❶
    keyrequest:                   ❷
      algo: ecdsa
      size: 256
    names:                        ❸
      - C: US
        ST: "New Jersey"
        L: "New Brunswick"
        O: Biotor
        OU: IT
    hosts:                        ❹
      - rca.biotor.com
      - localhost
    ca:
      expiry: 131400h
      pathlength: 1               ❺
```

❶ This has to be the same as the username of the bootstrap user. You can just leave it as empty and `fabric-ca-server` will auto-set it to correct value.

❷ Do not make any changes to keyrequest. This will generate a 256 bit ECDSA key. fabric-ca-server requires an ECDSA key to bootstrap.

❸ The names section can be modified to insert custom metadata pertaining to your organization.

❹ Use the hosts section to list all names and IP addresses by which your server can be accessed. These will appear as SANs in the certificate. localhost will allow accessing the server from the same machine on which its hosted as it happens in a dev setup.

❺ pathlength controls maximum number of CAs that can appear between this CA and an end entity certificate. A pathlength of 1 allows one intermediate CA to exist in the chain between this and an end entity certificate.

The rest of the sections in the config file can be ignored for now. The `operations` section spins up an operations server that is a black box for us. There is a `metrics` section in the default config but it is disabled by default. Its used to emit metrics to a `statsd` or `prometheus` server and we don't do that for now.

13.3.9. Deploying multiple CAs in one instance of `fabric-ca-server`

Now comes something mind-bending. *It is possible to run multiple CAs without having to spin multiple instances of* `fabric-ca-server`. How you ask. The answer is to use the **cafiles** option in the config file. The `cafiles` provides a list of config files of the other CAs. We can use this technique to deploy the two TLS CAs we have - `donald` and `goofy`.

Begin by creating two directories under the `mickey` folder. Call them `donald` and `goofy`. Now repeat the steps as above making modifications as necessary as if you were going to run independent `fabric-ca-server` instances in these directories. Both these directories will have a `fabric-ca-server-config.yaml`. Delete the `tls`, `port`, `debug`, `operations` and `metrics` sections in the config files. *Donald and Goofy's certs are not self-signed so you will need to create and provide a chainfile in their* `fabric-ca-server-config.yaml` *under* `ca.chainfile`. The chainfile for Donald can be created by simply running:

```
$ cat donald_ca_cert.pem mickey_ca_cert.pem > donald_mickey_chain.pem
```

Do same for Goofy. The chainfile always starts with the leaf or least authoritative cert and ends with the root or trusted CA. If you do not provide a chainfile there is no error at startup but registration requests will fail (being a bad programmer I have made all these mistakes so I know; learn from my experience).

Now let's go back to the `fabric-ca-server-config.yaml` under `mickey` and edit the `cafiles` section like so:

```
cafiles:
  - donald/fabric-ca-server-config.yaml
  - goofy/fabric-ca-server-config.yaml
```

We call this setup a "triple-headed CA" as a single instance of `fabric-ca-server` is being used to serve three CAs.

 Can you have a `cafiles` section in `fabric-ca-server-config.yaml` of `donald` or `goofy`? I don't think so. Try it if you like and let me know how it goes.

13.4. *Running* `fabric-ca-server`

You are now ready to start the `fabric-ca-server`. Do it as follows from `mickey` directory:

Listing 13. 30. Command to start `fabric-ca-server`

```
$ fabric-ca-server start
```

This is the same command as Listing 13. 1 except for the -b switch. We don't use the -b switch as the bootstrap user will come from config file. Even if we used a -b switch it will have no effect if a config file is present in the search path. The reason for this odd behavior is that internally `fabric-ca-server` always takes username and password from the config file. When the config file does not exist, one is auto-generated and the username and password specified on the command line using the -b switch is used to fill in the `registry.identities` in the config file. [158]

A partial result of running the `fabric-ca-server start` command when is shown below (full log at git.io/Jk28u):

Listing 13. 31. Output from `fabric-ca-server start` **command for Biotor's Root CA (Mickey)**

```
[INFO] Configuration file location: /Users/siddjain/phf/fabric-ca-
lesson/biotor/mickey/fabric-ca-server-config.yaml ❶
[INFO] Starting server in home directory: /Users/siddjain/phf/fabric-ca-
lesson/biotor/mickey
[INFO] Server Version: 1.4.6
[INFO] The CA key and certificate files already exist        ❷
[INFO] Key file location: /Users/siddjain/phf/fabric-ca-
lesson/biotor/mickey/mickey_ca_key.pem   ❸
[INFO] Certificate file location: /Users/siddjain/phf/fabric-ca-
lesson/biotor/mickey/mickey_ca_cert.pem ❸
[DEBUG] DB: Add identity mickey
[DEBUG] Successfully added identity mickey to the database  ❹
[INFO] Initialized sqlite3 database at /Users/siddjain/phf/fabric-ca-
lesson/biotor/mickey/fabric-ca-server.db ❺
[INFO] Home directory for default CA: /Users/siddjain/phf/fabric-ca-lesson/biotor/mickey
[DEBUG] 3 CA instance(s) running on server                  ❻
[INFO] Operation Server Listening on 127.0.0.1:9443         ❼
[INFO] Listening on https://0.0.0.0:6000                    ❼
```

❶ This confirms fabric-ca-server was able to find a config file. If its not able to find a config file we see a message that says Created default configuration file.

❷ This confirms fabric-ca-server will use the identity we have provided it instead of generating one on its own.

❸ The CA server's identity. This could be self-generated or it could come from cryptogen, openssl or using fabric-ca-server itself during a bootstrap phase.

❹ The bootstrap user is auto-registered in the database (when not using LDAP) without the need for any explicit registration step from fabric-ca-client.

❺ By default fabric-ca-server stores its data in sqlite3 database.

❻ Voila! We are running 3 CAs on one server. Pat! Pat!

❼ Take care that the ports are available and no one else is using them. Ports can be changed in yaml or through environment variables.

When you restart the server you will see:

```
[DEBUG] Identity 'mickey' already registered, loaded identity
```

since the user already exists in the database (i.e., has been previously registered). You should see following files created in each CA's directory when the `fabric-ca-server` starts:

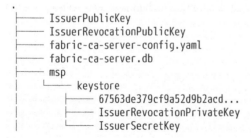

```
.
├────── IssuerPublicKey
├────── IssuerRevocationPublicKey
├────── fabric-ca-server-config.yaml
├────── fabric-ca-server.db
├────── msp
│       └────── keystore
│               ├────── 67563de379cf9a52d9b2acd...
│               ├────── IssuerRevocationPrivateKey
│               └────── IssuerSecretKey
```

The files prefixed with `Issuer` have to do with Idemix and can be safely ignored as we don't use it in the book. That leaves the yaml and db file and we know what they are. *Note carefully that each CA is using a separate database.* We now have a `fabric-ca-server` running and hosting 3 CAs. In next chapter we will see how to make requests against this server.

13.5. Summary

- `fabric-ca-server` can be provisioned without providing any bootstrap certificates for its identity or TLS. It automatically generates the necessary certificates and keys in that case but the auto-generated certs may not have the attributes you want. For this reason it is sometimes necessary to go through a bootstrap phase where we generate necessary keys and certs to bootstrap the server itself.
- `fabric-ca-server` only supports ECC keys and ECDSA signatures for the identity used to bootstrap the CA. [159]
- The certs and keys generated by `cryptogen` under the `ca` and `tlsca` folders can be used to bootstrap `fabric-ca-server`. This option provides a way to migrate an existing setup from `cryptogen` to `fabric-ca-server` without losing your work or having to make any configuration changes to the blockchain. Both the `ca` and `tlsca` are self-signed and have identical key usages so using `tlsca` to issue TLS certificates is a matter of convention not a requirement.
- The client cannot specify arbitrary key usages in the CSR. The client has to choose amongst one of the predefined profiles and `fabric-ca-server` will set the key usages according to that profile. The profiles are defined in `fabric-ca-server-config.yaml`. The default config file comes populated with three profiles - `default`, `ca`, and `tls`. You can change key usages of existing profiles as per your needs but it is not possible to declare new profiles without making source code level changes to `fabric-ca-server`.
- `fabric-ca-server` derives much of its functionality from `cloudflare/cfssl` package.
- It is recommended to start `fabric-ca-server` with `FABRIC_CA_SERVER_COMPATIBILITY_MODE_V1_3=false` which fixes a security vulnerability (FABC-174).
- The private key and public cert used to bootstrap the Fabric CA make up identity of the CA which is *different* from the identity of the user used to bootstrap the CA.
- When you restart `fabric-ca-server`, ensure it is using the same identity with which it was started earlier otherwise all new certificates are being issued by a different CA. Practically this means you should self-generate the server's identity only once. If you are self-generating the server's identity on restarts, then you are using a different CA each time!
- `fabric-ca-server` supports an `init` command that is intended to be run from an empty directory to get a default config that can then be customized before starting the CA. It also generates a ECDSA key and cert and initializes a sqlite3 database. The `start` command does an automatic `init` as well and will skip generating a config file or database if they already exist.

13.6. Further Reading

- Fabric CA Official Guide: hyperledger-fabric-ca.readthedocs.io/en/release-1.4/users-guide.html
- Checklist for a Production CA server: hyperledger-fabric-ca.readthedocs.io/en/release-1.4/deployguide/ca-config.html

[147]   hyperledger-fabric-ca.readthedocs.io/en/release-1.4/deployguide/ca-deploy-topology.html#how-many-cas-are-required

[148] github.com/cloudflare/cfssl

[149] If you are curious, the code that does this can be found at github.com/hyperledger/fabric-ca/blob/v1.4.6/cmd/fabric-ca-server/config.go#L564

[150] en.wikipedia.org/wiki/LibreSSL

[151] See section 2.3.3 in www.secg.org/SEC1-Ver-1.0.pdf

[152] for details see stackoverflow.com/a/29707204/147530

[153] see complete list at www.openssl.org/docs/man1.0.2/man1/ca.html

[154] The code which does this can be seen at github.com/hyperledger/fabric-ca/blob/v1.4.6/util/util.go#L463

[155] see github.com/hyperledger/fabric-ca/blob/v1.4.6/lib/ca.go#L1198

[156] golang.org/pkg/crypto/tls/#ClientAuthType

[157] github.com/hyperledger/fabric-ca/blob/v1.4.6/lib/ca.go#L423

[158] github.com/hyperledger/fabric-ca/blob/v1.4.6/cmd/fabric-ca-server/config.go#L667

[159] github.com/hyperledger/fabric-ca/blob/v1.4.6/util/csp.go#L241

Chapter 14. Using Fabric CA Client to obtain X.509 Certificates

This chapter covers:

* Using the command line and Node.js `fabric-ca-client` to register and enroll users
* Inspecting sqlite3 database of registered users

Code for this chapter is in `$/fabric-ca-lesson`

The previous chapter provisioned three Fabric CAs - Mickey, Donald and Goofy. Now let's use these CAs to get X.509 certificates! After all, that's what they are for. We use the `fabric-ca-client` to make requests to `fabric-ca-server`. There are primarily two things we do with `fabric-ca-client` - register users and then enroll them. Other things are also possible. The complete list is shown below:

```
Available Commands:
  affiliation Manage affiliations
  certificate Manage certificates
  enroll      Enroll an identity
  gencrl      Generate a CRL
  gencsr      Generate a CSR
  getcainfo   Get CA certificate chain and Idemix public key
  identity    Manage identities
  reenroll    Reenroll an identity
  register    Register an identity
  revoke      Revoke an identity
  version     Prints Fabric CA Client version
```

Fabric provides us with a command-line client as well as a Node.js client and we will cover both in this chapter beginning with the command-line client. Both clients make HTTP REST calls to `fabric-ca-server`.

14.1. Using the command-line `fabric-ca-client`

We work from `$/fabric-ca-lesson/biotor/client` in this section.

Start by making sure you have the right version of `fabric-ca-client` installed:

```
$ fabric-ca-client version
fabric-ca-client:
 Version: 1.4.6
 Go version: go1.13.4
 OS/Arch: darwin/amd64
```

Imagine we need to provision the peer and orderer of Biotor. To do that we need certificates of peer and orderer. Not only that, if TLS will be enabled then we need TLS certificates as well. Let's see how to do that. Note that there is no admin certificate needed to provision peer or orderer. The admin certificate is needed only when you come to the stage of creating a channel, joining peer nodes, committing chaincode etc. Begin by changing your directory to $/fabric-ca-lesson/biotor/client and copy over the client cert, key from the bootstrap/client folder to the directory. You will also need Donald's CA certificate. We generated these in previous chapter. You should have following files under client when you are done:

```
$ ls
client_tls_cert.pem client_tls_key.pem  donald_ca_cert.pem
```

Similar to fabric-ca-server-config.yaml, fabric-ca-client uses a corresponding file named fabric-ca-client-config.yaml. A sample file is provided under $/sample-configs. fabric-ca-client looks for this file under following folders in order: FABRIC_CA_CLIENT_HOME, FABRIC_CA_HOME, CA_CFG_PATH and if it still cannot find a config file it will look under $HOME/.fabric-ca-client as last resort. If it still can't find the config file, a default config will be auto-generated. [160] As before, the values in the config file can be *overridden* using environment variables. The environment variables should be uppercase, start with FABRIC_CA_CLIENT prefix and use underscores to delimit the keys in the config file. Copy the sample config file into the client directory and edit the tls section in it:

Listing 14. 1. TLS settings on fabric-ca-client

```
tls:
  certfiles: donald_ca_cert.pem    ❶
  client:
    certfile: client_tls_cert.pem   ❷
    keyfile: client_tls_key.pem     ❸
```

❶ The TLS server certs are issued by Donald, so his certificate must be added to the list of trusted CAs.

❷ The TLS client cert. This is used only if client authentication is enabled on the server. This cert must have clientAuth enabled.

❸ The private key corresponding to the public cert.

We can now see the contrast between server-side and client-side when it comes to TLS. The server needs to have certificate of the CA that issues client certs (goofy_ca_cert.pem as in Section 13.3.2) whereas the client needs to have the certificate of the CA that issues server certs (donald_ca_cert.pem). We used distinct CAs for the two to illustrate the difference. This is a choice not a necessity.

14.1.1. Enrolling bootstrap user: The enroll *command*

The very first step is to obtain X.509 certificate of the bootstrap user i.e., enrolling the bootstrap user. We do that by running following command. We assume you have exported FABRIC_CA_HOME or another env variable so fabric-ca-client can find the config file and tls settings in it. Substitute localhost:6000 with the address of your fabric-ca-server and mickey:mickeypw with username:password of your bootstrap user if they are different.

Listing 14. 2. Enrolling the bootstrap user.

```
$ fabric-ca-client enroll -d \
-u https://mickey:mickeypw@localhost:6000 \
-M msp/mickey \
--caname mickey-mouse \
--csr.names C=US --csr.names ST=WA --csr.names L=Bellevue --csr.names O=Biotor
```

The `-d` flag is used to turn on debug output. The `-u` flag is used to provide address of the `fabric-ca-server` to which the client will connect. It also contains the username and password of the user we are trying to enroll. `fabric-ca-server` will first *authenticate this user against its database before issuing a certificate to it.* The `-M` flag is used to specify an *output* directory where the client will store the certificate and other files. The `--caname` is used to provide the CA we want to target. Recall we have 3 CAs running on same server in previous chapter. The `--csr.names` is used to customize the Country, STate, Location and Organization attributes in the X.509 certificate.

When the `enroll` command is run, `fabric-ca-client` will generate a public private key pair on the client side. The type of key is governed by the `csr.keyrequest.algo` setting in the config file and set to `ecdsa` by default. The `csr.keyrequest.size` controls the size of the key and is set to 256 by default (units: bits). A CSR is also drafted and sent to the `fabric-ca-server` for endorsement. We see this in below output:

```
[DEBUG] generate key from request: algo=ecdsa, size=256
[INFO] encoded CSR
[DEBUG] Sending request
POST https://localhost:6000/enroll
...
```

The most important thing you need to understand is that the private key is never sent to the server. This will not make any difference when both server and client are running on the same machine, but is paramount otherwise. The private key is the client's property and should never be exposed to anyone. Running the above command should end in following output:

```
[INFO] Stored client certificate at /Users/siddjain/phf/fabric-ca-
lesson/biotor/client/msp/mickey/signcerts/cert.pem
[INFO] Stored root CA certificate at /Users/siddjain/phf/fabric-ca-
lesson/biotor/client/msp/mickey/cacerts/localhost-6000.pem
[INFO] Stored Issuer public key at /Users/siddjain/phf/fabric-ca-
lesson/biotor/client/msp/mickey/IssuerPublicKey
[INFO] Stored Issuer revocation public key at /Users/siddjain/phf/fabric-ca-
lesson/biotor/client/msp/mickey/IssuerRevocationPublicKey
```

Let's look at the `msp/mickey` directory. It has a predefined structure:

Listing 14. 3. The MSP directory of bootstrap user.

```
$ tree msp/mickey
msp/mickey
├────── IssuerPublicKey
├────── IssuerRevocationPublicKey
├────── cacerts
│       └────── localhost-6000.pem   ❶
├────── keystore
│       └────── 3dbe5f8d8b8babaa7c0d5e06da556c7de144935b917711282d0d535ad420c433_sk  ❷
├────── signcerts
│       └────── cert.pem          ❸
└────── user
```

❶ A copy of the CA's cert is stored in this directory. This will be nothing but `mickey_ca_cert.pem` - the cert we used to bootstrap the `fabric-ca-server`.

❷ The private key generated by `fabric-ca-client`. The name will obviously be different in your case.

❸ The X.509 certificate issued by `fabric-ca-server`

As exercises, print out `cert.pem` and verify it has the key usages associated with the default signing profile and the C, ST, L, O attributes we defined. Also verify `localhost-6000.pem` is nothing but `mickey_ca_cert.pem`. Next, verify the private key and public key inside `cert.pem` are a matching pair.

A user can be enrolled multiple times by running the enroll command again. Do that as exercise and change the C, ST, L, O to something else as shown below for example:

```
$ fabric-ca-client enroll -d -u https://mickey:mickeypw@localhost:6000 -M msp/mickey
--caname mickey mouse --csr.names C=CA --csr.names ST=BC --csr.names L=Vancouver
--csr.names O="Express Medicinals"
```

You will see a new private key and the old certificate will be overwritten:

```
$ tree msp/mickey
msp/mickey
├────── IssuerPublicKey
├────── IssuerRevocationPublicKey
├────── cacerts
│       └────── localhost-6000.pem
├────── keystore
│       ├────── 3dbe5f8d8b8babaa7c0d5e06da556c7de144935b917711282d0d535ad420c433_sk
│       └────── c1cf5972275bbb22bf5ffa0412ccbc95e7a3a6cccb0016fd743836b49bb56457_sk
├────── signcerts
│       └────── cert.pem
└────── user
```

Verify the old private key does not match the public key stored inside the new `cert.pem`. *The user has been issued a new identity.* The ramifications of this are important to keep in mind. The `maxenrollments` attribute controls how many times a user can enroll without changing his or her password. A default value of this attribute is set in `fabric-ca-server-config.yaml` and can be changed when a user is registered. Note that one can specify whatever Organization one wants in the `enroll` command. *The smart contract should never rely on the* 0 *attribute in X.509 cert to decide the organization a user belongs to.*

 The enrollment request is processed on the server by function `handleEnroll` in `lib/serverenroll.go`. Stick a breakpoint in that function to debug issues with enrollment.

Enroll bootstrap users of Donald and Goofy. We will need them when we want to get TLS certificates. You will have to specify different `caname` in your enrollment requests. If you print out the `msp` directories of `donald` and `goofy` you will see something different. For example, below is Donald's `msp` directory:

Listing 14. 4. MSP directory of bootstrap user of an intermediate CA.

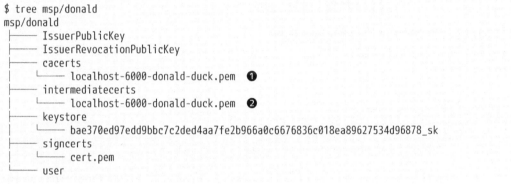

```
$ tree msp/donald
msp/donald
├── IssuerPublicKey
├── IssuerRevocationPublicKey
├── cacerts
│   └── localhost-6000-donald-duck.pem    ❶
├── intermediatecerts
│   └── localhost-6000-donald-duck.pem    ❷
├── keystore
│   └── bae370ed97edd9bbc7c2ded4aa7fe2b966a0c6676836c018ea89627534d96878_sk
├── signcerts
│   └── cert.pem
└── user
```

❶ This will be same as `mickey_ca_cert.pem`

❷ This will be same as `donald_ca_cert.pem`

Verify `cacerts/localhost-6000-donald-duck.pem` *is nothing but* `mickey_ca_cert.pem` *whereas* `intermediatecerts/localhost-6001.pem` *is nothing but* `donald_ca_cert.pem`.

Fabric also provides a `reenroll` command in addition to `enroll`. What's the difference? The `enroll` command authenticates the user against `fabric-ca-server` using the username and password (`http(s)://<username>:<password>@@<ca-server>:<port>`) whereas the `reenroll` command authenticates the user using his or her X.509 identity in the provided MSP directory. *It is thus not necessary to provide username and password when using* `reenroll` *but you must already be in possession of the user's X.509 identity.* And the only way you can be in possession of a user's identity is if the user has been enrolled in the past. That's why the command is called `reenroll`. *Why would anyone want to use* `reenroll` *when they are already in possession of user's identity?* The answer is that perhaps you made a mistake in the `--csr.names` metadata when enrolling the user. The `reenroll` command will first read user's identity from provided MSP directory, [161] make call to `fabric-ca-server` and then *overwrite* the user's identity in the MSP directory. With the `enroll` command, the MSP directory is expected to point to an *output* folder that is ideally *empty* or even *non-existent* whereas with `reenroll` the MSP directory is both *input* as well as *output*. Use it with caution. The only advantage it offers over `enroll` is that you don't have to expose/transmit the user's password again. *The* maxenrollments *check applies only to the* enroll *command. It does not apply to* reenroll. Like the enroll command, the reenroll command also issues a new identity to the user. It creates a new private and public key pair when it sends CSR to the server and does not reuse the existing keys.

> If you lose a X.509 certificate, instead of enrolling or re-enrolling the user - which would issue a new identity to the user - run the certificate list command with the --id.name option to retrieve the certificate from the server. This does assume that you have not lost the private key. If you have lost the private key, then you have lost the identity and the certificate by itself won't help much.

14.1.2. Registering peer0.biotor.com: *The* register *command*

Now that the bootstrap user is enrolled, he or she can enroll other users in the system. Run following command to register Biotor's peer node:

Listing 14. 5. Registering Biotor's peer node

```
$ fabric-ca-client register -d \
-M msp/mickey \
--url https://localhost:6000 \
--caname mickey-mouse \
--id.name peer0.biotor.com \
--id.type peer \
--id.affiliation "biotor.Supply Chain" \
--id.attrs "foo=bar:ecert,email=peer0@biotor.com"
```

The -d flag turns on debug output. --url or -u is used to provide URL of the fabric-ca-server. --id.name provides the username of the user that we are registering. As far as fabric-ca-server is concerned peer0.biotor.com is a user just like anyone else. --id.type sets the type of the user and will appear as OU=peer in the user's X.509 certificate. For demonstration, we have used the --id.affiliation option to show how to use it. Its not necessary to use it. The affiliations will appear as OU=biotor, OU=Supply Chain in the X.509 certificate. Once again for demonstration purposes, we use the --id.attrs option to illustrate its usage. The attribute foo will appear in the X.509 certificate as indicated by the ecert keyword (ecert stands for enrollment certificate). The email attribute will not appear in the enrollment certificate (unless explicitly requested in an enrollment request) but will be part of the user's profile in the CA server's database. *The* -M *flag is important and is used to specify the MSP directory of the registrar (*mickey *in our case).* We generated this in previous section when we enrolled mickey. We can thus see a user (mickey) has to be registered and enrolled themselves before they can begin registering other users.

> The -M flag is used to provide an *input* directory in case of register command whereas it provides an *output* directory in case of enroll command.

When the command above is run, you should see it end in an output resembling below:

```
[DEBUG] Sending request
POST https://localhost:6000/register
{"id":"peer0.biotor.com","type":"peer","affiliation":"biotor.Supply
Chain","attrs":[{"name":"foo","value":"bar","ecert":true},{"name":"email","value":"peer0@bi
otor.com"}]}
[DEBUG] Received response
statusCode=201 (201 Created)
[DEBUG] The register request completed successfully
Password: RapHsYNCJifs
```

The `register` command basically creates a user account in the CA server's database. Note that it returned a random password in the output above. This is the user's password and will be needed at time of enrollment. It is possible to specify a password at time of registration using the `--id.secret` option. In that case, `fabric-ca-server` will not generate a random password. Also the settings can be defined in the config file vs. having to specify them on the command line. If you check the server logs, they should show following messages:

```
[DEBUG] canRegister - Check to see if user 'mickey' can register
[DEBUG] Checking to see if caller 'mickey' can act on type 'peer'
[DEBUG] Checking to see if caller 'mickey' is a registrar
[DEBUG] Validating affiliation: biotor.Supply Chain
[DEBUG] Checking to see if affiliation 'biotor.Supply Chain' contains caller's affiliation
''
[DEBUG] Caller has root affiliation
[DEBUG] DB: Get affiliation biotor.Supply Chain
[DEBUG] Registering user id: peer0.biotor.com
[DEBUG] Max enrollment value verification - User specified max enrollment: 0, CA max
enrollment: -1
[DEBUG] DB: Getting identity peer0.biotor.com
[DEBUG] DB: Add identity peer0.biotor.com
[DEBUG] Successfully added identity peer0.biotor.com to the database
[INFO] 127.0.0.1:52819 POST /register 201 0 "OK"
```

This confirms `peer0.biotor.com` has been successfully registered. Congratulations! Table 14. 1 summarizes the different settings you can specify when registering a user.

Table 14. 1. Parameter's affecting a user's registration. From hyperledger-fabric-ca.readthedocs.io/en/release-1.4/users-guide.html. Reproduced under terms of CC license.

Fields	Required	Default Value
ID	Yes	
Secret	No	
Affiliation	No	Caller's Affiliation
Type	No	client
Maxenrollments	No	0
Attributes	No	

The register request is processed on the server by function `register` in `lib/serverregister.go`. Stick a breakpoint in that function to debug issues with registration.

14.1.3. Modifying, Deleting and Listing users: The `identity` *command*

Oddly enough, to add confusion, Fabric provides one than one way to register a user. A user can also be registered using the `fabric-ca-client identity add` command as shown below for a `test` user:

Listing 14. 6. Alternate way to register users.

```
$ fabric-ca-client identity add test -d \
-M msp/mickey \
--url https://localhost:6000 \
--caname mickey-mouse \
--type peer \
--affiliation "biotor.Supply Chain" \
--attrs "foo=bar:ecert,email=peer0@biotor.com"
```

Run the above command and compare the output to what you get from `register` command. The `identity add` command also supports a `--json` option that provides an alternative way to provide a user's registration settings. An example is shown below:

Listing 14. 7. Yet another way to register users.

```
$ fabric-ca-client identity add ... \
--json '{"type":"peer","affiliation":"biotor.Supply
Chain","attrs":[{"name":"email","value":"peer0@biotor.com"},{"name":"foo","value":"bar","ec
ert":truc}],"max_enrollments":0}'
```

Both `register` and `identity add` commands use the `registerUser` function in `lib/serverregister.go`. The entry point for `identity add` command is `processPostRequest` in `lib/serveridentities.go`. I would suggest sticking to one command and forget the other.

It is possible to modify the profile of a registered user using the `identity modify` command as shown below for example:

Listing 14. 8. Modifying attributes of a registered `test` user.

```
$ fabric-ca-client identity modify test -d \
-M msp/mickey \
-u https://localhost:6000 \
--caname mickey-mouse \
--attrs "email=test@biotor.com:ecert"
```

Note that we did not have to specify the password of the user. Indeed if we had specified a `--secret` that would have set the password of `test` user to the secret we specified. To remove an attribute set it to blank like so `--attrs email=`. This would remove the `email` attribute from the user's profile. Try running the command and see what it gives.

To unregister a user i.e., remove them from the database use the `identity remove` command like so:

Listing 14. 9. Unregistering (removing or deleting) a `test` **user**

```
$ fabric-ca-client identity remove test -d -M msp/mickey -u https://localhost:6000 --caname
mickey-mouse
```

This will remove **test** user and also revoke any certificates associated with the **test** user. *The removal of identities is disabled in the* `fabric-ca-server` *by default for protection. It has to be enabled by starting the* `fabric-ca-server` *with the* `--cfg.identities.allowremove` *command-line option.*

Finally, to get a list of all the users `mickey` is authorized to see, run following command:

Listing 14. 10. Getting a list of registered users.

```
$ fabric-ca-client identity list -d -M msp/mickey -u https://localhost:6000 --caname
mickey-mouse
```

It is also possible to specify a particular user to the `list` command using the `--id` option like so:

Listing 14. 11. Getting details of a particular user using the `--id` **option.**

```
$ fabric-ca-client identity list --id peer0.biotor.com -u https://localhost:6000 --caname
mickey-mouse
```

 `fabric-ca-server` allows users to re-enroll but not re-register. `fabric-ca-server` returns a 500 error if you try to re-register a user. If you need to re-register a user, remove them first using the `identity remove` command.

14.1.4. *Getting identity and TLS certs for* `peer0.biotor.com`

Let's use the `enroll` command again but this time to get the ID and TLS certs of `peer0.biotor.com`. Begin by running as example:

```
$ fabric-ca-client enroll -d \
-M msp/peer0.biotor.com \
-u https://peer0.biotor.com:RapHsYNCJifs@localhost:6000 \
--caname mickey-mouse \
--csr.names C=US --csr.names ST="New Jersey" --csr.names O=Biotor
```

In above we have used the password we obtained earlier as part of registration step. Above command would enroll `peer0.biotor.com` against the `default` profile and you should see an output that ends in following:

```
[INFO] Stored client certificate at /Users/siddjain/phf/fabric-ca-
lesson/biotor/client/msp/peer0.biotor.com/signcerts/cert.pem
[INFO] Stored root CA certificate at /Users/siddjain/phf/fabric-ca-
lesson/biotor/client/msp/peer0.biotor.com/cacerts/localhost-6000.pem
```

Open `cert.pem` and verify it has all the attributes you expect. See Listing 14. 12 for reference.

Listing 14. 12. ID certificate of `peer0.biotor.com`. **An ID certificate is characterized by presence of** `digital signature` **bit and** `id-ecPublicKey`.

```
Certificate:
    ...
        Subject: C=US, ST=New Jersey, O=Biotor, OU=peer, OU=biotor, OU=Supply Chain,
CN=peer0.biotor.com
        Subject Public Key Info:
            Public Key Algorithm: id-ecPublicKey
            ...
        X509v3 extensions:
            X509v3 Key Usage: critical
                Digital Signature
            X509v3 Basic Constraints: critical
                CA:FALSE
            ...
            1.2.3.4.5.6.7.8.1:
                {"attrs":{"foo":"bar","hf.Affiliation":"biotor.Supply
Chain","hf.EnrollmentID":"peer0.biotor.com","hf.Type":"peer"}}
    ...
```

We see that the `type` of the user appears as a OU (i.e., `OU=peer`) in the X.509 cert. `OU=peer` will provide privileges associated with the `peer` role when Node OUs are enabled as we saw in Section 7.3.2. We also see that all `hf` attributes are listed in the certificate and any custom attributes that were marked with `ecert` keyword also appear in the certificate.

- You cannot change or customize the subject's `CN` in your enrollment request. `fabric-ca-client` sets the `CN` to the registered username irrespective of whatever you may define on the command-line or in the config file, when it submits the request to `fabric-ca-server`. [162]
- You cannot change or customize the subject's OUs. `fabric-ca-server` follows a prescribed procedure where it sets the `OU` according to the registered `type` and `affiliation` of the user ignoring whatever OUs may be set in the CSR. [163]

Now let's get the TLS certificate of `peer0.biotor.com` which will come in handy if we want to run the peer with TLS enabled. First, we need to register `peer0.biotor.com` against Donald and Goofy as we have adopted a convention that Mickey will issue ID certs and Donald and Goofy will issue TLS certs. Do that as exercise. You will need to enroll Donald and Goofy's respective bootstrap users as first step if you haven't done that. *When you are done,* `peer0.biotor.com` *will have an entry as a registered user in databases of all 3 CAs. The 3 CAs are hosted on same server but their databases are independent.* You can now see that using multiple CAs also increases the work that needs to be done by that much amount. After registering `peer0.biotor.com` against Donald and Goofy, *we repeat the same* `enroll` *command as before except that we change the enrollment profile using the* `--enrollment.profile` *command-line option.* There are a few gotchas to be aware of. *If you specify the same* `-M` *directory that we used before, the ID certificate we obtained previously will get overwritten with the TLS certificate.* So make sure to enter a new directory for the different enrollment profile. The next thing is to make sure you enter all the names and IP addresses by which you want `peer0.biotor.com` to be accessible. These are specified using the `--csr.hosts` option and will appear in the SAN section of the X.509 certificate. The SAN section is not applicable for a client cert but it is paramount for a TLS certificate used on the server since the hostname validation depends on it. A complete example is shown below where I have entered `localhost` and `microsoft.com` as the hostnames just for demonstration. The `localhost` is useful in dev setup when the client is on the same machine as the server.

Listing 14. 13. Getting TLS certificate for `peer0.biotor.com`. **Note that we now use** donald-duck **CA and have changed the** enrollment.profile **to** tls.

```
$ fabric-ca-client enroll -d \
-M msp/peer0.biotor.com/tls \
-u https://peer0.biotor.com:RapHsYNCJifs@localhost:6000 \
--caname donald-duck \
--enrollment.profile tls \
--csr.names C=CA --csr.names ST="British Columbia" --csr.names O=Biotor \
--csr.hosts peer0.biotor.com \
--csr.hosts localhost \
--csr.hosts microsoft.com
```

I used different Country and STate attributes (instead of US/New Jersey) for demonstration in above command. Also when I had registered the peer against Donald and Goofy I manually specified the enrollment secret (RapHsYNCJifs) instead of letting it be auto-generated. That is why you see the same password we saw earlier being re-used in listing above. When you run above command, it should end with an output like below:

```
[INFO] Stored client certificate at /Users/siddjain/phf/fabric-ca-
lesson/biotor/client/msp/peer0.biotor.com/tls/signcerts/cert.pem
[INFO] Stored TLS root CA certificate at /Users/siddjain/phf/fabric-ca-
lesson/biotor/client/msp/peer0.biotor.com/tls/tlscacerts/tls-localhost-6000.pem
```

Open `cert.pem` and verify it has the key usages corresponding to the `signing.profiles.tls` profile defined in Donald's `fabric-ca-server-config.yaml`. Also verify all the `--csr.hosts` you entered are listed as Subject Alternative Names in `cert.pem`. See below for comparison:

Listing 14. 14. TLS certificate of `peer0.biotor.com`.

```
Certificate:
    ...
        Issuer: C=US, ST=WA, O=Biotor, OU=IT, CN=Donald Duck (Director of IT)
        ...
        Subject: C=CA, ST=British Columbia, O=Biotor, OU=peer, OU=biotor, OU=Supply Chain,
CN=peer0.biotor.com
        ...
        X509v3 extensions:
            X509v3 Key Usage: critical
                Digital Signature, Key Encipherment, Key Agreement        ❶
            X509v3 Extended Key Usage:
                TLS Web Server Authentication, TLS Web Client Authentication ❷
            ...
            X509v3 Subject Alternative Name:                                 ❸
                DNS:peer0.biotor.com, DNS:localhost, DNS:microsoft.com
            1.2.3.4.5.6.7.8.1:
                {"attrs":{"foo":"bar","hf.Affiliation":"biotor.Supply
Chain","hf.EnrollmentID":"peer0.biotor.com","hf.Type":"peer"}}
    ...
```

❶ The only key usage that is necessary for a TLS server certificate is `Key Encipherment`

❷ The only EKU (extended key usage) that is necessary for a TLS server certificate is `TLS Web Server Authentication`

❸ SAN section must contain all names and IP addresses by which the server should be accessible

If you print out the MSP directory, you will see following directory structure:

```
$ tree msp/peer0.biotor.com/tls
msp/peer0.biotor.com/tls
├────── IssuerPublicKey
├────── IssuerRevocationPublicKey
├────── cacerts
├────── keystore
│       └────── 40a9859b5056a17aac79706fd4180e93297fc8cf4010ac4741d3c58dae1999a0_sk
├────── signcerts
│       └────── cert.pem
├────── tlscacerts
│       └────── tls-localhost-6000-donald-duck.pem   ❶
├────── tlsintermediatecerts
│       └────── tls-localhost-6000-donald-duck.pem   ❷
└────── user
```

❶ Same as `mickey_ca_cert.pem`

❷ Same as `donald_ca_cert.pem`

Note very carefully that the `cacerts` *folder is empty and that Donald's cert is in* `tlsintermediatecerts` *and Mickey's cert (who issued Donald his certificate) is in* `tlscacerts`.

> ℹ The MSP directory structure you will end up with when using `fabric-ca-client` will be different from the MSP directory structure you had with `cryptogen`.

Congratulations! You now have all the knowledge necessary to be able to obtain X.509 certificates for Biotor's orderer, user and admin. `fabric-ca-client` supports a handful of more commands. We won't be able to cover them in the book and refer the reader to online documentation. One last command we cover is the `getcainfo` that comes in handy when debugging. It returns the complete certificate chain of the CA. There is no username, password or MSP directory that you need to provide. You can run the command as follows to get the CA chains of all 3 CAs:

Listing 14. 15. Getting CA certificates of our 3 CAs.

```
$ fabric-ca-client getcainfo -u https://localhost:6000 --caname mickey-mouse -M mickey
$ fabric-ca-client getcainfo -u https://localhost:6000 --caname donald-duck -M donald
$ fabric-ca-client getcainfo -u https://localhost:6000 --caname goofy-ca -M goofy
```

In all three cases, `-M` provides output directory. The certificates are stored in `cacerts` and `intermediatecerts` folders under the directory. This command is useful in conjunction with `openssl verify` to debug certificate validation errors.

14.2. Using the Node.js `fabric-ca-client`

We work from `$/fabric-ca-lesson/biotor/ts-client` in this section.

Let's move on to the Node.js `fabric-ca-client`. You are more likely to use the Node.js client in production as part of an application rather than the command-line client. Begin by creating a directory `ts-client` under `$/fabric-ca-lesson/biotor` and copy over the `package.json`, `tsconfig.json` and `tslint.json` files from Chapter 3 into this directory. Edit the `dependencies` section of `package.json` file to include `fabric-ca-client` and `fabric-network` packages like so:

```
"dependencies": {
    "fabric-ca-client": "~2.2.2",
    "fabric-network": "~2.2.2"
},
```

Now run `npm i` to install the dependencies. This will install `fabric-ca-client` under `node_modules` directory. From there you can see all the source code of `fabric-ca-client` under `fabric-ca-client/lib` folder. The starting point for the Node.js `fabric-ca-client` is the **FabricCAServices** class. This class in turn holds an instance of `FabricCAClient` inside it. `FabricCAServices` also provides entry point to three other services - **AffiliationService**, **IdentityService** and **CertificateService** via the `newAffiliationService`, `newIdentityService` and `newCertificateService` methods. These three services are analogous to the respective `affiliation`, `identity` and `certificate` commands of the command-line `fabric-ca-client`. Listing 14. 16 provides an overview of the `FabricCAServices` class. You can see there is a 1:1 mapping between the class and the command-line `fabric-ca-client`.

Listing 14. 16. The `FabricCAServices` **class is the entry point to the Node.js** `fabric-ca-client`

```
const FabricCAServices = class extends BaseClient {
    constructor(url, tlsOptions, caName, cryptoSuite)
    getCaName()
    async register(req, registrar)
    async enroll(req)
    async reenroll(currentUser, attrReqs)
    async revoke(request, registrar)
    async generateCRL(request, registrar)
    newCertificateService()
    newIdentityService()
    newAffiliationService()
}
```

The `newCertificateService` method is not exposed in the TypeScript declarations file `index.d.ts`. Edit the file to expose the method.

The logging of Node.js `fabric-ca-client` is controlled by the same **HFC_LOGGING** variable that we encountered in Chapter 8 in relation to the `fabric-network` package.

14.2.1. Creating a new instance of `FabricCAServices`

A new instance of `FabricCAServices` is created by providing the constructor the `url` of the `fabric-ca-server`. The `tlsOptions` is used to configure TLS and has the information corresponding to the `tls` section in the `fabric-ca-client-config.yaml` file. That yaml file is not used by the Node.js client. Remember this is a separate client and none of the env variables like `FABRIC_CA_HOME` and yaml file apply to it. `tlsOptions` can be created quite simply as follows:

Listing 14. 17. `tlsOptions` **is needed to connect to a server with TLS enabled.**

```
const tlsOptions: TLSOptions = {
    trustedRoots: [fs.readFileSync(cacert)],
    verify: true
}
```

There are several things to note. In case of the command-line client we provided `donald_ca_cert.pem` in `tls.certfiles` but that will not work here. The Node.js client needs to be provided with the full chain leading up to the self-signed certificate. So the `cacert` variable in above needs to point to `donald_mickey_chain.pem` which will have PEM encoded certificate of `donald` followed by PEM encoded certificate of `mickey`. The `verify` flag in Listing 14. 17 is quite important. If you set it to `false` or leave it undefined then the client will not validate the server's certificate against trusted CAs. *I recommend never to do that.* The `trustedRoots` and `verify` variables are passed as-is to the `ca` and `rejectUnauthorized` options of Node.js `https.request` object which makes the actual HTTPS request to `fabric-ca-server`. [164] And the `https` object in turn uses Node.js `tls.connect` to establish TLS connection with a server. [165]

The TypeScript compiler is going to throw an error (Type 'Buffer' is not assignable to type 'string | number') with above declaration of `tlsOptions`. This is yet another bug in Fabric having to do with incorrect TypeScript definition file. Ignore the error. The TypeScript compiler still compiles the file to JavaScript. You also have the option to fix the error by editing the `index.d.ts` file of `fabric-ca-client` module.

Another thing to note is that the Node.js client has no support for connecting to a server with client authentication enabled (FABN-1234). The `tlsOptions` struct does not expose any fields related to client authentication. There is a workaround for this which is to set the `key` and `cert` on the global `https` agent in your TypeScript like so:

Listing 14. 18. Connecting to a server that has client authentication enabled by setting the key and cert on global https agent.

```
import https = require('https');
...
https.globalAgent.options.key
        = fs.readFileSync('client_tls_key.pem');   ❶
https.globalAgent.options.cert
        = fs.readFileSync('client_tls_cert.pem');   ❷
```

❶ The PEM encoded key
❷ The PEM encoded client TLS certificate

The `caName` in `FabricCAServices` constructor is used to provide the name of the CA to target and is useful when you have multiple CAs deployed on the same server. The `cryptoSuite` is an optional field and controls the crypto algorithm used by the client when it generates key pairs. The default algorithm is set to `ecdsa` with 256 bit key size which is the same setting that we have been using with the command-line client. A new `cryptoSuite` can be constructed using the `Utils.newCryptoSuite` method from the `fabric-common` package. [166] This method takes input a struct of the form:

```
export interface CryptoSetting {
    algorithm: string;      ❶
    hash: string;           ❷
    keysize: number;        ❸
    software: boolean;      ❹
}
```

❶ Only 'EC' (standing for ECDSA) is supported
❷ 'SHA2' or 'SHA3'
❸ Use 256 or 384 bit keys
❹ Set to `false` to use a Hardware Security Module (HSM)

Since `fabric-ca-client` only supports the ECDSA algorithm, *practically speaking the only time you need to explicitly construct a* `cryptoSuite` *is when you want to use a Hardware Security Module or HSM.* From Wikipedia: A hardware security module is a physical computing device that safeguards and manages digital keys, performs encryption and decryption functions for digital signatures, strong authentication and other cryptographic functions. [167] Thus instead of using software libraries, one relies on hardware for cryptographic functions. To use a HSM the software field of the CryptoSetting struct is marked false. Using HSM is outside the scope of this book. Its not something I have tried.

14.2.2. Registering a new user

Before we can register a new user, we need to load the identity of the registrar into the system. And before we can do that, we need to store the identity in a Wallet. This can be done using the addToWallet script provided in Section 8.10.4. In what follows we assume you have stored Mickey or another registrar's identity into a wallet. An identity stored in the wallet can be loaded using following code:

Listing 14. 19. Load an identity from the wallet.

```
async function loadIdentity(wallet: Wallet, username: string) {   ❶
    const identity = await wallet.get(username);                   ❷
    if (!identity) {
        throw `Could not find ${username} in the wallet`;
    }
    const provider = wallet.getProviderRegistry()
                            .getProvider(identity.type);
    return await provider.getUserContext(identity, username);      ❸
}
```

❶ The function is provided a wallet instance and id of user to be retrieved from the wallet.

❷ Load identity of the user from the wallet.

❸ This method creates a SigningIdentity. The SigningIdentity is what allows a user to sign requests.

We have seen how to obtain an instance of Wallet earlier in Section 8.10.4. Now that we have the registrar's identity, we can register a new user using the register method:

```
register(req: FabricCAServices.IRegisterRequest, registrar: User): Promise<string>;
```

This method takes input a IRegisterRequest shown below:

```
export interface IRegisterRequest {
    enrollmentID: string;
    enrollmentSecret?: string;
    role?: string;
    affiliation: string;
    maxEnrollments?: number;
    attrs?: IKeyValueAttribute[];
}
```

and returns the password of the user on success. Here is a code snippet showing it in action:

Listing 14. 20. Registering a new user using the Node.js `fabric-ca-client`

```
const ca = new FabricCAServices(url, tlsOptions, caName);      ❶
const walletPath = './wallet';
const wallet = await Wallets.newFileSystemWallet(walletPath);  ❷
const adminUser = await loadIdentity(wallet, registrar);       ❸
console.log("Making registration request...");
const secret = await ca.register({                             ❹
    affiliation: affiliation,                                  ❺
    enrollmentID: username,                                    ❻
    role: type,                                                ❼
    attrs: [{name: "email", value: email, ecert: true}]        ❽
}, adminUser);                                                 ❾
console.log(`Successfully registered ${username} with password ${secret}`);
```

❶ Create instance of `FabricCAServices` which will provide entry point to all functions related to Node.js `fabric-ca-client`.

❷ Create instance of a wallet.

❸ Load identity of registrar. Assumes identity has been previously stored in the wallet.

❹ Make asynchronous call to `fabric-ca-server` to register new user. The function will return the user's password. A password will be generated by the server if its not provided by the client.

❺ The affiliation of the user (optional). Same rules apply as with command-line client.

❻ The username of the new user.

❼ The type of user. Fabric supports `client`, `admin`, `member`, `peer` or `orderer` types. Default type is `client`.

❽ For demonstration we add an email attribute to the user's profile. This attribute will also appear in the user's X.509 certificate by virtue of marking it as `ecert:true`.

❾ A registrar (`adminUser`) is needed to register new users.

One thing to note is that *whereas the command-line client sets the* `maxEnrollments` *to 0 allowing the user to enroll unlimited number of times, the Node.js client by default sets* `maxEnrollments` *to 1. This means the user will be able to enroll only once using the default setting.* If you need to enroll again for some reason you can do that using the `reenroll` command. A complete script to register a user is provided in `$/fabric-ca-lesson/biotor/ts-client/src/register.ts`. Go ahead and register the orderer, admin and user of Biotor as exercises using that script.

14.2.3. Enrolling a user

Once a user is registered, they can be enrolled i.e., we can obtain their X.509 certificate. To do this we do not need any registrar, only the username and password of the user are required. The user is enrolled using the `enroll` method on `FabricCAServices`.

```
enroll(req: FabricCAServices.IEnrollmentRequest):
Promise<FabricCAServices.IEnrollResponse>;
```

The method takes input an `IEnrollmentRequest` shown below:

```
export interface IEnrollmentRequest {
    enrollmentID: string;
    enrollmentSecret: string;
    profile?: string;
    attr_reqs?: IAttributeRequest[];
    csr?: string;
}
```

In above, the enrollmentID is nothing but the username of the user. The enrollmentSecret is the password of the user. These are the only two fields which are required. Rest of the fields are optional. The profile maps to the signing profile to use. Leave it unset to use the default profile. The attr_reqs is an array of attributes that you would like to appear in the X.509 certificate. Any attributes that were marked ecert:true at time of registration automatically appear in the X.509 certificate. attr_reqs can be used to select any attributes that were not marked with ecert:true at time of registration but which you still want to be listed in the X.509 certificate. The IAttributeRequest interface is shown below:

```
export interface IAttributeRequest {
    name: string;
    optional: boolean;
}
```

You only need to set the name field of this interface equal to the attribute you want listed in the X.509 certificate.

This takes us to the csr field in IEnrollmentRequest. *Contrary to what you might expect this is not the same as the* csr *option of the command-line* fabric-ca-client. *In case of the Node.js client,* csr *field if set is supposed to contain a PEM encoded certificate signing request like the one we generated using* openssl *in Section 13.2.3.* When the csr is left empty Node.js client automatically generates a CSR. The thing to note is that the Node.js client does not allow the developer to set any Subject attributes in the CSR it generates. The command-line client allows us to use --csr.names to set the Country, STate, Location, Organization attributes. The Node.js client supports none of that. It is unfortunate. The CSR it will generate will just have CN=<enrollmentID> where enrollmentID is replaced by actual username of the user and *the* Subject *is empty.* This behavior is hardcoded and not something you can change.

 You will have to generate your own csr if you want to customize the Country, State, Location, Organization attributes of the X.509 certificate. A better option is to modify the fabric-ca-client itself as shown in exercises.

The enroll command returns a Promise to an IEnrollResponse shown below:

```
export interface IEnrollResponse {
    key: IKey;
    certificate: string;
    rootCertificate: string;
}
```

The `key` *is set only if the* `csr` *was empty in the* `enroll` *request.* The reason is that if you specified your own CSR then you are in possession of the private key yourself. The `certificate` stores the X.509 certificate issued by `fabric-ca-server` and `rootCertificate` will contain the issuing CA chain.

With this background we can simply enroll a user like so:

Listing 14. 21. Enrolling a user using the Node.js `fabric-ca-client`

```
const res = await ca.enroll({
    enrollmentID: username,
    enrollmentSecret: password,
    profile: profile
});
```

The certificate returned by the `enroll` command can then be stored in the `Wallet` as follows:

Listing 14. 22. Storing X.509 cert and private key in a wallet

```
const x509Identity = {
    credentials: {
        certificate: res.certificate,       ❶
        privateKey: res.key.toBytes()       ❷
    },
    mspId: 'BiotorMSP',
    type: 'X.509'
};
await wallet.put(username, x509Identity); ❸
console.log(`Successfully enrolled ${username} and imported it into the wallet`);
```

❶ The certificate returned by the `fabric-ca-server`

❷ The private key generated on the client. Contrary to what the name suggests, `toBytes()` does not convert into bytes. It converts to a PEM string which is what we need.

❸ Save the identity into a wallet for later use

A complete script to enroll a user is provided in `src/enroll.ts`. Run the script using the default profile to obtain the ID certs of Biotor's user, admin and orderer. Print out the certs and verify there are no Country, State, Location, Organization attributes in them. Verify the `CN` is set to the username and the `OU` are set according to the type and affiliation of the user when the user was registered in the system.

14.2.4. Obtaining TLS certs with Node.js client

To obtain a TLS certificate, simply change the `profile` when making `enroll` request to `tls` and the client will request server to use the `tls` signing profile. You will also need to set the `caName` in constructor of `FabricCAServices` to target appropriate CA. We run into a problem though. Where do we specify the `hosts`? The Node.js client has no support for specifying `hosts` that appear in SAN section of TLS certificate and are crucial part of the TLS cert. The command-line client allowed to specify hosts using the `--csr.hosts` option. *You can't get around this limitation even by generating your own* `csr` *in the* `IEnrollmentRequest`. As an exercise modify Node.js `fabric-`

`ca-client` to fix this limitation. *Hint*: You will need to add a `hosts` field to the `enrollRequest` in `fabric-ca-client/lib/FabricCAClient.js::enroll` method: [168]

```
async enroll(enrollmentID, enrollmentSecret, csr, profile, attr_reqs) {
    ...
    const res = await this.request('POST', 'enroll', undefined, enrollRequest,
requestOptions);
}
```

The `enrollRequest` becomes the body of the `POST` request made to `fabric-ca-server`. *The* `fabric-ca-server` *expects all hostnames to be listed as a* `hosts` *array in the request body.* Here is what a sample request body looks like for reference where the `hosts` has been set:

```
{
    hosts: [ 'orderer0.biotor.com' ],
    certificate_request: '-----BEGIN CERTIFICATE REQUEST-----\n' +
        ...
        '-----END CERTIFICATE REQUEST-----\n',
    profile: 'tls',
    crl_override: '',
    label: '',
    NotBefore: '0001-01-01T00:00:00Z',
    NotAfter: '0001-01-01T00:00:00Z',
    CAName: 'mickey-mouse'
}
```

The `NotBefore` and `NotAfter` fields are don't care because *the certificate expiry is configured on the server and its not something the client can choose.* In addition, the `POST` request has to contain a `Authorization` header followed by base64 encoded credentials of the user prefixed with `Basic` keyword. An example is shown below:

```
Header: net/http.Header [
    "Authorization": [
        "Basic bWlja2V50m1pY2tleXB3Cg==",
    ],
]
```

`fabric-ca-client` inserts this header with following code in the `enroll` method of `FabricCAClient.js`:

```
const requestOptions = {
    auth: `${enrollmentID}:${enrollmentSecret}`,
};
```

This is a standard way of authentication built into HTTP protocol itself and is known as `Basic Authentication`. [169] The TLS connection between client and server protects an eavesdropper from spying on the password.

Exercise 14.1

This exercise asks you to modify the Node.js fabric-ca-client to expose a friendly enroll API where the IEnrollmentRequest is augmented as follows:

```
export interface IEnrollmentRequest {
    enrollmentID: string;
    enrollmentSecret: string;
    profile?: string;
    attr_reqs?: IAttributeRequest[];
    csr?: string;
    subjectDN?: string;
    hosts?: string[];
}
```

The subjectDN should allow the user to specify the Subject field of X.509 certificate in LDAP(RFC 2253) format e.g., CN=Steve Kille,O=Isode Limited,C=GB. The hosts field should allow the user to set the hostnames to appear in a TLS certificate (see previous exercise). *Hint*: Instead of the hardcoded:

```
csr = privateKey.generateCSR('CN=' + req.enrollmentID);
```

line in fabric-ca-client/lib/FabricCAServices.js::enroll, you would use the subjectDN as argument to generateCSR.

Exercise 14.2

This exercise asks you to add support for client authentication to the Node.js fabric-ca-client (FABN-1234). To do this, the developer should be able to provide a keyfile and associated certificate to FabricCAServices and it would use them in FabricCAClient.js::request method as follows

```
const requestOptions = {
    hostname: this._hostname,
    port: this._port,
    path,
    method: http_method,
    ca: this._tlsOptions.trustedRoots,
    rejectUnauthorized: this._tlsOptions.verify,
    key: pemKey,
    cert: pemCert,
    timeout: CONNECTION_TIMEOUT
};
```

where pemKey and pemCert are PEM encoded strings containing the private key and public cert respectively to be used for client authentication.

Registering and enrolling users are the two most common tasks performed with the fabric-ca-client. We leave the other endpoints as exercises for the reader to explore.

14.3. Inspecting the sqlite3 database

Let's see how to inspect the registered users' database. Begin by running `sqlite3` command (install it if you don't have it) from the directory that contains `fabric-ca-server.db`. This directory should be `$/fabric-ca-lesson/biotor/mickey`.

```
$ sqlite3 fabric-ca-server.db
SQLite version 3.22.0 2018-12-19 01:30:22
Enter ".help" for usage hints.
sqlite>
```

The command takes us to the `sqlite3` shell. From here we can see a list of tables by running `.tables` as shown below:

```
sqlite> .tables
affiliations              properties
certificates              revocation_authority_info
credentials               users
nonces
```

Note there is no semicolon at end of `.tables`. The commands beginning with a dot (`.`) do not end in a semicolon. We can see the schema of a table using the `.schema` command:

```
sqlite> .schema users
CREATE TABLE users (id VARCHAR(255), token bytea, type VARCHAR(256), affiliation
VARCHAR(1024), attributes TEXT, state INTEGER,  max_enrollments INTEGER, level INTEGER
DEFAULT 0, incorrect_password_attempts INTEGER DEFAULT 0);
```

To list the rows in a table we use the familiar `select` command:

```
sqlite> select * from users;
mickey|$2a$10$biorB.lFveuYY1JnGAAMmutG1h9xKtzNuvutCGxaugglPnUDSfb0m|client||[{"name":"hf.Ge
nCRL","value":"1"},{"name":"hf.Registrar.Attributes","value":"*"},{"name":"hf.AffiliationMg
r","value":"1"},{"name":"hf.Registrar.Roles","value":"*"},{"name":"hf.Registrar.DelegateRol
es","value":"*"},{"name":"hf.Revoker","value":"1"},{"name":"hf.IntermediateCA","value":"1"}
]|2|-1|2|0
...
```

Table 14. 2 displays the schema and sample row in friendly form. Remember `max_enrollments` only applies to `enroll`. It does not apply to `reenroll`.

Table 14. 2. Schema of the `users` table

Column	Type	Example	Notes
id	VARCHAR(255)	mickey	username (aka enrollment ID) provided at time of registration

Column	Type	Example	Notes
token	bytea	$2a$10$biorB...	hashed password. The $2a$ prefix indicates the use of bcrypt algorithm to hash passwords.
type	VARCHAR(256)	client	client, admin, member, peer or orderer
affiliation	VARCHAR(1024)	biotor.Supply Chain	affiliations appear as OUs in X.509 certificate (OU=biotor, OU=Supply Chain)
attributes	TEXT	[{"name":"hf.GenCRL"," value":"1"}...]	hf. attributes affect what a registrar can do. We can set other attributes as well. Attributes marked ecert:true will appear in X.509 certificate.
state	INTEGER	2	# of previously successful logins
max_enrollments	INTEGER	-1	# of times user can enroll. -1 means unlimited.
level	INTEGER	2	used to verify if the user needs migration.
incorrect_password_atte mpts	INTEGER	0	# of incorrect password attempts

It is instructive to inspect the schema of the certificates table as well:

```
sqlite> .schema certificates
CREATE TABLE certificates (id VARCHAR(255), serial_number blob NOT NULL,
authority_key_identifier blob NOT NULL, ca_label blob, status blob NOT NULL, reason int,
expiry timestamp, revoked_at timestamp, pem blob NOT NULL, level INTEGER DEFAULT 0, PRIMARY
KEY(serial_number, authority_key_identifier));
```

Table 14. 3 displays the schema of certificates table and sample row in friendly form.

Table 14. 3. Schema of certificates table

Column	Type	Example	Notes
id	VARCHAR(255)	mickey	username
serial_number	blob NOT NULL	5dcaa38b261...	serial # of certificate
authority_key_identifier	blob NOT NULL	d462f39a36a...	identifier of the CA

Column	Type	Example	Notes
ca_label	blob		
status	blob NOT NULL	good	whether certificate is valid or revoked etc.
reason	int	0	reason for revocation
expiry	timestamp	2021-09-14 22:27:00+00:00	when certificate expires
revoked_at	timestamp	0001-01-01 00:00:00+00:00	when certificate was revoked
pem	blob NOT NULL		PEM encoded certificate
level	INTEGER DEFAULT 0	1	

The authority_key_identifier (AKI) is the identifier of the CA. It will be the same for all the rows in our case. If multiple CAs were using the same database or if a CA owned multiple signing keys then the AKI can vary between rows. The AKI provides a means of identifying the public key corresponding to the private key used to sign a certificate. The thing to note w.r.t. the certificates table is that the table does not contain any private key. That is never sent to the server as mentioned earlier. It is generated on the client and is confidential information like a password.

 Advanced readers might be tempted to modify fabric-ca-server.db directly without going through the fabric-ca-server. The usual caveats apply here. Do it at your own risk.

To log out of sqlite3 shell, use Ctrl+D combination.

14.4. Summary

* Fabric provides a command-line and a Node.js fabric-ca-client. Both clients are written in different programming languages and use altogether different dependencies but both make the same HTTP REST calls to fabric-ca-server.
* When a user is enrolled, the private key is generated on the client and never sent to the fabric-ca-server. It is a secret like a password and should never be shared with anybody.
* If you enroll or reenroll a user, they are issued a brand new identity and a new set of keys. If you lose a X.509 certificate, use the certificate list command to recover the certificate instead of enrolling the user again.
* The only difference between enroll and reenroll has to do with the way the user is authenticated. enroll authenticates the user using the username and password whereas reenroll authenticates the user using a token generated from the user's X.509 credentials. [170] The only way you can have these credentials is if you have enrolled the user in the past. That is why the command is called reenroll. In both cases, the username/password or token are placed

inside an HTTP Authorization header.

* The maxEnrollments check applies only to the enroll endpoint not to reenroll.
* Use the identity command to unregister users or change their password (aka enrollment secret) etc.
* You cannot change or customize the user's OUs in your enrollment request. fabric-ca-server follows a prescribed procedure where it sets the OU according to the registered type and affiliation of the user ignoring whatever OUs may be set in the CSR.
* You cannot customize the Common Name (CN) of the user in your enrollment request. Both clients set the CN equal to the enrollment ID (aka username) of the user when they make HTTP request to the server.
* The logging level of the command-line client can be controlled using the -d or --loglevel flags or FABRIC_CA_CLIENT_LOGLEVEL env variable or loglevel setting in fabric-ca-client-config.yaml whereas the logging level of the Node.js client is controlled with the HFC_LOGGING env variable or hfc-logging setting in default.json.
* The Node.js client comes with three limitations: no support for client authentication, no support for setting hostnames, no support for setting subject metadata. The last limitation is cosmetic and a workaround exists for the first limitation. The leaves the hostnames limitation which applies only to TLS (server) certs. We show how to fix it in the chapter.

[160] The code that does this can be seen at github.com/hyperledger/fabric-ca/blob/v1.4.6/util/util.go#L474
[161] github.com/hyperledger/fabric-ca/blob/v1.4.6/cmd/fabric-ca-client/command/reenroll.go#L62
[162] github.com/hyperledger/fabric-ca/blob/v1.4.6/lib/client.go#L204
[163] github.com/hyperledger/fabric-ca/blob/v1.4.6/lib/serverenroll.go#L304
[164] github.com/hyperledger/fabric-sdk-node/blob/v2.2.2/fabric-ca-client/lib/FabricCAClient.js#L263
[165] nodejs.org/api/tls.html#tls_tls_connect_options_callback
[166] github.com/hyperledger/fabric-sdk-node/blob/v2.2.2/fabric-common/lib/Utils.js#L82
[167] en.wikipedia.org/wiki/Hardware_security_module
[168] github.com/hyperledger/fabric-sdk-node/blob/v2.2.2/fabric-ca-client/lib/FabricCAClient.js#L388
[169] en.wikipedia.org/wiki/Basic_access_authentication
[170] github.com/hyperledger/fabric-ca/blob/v1.4.6/lib/identity.go#L583

Chapter 15. Authenticating Users using LDAP

This chapter covers:

- Provisioning an OpenLDAP server
- Communicating with an LDAP server from Node.js
- Authenticating users against LDAP from Node.js
- Password hashing schemes
- How to use `fabric-ca-server` with LDAP

> Code for this chapter is in `$/ldap-lesson`

This chapter has two entry points: one if you want to learn how to use `fabric-ca-server` with LDAP and another if you want to learn how to use LDAP in general to authenticate users and implement an identity and access management (IAM) system. Most of the chapter will cover LDAP in its own right without any relation to Fabric. We will show how to connect `fabric-ca-server` to LDAP at end of the chapter.

The whole chapter can be said to be inspired by a question I saw on StackOverflow asking if the `fabric-ca-server` can be used to authenticate users. [171] The question refers to following problem: consider the Node.js code we wrote for example in Section 8.10 to perform transactions. Where does that code run? *Does it run on the end user's device or does it run on a web server in production?* In most cases you would want it to run on a web server and your users will access this web server from a browser such as Chrome or a mobile app. This is known as a *thin client* architecture. *How do you authenticate your users before letting them perform transactions?* One way would be to do pretty much what Fabric does - use their X.509 certificates to authenticate them (Section 7.3); you may feel like we are running in circles. But this will require user to install a certificate on their device and runs into a *portability problem* when user wants to access the application from say a friend's machine or public kiosk at the airport. Users are much more used to authenticating themselves with a username and password. This is so common now-a-days that we take it for granted but have you ever wondered how that is actually done behind the scenes?

These days user authentication is handled by technologies like Single Sign On (SSO) and Identity Providers (IdP). Maybe your client application is for use by company employees and your company uses an identity provider with a SAML or OAuth interface. If that's the case, well and good and you should definitely use that. But what if this is a brand new system and no a-priori database exists to store and authenticate users? Before you run off to some enterprise selling SAML/OAuth solutions, consider doing it yourself (DIY) using LDAP. Or maybe your company has not jumped on the SAML/OAuth bandwagon and is using LDAP for identity management and you want to learn how to authenticate users against the company's LDAP server. This chapter will show how to do that. And if you are going to run a LDAP server why not re-use it so that it doubles down as the registry of `fabric-ca-server` too - we'll see how to do that as well in this chapter.

Before we dive in, two comments. *First*, note that in this architecture where we use username/password for authentication, the users' X.509 credentials which Fabric uses and relies on all the time are *never stored on the users' device*. They just reside on the web server in a wallet or secret store. The web application after authenticating the user, loads respective credentials from the wallet. *Second*, going back to the question with which we began this chapter, `fabric-ca-server` cannot be used for user authentication. Internally it does perform a username/password authentication when it gets a request for an `enroll` for example, but the `fabric-ca-server` does not expose this as an API. `fabric-ca-server` is not meant to be used for user authentication - that is not its purpose and use-case. Let us now dive into LDAP by understanding its history.

15.1. An Introduction to LDAP and its history

In the beginning there was *X.500* - a standard developed by telecommunications industry that defined how data can be stored in a directory, and *DAP - Directory Access Protocol* that defined how this data can be accessed. With the advent of internet, *LDAP* or *Lightweight Directory Access Protocol* was invented that allowed X.500 directories to be accessed over a TCP/IP (i.e., internet) connection. The LDAP protocol has been refined over the years in RFCs 1487, 1777, 2251 and 4510. There are three versions of the protocol with v3 (RFC 4510) being the latest.

LDAP as its name suggests is a protocol and then there are databases or solutions that support that protocol. The most popular and widely deployed LDAP database is of course the ubiquitous Microsoft Active Directory (AD). *Note that Azure AD which is Microsoft's cloud offering of Active Directory does not support the LDAP interface.* [172] There are paid as well as some free LDAP solutions out there. Some of the free open source LDAP solutions are:

- *OpenLDAP*: The first LDAP database/server was written at the University of Michigan (known as `slapd`). OpenLDAP is a fork of this code. OpenLDAP probably has the largest deployment footprint amongst the free LDAP solutions.
- *RedHat Directory Server*: Known more commonly as *Port 389*, this is also derived from the original University of Michigan `slapd` project. The project is named after the port LDAP uses for communication.
- *OpenDJ*: Written in Java and having its roots in the Sun Microsystems company.
- *Apache Directory Server*: also written in Java.
- *Ldapjs*: pure JavaScript implementation.

Both OpenLDAP and Port 389 are written in C/C++. We will not go into a discussion of which solution is the best as that is outside the scope of this book but we will use OpenLDAP to provision an LDAP server and show how to access it from Node.js using `ldapjs`.

15.1.1. How LDAP models Data

Whereas relational databases such as MySQL model data as tables, *LDAP models data as trees* - that is why the word *directory* is in its name, similar to the way we have a yellow pages directory that contains business names organized into alphabetical folders. So when it comes to LDAP there is always a root node known as *Base Domain* - this could be name of your organization - and then users would be child nodes of this root node. In general you can have an organizational hierarchy where users are segregated and grouped into organizational units etc. The nodes in a LDAP tree are also known as *directory objects*. Thus it is much more natural and common to talk in terms of a directory rather than a database and directory trees rather than tables when discussing LDAP. Table 15. 1 is a mapping of terms between RDBMS (Relational Data Base Management System) and LDAP.

Table 15. 1. Mapping of terms from RDBMS to LDAP

RDBMS	LDAP
Row	Directory object / entry
Table	Directory Tree
Database	Directory

There are a lot of acronyms you come across with LDAP. Table 15. 2 lists some of these. In fact the Subject and Issuer headers we have seen in X.509 certificates follow LDAP naming convention - not surprising when you consider that both X.509 and LDAP have their roots in X.500.

Table 15. 2. LDAP Abbreviations

Acronym	Full Form
dc	domain component
dn	distinguished name
cn	common name

We can have multiple trees inside a LDAP Directory just like we have multiple tables in a MySQL database. The full LDAP schema can be found in RFC 4512 and detailing it here is outside the scope of this book - it is quite complicated to say the least. But some key concepts are as follows: every node has to have a unique `Distinguished Name` (`DN`) which is nothing but the full path of the node in the directory tree starting from the node to the root. The Distinguished Name is very much like the fully qualified class name in Java which is the class name prefixed by the complete namespace the class lives in. Just like the fully qualified class name in Java disambiguates a class and provides name resolution when there is a conflict (e.g., think of same class `Foo` but in two different namespaces or packages) similarly the distinguished name in LDAP provides unique ID of a directory object. The next thing to note is that LDAP has the notion of an `objectClass` which is again quite similar to notion of classes in object oriented programming languages. A directory object or node can be associated with *multiple* object classes and will inherit their attributes and properties. An `objectClass` itself can inherit from other object classes. Again, just like Java has some well-known and built in classes similarly LDAP has some well-known and built-in object classes that you can find in its RFC. We will use one such class `inetorgperson` to describe a user.

15.1.2. Introduction to OpenLDAP: a free and open source LDAP server

OpenLDAP is a free LDAP v3 compliant database and server. We will see how to run an OpenLDAP server in this chapter. You don't have to pay anything to use OpenLDAP. OpenLDAP itself is made up of three main components:

- a *frontend* - `slapd` standing for the Standalone LDAP Daemon - which handles network access and protocol processing. The frontend exposes the database as an LDAP data store.
- a *backend* which deals strictly with data storage. This is the database.
- a command line *client* to make requests against the `slapd` server. This consists of CLI tools such as `ldapadd`, `ldapsearch`, `ldapmodify` and utilities such as `slapcat` and `slappasswd`.

The part where it can get confusing is that OpenLDAP itself can use a SQL database on the backend if you wanted! According to Wikipedia, currently 17 different backends are provided in the OpenLDAP distribution. [173]

15.1.3. MDB: OpenLDAP's Memory Mapped Database

We will use the `mdb` backend in this chapter which stores data in an *embedded memory mapped database*. `mdb` is at the heart of OpenLDAP and is its default backend. It is a *key-value store* and the basic idea behind `mdb` is to treat *all of computer storage as a single virtual address space*. Pages of storage may reside in RAM (primary storage) or disk (secondary storage) but `mdb` does not care about it. It maps all the storage as a single read-only virtual address space - that is why its known as a memory mapped database. It relies on the OS to bring a page in secondary storage into primary storage when needed. This may seem counter-intuitive and the backends that predate `mdb` (hdh and hdb) made heavy of caching to prevent having to read from the disk but as they say premature optimization is the root of all-evil. Those solutions ironically introduced a lot of performance issues (heap fragmentation, deadlocks) and required careful tuning of caches which were eliminated by having *no caching at all at the database level* in `mdb`. `mdb` only allows one writer at a time but multiple readers can read. This is because the readers are isolated from the writer. How? The writer writes to a new version of the database. This way of isolating the writer from the readers is known as *Multi Version Concurrency Control (MVCC)*. `mdb` does not retain full history of the database. It only retains two versions - current and the one immediately before it. The fact that `mdb` is optimized for read operations means it is ideally suited for applications such as a user management service where it is much more common to have to authenticate existing users than register new ones into the system. `mdb` makes use of *B+ trees* for efficient searches and retrieval. The idea of mapping all of storage into a single virtual address space is not new and dates back to Multics operating system. [174] The idea fell out of fashion because 32 bit processors can only handle virtual memory less than than 4GB. Thus if you have a hard disk that exceeds that amount, it cannot be mapped to a virtual address space. `mdb` is made possible only by the advent of 64 bit processors common in use today which can handle a virtual address space of 8 exabytes. `mdb` is available as a general purpose database under the name of Lightning MDB (LMDB) for use in your non-LDAP projects. [175]

15.2. Provisioning an OpenLDAP Server

We work from $ldap-lesson/server in this section.

You can provision an instance of OpenLDAP server using the slapd and ldap-utils package on Ubuntu and openldap, openldap-clients and openldap-servers packages on CentOS/RHEL. Refer to online documentation for details and examples. [176] We will instead jump directly to running OpenLDAP in a Docker container to mimic a production setup.

We will make use of the tiredofit/openldap Docker image published on Docker Hub to provision an OpenLDAP server. The latest version at time of this writing is 7.1.3 and that is what we will use. Always check if you are using the same version in case you run into any issues with installation. To demonstrate the most secure setup, we will run the OpenLDAP server with *TLS enabled and client authentication turned on*. So the first step would be to obtain the TLS certificates used to bootstrap the server. We leave this as exercise for the reader. You will first have to register the ldap server against donald - the fabric-ca-server that we have been using for TLS server certs - and then enroll to obtain TLS certificate and key. A dump of pre-generated crypto material can be found in $/ldap-lesson/crypto in case you want to use that. It has two files ldap.biotor.com_tls_cert.pem and ldap.biotor.com_tls_key.pem which are the certificate and key respectively. The subjectAltName in TLS cert is set to ldap.biotor.com so this has to match the hostname the client uses to connect to the server.

Once you have the TLS certs, execute the $/ldap-lesson/server/run-ldap-server.sh file making changes to it as necessary to get an instance of OpenLDAP server running on your machine. *The script assumes you have a Docker network provisioned previously.* It uses the a network named biotor_net by default. There are two passwords that you can customize: an ADMIN_PASSWORD and CONFIG_PASSWORD. Both are need at bootstrap. By default the server will listen to requests at port 389 and 636. There are other settings you can customize such as ORGANIZATION set to Biotor by default and BASE_DN set to dc=biotor,dc=com by default. This weird looking string is just how LDAP syntax works. Just like in Java we use namespaces delimited by period (.), LDAP uses tokens of the form dc=foo separated by commas and the order is reversed e.g., *Java's* com.biotor *becomes* dc=biotor,dc=com *in LDAP*. The script sets up a couple of bind mounts. One bind mount is used to inject TLS certs and keys into the container, and other bind mounts are used to persist data from the container. Once you are ready - make sure the file paths are setup correctly - run the script like so:

```
$ ./run-ldap-server.sh
```

The Docker image would be automatically downloaded and you should see a container named ldap.biotor.com up and running! A complete log can be found at git.io/Jk2Kd for comparison. This is where the server is started:

```
+ /usr/sbin/slapd -h 'ldap://localhost ldaps://localhost ldapi:///' -u ldap -g ldap -d 1
[INFO] /etc/services.available/10-openldap/run ** [openldap] Starting OpenLDAP 2.4.53
...
5f77a28a @(#) $OpenLDAP: slapd 2.4.53 (Sep 15 2020 00:56:49) $
...
5f77a28a daemon_init: listen on ldap://localhost
5f77a28a daemon_init: listen on ldaps://localhost
5f77a28a daemon_init: listen on ldapi:///
...
5f77a28a daemon_init: 3 listeners opened
...
5f77a28a slapd init: initiated server.
```

There are three listeners - any of which can be used to connect to and transact against the database.
The ldap listener is listening at port 389. The ldaps listener listens at port 636 and the ldapi
listener is listening at the unix socket similar to the unix:/// listener we have seen with Docker
daemon. At this point if you log into the Docker container and run slapcat you should see
following output:

Listing 15. 1. A bare-bones LDAP database with just a root node (dc=biotor,dc=com) **and an
admin user** (cn=admin,dc=biotor,dc=com)

```
bash-5.0# slapcat
dn: dc=biotor,dc=com
o: Biotor
dc: biotor
description: biotor
objectClass: top
objectClass: dcObject
objectClass: organization
structuralObjectClass: organization
entryUUID: 4cfad9b2-507e-40f6-97e1-423a6422f17c
creatorsName: cn=admin,dc=biotor,dc=com
createTimestamp: 20201002215833Z
entryCSN: 20201002215833.354707Z#000000#000#000000
modifiersName: cn=admin,dc=biotor,dc=com
modifyTimestamp: 20201002215833Z

dn: cn=admin,dc=biotor,dc=com
objectClass: simpleSecurityObject
objectClass: organizationalRole
cn: admin
description: LDAP administrator
userPassword:: e1NTSEF9Wjlzdm42U2w0dm44WnNVUGlzTm93WjQwSHhsYXF5Rkw=
structuralObjectClass: organizationalRole
entryUUID: f8ed0cde-0a2c-48d5-a17a-de1fc8edde7f
creatorsName: cn=admin,dc=biotor,dc=com
createTimestamp: 20201002215833Z
entryCSN: 20201002215833.403585Z#000000#000#000000
modifiersName: cn=admin,dc=biotor,dc=com
modifyTimestamp: 20201002215833Z
```

There are just two nodes in the tree. The root node dc=biotor,dc=com which is the BASE_DN and the admin node cn=admin,dc=biotor,dc=com. This confirms the database has been successfully initialized! Recall that LDAP has the notion of an objectClass and that a directory object or node can be associated with multiple object classes and will inherit their attributes and properties. We can see several object classes in Listing 15. 1. The LDAP schema files describing the various objectClasses are stored at /etc/openldap/schema on the server. Check out that directory. core.schema contains the core schema.

OpenLDAP's own configuration is stored in a cn=config tree. Config updates can be made dynamically using LDIF files. This inserts new nodes into the cn=config tree. LDIF stands for *LDAP Directory Interchange Format*. The old way of configuring the server was to edit slapd.conf file. The dynamic method is superior. To print out the config tree, run following command:

Listing 15. 2. Print out the config tree.

```
bash-5.0# slapcat -b cn=config
```

Next, its a good idea to check that the TLS is working as expected. To do that run following command from the client machine:

```
$ openssl s_client -connect ldap.biotor.com:636 -cert client_tls_cert.pem -key
client_tls_key.pem -state -nbio -CAfile donald_mickey_chain.pem -showcerts
```

Use the /etc/hosts trick to map ldap.biotor.com to appropriate IP address if you don't have actual DNS mapping setup. client_tls_cert.pem and client_tls_key.pem are the cert and key the client uses to authenticate itself to the server. The server's cert is signed by donald and so we have to provide the complete CA chain (donald_mickey_chain.pem) to openssl in the CAfile variable. The client's own certificate is signed by goofy and a copy of Goofy→Mickey chain was provided to the server at startup so it can validate the client cert. A sample output of running above command can be found at git.io/Jk2Kj for comparison. It gave me following session:

```
SSL-Session:
    Protocol  : TLSv1.2
    Cipher    : ECDHE-ECDSA-AES256-GCM-SHA384
    Session-ID: E4CF1EC211D1412B322BB490835795AC42D3877C6FFA6744ECD2D59A58FD8615
    Session-ID-ctx:
    Master-Key:
42753B7A7A43190207C48438E5690497935DB3551EEF5D586F6B49B93D48B37561AC6B880AA11E52511686D5E26
DCA1
```

This indicates success.

15.3. Querying OpenLDAP from Node.js

We work from $ldap-lesson/node-client in this section.

OpenLDAP comes with a few CLI tools but we will jump directly to the Node.js client. After all, we started down the path of LDAP as a means to authenticate and register new users from our client application. So let's see how to use LDAP from Node.js. The key library which makes this possible is ldapjs. The current version at time of this writing is 2.2.0 so that's what we will be using. This library can even spin up a LDAP server! It won't be the same as an OpenLDAP server. OpenLDAP and ldapjs are two separate projects having nothing to do with each other. We will only use the client API of ldapjs to run commands against any LDAP compliant server from Node.js. The way ldapjs works is that we create an instance of the Client object using the - you guessed it - createClient method. After that this client *binds* or authenticates to the server using some credentials. LDAP uses the term *bind* instead of authentication or log in but it has same meaning. Once a client has bound to a server it creates a *stateful session - LDAP unlike HTTP is a stateful protocol.* All subsequent commands against the server are executed with the privileges of that user. Finally the client *unbinds* itself from the server.

An LDAP server supports two kinds of authentication - a *simple authentication* where user specifies their username and password and a *SASL* (Simple Authentication and Security Layer) authentication where the client and server negotiate customized mechanisms for authentication, depending on the level of protection desired by the client and the server. *The SASL authentication is only supported by v3 of LDAP protocol.* We will only show simple authentication in this book and leave SASL as an exercise to explore. The SASL authentication is spec'd out in RFC 4422. The OpenLDAP 2.4 server supports both simple and SASL authentication.

There are two ways by which TLS is supported by LDAP. The recommended way is to use what is known as the *Start TLS* operation on the ldap:// endpoint (port 389 by default). The **starttls** operation *upgrades* the connection to use the TLS protocol between client and server. This method is *standardized* in Section 4.14 of the LDAP RFC 4511. *The client has to make a request to the server to initiate this operation.* Many servers including OpenLDAP also support TLS out-of-the-box on a ldaps:// endpoint (port 639 by default). This is similar to how we use TLS on any https:// server. This option might seem more enticing but its *not a part of the LDAP standard per se* and has led to some security vulnerabilities where it was found that the LDAP clients shipped with the Sun/Oracle and OpenJDK JVMs did not perform hostname verification when using ldaps. [177] We will use **starttls** in our code samples. *The lesson here is that you should enable* TLS_ENFORCE *env variable on the server in the* run-ldap-server.sh *script otherwise it can allow non-TLS connections on port* 389. (we do that by default so you don't have to make any changes). The TLS_ENFORCE flag inserts a olcSecurity: ssf=128 and olcLocalSSF: 128 in the server's configuration as you can see in install/assets/slapd/config/tls/tls-enforce-enable.ldif of tiredofit/openldap:7.1.3 repo. [178]

Listing 15. 3. Settings to enforce TLS on OpenLDAP server.

```
dn: cn=config
changetype: modify
replace: olcSecurity
olcSecurity: ssf=128
-
replace: olcLocalSSF
olcLocalSSF: 128
```

Cd into the `$/ldap-lesson/node-client` directory to execute the code in this section. Verify it contains following .js files:

```
$ git ls-files *.js
add-user.js
get-config-entry.js
get-user.js
hash-passwords.js
init.js
test-admin.js
use-crypt.js
verify-password.js
```

15.3.1. The `ldapjs-client` *module: creating a* `Client`

The `ldapjs` library does not have a very user-friendly interface and seems to be stuck in a pre-historic era when Node.js did not have any `Promises`. A lightweight wrapper around this library is provided in `$/ldap-lesson/node-client/ldapjs-client` which exposes it with a more user-friendly and modern API. We will be using this module in the book. Run `npm i` in `ldapjs-client` folder to install the module's dependencies. The starting point of `ldapjs-client` module is a config file that is written in `yaml`. You can name the config file anything and place it anywhere. A sample config that will work in our case is shown below:

Listing 15. 4. Config file for `ldapjs-client` module

```
ldap:
  base:
    dn: dc=biotor,dc=com              ❶

  server: ldap.biotor.com            ❷
  port: 389                          ❸

  admin:
    password: superman               ❹

  config:
    password: spiderman              ❺

  tls:
    ca: donald_mickey_chain.pem      ❻
    key: client_tls_key.pem          ❼
    cert: client_tls_cert.pem        ❽
    subjectAltName:  ldap.biotor.com ❾
```

❶ The `basedn` we used when we started the server. This forms the root of Biotor's directory tree.
❷ The URL (hostname) where the server is running
❸ The port where server is listening for connections
❹ Password of user who will have admin access to Biotor's directory tree
❺ Password to modify the `cn=config` tree
❻ Certificate chain of CA who issued server's TLS certificate

❼ The private key associated with client's TLS certificate
❽ Client's TLS certificate
❾ passed as-is to the `servername` property of Node.js `tls.connect` method

The `ldapjs-client` module supports using environment variables to override the settings in config file - the same pattern that we have seen with Fabric throughout this book. Once you have a config file it can be loaded like so from the `node-client` directory:

```
const { createConnectionOpts, createClient } = require("./ldapjs-client");
var opts = createConnectionOpts("config.yaml");
```

Above code will read the config file and convert it to a format that can be used to create a client. The creation of client is done by the `createClient` method as shown below:

```
var client = await createClient(opts);
```

The `createClient` method will automatically take care of starting TLS using the `starttls` operation if a CA cert file was given in the `config.yaml`. The presence of a CA cert file is meant to indicate that the user wishes to use TLS.

15.3.2. Authenticating as admin: Illustrating the `bind` operation

Once you have a `client` object, you can authenticate to the server by binding to it. The code to bind as admin is simply:

Listing 15. 5. The `bind` operation allows a user to log into a LDAP server.
```
await client.bind(opts.adminDN, opts.adminPassword);
```

Remember that in LDAP a DN *or* Distinguished Name *is needed to fully identify a node in a directory tree. So when we* bind *we have to use a* DN *not just the username (*common name *in LDAP parlance). The* DN *will contain the full path of the directory object.* This code will throw error if there is any problem - the problem could be related to TLS, wrong password or any number of other reasons - and otherwise will complete silently. You should always `unbind` the client when you are done. This is akin to logging out the user and is done by simply calling:

```
await client.unbind();
```

 The `client` object is useless after the `unbind` operation. Create a new `client` for any subsequent use.

There is a `test-admin.js` script provided in the `node-client` folder which puts everything together. Run this script now using `node test-admin.js` and verify there are no errors.

15.3.3. Initializing the database with a users *group: Illustrating the* add *and* modify *operations*

We are now ready to add or register new users into the system. Before we do that we will create a users group under which we will store users. This is done by creating a ou=users,dc=biotor,dc=com entry of type organizationalUnit in the directory tree as shown in the code below:

Listing 15. 6. Create a users **group in the directory tree**

```
var entry = {
    objectClass: ["top", "organizationalUnit"]
}
await client.add("ou=users," + config.baseDN, entry);
```

The top object class is just a base class from which every LDAP class descends or inherits. Above method illustrates the add operation. Another thing we will do as best practice is to set what algorithm will be used to hash passwords. We do that by specifying the olcPasswordHash directive as shown in the code below:

Listing 15. 7. Setting the hash algorithm for hashed passwords

```
var change = new ldapjs.Change({
    operation: 'add',
    modification: {
        olcPasswordHash: '{SSHA}'
    }
});
await client.modify("olcDatabase={-1}frontend,cn=config", change);
```

In above, ldapjs is the native ldapjs library without our wrapper. We use the Change class of that library to specify a changeset we want to make. The Change class is used to make a change to an attribute - the olcPasswordHash attribute in our case. The attribute and its value are specified in the modification struct. *The* Change *class only accepts one attribute at a time so the* modification *must list exactly one attribute and the value for that attribute.* The operation parameter of the Change object can have following values: add, replace and delete. add will add the attribute value - it is used when the attribute does not exist. replace will replace the value of the attribute and delete is used to delete the attribute. A Change to the server is made using a modify operation. The modify function can take a single Change object or an array of Change objects when you want to make multiple changes but don't want to make multiple calls to the server to do so. Note that the change to olcPasswordHash is made in the config tree (cn=config). SSHA stands for SHA1 secure hash algorithm and is one of the password hashing algorithms supported by OpenLDAP.

An init.js script is provided which puts everything together. Run this script using node init.js and verify there are no errors. On the server, you should now see following entry in Biotor's directory tree:

```
dn: ou=users,dc=biotor,dc=com
objectClass: top
objectClass: organizationalUnit
structuralObjectClass: organizationalUnit
ou: users
entryUUID: 08f21305-099b-42ed-bb68-943b1bacddbc
creatorsName: cn=admin,dc=biotor,dc=com
createTimestamp: 20201005234305Z
entryCSN: 20201005234305.088177Z#000000#000#000000
modifiersName: cn=admin,dc=biotor,dc=com
modifyTimestamp: 20201005234305Z
```

15.3.4. Adding, Deleting and Authenticating a user: using the `inetOrgPerson` *object class*

Let us now see how to add or register a new user. Given a username and password, a new user is created in the directory tree by adding an entry of the form `uid=<username>,ou=users,dc=biotor,dc=com`. Similar to how we needed a registrar to register new users when using the `fabric-ca-server`, here also only a user with sufficient privileges can register new users. Thus we will be using the admin user to register a new user. The code to add a new user is shown below:

Listing 15. 8. Adding a new user to the directory tree.

```
var newUser = {
    cn: 'Bob Smith',
    sn: 'Smith',
    uid: 'bobs',
    objectClass: 'inetOrgPerson',
    userPassword: "bob's cat"
};
await client.add(
    'uid=bob,ou=users,dc=biotor,dc=com', newUser);
```

In above we have done `bind` operation with credentials of Biotor's admin (not shown in the code). Note the use of `inetOrgPerson` class which defines the object type. This is one of the built-in LDAP classes. Its schema can be found in `/etc/openldap/schema` on the server. We use the same `client.add` method we have used before.

Write a Node.js script to add this user as exercise. Don't forget to `unbind` when you are done. Run `slapcat` on the server to verify new user entry is successfully created.

Once you have added a new user you can log in as that user by executing the `bind` operation as illustrated earlier. The `bind` operation will throw error if there is any problem with user credentials or complete successfully otherwise. Do it as exercise. *This way your client application can log in and authenticate a user.* Note that the `bind` operation can also throw if there are problems unrelated to incorrect user credentials.

An existing entry in the directory tree can be *deleted* using the `del` method on the `client` object.

The input to the method is the distinguished name of the directory object.

15.3.5. Checking to see if a user exists and getting user details: Illustrating the search *operation*

A common use-case of LDAP directory is to search if an entry exists. In fact remember that is what directories like yellow pages are used for. This can be done via the search method of ldapjs library which takes as input the node where to start the search (the tree under the node will be searched including the node itself) and optionally some filters can be specified to filter the search results. The raw method on ldapjs has following syntax:

Listing 15. 9. The raw search **method on** ldapjs

```
search(base: string, options: SearchOptions, callback: SearchCallBack): void;
```

The ldapjs-client module wraps this method in a friendly API that takes input the distinguished name (dn) of the entry you want to search and returns a true or false depending on whether the entry exists or not. The new method is called exists. Check it out.

Following code shows how to get a user's details given the user's distinguished name:

Listing 15. 10. Getting a user's details

```
var result = await client.search(dn);
if (result) {
  var entries = result.entries;
  if (entries && entries.length === 1) {
     return entries[0].object;
  }
}
```

Here we are using the ldapjs-client search method, not the raw search method on ldapjs. ldapjs-client wraps the code above in a function getEntry. There is also a get-user.js script provided that you can run like so to get a user's details:

```
$ node get-user.js bob
```

Try it out. The getEntry function will be handy to get a user's full name to be displayed in a UI and any other profile information. Couple of things to note:

* *Getting user details does not require us to* bind *to the server.* You will notice there is no bind operation in get-user.js. This is by design and can be changed by reconfiguring the server if one wanted. The default configuration configures the server so that reading Biotor's directory tree does not require any authentication.
* get-user.js will not return the user's password. Thank goodness.

15.3.6. Putting it all together: add-user.js *script*

The add-user.js script puts together everything we have learned. It takes a username and password from the command line. It checks to see if a user with given username exists in the directory (search operation). If so, the user is deleted (del operation). A new user entry is created (add operation) in the directory tree and the program then tests that the username and password can be used to successfully log in (bind operation). The code for add-user.js looks like following:

Listing 15. 11. The add-user.js **script illustrates** bind, search, add, del **(delete), and** unbind **operations.**

```
var user = getDN(username, opts.baseDN);        ❶
var adminDN = opts.adminDN;
var adminPassword = opts.adminPassword;
var client = await createClient(opts);
await client.bind(adminDN, adminPassword);      ❷
console.log("logged in as admin");
var exists = await client.exists(user);         ❸
if (exists) {
    console.log(user + " already exists");
    console.log("deleting " + user);
    await client.del(user);                     ❹
}
await addUser(client, username, passwd, fullName, opts.baseDN);   ❺
console.log("added " + username);
await client.unbind();

client = await createClient(opts);                               ❻
await client.bind(user, passwd);                                 ❼
console.log("tested logging with " + username + " credentials");
await client.unbind();                                           ❽
```

❶ getDN is a helper method to get distinguished name of the user
❷ Log in as Biotor's LDAP administrator
❸ Check if user exists. This will make use of ldapjs' search method.
❹ Delete user
❺ addUser is a helper method that will call ldapjs' add method to add an entry in the directory tree.
❻ We must create a new client once we unbind
❼ Test credentials of new user
❽ Always remember to unbind when you are done

Run this script like so:

```
$ node add-user.js john 'attaboy!' "John Doe"
```

Go ahead and register a few users in the system.

15.4. Password Hashing

Let's take a moment to inspect the directory tree using slapcat. I see following entry for bob in the database:

```
dn: uid=bob,ou=users,dc=biotor,dc=com
cn: Bob Smith
sn: Smith
uid: bob
objectClass: inetOrgPerson
userPassword:: Ym9iJ3MgY2F0
structuralObjectClass: inetOrgPerson
...
```

See what happens if you run following command:

```
bash-5.0# echo Ym9iJ3MgY2F0 | base64 -d
bob's cat
```

Oops! we can see Bob's password stored in plain text! This is how hackers are able to steal passwords! The double colon (::) indicate the string is base 64 encoded. We decoded it using `base64 -d`. This seems like a clear bug since we set the hash algorithm in Listing 15. 7 (olcPasswordHash: '{SSHA}'). *Unfortunately what that does is set what algorithm will be used to hash passwords but does not turn on the hashing of passwords itself!* That requires us to do two things:

• *Condition 1: The password policy (known as* ppolicy*) module has to be loaded on the server*
• *Condition 2: A* ppolicy *overlay has to be added to the* mdb *backend and* olcPPolicyHashCleartext *has to be set to* TRUE.

Both these are config changes and so have to be made in the cn=config tree. Making changes to config tree requires us to bind with config password. The first change - loading ppolicy module - has to be made to the cn=module{0},cn=config entry and the second change will create a new entry under olcDatabase={1}mdb,cn=config. If you are wondering about the braces - these are used to create an order in an otherwise unordered list of config commands; we need some commands to execute before others. Refer to online documentation for details around their purpose.

15.4.1. Checking existing configuration

Before we make the config changes, its a good idea to check out the existing configuration. A get-config-entry.js script has been provided which enables us to inspect the config from a client machine. Run the script like so:

```
$ node get-config-entry.js cn=module{0},cn=config
```

This should return:

```
{
  dn: 'cn=module{0},cn=config',
  controls: [],
  objectClass: 'olcModuleList',
  cn: 'module{0}',
  olcModulePath: '/usr/lib/openldap',
  olcModuleLoad: [ '{0}back_mdb.so', '{1}memberof', '{2}refint' ]
}
```

We can see the `back_mdb`, `memberof` and `refint` modules are loaded on the server but *the* `ppolicy` *module is missing.* Let us also check the `olcDatabase` configuration. *Caution*: You might be thinking you can run following command to check if `ppolicy` overlay has been created under `mdb` database:

```
$ node get-config-entry.js olcDatabase={1}mdb,cn=config
```

However, that would be incorrect. The `get-config.entry.js` script will only print out details of `olcDatabase={1}mdb,cn=config` as shown below:

```
{
  dn: 'olcDatabase={1}mdb,cn=config',
  controls: [],
  objectClass: [ 'olcDatabaseConfig', 'olcMdbConfig' ],
  olcDatabase: '{1}mdb',
  olcDbDirectory: '/var/lib/openldap',
  olcSuffix: 'dc=biotor,dc=com',
  olcAccess: [
    '{0}to attrs=userPassword,shadowLastChange by self =xw by
dn="cn=admin,dc=biotor,dc=com" write by anonymous auth by * none',
    '{1}to * by self write by dn="cn=admin,dc=biotor,dc=com" write by * read'
  ],
  olcRootDN: 'cn=admin,dc=biotor,dc=com',
  olcRootPW: '{SSHA}RZ4QMqB3Ev2oJdRPgmyMCQ7HuWd1FfHl',
  olcDbIndex: [
    'uid eq',
    'mail eq',
    'memberOf eq',
    'entryCSN eq',
    'entryUUID eq',
    'objectClass eq'
  ],
  olcDbMaxSize: '1073741824'
}
```

Its not going to print out the child nodes and entire subtree under `olcDatabase={1}mdb,cn=config`. The correct command to check if `ppolicy` overlay has been created under `mdb` database (condition 2) is shown in Listing 15. 13. Using the command-line to inspect and browse the OpenLDAP directory can be difficult. Several free LDAP browsers with a graphical user interface (GUI) exist. For example, checkout *Apache Directory Studio*. However, it does not support connecting to a server with client auth enabled and so won't work for our setup.

Future releases of `tiredofit/openldap` may return different configs so its important you check the config before making changes to it.

15.4.2. Making changes to the config

We are now ready to make changes to the config! Listing 15. 12 shows the code to do so.

Listing 15. 12. Enable password hashing on OpenLDAP server.

```
await client.bind(config.configDN, config.configPassword);    ❶

var loadPasswordPolicyModule = new ldapjs.Change({            ❷
    operation: 'add',                                        ❸
    modification: {
        olcModuleLoad: 'ppolicy'                             ❹
    }
});
await client.modify("cn=module{0},cn=config",                ❺
    loadPasswordPolicyModule);

var pPolicyOverlay = {
    objectClass: ["olcConfig", "olcOverlayConfig", "olcPpolicyConfig"],
    olcOverlay: 'ppolicy',
    olcPPolicyDefault: `cn=default,ou=ppolicies,${config.baseDN}`,
    olcPPolicyUseLockout: 'TRUE',                            ❻
    olcPPolicyHashCleartext: 'TRUE'                          ❼
};
await client.add(                                            ❽
    "olcOverlay=ppolicy,olcDatabase={1}mdb,cn=config",
    pPolicyOverlay);
```

❶ We have to bind to the config tree with the config admin's password to make any changes to it

❷ We create a change object to make changes to an entry that already exists in the directory tree

❸ The add operation will add an attribute to the entry. It will not make any changes or deletions to any existing attributes.

❹ This tells OpenLDAP to load the ppolicy module

❺ This is where we make request to the server and wait for its response. We use the modify operation to make changes to existing entry.

❻ This is not going to lock out users for failed login attempts. That is done elsewhere. This merely turns on displaying a more helpful error message where user is notified that their account is locked due to failed attempts.

❼ This is the key setting that turns on password hashing. This is absolutely critical in any production environment.

❽ This is where we make request to the server and wait for its response. We use the add operation to add an entry into the directory tree.

A hash-passwords.js script is provided for you to turn on password hashing. Run the script and verify there are no errors. We are not done yet. It is always best practice to check the configuration to see your changes have been really applied. Let's check if ppolicy module is loaded:

```
$ node get-config-entry.js cn=module{0},cn=config
{
  dn: 'cn=module{0},cn=config',
  controls: [],
  objectClass: 'olcModuleList',
  cn: 'module{0}',
  olcModulePath: '/usr/lib/openldap',
  olcModuleLoad: [ '{0}back_mdb.so', '{1}memberof', '{2}refint', '{3}ppolicy' ]
}
```

This confirms ppolicy is indeed loaded. Next, check if ppolicy overlay is created:

Listing 15. 13. The olcPPolicyHashCleartext: 'TRUE' **attribute under** ppolicy **overlay is what turns on password hashing on OpenLDAP.**

```
$ node get-config-entry.js olcOverlay={2}ppolicy,olcDatabase={1}mdb,cn=config
{
  dn: 'olcOverlay={2}ppolicy,olcDatabase={1}mdb,cn=config',
  controls: [],
  objectClass: [ 'olcConfig', 'olcOverlayConfig', 'olcPPolicyConfig' ],
  olcOverlay: '{2}ppolicy',
  olcPPolicyDefault: 'cn=default,ou=ppolicies,dc=biotor,dc=com',
  olcPPolicyHashCleartext: 'TRUE',
  olcPPolicyUseLockout: 'TRUE'
}
```

If I had run:

```
$ node get-config-entry.js olcOverlay=ppolicy,olcDatabase={1}mdb,cn=config
```

where I skipped the {2} prefix the result would be empty. How did I know that I have to use olcOverlay={2}policy? Because I checked the server logs:

```
5f7df7df ldif_write_entry: wrote entry "olcOverlay={2}ppolicy,olcDatabase={1}mdb,cn=config"
5f7df8d1 <<< dnPrettyNormal: <olcOverlay=ppolicy,olcDatabase={1}mdb,cn=config>,
<olcOverlay=ppolicy,olcDatabase={1}mdb,cn=config>
```

You might have to do the same to pick up correct prefix. Now we are really done.

15.4.3. Test it works

Add some new users to the directory and then run slapcat on the server to see new user entries. For example, after these changes I can see following entry for a new user:

```
dn: uid=alice,ou=users,dc=biotor,dc=com
cn: Alice Brown
sn: Brown
uid: alice
objectClass: inetOrgPerson
userPassword:: e1NTSEF9TnJydTRKSW16aWNFMHdZeTk4Njd0NS9ZblRTL1EvY3Y=
...
```

Base64 decoding the userPassword string gives the hashed password like so:

Listing 15. 14. Hashed Password

```
bash-5.0# echo e1NTSEF9TnJydTRKSW16aWNFMHdZeTk4Njd0NS9ZblRTL1EvY3Y= | base64 -d
{SSHA}Nrru4JImzicE0wYy9867t5/YnTS/Q/cv
```

We can now see the original password is lost and cannot be derived from the userPassword string. *Even if a hacker steals this database, they will not be able to recover the original passwords.*

This brings up an interesting question which is that *if the original password is lost, then how does OpenLDAP itself authenticate the user?* The answer is that the original password is mixed with a *salt* (a random byte array or binary string of a fixed length) and the resulting byte buffer is then hashed. The hash is then compared to the string stored in userPassword to see if there is a match. We saw this pattern in the Handling Data Privacy chapter (Chapter 12). *A different random salt is used for each user for increased security so that the database is foolproof against rainbow attacks by a hacker.* OpenLDAP needs to store the salt somewhere so that it remembers its value when it has to perform the hashing. Where is that location? The answer is that its in the userPassword itself. The bytes of userPassword are broken up into two blocks. One block stores the salt and the other stores the hash. The {SSHA} prefix in Listing 15. 14 indicates the SHA1 algorithm has been applied to compute the hash.

How many bytes salt does OpenLDAP use and where is the salt stored in userPassword? To answer this, the password you see in Listing 15. 14 is such that:

```
Nrru4JImzicE0wYy9867t5/YnTS/Q/cv = Base64Encode(SHA1(salt + password) + salt)
```

where the + operator denotes concatenation of strings or bytes. To solve above equation for the salt, you will have to first base64 decode the Nrru.. string, then skip or discard the first 20 bytes in resulting byte buffer and the rest will be the salt. We skip 20 bytes because the SHA1 *operation produces a binary string of length 20 bytes.* Note the double dose of base64 decoding; first we decoded e1NTSEF.. to Nrru4J.. and now we have to decode Nrru4J... The data is just a series of bytes. Its just that it has to be encoded somehow when displayed in a UI and OpenLDAP is using Base64 encoding each time it displays the data to user in the CLI.

We can mimic the algorithm OpenLDAP uses to authenticate a user given their password as shown in the Node.js code below:

Listing 15. 15. Algorithm used by OpenLDAP to authenticate a user and verify user's password.

```
var crypto = require('crypto');
var argv = process.argv.slice(2);
let hashedPassword = argv[0];                        ❶
let actualPassword = argv[1];                        ❷
let buf1 = Buffer.from(hashedPassword, 'base64');
let observed = Buffer.allocUnsafe(20);               ❸
buf1.copy(observed, 0, 0, 20);
let n = buf1.length - 20;
let salt = Buffer.allocUnsafe(n);                    ❹
buf1.copy(salt, 0, 20, buf1.length);
let buf2 = Buffer.from(actualPassword);
let shasum = crypto.createHash('sha1');
shasum.update(buf2);
shasum.update(salt);                                 ❺
let expected = shasum.digest();
console.log(expected.equals(observed));              ❻
```

❶ This will be the base64 decoded `userPassword` string sans the `{SSHA}` prefix. i.e., `Nrru4JImzicE0wYy9867t5/YnTS/Q/cv` to take our example.

❷ This will be the original password which only the user knows

❸ `observed` will store the SHA1 hash (20 bytes)

❹ `salt` will store the salt extracted from `hashedPassword` (n=4)

❺ This is where we mix the `salt` with the user given password

❻ Test if the hashed password matches with what is stored on the server

This code forms the `verify-password.js` script. Try running the script as follows:

```
$ node verify-password.js Nrru4JImzicE0wYy9867t5/YnTS/Q/cv "magic mushrooms"
```

Boom! You should see a match! Substitute the `Nrru..` string with what you have in your database and `magic mushrooms` with password you used when you created your user entries in LDAP directory. *In future you should always execute* `hash-passwords.js` *before you add any users to the LDAP directory.*

Note that storing hashed passwords in `userPassword` as done above violates RFC 4519 schema specifications (refer to Section 2.41 in the RFC). It shouldn't be an issue as long as you stay within the OpenLDAP ecosystem but could create issues if you take OpenLDAP's database and use it to bootstrap another LDAP server (interoperability). A new attribute type, `authPassword`, to hold hashed passwords was defined as early as 2001 in RFC 3112, but is not implemented in OpenLDAP to my knowledge.

15.4.4. Alternate Hashing Schemes

In fact, now that you know how password hashing works, you could in principle use another database such as MySQL to store passwords if that's your cup of tea and if you find working with OpenLDAP challenging. Just make sure you are hashing and salting passwords. _In fact you can go a step further and use the **bcrypt** library to hash passwords._ [179] The safety of SHA1 hash for storing passwords is subject to some criticism and bcrypt is considered the gold standard when it comes to storing and hashing passwords.

If you want to harden the hash algorithm in OpenLDAP and go beyond {SSHA} to something that is more secure, that is also possible. To do this set the olcPasswordHash to **{CRYPT}**. OpenLDAP will now rely on the **crypt** function call to compute the password. Some caveats apply when using crypt. This is a system function call and its result can vary from system to system depending on the C library used to serve this call. Because of this OpenLDAP does not recommend using {CRYPT} in its official documentation. [180] With that disclaimer in place, the glibc (GNU C Library) version of crypt supports additional encryption algorithms summarized in Table 15. 3.

Table 15. 3. The crypt **function that comes with GNU C Library supports advanced hash algorithms listed here.**

ID	Method
1	MD5
2a	Blowfish (not in mainline glibc; added in some Linux distributions)
5	SHA-256 (since glibc 2.7)
6	SHA-512 (since glibc 2.7)

If you are running OpenLDAP in an environment that has glibc installed then you can use crypt to implement more sophisticated password hashing than what is provided by {SSHA}. For example the code below shows how to change the hash algorithm to SHA-512 with 8 bytes of salt:

Listing 15. 16. Use SHA-512 **algorithm to hash passwords with 8 byte salt.**

```
var change = new ldapjs.Change({
    operation: 'replace',
    modification: { olcPasswordHash: '{CRYPT}' }          ❶
});
await client.modify("olcDatabase={-1}frontend,cn=config", change);

change = new ldapjs.Change({
    operation: 'add',
    modification: { olcPasswordCryptSaltFormat: '$6$%.8s' } ❷
});
await client.modify("cn=config", change);
```

❶ {CRYPT} will delegate password hashing to the crypt function call.

❷ This will turn on using SHA-512 algorithm to hash passwords with an 8 byte salt.

Since the Blowfish (which is same a bcrypt) algorithm is only available on some Linux distributions, a better choice is to use the SHA-512 algorithm. A script use-crypt.js is provided that contains the code above and can be executed to enable SHA-512 passwords on the server. Try it. Note that the two changes in Listing 15. 16 are made to different parts of the cn=config tree. The decision to choose SSHA vs. CRYPT will be a personal choice and will depend on your preference between *portability and reliability vs. enhanced security*. For information, there are a few other choices besides SSHA and CRYPT offered by OpenLDAP for the `olcPasswordHash` directive, but we don't list them here as they are sub-optimal.

The `tiredofit/openldap:7.1.3` image that we use is based on Alpine Linux by the way and Alpine Linux uses `musl libc` instead of `glibc`. It does have the `crypt` function fortunately and supports SHA-512 hash. Whether its 1:1 compatible with `glibc` is something I don't know for sure and haven't tested.

Exercise 15.1

Modify the `tiredofit/openldap` image so that it supports SSHA password hashing out-of-the-box without user having to do any config changes. *Hint*: execute following LDIF entry as part of the server's bootstrap:

```
dn: cn=module{0},cn=config
changetype: modify
add: olcModuleLoad
olcModuleLoad: ppolicy

dn: olcOverlay=ppolicy,olcDatabase={1}${BACKEND},cn=config
objectClass: olcConfig
objectClass: olcOverlayConfig
objectClass: olcPpolicyConfig
olcOverlay: ppolicy
olcPPolicyDefault: cn=default,ou=ppolicies,${BASE_DN}
olcPPolicyUseLockout: TRUE
olcPPolicyHashCleartext: TRUE
```

Above LDIF is the equivalent of `hash-passwords.js` script. The BACKEND and BASE_DN are environment variables in `tiredofit/openldap`.

Exercise 15.2

As a bonus exercise to get a feel of how secure SSHA vs. CRYPT hashes are, use the `hashcat` utility (download from `hashcat.net`) to reverse engineer or guess passwords from the hashes.

15.5. Using LDAP as `fabric-ca-server` *registry database*

We work from `$ldap-lesson/fabric-ca-server` in this section.

`fabric-ca-server` supports using a LDAP database for its backend. So you could re-use your LDAP database and connect it to `fabric-ca-server`. `fabric-ca-server` would then use the LDAP directory to authenticate users instead of `sqlite3`. *It will still rely on a* `sqlite3` *or whatever db is defined in the* db *section of config file to store user certificates and other data*. The `fabric-ca-server` maintains two DB accessors - one for the registry and another for the certificates. We can see this in `lib/ca.go`: [181]

```
// CertDBAccessor returns the certificate DB accessor for CA
func (ca *CA) CertDBAccessor() *CertDBAccessor {
    return ca.certDBAccessor
}

// DBAccessor returns the registry DB accessor for server
func (ca *CA) DBAccessor() user.Registry {
    return ca.registry
}
```

When LDAP is disabled the same db is used for both registry and the certificate store. To use LDAP with `fabric-ca-server` we set `ldap.enabled` to `true` in the config file. *When* `ldap.enabled` *is* `true` *the* `registry` *section of the config is ignored. And you should not be making any* `register` *calls against the* `fabric-ca-server`. If you try to call the `register` endpoint with LDAP enabled, you will be greeted by an appropriate error that looks like following:

```
[INFO] 172.22.23.9:51200 POST /api/v1/register 403 72 "Registration is not supported when
using LDAP"
```

To connect `fabric-ca-server` to LDAP, we need to edit the `ldap` section of the `fabric-ca-server-config.yaml` file like so to give an example:

Listing 15. 17. Connecting `fabric-ca-server` **to a LDAP server.**

```
ldap:
    enabled: true
    url: ldaps://cn=admin,dc=biotor,dc=com:superman@ldap.biotor.com:636/dc=biotor,dc=com
    tls:
        certfiles: donald_mickey_chain.pem
        client:
            certfile: client_tls_cert.pem
            keyfile: client_tls_key.pem
    attribute:
        names: ['uid','member','cn']
        converters:
            - name: hf.Registrar.Roles
              value: map(attr("uid"),"roleMap")
            - name: hf.Registrar.DelegateRoles
              value: map(attr("uid"),"roleMap")
            - name: hf.Registrar.Attributes
              value: map(attr("uid"),"roleMap")
            - name: hf.GenCRL
              value: attr("uid") =~ "alice"
            - name: hf.Revoker
              value: attr("uid") =~ "alice"
            - name: hf.AffiliationMgr
              value: attr("uid") =~ "alice"
            - name: hf.IntermediateCA
              value: attr("uid") =~ "alice"
        maps:
            roleMap:
                - name: alice
                  value: '*'
```

The general syntax of `ldap.url` is `ldap(s)://<adminDN>:<adminPassword>@<host>:<port>/<base>`. `fabric-ca-server` *(at least v1.4.6) does not support the* `starttls` *operation (FABC-841) so we have to use the* `ldaps://` *endpoint (port 636) to establish a secure connection with the LDAP server.* The `adminDN` is the full distinguished name (DN) of the admin user and `base` will be the DN of Biotor's directory tree. The `tls` section should be well understood by now which takes us to the `attribute` section which is the main one to understand.

`ldap.attribute` is an optional section. Within it, `names` is supposed to provide a list of attributes that you would like to be read from the LDAP server. For example, a complete user record on the server is as follows:

```
dn: uid=alice,ou=users,dc=biotor,dc=com
cn: Alice Brown
sn: Brown
uid: alice
objectClass: inetOrgPerson
userPassword:: e1NTSEF9TnJydTRKSW16aWNFMHdZeTk4Njd0NS9ZblRTL1EvY3Y=
structuralObjectClass: inetOrgPerson
entryUUID: c31fdeed-89d6-447a-980b-585ea03b51cb
creatorsName: cn=admin,dc=biotor,dc=com
createTimestamp: 202010071829082
entryCSN: 20201007182908.3985992#000000#000#000000
modifiersName: cn=admin,dc=biotor,dc=com
modifyTimestamp: 202010071829082
```

Setting `names` to `['uid','member','cn']` will read those attributes from the record. We can see there is no `member` attribute in the record so that will be empty when read. Next we come to `converters`. This section is supposed to provide a mapping that can be used to convert LDAP attributes to Fabric attributes. You may or may not even need it. It depends on your scenario. Let's look at:

```
- name: hf.Registrar.Roles
  value: map(attr("uid"),"roleMap")
```

What this is saying is that we would like to set the `hf.Registrar.Roles` attribute on the user. If we were using `sqlite3`, `fabric-ca-server` stores the attribute in the database directly when user is registered but remember here the users will be registered externally - the LDAP will be a general purpose directory and its likely not to contain any Fabric specific properties in it. How do we set this attribute? That is defined by `value: map(attr("uid"),"roleMap")` which is saying please give it the value that is the result of `map(attr("uid"),"roleMap")` operation. `map` takes two arguments. The first argument is an LDAP attribute. `attr("uid")` returns the value of the `uid` attribute. So this will be `alice` in our example. The second argument is the name of a map. The maps are defined in `ldap.attribute.maps`. Thus there can be many maps which can potentially map the same attribute but in different ways. In our example, we are directed to the `roleMap`. If we look at it we see it has only one mapping:

```
maps:
  roleMap:
    - name: alice
      value: '*'
```

This mapping is saying if the input to the map is `alice` the output is `'*'`. So the net effect is that user `alice` will have `hf.Registrar.Roles` set to `'*'`. For all other users, the attribute will be empty or null as the `roleMap` only defines the mapping for `alice`. So the whole operation is more like:

```
set hf.Registrar.Roles = roleMap(uid);
```

to simplify the syntax a bit. But think how you would achieve this if you were the developer parsing a `yaml` file and then you can understand the need for the convoluted syntax. The `hf.Registrar.DelegateRoles` and `hf.Registrar.Attributes` work the same way. The only other form we see is:

```
- name: hf.GenCRL
  value: attr("uid") =~ "alice"
```

This is saying that we don't need to consult any `map` to determine the value of the `hf.GenCRL` attribute. Please set the value of attribute equal to `attr("uid") =~ "alice"`. As before `attr("uid")` will return the value of the `uid` attribute. The `=~` is used to indicate case-insensitive match. So the whole thing evaluates to a `true` for `alice` and `false` for other users. In summary. its saying:

```
set hf.GenCRL = (uid =~ "alice")
```

and the RHS (right-hand side) evaluates to `true` or `false`. Fabric does support use of `'*'` in the search string so `attr("uid") =~ "alice*"` will match all usernames that start with `alice`.

With this background in place we are ready to connect the `fabric-ca-server` of previous chapters to LDAP server we have provisioned in this chapter. The code to do so is provided in `$ldap-lesson/fabric-ca-server`. There is a script `run-ca-server.sh` in that folder which is a one-click installer that you can run to provision an instance of `fabric-ca-server` in a Docker container that will use LDAP for its registry. As before we provision three CAs - `mickey-mouse`, `donald-duck` and `goofy-ca`. The three CAs are configured by three distinct config files. For simplicity, *all three CAs are connected to the same LDAP server in the code provided in the repo but that does not need to be the case.* You are free to connect the different CAs to different LDAP servers. *The three CAs will use separate* `sqlite3` *dbs for their certificate store.* The script assumes a `biotor_net` Docker network has been created before. The network name can be overridden with the `NETWORK` environment variable. Take a look at the script and compare the config files to those of Chapter 13. Make any changes as necessary. When you are ready run the script like so:

```
$ ./run-ca-server.sh
```

A container named `mickey.biotor.com` will be provisioned. A full container log is shown at git.io/Jk26q for reference.

15.5.1. Enrolling Users

We work from `$ldap-lesson/fabric-ca-client` in this section.

Let's proceed to enroll `alice` - our canonical user. The script to do this is same as the one we used in Section 14.2.3 and present as `enroll.js` under `$ldap-lesson/fabric-ca-client`. Cd into that directory, `npm install` all dependencies and then run the `enroll-alice.sh` script modifying username and password as necessary in your case.

```
$ ./enroll-alice.sh
```

Boom! alice should be enrolled and her credentials saved to wallet. On the server you should see a log that resembles git.io/Jk263. In the log you should see messages like following which show successful conversion of LDAP attributes to Fabric attributes:

```
[DEBUG] Evaluated expression for attribute 'hf.Registrar.DelegateRoles'; parms:
map[DN:uid=alice,ou=users,dc=biotor,dc=com affiliation:[users]]; result: *
```

To get a TLS certificate for let's say orderer0.biotor.com, let's first create an account by running following from $ldap-lesson/node-client:

```
$ node add-user.js orderer0.biotor.com batman "Any Name You Like"
```

After that run enroll-orderer0.biotor.com.sh from $ldap-lesson/fabric-ca-client:

```
$ ./enroll-orderer0.biotor.com.sh
```

Boom! You should get a TLS certificate saved in wallet. *Verify the TLS certificate has the hostnames given in* enroll-orderer0.biotor.com.sh *in its SAN header.* Server log is shown in git.io/Jk26n. If you inspect the sqlite3 db on fabric-ca-server you will notice it will have all the tables we saw in Section 14.3 except that the users table is empty and does not store anything. This concludes our demo. Now you have seen how fabric-ca-server can be made to work with LDAP. To recap in LDAP mode:

* you should not be making register calls against the fabric-ca-server
* the registry section in the fabric-ca-server-config.yaml file is ignored and has no bearing on anything
* fabric-ca-server does not support starttls (FABC-841) so you should use the ldaps:// endpoint for secure communication
* the sqlite3 db is still needed by fabric-ca-server to store the certificates

15.6. Summary

* LDAP is a communication protocol like HTTP. There are databases or directory servers that support that protocol. The most popular paid LDAP server by far is Microsoft Active Directory and the most popular free option is OpenLDAP.
* It is much more common to speak in terms of directories, trees and entries (and sometimes nodes or directory objects) when it comes to LDAP rather than databases, tables and rows.
* LDAP unlike HTTP is a stateful protocol. A client binds to a LDAP server which establishes a session and unbinds to terminate the session.
* OpenLDAP is made up of a frontend - the slapd server or daemon and a backend which is the data store. mdb is the default backend used in OpenLDAP. It maps all of computer storage into a single virtual address space.
* mdb is only made possible by the advent of 64-bit processors that can provide access to 8 exabyte

virtual address space that is more than sufficient to cover capacity of modern hard disks.

- OpenLDAP configuration is stored in the `cn=config` tree and can be updated on-the-fly by loading new LDIF entries.
- To make a secure connection to a LDAP server we use the `starttls` operation. The client has to initiate this operation. Some servers including OpenLDAP expose a `ldaps://` endpoint that provides TLS out-of-the-box but this is not part of official standard and specification in the LDAP RFC.
- The `olcPasswordHash` sets the hashing algorithm in OpenLDAP whereas `olcPPolicyHashCleartext` is what actually turns on the hashing. `SSHA` is the recommended setting for `olcPasswordHash` and will salt passwords and hash them using the SHA1 algorithm. OpenLDAP uses a 4 byte salt. More sophisticated schemes are possible using `CRYPT` but its behavior can vary from system to system depending on which underlying library is being used.
- When `ldap.enabled` is `true` the `registry` section of `fabric-ca-server-config.yaml` is ignored. And you should not be making any `register` calls against the `fabric-ca-server` in this mode. The `fabric-ca-server` will use LDAP to authenticate users but still rely on a `sqlite3`, `mysql`, or `postgres` db to store user certificates and other data.
- Several free LDAP browsers with a graphical user interface (GUI) exist. For example, Apache Directory Studio. However, it does not support connecting to a server with client auth enabled.

15.7. Further Reading

- MDB: A Memory-Mapped Database and Backend for OpenLDAP. www.openldap.org/pub/hyc/mdb-paper.pdf
- LMDB: Lightning Memory-Mapped Database Manager (LMDB). www.lmdb.tech/doc/index.html

[171] stackoverflow.com/questions/48068565/store-user-credentials-and-validate-via-fabric-ca

[172] docs.microsoft.com/en-us/azure/active-directory/fundamentals/active-directory-faq

[173] en.wikipedia.org/wiki/OpenLDAP

[174] en.wikipedia.org/wiki/Single-level_store

[175] www.lmdb.tech/doc/index.html

[176] E.g., see www.digitalocean.com/community/tutorials/how-to-install-and-configure-openldap-and-phpldapadmin-on-ubuntu-16-04

[177] shibboleth.net/community/advisories/secadv_20120227.txt

[178] github.com/tiredofit/docker-openldap/blob/7.1.3/install/assets/slapd/config/tls/tls-enforce-enable.ldif

[179] www.npmjs.com/package/bcrypt

[180] www.openldap.org/faq/data/cache/344.html

[181] github.com/hyperledger/fabric-ca/blob/v1.4.6/lib/ca.go#L868

Chapter 16. Bonus Chapter: The Bitcoin

This chapter covers:

- What is Bitcoin?
- How does it work?

Code for this chapter is under **$/bitcoin-lab** directory

In this chapter we will do a deep dive on *Bitcoin* - the original and most ingenious application of blockchain technology. We begin with a quote from the New Yorker: [182]

> *There are lots of ways to make money: You can earn it, find it, counterfeit it, steal it. Or, if you're Satoshi Nakamoto, a preternaturally talented computer coder, you can invent it. That's what he did on the evening of January 3, 2009, when he pressed a button on his keyboard and created a new currency called bitcoin. It was all bit and no coin. There was no paper, copper, or silver—just thirty-one thousand lines of code and an announcement on the Internet.*

— The New Yorker, The Crypto-Currency

Bitcoin as we know is a peer-to-peer cryptocurrency. Any two people across the globe can exchange bitcoins with each other without any banks in-between to facilitate the transaction. Further, users are pseudo-anonymous. They have an *address* but its not linked to any *Personally Identifiable Information (PII)*. In fact they can use a different address for every transaction. Let's see how Bitcoin works.

16.1. Anatomy of a Bitcoin transaction

Bitcoin is an electronic currency. The Bitcoin blockchain records movement of bitcoins (i.e., transfer of ownership) from one address to another. There is a law in physics, and perhaps its most sacred law, known as *conservation of energy* which states that energy can neither be created, nor be destroyed - it can only be transformed from one form into another. Bitcoin transactions operate in much the same way. Each *transaction* refers to one or more bitcoins known as the *inputs* and creates one or more bitcoins known as the *outputs* subject to the constraint that *sum of outputs is less than sum of inputs*. The outputs of one transaction can be used as inputs to a future transaction and are known as *unspent transaction outputs (UTXO)*. Every transaction's inputs have to refer to some previous UTXOs - this is just a way of saying that money cannot be created out of thin air. And the UTXOs will get spent or destroyed once they are used as inputs of a transaction and the transaction is committed - this is just a way of saying that once you hand off a dollar bill to your friend, you no longer have it and cannot use it again - the dollar has been spent for you. For your friend, however, it is an unspent transaction output that he or she can use. *Think of it as your dollar bill getting a new serial number when you give it to your friend. The old serial number is marked invalid and cannot be used again.* The reason why bitcoin allows for sum of outputs to be less than sum of inputs is that the difference, if any, is automatically construed as *commission* or *transaction fees* which gets paid to people who operate the bitcoin network and create blocks of transactions. You can liken them to banks if you will. The operation of Bitcoin network requires a lot of energy;

there are people who provide hardware and resources to operate the network in hopes of earning a commission which would provide positive return on their investment - these people are known as *miners*. The paying of commission is not mandatory - miners have another income stream which is that new bitcoins get minted as new blocks are mined. However, a commission is certainly an incentive for miners to process a transaction.

In addition to the inputs and outputs, there are two other important pieces of a transaction - the *scriptSig* and the *scriptPubKey*. They serve the function of *From* and *To* respectively in a transaction (i.e., where are the bitcoins coming from and where are they going). The *scriptSig* is a piece of code that *proves ownership of the inputs (UTXOs)* and the *scriptPubKey* contains the *address* to which bitcoins should be transferred - it is the *hash* of a *public key*. This type of transaction is known as the P2PKH or *Pay-to-Public-Key-Hash*. Later on we will list the other transaction types available in Bitcoin.

16.1.1. Public keys and addresses

What do we mean by a public key? Bitcoin (and by extension blockchain) relies heavily on *public-private key cryptography* (also known as *asymmetric cryptography*). This is a deep field of computer science and discrete mathematics but we don't have to be an expert to understand the basics, especially what its used for. Think of the public key as the bank account and the private key as the password to unlock that bank account. Just like its safe to share your bank account with people from whom you want to accept money, it is safe to share your public key on the blockchain. In practice, for added security, it is the hash of the public key that gets shared on Bitcoin and is known as a bitcoin *address*, but even if you were to share your public key, it would not compromise anything. Using the hash also has added advantage of taking up less space than using the raw public key - it can be thought of as shortening and obfuscating the public key. But *you should never share or lose your private key*.

Note that Bitcoin addresses are used to receive payments, but not to send them: there is no concept of a "from" address in Bitcoin. [183] Figure 16. 1 shows example Bitcoin address.

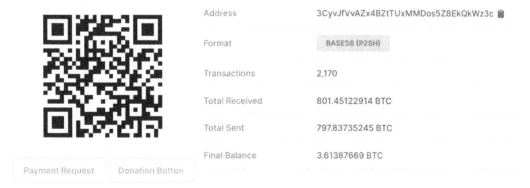

Address	3CyvJfVvAZx4BZtTUxMMDos5Z8EkQkWz3c 📋
Format	BASE58 (P2SH)
Transactions	2,170
Total Received	801.45122914 BTC
Total Sent	797.83735245 BTC
Final Balance	3.61387669 BTC

Payment Request   Donation Button

Figure 16. 1. An example Bitcoin address

Generating a Bitcoin address is easy. You first generate a new public-private key pair and then hash the public key two times to get the address. The first time it is hashed using SHA256 algorithm and second time it is hashed using RIPEMD160 algorithm. We can use the bitcoinjs-lib package (v5.1.6) to do the hard work for us. npm install it first if you don't have it already and then try running following piece of code:

Listing 16. 1. Generating public-private keys and Pay-to-Public-Key-Hash (P2PKH) address

```
const bitcoin = require("bitcoinjs-lib");
const keyPair = bitcoin.ECPair.makeRandom();            ❶
const { address } = bitcoin.payments.p2pkh({           ❷
      pubkey: keyPair.publicKey });
const publicKey = keyPair.publicKey.toString("hex");   ❸
const privateKey = keyPair.toWIF();                     ❹
```

❶ Generate a new public-private key-pair
❷ Generate a new P2PKH address
❸ Convert the public key byte buffer to a readable string
❹ Convert the private key byte buffer to a readable string

This gives me (as example):

```
> publicKey
'031d8aa8599312cca4dc176be873de51f8ee6321de5924965ff2c46108e70ac4fb'
> privateKey
'Ky2AxSGLxaNLkXUsC29Z74JYmVYmUsu8VutJALfPHDxzhNUiQ8Mh'
> address
'1GjLyxjReejXX8Ty4Rh1WrnXfGEG3NVhA4'
```

P2PKH addresses always start with 1 as you can verify above.

> - Public-private keys: Byte arrays to do crypto stuff.
> - P2PKH Address: Double-hash (ripemd160(sha256(.))) of public key.
> - *UTXO*: Unspent Transaction Output. In other words a bitcoin that has not been spent.
> - *scriptSig*: a piece of code that proves you own some UTXO.

16.1.2. How is the ownership of UTXOs proved?

Suppose Alice has sent some bitcoins to address *X*. The bitcoins can be thought of as sitting in a *digital locker. Anyone who can prove that they own the private key corresponding to the public key which hashes to X will gain ownership of those coins and will be able to spend them by means of a transaction.* This is how the locker gets unlocked. Note that it is necessary but not sufficient to know the public key corresponding to *X* to prove ownership. Indeed, public keys are meant to be shared and the system operates on the assumption that many people may know a key which hashes to *X*. But only the person who can prove they know the *private key* corresponding to the public key will gain ownership of the coins. Knowledge of the private key is thus equivalent to ownership of the UTXOs. *Your private keys are your bitcoins. You lose your private keys, you lose your bitcoins - this cannot be overemphasized.*

Let's take an example. Suppose Alice set X = 1N7CoyzoC3q61jN2DZas4riXeHnuFtwaer. This is the locker number. Let's say it contains 100 UTXOs. Now this much is public knowledge.

Everyone knows the locker number and even the UTXOs it contains. To spend these UTXOs, you just need to:

- Provide a key *k* such that `ripemd160(sha256(k))` = `1N7CoyzoC3q61jN2DZas4riXeHnuFtwaer`
- Prove you own the corresponding private key *s*

Along comes Bob, and he says `k=AoY3r6ug38pOz5M71VhXkFtKpP3g+uxpaow4a7eCpeJA`. *Exercise*: Verify this is indeed a solution to the equation. Providing *k* is not enough. Bob also has to demonstrate that he is in possession of the private key (*s*) corresponding to *k*. To do that, Bob will draft a transaction that tells how the UTXOs should be spent and sign it with a digital signature (Section 2.1.2). This signature can be verified by anyone using Bob's public key *k*.

By crafting a signature that can be verified using k, Bob has demonstrated he knows (or is in possession of) the private key s that corresponds to the public key k.

This is the crucial step. If someone knew Bob's public key (not impossible as the key is supposed to be public after all) but crafted a signature using a non-corresponding private key, that signature would not decrypt using Bob's public key. *The decryption process would raise an error. This then shows that there is a mechanism for Bob to prove ownership of private key without giving away the key itself. This is nothing but a zero-knowledge proof (ZKP) in action. The essence of a ZKP is to prove you have or know something without giving away the thing itself.* This is just one of the genius behind Bitcoin and all driven by properties of digital signatures.

The public key k plus the signature is what constitutes the scriptSig.

The exact details of what's in a transaction can be found online and Blockchain Explorer can be used to inspect transactions happening on the Bitcoin network. [184] [185]

It is common for people using Bitcoin to create a new key-pair for each transaction. This has several advantages:

- In the unfortunate event that someone loses a private key, only those UTXOs associated with that private key will be lost.
- Using distinct key for every transaction also increases the anonymity of the user. Otherwise it is possible using machine-learning algorithms to group all transactions associated with a key and build a profile of the user. The real identity may even be unmasked by clever algorithms.

If you are going to use a new key-pair for every transaction, you are going to need a safe place to store the myriad keys. This is where *digital wallets* come in. Just like a physical wallet is used to store paper currency bills, a digital wallet is used to store cryptocurrencies - more accurately it stores the private keys, but its the private keys that allow you to be able to spend your bitcoins. *The public key can be generated from private key - the reverse is not possible.* So storing private key is enough. Digital wallets have been hacked however. Usually whenever you read in the news that Bitcoin has been hacked, its invariably some user's digital wallet that has been hacked and the poor fellow's private keys and associated coins have been stolen. Bitcoin itself is very secure as we will see in this chapter.

16.1.3. Transaction Validation

Figure 16. 2 shows how a transaction is validated by an auditor.

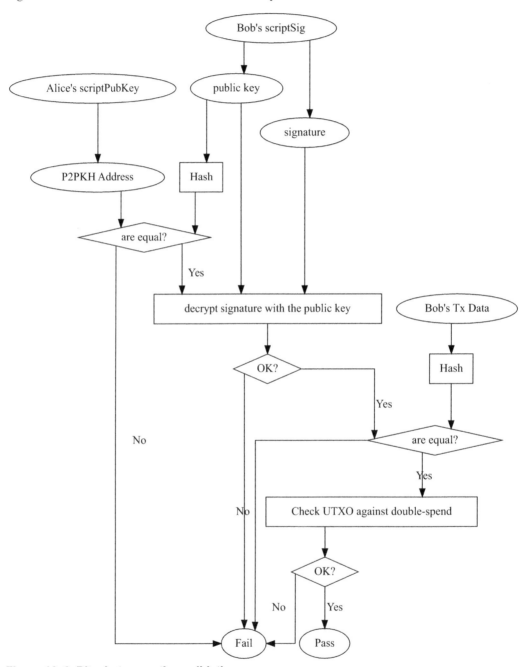

Figure 16. 2. Bitcoin transaction validation

- First, the auditor will crack open the *scriptSig* and hash the public key found in it to convert it to a P2PKSH address. The hash will be compared to the address in the *scriptPubKey* Alice posted in her transaction. If there is no match, the validation fails, otherwise it continues to the next step.
- Next, the signature found in the *scriptSig* will be decrypted using the public key. If the decryption fails, the validation fails as well, otherwise it proceeds to next step.
- At this point, since the decryption succeeded, it has been proved that Bob owns the private key corresponding to the public key. The locker has been unlocked. *Alice's scriptPubKey can be thought of as a puzzle and Bob's scriptSig is the solution to the puzzle. Note that the puzzle and its solution don't appear in the same transaction. The puzzle appears first in Alice's transaction and the solution appears later in Bob's transaction.*
- Now the auditor will hash the transaction data *D* he or she finds and compare it to the decrypted signature. If the two match, it is proved the data has not been tampered with. Otherwise, what this means is that the transaction data that Bob signed is different from the data the auditor observed when he or she opened the locker. This is bad and the transaction will be deemed invalid. Maybe Bob had authorized transfer of 1 Bitcoin but someone changed it to 5 Bitcoins. Bob would not want this transaction to be committed to the ledger. It is impossible for an attacker to change the transaction data without invalidating the original signature. And they cannot compute a new signature if they don't have Bob's private key. This is the second genius behind blockchain (many more to follow) and the essence of how data is secured on the blockchain, made tamper proof and permanent. Once the transaction is recorded, Bob cannot argue that he transferred 1 bitcoin to someone (nonrepudiation).
- Bob's transaction data will also be validated for accuracy. For example, the auditor will check that the bitcoins in the data *D* are not already spent. The serialization of transactions ensures that money cannot be *double spent*. For example, Bob may create two transactions at the same time in which he transfers the same bitcoins to two people. But when the time comes to commit these transactions to the ledger, the transactions will get *serialized* (i.e., sequenced) and the transaction that comes later will be invalidated as the system will detect that the bitcoins have already been spent. The first transaction will mark the UTXOs as spent and remove them from the index of UTXOs that is maintained by bookkeepers, and when the second transaction is validated, its inputs will no longer be found in database of UTXOs.

Some books and articles make a big deal of how Bitcoin solved the *double spend* problem. They usually go like this: it is very difficult to prevent double spending of digital assets as a digital asset (like a mp3) can be copied and used infinite times. Fact is Bitcoin prevents double-spending in exactly the same way as banks do. By serializing the transactions so that one happens after the other so that if someone tries to double-spend money only one transaction will succeed and the other one will fail. Our money in bank is also a digital asset. I used to think that at end of every month, banks send each other big trucks loaded with cash to reconcile accounts but no, nothing like that happens. All our money in banks is digital. They maintain a digital ledger in which they record movement of money - just like Bitcoin does. The difference is that in case of banks there is a different system altogether to reconcile the ledgers.

16.1.4. Types of Transactions

The combination of *scriptSig* and *scriptPubKey* as mentioned above is just one form of transaction on the Bitcoin blockchain also known as *pay-to-public-key-hash (P2PKH)*. There are other forms of transaction as well that Bitcoin supports. In fact, there are total 5 different types of transactions:

- Pay-to-public-key-hash (P2PKH): covered above
- Pay-to-public-key (P2PK): older version of P2PKH in which the public key is directly stored in *scriptPubKey* instead of the public key's hash. Rarely used but you can see it if you go back to the earliest blocks on the chain.
- M-out-of-N: There are N public keys stored in *scriptPubKey* object and M out of N must provide signatures for funds to be released. This is very useful for companies or corporations where more than one person in finance must approve for money to be spent to prevent theft of funds or embezzlement.
- Data Output (OP_RETURN): This type of transaction is used by someone to store some piece of data, limited to 40 bytes, on the Bitcoin blockchain. The Bitcoins involved in the transaction are not sent to any public address. They get *burned* and no one can spend them anymore. The data is usually hash of something intended to provide a proof of existence of something such as a person's will.
- Pay-to-script-hash (P2SH): a transaction type used to implement more complex transactions than can be implemented with the types above. This is now the default transaction type on Bitcoin.

Although Ethereum is usually credited with introducing *smart contracts*, Bitcoin's rich *scriptSig* and *scriptPubKey* API together with various transaction types is nothing but *smart contracts* in action.

16.2. Handling concurrency: The mining network

We have covered a lot of material, and you should be proud if you have made it so far. However we are only about half done and there is more to follow as we now consider the larger distributed system that makes up Bitcoin and how the problem of concurrent transactions is solved. Imagine a room full of stock brokers, buyers and sellers - perhaps you have seen one in the movies. The buyers and sellers are shouting orders to buy and sell and brokers are busy executing orders. Bitcoin is no different. Transactions are being generated by users like Alice and Bob who broadcast it to the network. A transaction has to be committed, just like a share order has to be executed, for it to have effect. Until the transaction is committed, it sits in an *unconfirmed* or *pending pool*. There are multiple copies of the ledger maintained by bookkeepers e.g., Alice may have her bookkeeper and Bob may have his, and each bookkeeper has his or her own copy of the ledger. *In a completely uncontrolled environment, the transactions can and will arrive in different order on the bookkeeping nodes.*

1. if each bookkeeper applies transactions as it receives them, and
2. the different bookkeepers don't receive them in same order,

Then it follows that the bookkeepers' copies will start to differ from each other - the ledger will *fork*. This has to be prevented. *The copies need to remain in sync and identical.* One way to achieve it is to change the completely uncontrolled environment to a controlled one and put in place *a system which ensures all bookkeepers receive transactions in the same order. Assuming the bookkeepers' copies start out in sync, they will remain in sync if all the copies record transactions in the same order.* This can be done by building a *mining network* that sits in between the *users* and *bookkeepers*.

Suppose we could build a throttling service - a *rate limiter* - that reduces the rate r at which transactions are produced such that $r \ll 1/\tau$ where τ *is the time it takes for a transaction to be absorbed and committed by all the bookkeepers.* That would mostly solve the problem, right? *The idea is that at any time there is only one transaction sitting in the unconfirmed or pending pool. That ensures that no two bookkeepers will apply transactions in different order from each other because for all the bookkeepers there is only one unique transaction to be dequeued from the pending pool.* Not convinced? Go through Exercise 16.1 at end of this chapter, and come back once you are convinced. Let's see how we can build such a *rate limiter*.

The first thing we will do is to *pack the transactions into blocks* - this is also known as *batching* - it simply refers to creating a bundle of items. To do this, we will have to insert some new entities into the system which we will call *miners* - they will collect transactions from users and bundle them into blocks. An individual user only has knowledge of transactions he or she is generating and can only batch those, so we need the *miner* entities who have knowledge of all the transactions generated across the pool of users.

We now have three entities in the ecosystem:

- the *users* generating the transactions. These are people tapping out orders on mobile devices, laptops and other thin clients with a digital wallet. The purpose of digital wallet is to securely store the private keys.
- the *bookkeepers* committing transactions and each possessing a copy of the ledger. These are also known as *full nodes* in Bitcoin literature. The Bitcoin ledger is large and continuously increasing in size as a new block (approx. 1MB) is added every 10 minutes on average. To become a full node you will need to download approx. 302GB of data as of Q3 2020. Anyone with sufficient storage and compute power can decide to become a full node. You do not need anyone's permission to join or participate. This is why we say the network is public or *permissionless*.
- and the *miners* who for now are collecting transactions and packing them into blocks and will be the backbone of the *mining network*.

A Bitcoin block contains about N transactions where N is somewhere around 1500-3000. And blocks are what get broadcasted to the bookkeepers by the miners.

16.2.1. Why batch transactions into blocks?

It is tempting to think that batching immediately reduces r by a factor of N. The actual effect is a little nuanced though. If transactions are generated at a constant rate of r txs/s (we use tx as shorthand for transaction) then the batching process will output bursts of transaction blocks. In between bursts, there will be periods of quietness. For example, before we might have a system producing 1 tx every second and if we have a batch size of $N=10$, then afterwards we get bursts of

10 transactions every 10 second. [186] Multiple transactions generated at rate of 1 tx every second, to continue our example, and a batch of 10 txs generated every 10s, both give the same overall transaction rate of 1 tx/s. *The transaction rate remains the same on average, but the block rate is reduced to r/N.* In fact that's exactly what we want. *We have successfully reduced the rate at which events are produced by a factor of N while keeping the overall transaction throughput the same.* And its the events we should aim to rate-limit not the transaction throughput itself. Less events means:

- Less network congestion. Batching reduces the amount of congestion in the network in much the same way as packing more people in a bus reduces congestion on roads vis-a-vis having them travel in cars.
- More time for a block to be disseminated and absorbed through the network before the next one is ready.
- Lesser collisions and forks (two miners generating blocks at the same time and different blocks getting committed by different bookkeepers i.e., the concurrency problem).

You might have wondered why transactions are batched into blocks in a blockchain. Well, now you know why.

In addition to batching, before a miner can broadcast a block, it is given a puzzle to solve. Solving the puzzle will take some time. The puzzle is very special in the sense:

- Its solution cannot be pre-computed by anyone, so no one can cheat and everyone has equal chance of solving the puzzle. The ability to solve the puzzle is directly proportional to the amount of CPU power one has. This is also referred to as 1 CPU = 1 vote in Bitcoin literature.
- Its difficulty can be adjusted so that we can tightly control the time it would take on average to solve the puzzle. This is important because computers get faster with time and our objective is to build a speed-bump that can keep up with this increase in computational power.

The difficulty is configured such that it takes on average `10 minutes` to produce or mine a block and solve the puzzle. There is a statistical spread in the time required to solve the puzzle and that is very important otherwise everyone would be finding the solution at same time and causing a spike of blocks - the very thing we set out to avoid. So now users are busy generating transactions. Miners are busy capturing these transactions into blocks and all of them get into a race to solve a puzzle. Due to variability in how traffic gets routed on the internet, it is very much possible that different miners will assemble blocks in which transactions are in different order. But they have to solve the puzzle and provide a *proof of work* before they can release their respective block. After about `10 minutes`, a random miner would find solution to the puzzle and broadcast it to everyone with the block it has assembled. The miner is rewarded with some bitcoins for the work they have done to mine the block - *this is how bitcoins get minted* and why these entities are called miners - similar to the gold miners of the gold rush era. The bookkeepers will start updating their copies and other miners will abort as they have lost the race and the associated reward. System will reset. 10 minutes gives sufficient time for all the bookkeepers to update their records, and be ready to receive the next block. All bookkeepers are receiving transactions in the same order now so their copies cannot diverge, assuming each of them is honest i.e., each of them is running identical code which gives same deterministic output given same input and initial state. Each block is about `1MB` in size and contains 1500-3000 transactions. This gives us a transaction rate of 2.5-5.0 tx/s - not a lot if you consider VISA processes 1700 tx/s. [187] We can see now why the batching of transactions is *also important from a performance standpoint*. One way to increase the throughput of Bitcoin is to increase the block size and pack more transactions into a block, but it requires approval and co-operation of the players making up the ecosystem.

The number of Bitcoins generated per block started at 50 with the first block and is halved every 210,000 blocks (about four years). [188] There will be a total of 21 million coins the Bitcoin mine will produce over time. After that no more coins can be mined and maybe users will advertise transaction fees as incentive for miners to keep mining.

16.2.2. Collisions, forks, conflict resolution and the myth of immutability

The scheme above mostly works. At any time, there is a unique block floating around and being disseminated amongst the bookkeepers. This goes back to the idea of *only one transaction sitting in the unconfirmed pool* (the transaction is replaced by a block). But occasionally it is possible that two miners will mine two blocks at the same time (a *collision*) and broadcast their respective blocks (call them block A and block B) amongst the bookkeepers. When this happens, the ledger does *fork* (or *branch*). One bookkeeper may receive block A and add the transactions in it to its copy of the ledger; it will deem block B invalid when it receives it. And another bookkeeper might do the opposite. There are two chains now and there could be *M* bookkeepers corresponding to chain 1 and *N* bookkeepers corresponding to chain 2. *How does the conflict between the two get reconciled?* Bitcoin's solution is just to be patient. As more blocks get mined and the two chains grow, a *longer* chain will eventually emerge - this can happen as soon as the next block is mined since the probability of two blocks getting mined at the same time, two times in a row is exceedingly small. *The Bitcoin software running on bookkeeper nodes will automatically switch the nodes having shorter chain to the longer when that happens thereby resolving the fork. The longest chain always wins*. The length of a chain is a direct reflection of the amount of work that has been done in producing it. ***The winning chain is determined not by the number of bookkeepers that have it (i.e., by number of copies) but by its length***.

Wait. Did we say Bitcoin software will automatically switch the nodes having the shorter chain to the longer? Do you see what it means - it means some transactions might get *voided*! This should be setting off alarm bells in minds of readers who were told blockchain is an append-only ledger - data once written cannot be erased. Well yes, it can. We lied. Sorry. However, the probability of this happening decreases very rapidly and exponentially the more a transaction gets buried in the ledger i.e., the more other transactions happen on top of it. What all this means in practical terms is that as a rule of thumb, if you are selling something and accepting Bitcoin as a form of payment, do not ship or deliver the product unless your transaction has been buried under 5 blocks or more. After that, chances of the transaction getting voided are considered close to zero. Five blocks translates to waiting for 5+1=6 *confirmations* or 60 minutes. We add 1 for the block in which the transaction resides, and 5 for the number of blocks which are on top of it i.e., number of blocks under which it is buried. So no transaction on Bitcoin can be considered confirmed 100% for sure for an hour (as rough rule of thumb). This is definitely one challenge facing Bitcoin. If you go to a restaurant, you don't want to be waiting for an hour before they are willing to serve you food. This kind of forking and reconciliation of forking by switching nodes from one branch to another, never happens with Fabric. This is because in case of Fabric the miner entities work in unison rather than competing with each other as in case of Bitcoin.

16.3. Making the ledger secure and tamper-proof: The Proof of Work

Now let's take some time to go over the details of the puzzle that miners have to solve and more importantly *why Bitcoin does that*. The puzzle to solve is this: ***the miner has to find a nonce, ν which gives a block header, H that when hashed is less than a certain number known as the target,*** t.

What is nonce? A *nonce*, also known as *salt* denoted by ν, is a binary string (i.e., byte array or buffer) that is prefixed to the input of a hash function before running the hash on it. Normally we have some input X and we hash it to give $\phi(X)$. The nonce would modify the hashing process so that first we prefix X by ν to give (ν, X) and apply the hash on this combination to give $\phi((\nu, X))$.

What is block header? It is an 80 byte long string denoted by H_i for the *i*-th block made up of following 6 fields:

- 4-byte long nonce ν_i which is the unknown for which we have to solve
- 32-byte previous block hash ϕ_{i-1} (i.e., hash of previous block's header, $\phi(H_{i-1})$)
- 32-byte long root of a *Merkle tree* m_i. Think of this as a *hash or fingerprint of the contents of this block. Any change to the contents will change the fingerprint. Merkle tree is just a binary tree of the hashes of each transaction in the block i.e., we first hash each transaction and that gives us leaf nodes in the tree. So each leaf node is a hash. Then we pair the leaf nodes (i.e., just concatenate their hashes) and run the hash function on each pair. That gives us next level in the tree. We keep continuing until we are left with only one node - the root. This is illustrated in Figure 16. 3. [189]

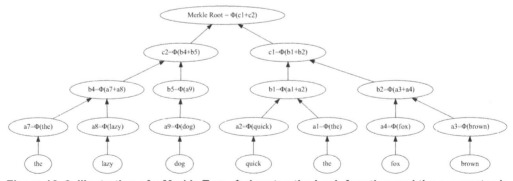

Figure 16. 3. Illustration of a Merkle Tree. Φ denotes the hash function and the + operator is used to mean string (or byte) concatenation.

The thing to note here is that m_i varies depending on what transactions are included in the block and their order. So this gives us additional degree of freedom in solving the puzzle.

- 4-byte long Bitcoin version number
- 4-byte long timestamp of the block
- 4-byte long truncated version of the target t

The puzzle can be mathematically stated as, for the i-th block, find ν_i s.t.

$$\text{ProofofWorkFormula} : \phi(H(\nu_i, \phi_{i-1}, m_i)) = \phi_i < t \qquad (1)$$

ϕ_i becomes the i-th block's identifier. Blocks can be identified two ways. Either using their height in the chain (positional indexing) or using their identifier. The block header is not the identifier of the block. Note that a block never stores its own identifier. It can be easily computed though by just hashing the block header. Bitcoin actually reverses the bytes of the hash to get the block id but that's just a bug that happened and we are stuck with it. [190] *So ignore that detail for now and consider the block id to be same as the hash of the block header.* [191] *A block does store the previous block's identifier (i.e., ϕ_{i-1}) in its header. So given a block we can navigate to the previous block. Since a block's identifier can be used to navigate to it, it can also be thought of as pointer to the block.*

Finally as if hashing once is not enough, the hash function ϕ that Bitcoin uses to hash the block header is the double `sha256` hash:

$$\phi(x) = sha256(sha256(x)) \qquad (2)$$

On the right-hand-side of Equation 16.1, t is a 256-bit number known as the *target* which is representative of the difficulty of the puzzle. Example target would be `0x00000000FFFFFFFFFFFFFFFFFFFFFFFFFFFFFFFFFFFFFFFFFFFFFFFFFFFFFFFFFF`. More difficult puzzle means lesser t i.e., t has to be decreased to increase difficulty of the puzzle. By virtue of SHA256 being a cryptographic hash, there is no way to solve this puzzle other than brute-force trial-and-error i.e., just keep trying different nonces until you hit the magic one that satisfies the inequality. t is set so that on average it will take 10 minutes to find the solution. As computational power increases, t is adjusted so that time required to solve the puzzle remains constant at 10 minutes.

Note that ϕ_i, which is pointer to the i-th block, is dependent on ϕ_{i-1}. And ϕ_{i-1} depends on ϕ_{i-2} and so on until we reach the very first block whose ϕ_0 is set to 0 by convention. So we see a genealogy where each block's "DNA" percolates to its child and so on until the latest or current block. As a corollary, if ϕ_i is changed, it affects all ϕ_j where $j > i$.

One can immediately see how this scheme makes the blockchain extremely secure and tamper-proof. If someone wants to fabricate an alternate longer chain than the currently accepted one, it is very difficult. First of all note that the individual transactions themselves are protected by means of digital signatures as we covered earlier. This means an attacker cannot change the contents of others' transactions. The only thing an attacker may conceivably want to do is to remove transactions e.g., removing a transaction to undo payment to someone. Every Bitcoin transaction spends money. Any change to a block, however minor, such as removing a transaction for example, will necessitate computing a new nonce for that block since the block's fingerprint (the Merkle root) will change. The new nonce will give a new hash and a new pointer. *All successive blocks*

will be broken as the pointer will not match for the immediate next block - this is key to understand.
If you are having difficulty understanding this, try watching the video at anders.com/blockchain/.
Do not proceed further until you understand this. So the attacker now has to solve a new puzzle for
the next block to fix the broken pointer and so on until he or she reaches the end of the chain. In the
meantime, the rest of the nodes are already extending the chain with more and more additional
blocks. It is a race the attacker cannot win. To remove a transaction that is buried under N blocks,
[192] there are $N + 1 + 1 = N+2$ new hash puzzles that need to be solved by an attacker and he or
she has to do it in less than 10 minutes - the average time for a new block to be generated by the
miners. N for the N blocks under which the transaction is buried. 1 for the block containing the
transaction itself. And 1 to counter the block that would be mined by the miners in the next 10
minutes. So the poor fellow needs to mine blocks at the rate of $1/(N + 2)$th the amount of time it
takes to mine a block. The probability of someone being able to do this becomes so low with
increasing N that $N=5$ has been deemed as a safe rule of thumb to wait to consider a transaction to
be completely *tamper-proof, immutable and permanent* on the Bitcoin blockchain. *The genius of
Bitcoin is that an attacker is pitted against the cumulative power of the entire network if they want
to execute an attack* (Exercise 16.2). As a corollary, the only way to subvert the system is to seize
control of more than 50% of the compute power - also known as the *51% attack* in Bitcoin
literature. With current size of the network, this is impossible and economically infeasible for
anyone to try to do.

Above is also the reason *why all the miners abort once a new valid block is announced by
someone.* The bookkeepers will immediately add it to their chain. Another one will come in the
next 10 minutes. If some miner wants to compete, he or she has to generate 2 blocks in next 10
minutes to stand a chance to win. Its better off to abort and instead spend resources in finding the
next block that can extend the established chain rather than taking on the arduous task of finding 2
blocks to create an alternate chain.

There is no such puzzle solving that happens in case of Fabric as the ordering service nodes do not
compete with each other. The blocks are still linked into a chain, but there is no puzzle to be solved
and *proof of work* to be demonstrated to "mine" a block. As a consequence, *Fabric can support
much higher transaction rates since the proof of work process is very time consuming and Fabric
does not have to do that.* The downside is that the blockchain is not as secure as Bitcoin (but its
secure enough, at least in my opinion). In Fabric, if someone could steal the private keys of every
peer organization plus the orderer, then they could easily manufacture a different chain. In case of
Bitcoin even if a hacker steals private keys of some users they will still not be able to change the
history of what's written onto the chain e.g., they won't be able to undo coins that have been spent.

From a hacker's perspective, there is actually little incentive to hack the Bitcoin blockchain. Its
better to spend one's time and energy trying to steal the private keys - which are never recorded
onto the chain by the way. If you steal some private keys and the associated coins have not been
spent, then you effectively gain ownership of those coins.

16.4. Bitcoin Lab

Do you think you understand how Bitcoin works? Let's do a lab where we put your knowledge and
understanding of Proof of Work (PoW) to the test. Go ahead and clone the code repository that

comes with the book and `cd` into the `$/bitcoin-lab` folder. There you should see a `src` folder with three files in it: `Block.ts`, `BlockHeader.ts` and `Blockchain.ts` which can be used to construct and demonstrate a Bitcoin like PoW based blockchain. Your goal in the lab is to fill out the missing functions in the classes above and see for yourself how easy or difficult it is to hack a PoW based blockchain.

16.4.1. `BlockHeader.ts`

Let's start with how to represent a block header. As we saw in previous section, the block header is a 80 byte long string consisting of the nonce, previous block hash, merkle root, timestamp, version number and target. For purposes of this exercise, we will consider a simplified header that is 68 byte long and consists of just the nonce, previous block hash and the merkle root. This will simplify the code a bit and we don't lose much in terms of demonstration of how PoW works. To get you started, I have already created a `BlockHeader.ts` file to represent the block header. You can see it has following properties (this is not an exhaustive list):

```
export class BlockHeader {
    public readonly nonce: Buffer;
    public readonly prevHash: Buffer;
    public readonly merkleRoot: Buffer;
}
```

Binary strings or byte buffers in Node.js are represented using the `Buffer` class. This is a built-in class in Node.js and you don't need to import any dependency to use the `Buffer` class. Let's look at the constructor of `BlockHeader` class:

```
constructor(nonce: Buffer, previousHash: Buffer, merkleRoot: Buffer) {
    this.setProperty("nonce", 4, nonce);
    this.setProperty("prevHash", 32, previousHash);
    this.setProperty("merkleRoot", 32, merkleRoot);
    this.blockHash = bitcoin.crypto.hash256(
        Buffer.concat([nonce, previousHash, merkleRoot]));
}
```

The constructor does some basic checking and concatenates the passed in nonce, hash of previous block and the merkle root of this block to create the 68 byte long block header. It then hashes the block header to get the hash of this block and stores it in the `blockHash` variable. To calculate the hash, we use the `bitcoinjs-lib` library which is listed as a dependency in `package.json`:

```
"dependencies": {
    "bitcoinjs-lib": "5.1.6"
}
```

This dependency and others can be installed by running following command from the root folder (`$/bitcoin-lab`):

```
$ npm install
```

Next, we have defined a method which can compare the block hash to a target to check if the hash is less than the target. This is the proof of work that appeared in Equation 16.1.

```
checkProofOfWork(target: number): boolean {
    return this.blockHash
        .compare(bitcoin.Block.calculateTarget(target)) <= 0;
}
```

The target *t* in Equation 16.1 is a 32 byte (i.e., 256 bits) number. To get a sense of how big this number can be, let's do some math:

```
> Math.pow(2,256)
1.157920892373162e+77
```

Bitcoin defines a 4 byte compact representation of the 32 byte number and this is what is used as input to the `checkProofOfWork` method above. This compact representation is explained in en.bitcoin.it/wiki/Difficulty#How_is_difficulty_stored_in_blocks.3F. We will work through it using an example. Suppose the 4 byte number is `0x1b0404cb`. Then to convert it into the 32 byte actual target:

1. We take the first byte `0x1b` (or 16+11=27 in decimal) and subtract 3 from it to give 24.
2. Next, we multiply the result by 8 to give 24*8=192.
3. Now, we simply take the remaining three bytes `0x0404cb` and left-shift them by 192 bits to give the result which is `0x00000000000404CB000000000000000000000000000000000000000000000000`. Note this has 24*2=48 zeros in the end which is consistent with left-shifting by 192 bits. Remember that in the `0x` string representation of a binary number, it takes 2 digits or characters to form 1 byte e.g., `0x0404cb` has 6 digits and corresponds to 3 bytes.
4. The easy way to remember this is that if the 4 byte target (also known as *bits* in Bitcoin parlance) starts with `0x1f` then the block hash will start with 2 zeros or `0x00`. If it starts with `0x1e` then the hash will start with 4 zeros (`0x0000`) and so on.

The call to `bitcoin.Block.calculateTarget` in the code above performs these steps and converts the 4 byte packed representation into a 32 byte number. Remember the greater the 32 byte target numerically, the easier it is to solve Equation 16.1 for the unknown nonce.

I have also defined a `getId` method inside the `BlockHeader` class which can return the the block's id which is nothing but the hex representation of the block hash:

```
getId(): string {
    return this.blockHash.toString('hex');
}
```

Above ignores the fact that in the real-world Bitcoin actually reverses the bytes in the hash (bytes; not bits. so `0x1b040e0c4bd0` becomes `0xd04b0c0e041b` to give an example) to get the block id but that is the artifact of a historical mistake and we don't make the same mistake in our code.

16.4.2. Block.ts

The Block.ts class is supposed to represent a block. Again, to get you started, parts of this class have already been written for you. There are 3 properties defined in the class:

```
export class Block {
    private nonce: Buffer;                       ❶
    public readonly prevHash: Buffer;            ❷
    public readonly transactions: string[];  ❸
}
```

❶ The block's 4 byte nonce.

❷ Hash (or identifier) to the block that comes before this block in the chain. For the very first block this would be a 32 byte buffer of zeros.

❸ List of transactions this block contains.

For purposes of this exercise, we can consider a transaction to be a string of the form From: Alice, To: Bob, Amount: $1. You can use any other string you like. Since the focus of this lab is proof of work, we won't be getting into the internals of the transactions and their validation etc. The list of transactions can be considered as the block's data. As has been mentioned in the chapter each transaction is protected by a digital signature and all that a hacker can do if s/he wants to hack the block is to change the order of transactions or possibly remove them from the block. The attacker won't be able to change what is inside a transaction.

The constructor of the class takes input a list of transactions and the id of the previous block expressed as a 32-byte hex string.

```
constructor(transactions: string[], previousBlockId: string) {
    this.transactions = transactions;
    this.nonce = Buffer.alloc(4);
    this.prevHash = Buffer.from(previousBlockId, "hex");
}
```

It does some error checking (omitted in listing above for brevity) and initializes the 3 properties of the class. You are also provided with a function to check if this is a valid block i.e., if the block header passes the PoW check:

```
public isValid(target: number): boolean {
    return this.getHeader().checkProofOfWork(target);
}
```

Your first task in the lab is to fill out the missing functions in Block.ts. These are as follows:

```
/**
 * The Block header (68 bytes) consist of:
 * 4 byte nonce
 * 32 byte previous block id
 * 32 byte root of Merkle tree of the transactions in this block
 */
public getHeader(): BlockHeader {
    throw new Error("Not implemented exception");
}

/**
 * The block id is nothing but the double sha256 hash of the block header
 */
public getId(): string {
    throw new Error("Not implemented exception");
}

/**
 * return id of the previous block in the chain
 */
public getPreviousBlockId(): string {
    throw new Error("Not implemented exception");
}

/**
 * Find a nonce such that the block header hashes to less than @param target
 * @param target expressed as 4 bytes packed representation. see
 * https://en.bitcoin.it/wiki/Difficulty#How_is_difficulty_stored_in_blocks.3F
 * @returns true if a nonce has been found, false if no solution exists for
 * given @param target
 */
public mineNonce(target: number): boolean {
    throw new Error("Not implemented exception");
}
```

Here are some hints to help you in the exercise:

- To get the block header you will need to calculate root of the Merkle Tree corresponding to the block's transactions. You can use the `fastRoot` function in the `merkle-lib` library to do this work for you. The `merkle-lib` library will get installed as part of `bitcoinjs-lib` dependencies.
- If your target is very aggressive, it is possible that no 4 byte nonce may exist that can give a header that hashes to less than target. When that happens in the real-world, the problem is taken care of by the timestamp property in the block header which can be changed and the miner can re-try finding a nonce that satisfies PoW with new timestamp. We don't have a timestamp in our block header in this exercise for simplicity. Miners can also re-order the transactions to address the problem. Changing the order of transactions changes the 32 byte Merkle root.

Write some unit tests under the `test` folder as you are implementing the methods to make sure they are working correctly. See Section 16.4.4 for how to run and debug tests.

16.4.3. Blockchain.ts

The Blockchain class represents a blockchain. This class could also be called Bookkeeper as it plays the role of a bookkeeper. It contains the blocks stored in an associative array (aka dictionary or JavaScript object) and the last block in the chain:

```
export class Blockchain {
    // the chain of blocks
    private blocks: { [id: string]: Block };

    // the last block in the chain
    private lastBlock: Block;

    // the blockchain difficulty expressed as 4 byte target. In the real
    // world, the Bitcoin block difficulty changes with time but we use a
    // constant difficulty in this exercise.
    private readonly target: number;
}
```

You are provided with a constructor and a validate method to check if this blockchain is valid:

```
validate(): boolean {
    let len = 0;
    if (this.lastBlock) {
        let id = this.lastBlock.getId();
        while (id !== Blockchain.GENESIS_BLOCK_HASH) {
            let block = this.blocks[id];
            if (block && block.isValid(this.target)) {
                len++;
            } else {
                return false;
            }
            id = block.getPreviousBlockId();
        }
    }
    if (len === this.getLength()) {
        return true;
    } else {
        return false;
    }
}
```

It traverses the chain from back to front (i.e., from the last block added to the chain to the very first or genesis block) and at each step checks that the block's hash is less than the target.

Fill out the missing methods in this class:

```
/**
 * returns the number of blocks in this chain. The return value from
 * this method should be trusted only if this chain is valid.
 * If the chain is invalid, the return value does not mean anything.
 */
public getLength(): number {
    throw new Error("Not implemented exception");
}

/**
 * Adds given block to the chain of blocks
 * @param block the block to add
 */
public addBlock(block: Block): void {
    throw new Error("Not implemented exception");
}

public getLastBlock(): Block {
    throw new Error("Not implemented exception");
}

public getTarget(): number {
    throw new Error("Not implemented exception");
}

/**
 * return block corresponding to given @param id
 * @param id id of the block you want
 */
public getBlockById(id: string): Block {
    throw new Error("Not implemented exception");
}
```

16.4.4. Putting it all together

Compile your code by executing following command from the root folder (`$/bitcoin-lab`):

```
$ npm run build
```

It should output a folder `dist` which stores the compiled code. The compiled code is nothing but converting TypeScript to JavaScript. The build process does not generate any machine executable (binary) code.

Let's write some code now to see it all working in action. There are two ways to do this. One is to write a standalone file which considers the module we have written as a dependency and imports it from the `dist` folder. You can then run this file using `node` if its written in JavaScript or using `ts-node` if its written in TypeScript. The `ts-node` binary itself can be accessed via `$(npm bin)/ts-node` from the root folder. Another way is to write an end-to-end test under the `test` folder. This is shown in the `Blockchain.spec.ts` file under the `test` folder. It creates 3 arrays of transactions:

```
// transactions in first block
let transactions1 = ["From: Alice, To: Bob, Amount: $1",
"From: Bob, To: George, Amount: $1",
"From: George, To: Johnny, Amount: $1"];

// transactions in second block
let transactions2 = ["From: Johnny, To: Dick, Amount: $1",
"From: Dick, To: Harry, Amount: $1",
"From: Harry, To: Peter, Amount: $1"];

// transactions in third block
let transactions3 = ["From: Peter, To: Dia, Amount: $1",
"From: Dia, To: Sasha, Amount: $1",
"From: Sasha, To: Vivek, Amount: $1"];
```

and then inserts these blocks into a blockchain as illustrated below:

```
let target = EASY_TARGET;
console.log("target = " + target.toString(16));
let chain = new bitcoin.Blockchain(target);
let blocks: bitcoin.Block[] = [];
console.log("Block | Nonce | PrevBlockId")
blocks.push(mineBlock(transactions1, chain, 1));
blocks.push(mineBlock(transactions2, chain, 2));
blocks.push(mineBlock(transactions3, chain, 3));
```

There are three pre-defined targets in the file named EASY_TARGET, MEDIUM_TARGET and DIFFICULT_TARGET with values set to 0x1fffffff, 0x1efffffff and 0x1dfffffff respectively. Use this file to test that the methods you implemented are working correctly. The tests in this class can be run by executing following command from the root folder ($/bitcoin-lab):

```
$ npm run test
```

To debug the tests from VS Code, select the mocha tests configuration defined in .vscode/launch.json:

```
{
    "name": "mocha tests",
    "type": "node",
    "protocol": "inspector",
    "request": "launch",
    "program": "${workspaceRoot}/node_modules/mocha/bin/_mocha",
    "stopOnEntry": false,
    "args": [ "-r", "ts-node/register", "${workspaceRoot}/test/**/*.spec.ts", "--no-
timeouts"],
    "cwd": "${workspaceRoot}"
}
```

and debug using F5 or the green debug button ( ) in VS Code.

16.4.5. Hacking the blockchain

Let's see how easy it is to hack the blockchain. Imagine you are Bob and you want to change the first transaction in the chain where Alice transfers $1 to Bob. So you go ahead and make following change:

```
let block = blocks[0]; // the block to hack
block.transactions[0] = "From: Alice, To: Bob, Amount: $100";
```

The first thing to keep in mind is that in real-world the transaction will be protected by a digital signature so Bob won't be able to change its contents but we ignore that for now in this exercise for demonstration purposes. Verify making this change will invalidate the blockchain because the Merkle root will change which will change the header which in turn will change the hash so it is no longer less than the target:

```
assert(!block.isValid(target));
assert(!chain.validate());
```

Write a method `fixChain` to repair the broken chain so following code passes:

```
let chain2 = fixChain(chain);
assert(chain2.validate());
```

Some hints to help you out are provided below:

- For Bob to fix the chain, he will have to find a new nonce for the block he changed. But this will change the block's hash and the next block will no longer be pointing to a valid block. It will have a "dangling pointer" to nowhere. So Bob will need to fix the next block and so on until he reaches end of the chain.
- You might need to traverse the chain from front to back and might need to use additional data structures for that purpose.

Remember in order for Bob to make his version of the blockchain gain acceptance by the community of bookkeepers he has to manufacture a *longer* chain than the current chain. So just fixing is not enough. He also needs to add another block before the next one gets mined. While Bob is fixing the chain, the rest of the miners are busy extending the established one. Try changing the target difficulty and see how long it takes for Bob to fix the chain.

We began this chapter with a quote from The New Yorker and end this chapter with a quote from The New York Times:

Bitcoin at its most fundamental level is a breakthrough in computer science – one that builds on 20 years of research into cryptographic currency, and 40 years of research in cryptography, by thousands of researchers around the world.

— Marc Andreessen founder of Andreessen-Horowitz VC and thought leader, NY Times 2014 - Why Bitcoin Matters

16.5. Summary

- Blockchain technology has its origins in Bitcoin which establishes a decentralized system or marketplace where people can perform monetary transactions without requiring any banks in between.
- Identity of participants in Bitcoin is pseudo-anonymous. Participants have a To address to which bitcoins should be sent but that address is not linked to any Personally Identifiable Information (PII).
- There is no concept of a From address in Bitcoin.
- The P2PKH (pay to public key hash) address is like a locker in which bitcoins sit and the scriptSig is used to unlock that locker. It is the key to the lock.
- Your private keys are your bitcoins. You lose your private keys, you lose your bitcoins.
- Transactions are protected by digital signatures.
- Proof of work protects against someone changing the order of transactions.
- Together digital signatures and proof of work secure the data in the blockchain.
- The proof of work protocol effectively establishes a hack-proof ledger and an ordering service that is not under control of any single person or organization.
- Whenever there are two competing blockchains, the longer chain wins. This is how forks caused due to simultaneous generation of blocks get resolved.

16.6. Further Reading

- The original Bitcoin paper by Satoshi is a classic and highly recommended: bitcoin.org/bitcoin.pdf
- A very good video explaining proof of work can be found at anders.com/blockchain/.
- Another excellent video explaining how Bitcoin works under the hood can be found at www.imponderablethings.com/2013/07/how-bitcoin-works-under-hood.html
- Why Bitcoin Matters by Marc Andreessen dealbook.nytimes.com/2014/01/21/why-bitcoin-matters/

16.7. Exercises

Exercise 16.1

In this exercise we will try to better understand the consensus problem and how building a rate limiter can solve it. The exercise assumes knowledge of multi-threaded programming. If you have never done it, use this exercise to get a fun introduction to it! Write a program that creates N users who produce transactions independently running in N independent threads. The transaction data could be anything. You could mimic money transfer by generating transactions of the form From: Alice, To: Bob, Amount: $2. Also initialize the users with $100 each in that case. But that is not crucial. Your users might just be producing some random text string and you will still be able to do the exercise. Now create M bookkeepers which act as consumers of the messages or transactions that are being produced. Each bookkeeper will have a register object stored in a private variable. Think of it as the bookkeeper's copy of the blockchain ledger. This register could be a dictionary of users and their account balance if you choose to work with money transfer, or it could simply be a message log (think WhatsApp) that can be implemented as a string buffer. Don't forget to initialize the register or string buffer. These M bookkeepers will run in their own M threads. We thus have a system of N producers and M consumers.

When you generate a transaction, make M copies of it, and broadcast it to each of the consumers using M *blocking queues* or any other programming construct you like. The queue acts as the *unconfirmed transaction pool*. The reader who is familiar with *producer-consumer* pattern will notice that we are using M queues instead of a *single* blocking queue. This is because in our case we want the transaction to be processed by *each* consumer. If we used a single queue that is *shared* across the consumers, then when a consumer dequeues a transaction, the transaction will be unavailable to other bookkeepers and that is not what we want. The Bookkeeper class will have some method which dequeues a message from the queue and processes it. Put in some artificial time delay into that method - call it τ - using a sleep statement. The purpose of τ is to mimic the time it takes to process a transaction or block. Also to mimic the fact that in a real-world uncontrolled environment the transaction can arrive in *different order on different nodes*, write your code so that the Bookkeeper dequeues a *random* item from its associated queue instead of first-in-first-out (FIFO) - there might not be a readily available class to provide this functionality and you may have to do some search or come up with some work around. For example, you can randomize the order of the M queues when a consumer has to broadcast (enqueue) a transaction as shown in the pseudocode below:

```
var tx = createTransaction();
var order = shuffle([0:M-1]);
for (var i = 0; i < M; i++) {
    Q[order[i]].enqueue(tx);
}
```

This would help (but not guarantee) in achieving a different order of transactions in the M queues.

Now let this system run for a while and then compare the contents of the registers across the bookkeepers. What do you find? Are the registers the same? That is the consensus problem. Now keeping everything the same, just insert a time delay with some randomness into the method that is producing transactions such that it is $\gg \tau N$. This is the *rate limiter*. The randomness is very important to break up the "lock-step", otherwise we succeed in rate-limiting the transactions but don't break their spikes. Run again. What do you find? Are the registers the same now? Congratulations, you now have built consensus into the system. If you inspect the size of the queues, you will find it is always zero. If you are familiar with the Go programming language, this corresponds to an *unbuffered channel*.

Exercise 16.2

In this exercise we try to calculate the probability that someone can attack the Bitcoin blockchain. [193] The only way this is possible, is for an attacker to manufacture an alternative longer chain as discussed in the chapter since in the Bitcoin world the longest chain always wins. The first part of this exercise is to calculate the probability distribution of the time it would take to solve the "hash challenge" i.e., finding appropriate nonce. As mentioned in the chapter, by virtue of SHA256 being a cryptographic hash, the only way to solve this problem is by brute-force trial-and-error. And the chances the nonce we try in the *i* th trial solves the challenge is the same irrespective of *i* i.e., irrespective of how many times we have tried in the past. It is like independent tossing or flipping of a coin trying to find occurrence of a heads with probability of heads in a toss given by *p*. In our case *p* is the probability that a random nonce we try will solve the "hash challenge".

- Begin the exercise by calculating *p*. A common newbie mistake is to note that the nonce is 4 byte long and assume that we have 2^{32} possibilities and one of them is the answer. This is not correct. If our choices were limited to 32 bits, we might not even find any answer - there might not be any nonce which gives a hash less than the target *t*. The block header is made up of many things - even the order of transactions in the block matters when calculating the hash ϕ and the same nonce will give a different hash if the order of transactions is changed. Another parameter is the timestamp. Any change to the timestamp gives a new range of 32 bits to try. So the effective input space of nonces is actually much larger.
- Now calculate the probability distribution function (pdf) of the # of trials it will take to solve the hash puzzle. [194] Calculate its mean and denote it by μ. μ is thus the expected number of trials it would take to solve the problem. This can be converted into time by multiplying by a constant which is the time taken by a trial - basically the time to compute a SHA256 hash twice. In case of Bitcoin, the target *t* is set so that $\mu = 10$ minutes - this is now *t* gets computed and is adjusted every 2016 blocks to keep μ constant.
- Now suppose that there are *n* independent miners each having identical hardware and compute power trying to solve the hash puzzle. Calculate the new pdf in this case.
- Now, suppose an attacker wants to change the history from *k* blocks behind (*k=1* means changing the last block; *k >= 1*). This means the attacker will have to manufacture *k+1* new blocks before a honest miner can produce the next block. *k* for the blocks that the attacker wants to re-write and 1 to counter the block a miner will produce in next *x* minutes or trials. What is the probability of this to happen? *Hint*: Start by assuming that some random miner will produce a block in *x* minutes or trials and calculating the probability that an attacker can manufacture *k+1* blocks in *x* minutes or trials. Then calculate probability of your assumption and sum over range of *x*. i.e., calculate $\Sigma P(B|A)P(A)$ where *P(A)* = Prob. of miner producing a block in *x* time (already calculated in previous part of the exercise) and *P(B|A)* = Prob. of attacker mining *k+1* blocks in *x* amount of time = $f(k; x)$. Technically, we have to consider *k+1 or more* when calculating *P(B|A)* to cover the case when the attacker is lucky enough to mine more than the *k+1* minimum required. Plot a graph of the probability of attack vs. *k*. You might find the problem more tractable by making *x* continuous and using a probability density function for *P(A)* instead of a probability mass function. *P(B|A)* will also change depending on whether *x* is continuous or discrete.
- Suppose you want to get into the mining "business". Use the result from previous exercise and calculate the probability of your success i.e., what are the chances you will be able to mine the next block, given a pool of *n* other independent miners with identical hardware and compute power.

Exercise 16.3

In this exercise we calculate the probability that an unfortunate seller has their transaction revoked due to reconciliation of a *fork* in the Bitcoin blockchain. As explained in the chapter, forks in

Bitcoin blockchain can happen when two miners mine two blocks at the same time (i.e., simultaneously - so each block is as good as the other and there is no winner). What is the probability of this event to happen? Use the learnings from previous exercise. The ledger will continue to be in a forked state for as long as blocks are mined simultaneously. Calculate the probability that the simultaneous generation of blocks continues for N occurrences i.e., the event whose probability you just calculated continues to repeat itself N times. Eventually the fork will be resolved when there is no more simultaneous generation of blocks. The *longer* chain will win as explained in the chapter. But this can impact some transactions which might get *voided* if someone was trying to *double-spend* their coins. Merchants should therefore not consider their transaction as confirmed as long as the ledger is in a forked state.

Both previous exercises are aimed at giving the reader a better understanding of the chances or likelihood that a transaction might become invalid. In Exercise 16.2, this can happen due to someone attacking the blockchain whereas in Exercise 16.3 it can happen just due to bad luck. The distinction between two must be kept in mind and understood. The original Bitcoin paper contains probabilistic calculations of the attack scenario.

Exercise 16.4

If you have followed the anatomy of a Bitcoin transaction closely, you must have observed that a Bitcoin transaction stores the amount of money transferred from one address to another. This means that if you want to know your account balance, you have to run through all your transactions and add up the deposits and subtract the withdrawals. Why do you think Bitcoin opted for this approach rather than storing the account balance in a transaction? E.g., say a user's account balance was 100 and they transferred 10 to someone. The transaction could debit the account balance by 10 and store 90. There would be no need to run through the user's entire transaction history to calculate his/her account balance. What are the pros and cons of this approach and its implications?

[182] www.newyorker.com/magazine/2011/10/10/the-crypto-currency

[183] en.bitcoin.it/wiki/From_address

[184] en.bitcoin.it/wiki/Transaction

[185] www.blockchain.com/explorer

[186] Readers with neuroscience background may notice an analogy with integrate-and-fire neurons, e.g. neuronaldynamics.epfl.ch/online/Ch1.S3.html

[187] hackernoon.com/the-blockchain-scalability-problem-the-race-for-visa-like-transaction-speed-5ccc48f9d44

[188] en.bitcoin.it/wiki/Block

[189] also see dev.to/damcosset/blockchain-what-is-in-a-block-48jo for a code example.

[190] E.g., reversing 0x12345678 gives 0x78563421. see learnmeabitcoin.com/guide/txid for more info.

[191] The hash of the block header is also referred to as the block hash for brevity. Thus block id, block hash and hash of block header all refer to the same thing.

[192] or equivalently $N+1$ confirmations. The # of confirmation = # of buried + 1. Some authors prefer to speak in terms of # of confirmations, and others use # of blocks buried underneath. Both are correct.

[193] This exercise assumes reader has had an undergraduate course in probability and statistics. If not, use this exercise as a fun way to learn probability! A good theoretical book is Introduction to Probability by Bertsekas and Tsitsiklis. For a more practical or applied book, refer to Miller and Freund's Probability and Statistics for Engineers.

[194] Note on terminology: some authors use the term probability mass function for pdf of discrete random variables, and the term probability density function is used for pdf of continuous random variables.

Appendix A: Installing Software and Prerequisites

This appendix covers installing software needed for developing applications on top of Hyperledger Fabric. The instructions here are w.r.t. a Mac. Please consult online resources for instructions on other platforms. Installing software needs patience and its not unusual to run into difficulties. Expect to spend a day on this. Please follow the instructions carefully and for a frictionless experience please install the same versions of software as mentioned in the instructions.

A.1. Installing Xcode CLI tools

If you are using a Mac for development, I'd recommend installing the Xcode CLI tools if you don't have them already (e.g., if you have a brand new Mac). You don't have to install full Xcode. The Xcode CLI tools bundle installs many useful utilities such as the GNU C compiler `gcc`, `clang` and `Git`. Check if you have the tools already installed by running:

```
$ xcode-select -v
```

If Xcode CLI tools are already installed you will see output that looks something like:

```
xcode-select version 2354.
```

To install the Xcode CLI tools, I'd recommend heading over to the Apple Developer portal. [195] You will need an Apple ID to sign in. From there download the Command Line Tools for Xcode available as a `.dmg` file and double-click to install. See screenshot below:

– Command Line Tools (macOS 10.13) for Xcode 9.4.1	Jun 12, 2018

This package enables UNIX-style development via Terminal by installing command line developer tools, as well as macOS SDK frameworks and headers. Many useful tools are included, such as the Apple LLVM compiler, linker, and Make. If you use Xcode, these tools are also embedded within the Xcode IDE.

Command Line Tools (macOS 10.13) for Xcode 9.4.1.dmg
183.6 MB

After installation, verify:

```
$ xcode-select -p
/Library/Developer/CommandLineTools
```

You can see all the tools by listing the contents of `/Library/Developer/CommandLineTools/usr/bin`. [196]

Linux Users: For Linux users I would recommend installing the C/C++ compiler toolchain, `make` and Python v2.7, v3.5, v3.6, or v3.7. These are listed as dependencies of `node-gyp`. [197] `node-gyp` is a cross-platform command-line tool for compiling native addon modules for Node.js and some Node.js packages that you install might require compiling C/C++ code.

Windows Users: On Windows the C/C++ build tools can be installed by running following command *after* you have installed Node.js in Section A.4.   [198] If not already installed, the command will also install Python 3.8, configuring your machine and npm appropriately.

```
$ npm install --global windows-build-tools
```

A.2. Installing Homebrew

This section only applies to Mac users. Check if you have Homebrew already installed:

```
$ brew -v
Homebrew 2.1.9
Homebrew/homebrew-core (git revision a9f09; last commit 2019-08-08)
```

If you don't have it installed, install Homebrew by following the instructions at brew.sh/:

```
$ /usr/bin/ruby -e "$(curl -fsSL
https://raw.githubusercontent.com/Homebrew/install/master/install)"
```

Part of Homebrew's prerequisites is Xcode CLI tools which you installed in previous step.

A.3. Installing Git

If you installed Xcode CLI tools, you should already have Git. Check the version of Git you have by running:

```
$ git --version
git version 2.20.1 (Apple Git-117)
```

Apple ships its own version of Git. Git can also be installed using homebrew on the Mac:

```
$ brew install git
```

Linux and Windows Users: Please consult online resources for installing Git and rest of software in the appendix.

A.4. Installing Node.js

Since we will be writing our smart contracts in JavaScript, we will need to install Node.js. Some of the packages we use in our work such as fabric-shim:2.1.2 require "node": "^12.16.1".   [199] This translates to using 12.16.1 or higher of Node.js but less than 13. We will install latest version of Node.js 12 which is 12.16.3 at time of this writing. The best way to install Node.js is to use nvm the Node.js Version Manager. Begin by checking if you have nvm installed already by running:

```
$ nvm --version
```

If nvm isn't installed, install it by running the command below:

```
$ curl -o- https://raw.githubusercontent.com/nvm-sh/nvm/v0.35.3/install.sh | bash
```

This should give an output ending in: [200]

```
=> Close and reopen your terminal to start using nvm or run the following to use it now:
```

```
export NVM_DIR="$HOME/.nvm"
[ -s "$NVM_DIR/nvm.sh" ] && \. "$NVM_DIR/nvm.sh"  # This loads nvm
[ -s "$NVM_DIR/bash_completion" ] && \. "$NVM_DIR/bash_completion"  # This loads nvm
bash_completion
```

NVM installs itself and adds the above lines to your ~/.bash_profile. Its asking you to close and reopen the terminal so that above settings can come into effect. However, you don't have to close and re-open the terminal to apply the settings. You can do this trick instead which re-loads the ~/.bash_profile containing the commands above:

```
$ . ~/.bash_profile
```

Verify nvm is installed by running command below:

```
$ nvm --version
0.35.3
```

Do not forget the --. nvm version returns the version of Node.js not nvm. To see all versions of Node.js available run:

```
$ nvm ls-remote
```

This displays a long output among which I can see:

```
v12.16.3   (Latest LTS: Erbium)
```

To install this version of Node.js run:

```
$ nvm install 12.16.3
```

Verify:

```
$ node -v
v12.16.3
$ which node
/Users/siddjain/.nvm/versions/node/v12.16.3/bin/node
$ npm -v
6.14.4
```

Running npm version instead of npm -v will show you a more verbose output. Try it.

If you are installing Node.js 12 on top of a pre-existing version of Node.js, you will observe following. *Running* node -v *in the same terminal window that you used to install v12 will give 12.16.3. But if you open a new terminal window and run* node -v *you will be back to the pre-existing version.* This is because when nvm installs on top of a pre-existing version, it does not update the default alias which tells it what default version to use. Thus the solution is to update that alias by running following command:

```
$ nvm alias default 12.16.3
default -> 12.16.3 (-> v12.16.3)
```

Now when you open a new window you should see 12.16.3 as the current version. Multiple versions of Node.js can be installed side by side and you can switch between them anytime using the nvm use command like so to give an example:

```
$ nvm use 10.20.1
Now using node v10.20.1 (npm v6.14.4)
```

Run nvm ls to see what versions you have installed on your system.

There are many Node.js packages that you might need to install in course of your work. For example, below shows how to install the eslint package in the global package directory that is useful for enforcing coding guidelines and best-practices:

```
$ sudo npm install -g eslint
```

Also go ahead and install the typescript package as we will use it in the book:

```
$ npm i typescript -g
```

The globally installed packages can be found in /usr/local/lib/node_modules directory.

A.5. Installing Go and Delve

Go installation would be needed if you intend to debug Fabric code. Fabric is written in Go. Contrary to what Fabric documentation might say, you do not need to install Go if you just want to run Fabric and will be writing smart contracts in JavaScript. To install or upgrade Go on the Mac follow these steps:

• Uninstall any previous version of Go by following below steps: [201]

  ◦ Remove the directory in which Go is installed. By default this directory is /usr/local/go:

```
$ sudo rm -rf /usr/local/go
```

  ◦ Also remove path to this directory by deleting following file:

```
$ sudo rm /etc/paths.d/go
```

- Download latest installer for your machine from golang.org/doc/install. In my case it is golang.org/doc/install?download=go1.13.3.darwin-amd64.pkg
- Double-click the installer and follow the prompts. The installer will install Go under `/usr/local/go/bin` and also add this path to `/etc/paths.d/go` file.

- Verify your installation is successful:

```
$ go version
go version go1.13.3 darwin/amd64
```

- Set your `GOPATH` environment variable. [202] `GOPATH` is not the location of the Go binary. Rather it is the location of your projects workspace. You are not limited to storing just Go projects in this workspace. If no `GOPATH` is defined, Go implicitly assumes it to be `$HOME/go` which may be good enough for your use-case. If you want to specify a different `GOPATH`, the simplest way to set it in Bash is to edit the `.bash_profile` file. Please also add `$GOPATH/bin` to your `PATH` environment variable like so e.g.:

```
export GOPATH=$HOME/go
export PATH=$GOPATH/bin:$PATH
```

Save the file, exit and remember to source it again for changes to take effect:

```
$ . ~/.bash_profile
```

- Install Delve - the Go debugger:

```
$ go get -u github.com/go-delve/delve/cmd/dlv
```

Verify:

```
$ ls -al $GOPATH/bin/dlv
-rwxr-xr-x  1 siddjain  staff  25780476 Oct 25 15:54 /Users/siddjain/go/bin/dlv
$ dlv version
Delve Debugger
Version: 1.3.2
Build: $Id: 569ccbd514fc47c8b4c521b142556867ec5e6917 $
```

A.6. Installing Docker CE

Docker containers provide a standalone execution environment that is pre-packaged and configured with necessary dependencies and binaries. The Community Edition (CE) of Docker is free and can be used for development. There is also an Enterprise Edition (EE). To install Docker please select your OS from below and follow the corresponding steps.

A.6.1. Mac

Please follow the steps in docs.docker.com/docker-for-mac/install/. You might need to create a Docker ID on Docker Hub. Once installed you should see (the latest version might be different by the time you read the book):

Listing A. 1. Docker on Mac

```
$ docker version
Client: Docker Engine - Community
 Version:           19.03.4
 API version:       1.40
 Go version:        go1.12.10
 Git commit:        9013bf5
 Built:             Thu Oct 17 23:44:48 2019
 OS/Arch:           darwin/amd64
 Experimental:      false

Server: Docker Engine - Community
 Engine:
  Version:          19.03.4
  API version:      1.40 (minimum version 1.12)
  Go version:       go1.12.10
  Git commit:       9013bf5
  Built:            Thu Oct 17 23:50:38 2019
  OS/Arch:          linux/amd64
  Experimental:     true
 containerd:
  Version:          v1.2.10
  GitCommit:        b34a5c8af56e510852c35414db4c1f4fa6172339
 runc:
  Version:          1.0.0-rc8+dev
  GitCommit:        3e425f80a8c931f88e6d94a8c831b9d5aa481657
 docker-init:
  Version:          0.18.0
  GitCommit:        fec3683
```

The Docker Desktop installation includes Docker Engine, Docker CLI client, Docker Compose, Notary, Kubernetes, and Credential Helper. If you examine above carefully, you will notice the OS/Arch for the server is linux/amd64 even though its installed on a Mac. This is because there is currently no such thing as Mac containers. *Docker for Mac runs containers inside a lightweight Linux VM on your Mac!*

 Where does Docker get installed? On the Mac you should find it under /usr/local/bin. On Linux it should be under /usr/bin. You can use the which Unix command to know the location.

A.6.2. Linux

Goto docs.docker.com/install/ and from there select your OS - Docker supports CentOS, Debian, Fedora and Ubuntu. On Red Hat you can use the CentOS image.

SERVER

Platform	x86_64 / amd64	ARM	ARM64 / AARCH64	IBM Power (ppc64le)	IBM Z (s390x)
CentOS	⊘		⊘		
Debian	⊘	⊘	⊘		
Fedora	⊘		⊘		
Ubuntu	⊘	⊘	⊘	⊘	⊘

Click on the corresponding link and follow the steps from there. For example, on Ubuntu I ran following commands:

```
$ sudo groupadd docker
$ sudo usermod -aG docker $USER
$ sudo apt-get update
$ sudo apt-get install apt-transport-https ca-certificates curl gnupg-agent software-properties-common
$ curl -fsSL https://download.docker.com/linux/ubuntu/gpg | sudo apt-key add -
$ sudo add-apt-repository "deb [arch=amd64] https://download.docker.com/linux/ubuntu $(lsb_release -cs) stable"
$ sudo apt-get update
$ sudo apt-get install docker-ce=18.06.1~ce~3-0~ubuntu containerd.io
```

The first command creates a group named docker and the second command adds current user to this group. This enables the user to execute Docker tasks such as create and launch containers. *The user needs to log out and log back in for changes to the groups to take effect.* Without adding the user to the docker group, whenever you will try to execute any docker command you will get a permission denied error:

```
$ docker ps
Got permission denied while trying to connect to the Docker daemon socket at
unix:///var/run/docker.sock: Get http://%2Fvar%2Frun%2Fdocker.sock/v1.38/containers/json:
dial unix /var/run/docker.sock: connect: permission denied
```

If the user you are trying to add has their credentials stored in a remote server such as Microsoft Active Directory, you might get an error like following when you try to run usermod command:

```
$usermod -aG docker $USER
usermod: user 'siddjain' does not exist
```

This is because the user does not exist in the local /etc/passwd file which stores the local users. You can try to add the user using the useradd command and after that the usermod will work but what you have done now is created a duplicate user with same username. *Don't do that.* Try using the gpasswd command to add the user to the group:

```
$ gpasswd -a $USER docker
```

If the same `user does not exist` error persists, the solution is simple. Manually edit the /etc/group file (requires `root` privileges) and add yourself to the `docker` group in it like so:

```
docker:x:500:siddjain
```

The meaning of the fields is as follows:

- `docker` is name of the group
- `x` is the password field
- `500` is the group ID (GID) which can be different in your case
- `siddjain` is now a member of the group. Additional members can be added separated by commas

Once you make the changes, you can verify that the user is indeed a member of `docker` group by running the `id` command:

```
$ id siddjain
uid=48081(siddjain) gid=101(zusers) groups=101(zusers),8652(seacct),500(docker)
```

It is not uncommon to run into unexpected errors during installation. Let StackOverflow and Docker Forums be your friends. Verify:

Listing A. 2. Docker on Linux (Ubuntu)

```
$ docker version
Client: Docker Engine - Community
 Version:           19.03.4
 API version:       1.40
 Go version:        go1.12.10
 Git commit:        9013bf583a
 Built:             Fri Oct 18 15:54:09 2019
 OS/Arch:           linux/amd64
 Experimental:      false

Server: Docker Engine - Community
 Engine:
  Version:          19.03.4
  API version:      1.40 (minimum version 1.12)
  Go version:       go1.12.10
  Git commit:       9013bf583a
  Built:            Fri Oct 18 15:52:40 2019
  OS/Arch:          linux/amd64
  Experimental:     false
 containerd:
  Version:          1.2.10
  GitCommit:        b34a5c8af56e510852c35414db4c1f4fa6172339
 runc:
  Version:          1.0.0-rc8+dev
  GitCommit:        3e425f80a8c931f88e6d94a8c831b9d5aa481657
 docker-init:
  Version:          0.18.0
  GitCommit:        fec3683
```

 On Ubuntu you will get following message if you try to run a Docker command and Docker is not installed.

```
$ docker version

Command 'docker' not found, but can be installed with:

sudo snap install docker     # version 18.06.1-ce, or
sudo apt  install docker.io

See 'snap info docker' for additional versions.
```

Resist installing Docker through sudo snap install docker. I once did it and ran into problems.

Verify Docker daemon is successfully running on the machine:

```
$ systemctl status docker
⍿ docker.service - Docker Application Container Engine
   Loaded: loaded (/lib/systemd/system/docker.service; enabled; vendor preset: enabled)
   Active: active (running) since Wed 2020-01-22 19:15:31 UTC; 1 months 4 days ago
     Docs: https://docs.docker.com
 Main PID: 1258 (dockerd)
    Tasks: 20
   CGroup: /system.slice/docker.service
           ├─  1258 /usr/bin/dockerd -H fd://
--containerd=/run/containerd/containerd.sock
           └─112844 /usr/bin/docker-proxy -proto tcp -host-ip 0.0.0.0 -host-port 8000
-container-ip 172.23.0.3 -container-port 80
```

Red Hat Enterprise Linux (RHEL) is a popular choice for enterprise deployments. It comes with its own version of Docker which can be installed by running

```
$ sudo yum install docker
```

However this version is different from Docker CE and I have run into few problems with it that are described later. I would therefore recommend installing Docker CE instead from the CentOS repo by running following commands that have worked for me:

```
$ sudo yum install -y yum-utils device-mapper-persistent-data lvm2
$ sudo yum-config-manager --add-repo https://download.docker.com/linux/centos/docker-
ce.repo
$ sudo yum -y install docker-ce-18.06.2.ce-3.el7 docker-ce-cli-18.06.2.ce-3.el7
containerd.io
$ sudo systemctl enable docker
$ sudo systemctl start docker
```

If you do end up installing Red Hat's version of Docker and run into following error when starting the Docker service

```
$ sudo systemctl start docker.service
Job for docker.service failed because the control process exited with error code. See
"systemctl status docker.service" and "journalctl -xe" for details.
```

Try editing the following files: [203]

```
bash # vi /etc/sysconfig/docker-storage
...
DOCKER_STORAGE_OPTIONS="--storage-driver devicemapper "
...

bash # vi /etc/sysconfig/docker-storage-setup
...
STORAGE_DRIVER=devicemapper
...
```

and restart the service.

A.7. Installing Fabric Source Code

Installing Fabric source code would be needed if you intend to debug Fabric code. In my case I have cloned following Fabric repos under `$GOPATH/src/github.com/hyperledger`:

- `fabric`: has `peer`, `orderer` and utilities like `cryptogen` and `configtxgen`
- `fabric-ca`: has Fabric CA
- `fabric-baseimage`: has base Docker images. Deprecated with 2.0.
- `fabric-chaincode-node`: contains `fabric-contact-api` used to write smart contracts in Node.js
- `fabric-sdk-node`: contact `fabric-network` API to develop client applications in Node.js

To give a complete example, below is how I downloaded the `fabric` repo: first create the `$GOPATH/src/github.com/hyperledger` directory if it doesn't exist. Then:

```
$ cd $GOPATH/src/github.com/hyperledger
$ git clone https://github.com/hyperledger/fabric.git
```

This book uses version 2.0 of Fabric which is under `release-2.0` branch. Make sure you checkout this branch:

```
$ cd fabric
$ git checkout release-2.0
```

Note that the `release-2.0` branch is not a snapshot in time. Commits will continue to be made to it as Fabric developers are working on `2.0.x`. If you want to sync to the source code that was used to compile binaries shipped with a specific release, check out the appropriate tag. For us it would be:

```
$ git checkout tags/v2.0.1
Note: checking out 'tags/v2.0.1'.
You are in 'detached HEAD' state. You can look around, make experimental
...
HEAD is now at 1cfa5da98 Updates for fabric release v2.0.1
```

Since a tag is a snapshot in time, you cannot make commits on top of it. This is what Git is trying to tell when it says `You are in 'detached HEAD' state`. Think of the detached state as a read-only state since you are in a frozen snapshot in time. If you want to make commits on top of a tag, you need to fork out a new branch. This can be done as follows:

```
$ git checkout tags/v2.0.1 -b mybranch
Switched to a new branch 'mybranch'
```

A.8. Installing Fabric Binaries, Samples and Docker Images

Let's first understand what each of these are:

- **Binaries**: The Fabric binaries consist of following executables:

  Listing A. 3. Binaries that ship with Fabric

  ```
  configtxgen     cryptogen      fabric-ca-client    idemixgen      peer
  configtxlator       discover        fabric-ca-server   orderer
  ```

- **Samples**: The Fabric samples are a set of code examples showing how to develop Fabric applications. They can be found at github.com/hyperledger/fabric-samples.
- **Docker Images**: These are Docker images to run Fabric components such as peer, orderer, fabric-ca-server etc. and can be found online at hub.docker.com/search? q=hyperledger%2Ffabric&type=image.

Fabric provides a script that can be used to download one or more of the above. Before continuing, decide on a directory where you will store the binaries and samples. In my case I am storing them under ~/hyperledger. So create this directory or your preferred location where you want to install.

- cd into this directory.
- Now you have two ways to get the install script - either from official repo or using the $/install-fabric.sh script checked under the book's code repo. Install wget if you don't have it already:

  ```
  $ brew install wget
  ```

  wget is a friendly command to download files from the internet.

- To get the install script from official distribution, run:

  ```
  $ wget https://raw.githubusercontent.com/hyperledger/fabric/master/scripts/bootstrap.sh
  ```

  This will save a file bootstrap.sh on your machine.

- Check VERSION and CA_VERSION strings in bootstrap.sh. By the time you read this book, there would likely be a new version of Fabric, but this book is locked to version 2.0.1 of main Fabric and version 1.4.6 of the Fabric CA so change VERSION and CA_VERSION to 2.0.1 and 1.4.6 respectively if you want exact same experience and output as the code snippets in the book.
- Make bootstrap.sh executable by running:

  ```
  $ chmod 755 bootstrap.sh
  ```

- Downloading Docker images may not work if you are not signed into your Docker account, so sign in using the account you created earlier when you installed Docker CE:

  ```
  $ docker login
  ```

- If you run the bootstrap.sh script, it will install all three components - samples, binaries and Docker images - by default unless you made some changes to the script. We don't use Fabric samples in this book and Docker images can be downloaded at runtime, so let's just install the binaries for now. This is done by specifying -ds in the command below (d for Docker and s for samples):

```
$ ./bootstrap.sh -ds
```

Above skips installation of Docker images and the samples.

Troubleshooting: Last time I tried it, the script did not work on a Mac because it had problems parsing command line options. The bug seems to have been fixed but in case you are having issues with the script, you can either use the script that comes with the book's repo or try deleting the command line argument parsing code in the script and manually set SAMPLES, BINARIES, DOCKER to true or false depending on whether you want to install them or not. By default all three are set to true in the script.

Verify:

* The binaries will get installed in a directory named bin under the directory from where bootstrap.sh is executed. If you ls this directory it should have the executables listed in Listing A. 3. Please add this directory to the PATH variable in ~/.bash_profile as we will use the binaries in this folder in the book.
* In addition a directory named config will be created that contains following files:

```
$ ls config
configtx.yaml   core.yaml   orderer.yaml
```

This happens as part of the BINARIES installation.

* Fabric samples - if you installed them - will get downloaded into a directory named fabric-samples. You might want to move this directory to $GOPATH/src/github.com/hyperledger so that all code you download from github.com is under one place.
* The Docker images - if you installed them - can be verified by running:

```
$ docker image ls
```

Troubleshooting: if you are getting an error similar to below:

```
Error response from daemon: Get https://registry-1.docker.io/v2/hyperledger/fabric-zookeeper/manifests/0.4.10: unauthorized: incorrect username or password.
```

Please try logging into Docker by running docker login.

A.9. Installing VS Code

I use the VS Code editor to write code and debug. It was the most popular IDE in the 2019 Stack Overflow developer survey (maybe because its free). [204] Its also popular among Fabric developers. If you want to use VS Code, install it from code.visualstudio.com/download. If you are completely new to VS Code, I'd recommend going through the tips & tricks to get comfortable with it. [205] The VS Code itself is a lightweight editor and it comes with a large set of *extensions* which can be used to extend its behavior and functionality. Below are some of the extensions I have installed:

- **ms-vscode.go**: adds language support for Go. Will be required if you will be debugging Fabric code written in Go
- **mads-hartmann.bash-ide-vscode**: allows IDE experience while writing Bash scripts such as jump to declaration, find references etc. I remember this was a difficult extension to get working. It requires installing `bash-language-server` separately as a prerequisite and the `bashIde.path` should be set to location of `bash-language-server`. Follow below steps to get it working:
  - `Cd to ~./vscode/extensions`
  - Run `npm install bash-language-server`
  - The `bashIde.path` can be found under `Code→Preferences→Settings` on the Mac. Set it to `~/.vscode/extensions/mads-hartmann.bash-ide-vscode-1.3.3/node_modules/.bin/bash-language-server`. You may want to substitute `~` with absolute path and `1.3.3` with version number in your case.
- **rogalmic.bash-debug**: allows debugging Bash scripts
- **donjayamanne.githistory**: view git log, file history, compare branches or commits
- **ms-azuretools.vscode-docker**: adds syntax highlighting, commands, hover tips, and linting for Dockerfile and docker-compose files
- **visualstudioexptteam.vscodeintellicode**: provides IntelliSense support (also known as code completion)
- **ms-vscode-remote.vscode-remote-extensionpack**: allows you to open any folder in a Docker container or on a remote machine and take advantage of VS Code's full feature set

Each of the extensions above can be installed from the Extensions tab. First, navigate to the Extensions tab by clicking on the Extensions icon in the left vertical sidebar of VS Code (Keyboard shortcut: `Cmd+Shift+X`). Then type the extension name in the search bar. This should bring up the extension in search results. Select it and click on Install. All the extensions get installed under `~/.vscode/extensions` on the Mac. It is possible to install a specific version of an extension using the context menu that appears besides the extension. [206]

A.10. Other tools

VS Code has integrated source control and includes Git support out of the box but if for some reason - such as if you are not using VS Code - you find yourself wanting another GUI for Git, you may want to try out SourceTree from Atlassian.

Ensure you have `ssh` and `openssl` installed as they will come in handy. They should come with your Mac and not require any installation from your side.

```
$ ssh -V
OpenSSH_7.9p1, LibreSSL 2.7.3
$ openssl version
LibreSSL 2.6.5
```

*A.11. ~/.*bash_profile

For reference this is what my ~/.bash_profile looks like when I am done with all the installation. Use below only as a guideline to help you in troubleshooting. Your ~./bash_profile does not need to match exactly with what I have below. For example, if you don't have Java and Maven installed you don't need JAVA_HOME and M2_HOME in your ~./bash_profile. Same goes for Ruby and Android.

Listing A. 4. ~/.bash_profile

```
export M2_HOME=/Library/apache-maven-3.6.1
export ANDROID_HOME=/Users/siddjain/Library/Android/sdk
export JAVA_HOME=/Library/Java/JavaVirtualMachines/jdk1.8.0_212.jdk/Contents/Home
export GEM_HOME=$HOME/.gem/ruby/2.6.0
export GOPATH=$HOME/go
export PATH=$ANDROID_HOME/platform-
tools:$M2_HOME/bin:$GEM_HOME/bin:$GOPATH/bin:$HOME/hyperledger/bin:/usr/local/opt/ruby/bin:
$PATH
alias sha256sum='shasum --algorithm 256'
test -e "${HOME}/.iterm2_shell_integration.bash" && source
"${HOME}/.iterm2_shell_integration.bash"
export NVM_DIR="$HOME/.nvm"
[ -s "$NVM_DIR/nvm.sh" ] && \. "$NVM_DIR/nvm.sh"  # This loads nvm
[ -s "$NVM_DIR/bash_completion" ] && \. "$NVM_DIR/bash_completion"  # This loads nvm
bash_completion
```

[195] developer.apple.com/download/more/

[196] A copy of what I see on my system is at git.io/JIvZb

[197] www.npmjs.com/package/node-gyp

[198] github.com/felixrieseberg/windows-build-tools#windows-build-tools

[199] see the engines section in github.com/hyperledger/fabric-chaincode-node/blob/v2.1.2/libraries/fabric-shim/package.json

[200] see git.io/JIvnq for full output

[201] taken from golang.org/doc/install#uninstall

[202] github.com/golang/go/wiki/SettingGOPATH

[203] refer forums.docker.com/t/unable-to-install-run-docker-on-red-hat-linux-7/92020/2 for full details

[204] insights.stackoverflow.com/survey/2019

[205] code.visualstudio.com/docs/getstarted/tips-and-tricks

[206] stackoverflow.com/a/53755378/147530

Appendix B: Summary of Commands

Table B. 1. Summary of commands used to provision a network

Command	Purpose	Dependency
`cryptogen generate --config=./crypto -config.yaml`	Generate necessary MSP directories and user, admin, peer and orderer identities. In real-world you will use a CA server such as Fabric CA.	`crypto-config.yaml`
`configtxgen -profile Genesis -outputBlock foo.block -channelID foo`	Generate genesis block for the system channel foo.	`configtx.yaml`
`configtxgen -profile Channel -outputCreateChannelTx channel.tx -channelID tracktrace`	Generate transaction which when committed on the system channel will provision the application channel.	`configtx.yaml`
`orderer`	Run orderer	`orderer.yaml, foo.block` (genesis block)
`peer node start`	Run peer	`core.yaml`
`docker network create --attachable -d bridge pharmanet`	Create a bridge network for single-node deployment	
`docker network create --attachable -d overlay pharmanet`	Create an overlay network for multi-node deployment	`docker swarm init` (only swarm manager can create an overlay network)

Table B. 2. List of Docker images for Fabric deployment

Image	Purpose
`couchdb:2.3.1`	CouchDB
`hyperledger/fabric-peer:2.0.1`	peer
`hyperledger/fabric-orderer:2.0.1`	orderer
`hyperledger/fabric-ca:1.4.6`	Fabric CA

Table B. 3. Table summarizing channel and chaincode administration commands and whether orderer is involved. The join operation requires the involvement of the orderer but the orderer endpoint is inferred from the genesis block passed to it rather than a command line argument.

Operation	Command	Orderer	Lifecycle function in `scc.go`
Create channel	`peer channel create`	✓	-
Fetch genesis block	`peer channel fetch`	✓	-
Join peer node	`peer channel join`	✓	-
List channels a peer has joined	`peer channel list`	✗	-
Install chaincode	`peer lifecycle chaincode install`	✗	`InstallChaincode`
List chaincodes	`peer lifecycle chaincode queryinstalled`	✗	`QueryInstalledChaincodes`
Approve chaincode	`peer lifecycle chaincode approveformyorg`	✓	`ApproveChaincodeDefinitionForMyOrg`
Check commit readiness	`peer lifecycle chaincode checkcommitreadiness`	✗	`CheckCommitReadiness`
Commit chaincode	`peer lifecycle chaincode commit`	✓	`CommitChaincodeDefinition`

Table B. 4. `peer` commands in "client mode" and whether orderer is involved.

Command	Purpose	Orderer	Need administrator privileges
`peer chaincode invoke`	submit a transaction, write to the ledger and world db	✓	✗
`peer chaincode query`	read from the world db	✗	✗
`peer channel update`	update channel configuration	✓	✓

Table B. 5. Summary of commands involved in updating a channel's configuration.

Command	Purpose	Admin privileges
`peer channel fetch config`	fetch latest channel config	✗
`configtxlator proto_decode`	decode protobuf to JSON	NA
`configtxlator proto_encode`	convert JSON to protobuf	NA
`configtxlator compute_update`	diff two protobufs	NA
`peer channel signconfigtx`	sign a channel update transaction	✗
`peer channel update`	update channel configuration	✓

Table B. 6. Summary of commonly used `openssl` **commands.**

Command	Purpose
`openssl x509 -in cert.pem -text -noout`	print out X.509 certificate
`openssl x509 -in cert.pem -pubkey -noout`	print out public key inside PEM encoded X.509 certificate
`openssl crl2pkcs7 -nocrl -certfile ca-chain.pem | openssl pkcs7 -print_certs -text -noout`	decode (print) a chain of certificates
`openssl ec -in private.key -pubout`	print public key corresponding to ECDSA private key
`openssl verify -CAfile ca-cert.pem test-cert.pem`	verify `test-cert.pem` is signed by the CA (or optionally chain of CAs) in `ca-cert.pem`. Supports a `-CApath` option to provide a directory. Use `-CRLfile` to supply a certificate revocation list.
`openssl req -new -x509 -newkey ec:<(openssl ecparam -name prime256v1) -nodes -keyout key.pem -out cert.pem -days 3650 -config ./openssl.cnf`	generate self-signed ECDSA certificate using settings in `openssl.cnf`. If the `-x509` switch is left out a certificate signing request (CSR) is generated instead.
`openssl req -newkey rsa:2048 -nodes -keyout key.pem -x509 -days 365 -out cert.pem -config ./tls.cnf -extensions 'v3_req'`	generate self-signed RSA certificate using settings in `tls.cnf` and adding extensions. If the `-x509` switch is left out a certificate signing request (CSR) is generated instead.
`openssl req -new -key key.pem ···`	generate a certificate or CSR using existing private key in `key.pem`
`openssl req -noout -text -in csr.pem`	print out a CSR
`openssl x509 -noout -modulus -in cert.pem | openssl md5`	verify if a RSA based cert and private key pair match by checking the MD5 hash of the modulus
`openssl rsa -noout -modulus -in key.pem | openssl md5`	
`openssl s_client -connect foo.com:443 -state -nbio -CAfile foo-ca-chain.pem -key client.key -cert client.crt -showcerts`	verify TLS certificate returned from `foo.com` validates against `foo-ca-chain.pem`. The `-key` and `-cert` are optional and are to be used when client authentication is enabled on the server.
`openssl ecparam -name secp256r1 -genkey -param_enc explicit -out ecdsa-private.pem`	generate private ECDSA key using the `secp256r1` also known as `prime256v1` (NIST P-256) curve. The curve parameters are explicitly encoded in the key.

Command	Purpose
`openssl ca -config signing.cnf -extensions v3_ca -create_serial -out cert.pem -notext -infiles csr.pem`	sign a CSR.

Table B. 7. Docker cheat sheet

Command	Purpose
`docker ps`	List containers
`docker ps -a`	List running and non-running (exited) containers
`docker ps -f "status=exited"`	Only list exited containers
`docker ps --format "{{.Names}}"`	Only list container names
`docker ps -a -f name=foo`	Check if container `foo` exists - could be running or exited. Note this will use regex matching and may return more results than you intended. If you want to do exact matching use `name=^foo$`.
`docker ps -q`	Quiet mode. Only return container IDs.
`docker container create`	Create container
`docker network create`	Create a network
`docker volume create`	Create a volume
`docker cp`	Copy files between host and container
`docker start`	Start container
`docker run`	Same as `create` followed by immediate `start`
`docker stop`	Stop a container. The main process inside the container will receive `SIGTERM`, and after a grace period, `SIGKILL`.
`docker rm`	Remove (delete) a container
`docker network rm`	Remove a network
`docker volume rm`	Remove a volume
`docker exec`	Execute a command against a running container
`docker logs`	Inspect logs
`docker logs <container> 2>&1 | grep <pattern>`	Search logs

Command	Purpose
`docker inspect`	Inspect a Docker object - could be container, image, volume etc.
`docker image ls`	List images
`docker volume ls`	List volumes
`docker network ls`	List networks
`docker pull`	Download an image
`docker image build`	Build an image
`docker history`	Reverse engineer an image
`docker volume prune`	Remove unused volumes
`docker system prune`	Remove all unused containers, networks, images, and optionally, volumes
`docker rename`	Rename a container
`docker swarm`	Manage Docker swarm
`docker service`	Manage a service
`docker stack`	Manage a stack of services

The general command to debug Fabric - or a Go program - is

```
dlv debug $SRC $OPTIONS --api-version=2 --log=true -- $ARGS
```

where `$SRC` should point to a directory containing a `main.go` file (`main` package). `$ARGS` gives the arguments that will be passed to the `main` function. The `SRC` and `ARGS` for various programs is given below.

Program	SRC	ARGS
`peer`	`github.com/hyperledger/fabric/cmd/peer`	`node start`
`orderer`	`github.com/hyperledger/fabric/cmd/orderer`	-
`fabric-ca-server`	`github.com/hyperledger/fabric-ca/cmd/fabric-ca-server`	`start`
`fabric-ca-client`	`github.com/hyperledger/fabric-ca/cmd/fabric-ca-client`	will depend on what you want to do

set `OPTIONS="--headless=true --listen=127.0.0.1:41305"` to be able to attach VS Code debugger. Substitute port as necessary. Replace `debug` with `exec` to debug a pre-compiled binary.

Index

Made in United States
North Haven, CT
21 November 2021